COMMON CORE MATHEMATICS

A Story of Units

Grade K, Module 4: Number Pairs, Addition and Subtraction to 10

consider the source

A Wiley Brand

Cover design by Chris Clary

Published by Jossey-Bass
A Wiley Brand
One Montgomery Street, Suite 1200, San Francisco, CA 94104-4594—www.josseybass.com

ISBN: 978-1-118-81120-7

Printed in the United States of America
FIRST EDITION
PB Printing   10 9 8 7 6 5 4 3 2 1

WELCOME

Dear Teacher,

Thank you for your interest in Common Core's curriculum in mathematics. Common Core is a non-profit organization based in Washington, DC dedicated to helping K-12 public schoolteachers use the power of high-quality content to improve instruction.[1] We are led by a board of master teachers, scholars, and current and former school, district, and state education leaders. Common Core has responded to the Common Core State Standards' (CCSS) call for "content-rich curriculum"[2] by creating new, CCSS-based curriculum materials in mathematics, English Language Arts, history, and (soon) the arts. All of our materials are written by teachers who are among the nation's foremost experts on the new standards.

In 2012 Common Core won three contracts from the New York State Education Department to create a PreKindergarten–12th grade mathematics curriculum for the teachers of that state, and to conduct associated professional development. The book you hold contains a portion of that work. In order to respond to demand in New York and elsewhere, modules of the curriculum will continue to be published, on a rolling basis, as they are completed. This curriculum is based on New York's version of the CCSS (the CCLS, or Common Core Learning Standards). Common Core will be releasing an enhanced version of the curriculum this summer on our website, commoncore.org. That version also will be published by Jossey-Bass, a Wiley brand.

Common Core's curriculum materials are not merely aligned to the new standards, they take the CCSS as their very foundation. Our work in math takes its shape from the expectations embedded in the new standards—including the instructional shifts and mathematical progressions, and the new expectations for student fluency, deep conceptual understanding, and application to real-life context. Similarly, our ELA and history curricula are deeply informed by the CCSS's new emphasis on close reading, increased use of informational text, and evidence-based writing.

Our curriculum is distinguished not only by its adherence to the CCSS. The math curriculum is based on a theory of teaching math that is proven to work. That theory posits that mathematical knowledge is most coherently and

---

1. Despite the coincidence of name, Common Core and the Common Core State Standards are not affiliated. Common Core was established in 2007, prior to the start of the Common Core State Standards Initiative, which was led by the National Governors Association and the Council for Chief State School Officers.

2. *Common Core State Standards for English Language Arts & Literacy in History/Social Studies, Science, and Technical Subjects* (Washington, DC: Common Core State Standards Initiative), 6.

effectively conveyed when it is taught in a sequence that follows the "story" of mathematics itself. This is why we call the elementary portion of this curriculum "A Story of Units," to be followed by "A Story of Ratios" in middle school, and "A Story of Functions" in high school. Mathematical concepts flow logically, from one to the next, in this curriculum. The sequencing has been joined with methods of instruction that have been proven to work, in this nation and abroad. These methods drive student understanding beyond process, to deep mastery of mathematical concepts. The goal of the curriculum is to produce students who are not merely literate, but fluent, in mathematics.

It is important to note that, as extensive as these curriculum materials are, they are not meant to be prescriptive. Rather, they are intended to provide a basis for teachers to hone their own craft through study, collaboration, training, and the application of their own expertise as professionals. At Common Core we believe deeply in the ability of teachers and in their central and irreplaceable role in shaping the classroom experience. We strive only to support and facilitate their important work.

The teachers and scholars who wrote these materials are listed beginning on the next page. Their deep knowledge of mathematics, of the CCSS, and of what works in classrooms defined this work in every respect. I would like to thank Louisiana State University professor of mathematics Scott Baldridge for the intellectual leadership he provides to this project. Teacher, trainer, and writer Robin Ramos is the most inspired math educator I've ever encountered. It is Robin and Scott's aspirations for what mathematics education in America *should* look like that is spelled out in these pages.

Finally, this work owes a debt to project director Nell McAnelly that is so deep I'm confident it never can be repaid. Nell, who leads LSU's Gordon A. Cain Center for STEM Literacy, oversees all aspects of our work for NYSED. She has spent days, nights, weekends, and many cancelled vacations toiling in her efforts to make it possible for this talented group of teacher-writers to produce their best work against impossible deadlines. I'm confident that in the years to come Scott, Robin, and Nell will be among those who will deserve to be credited with putting math instruction in our nation back on track.

Thank you for taking an interest in our work. Please join us at www.commoncore.org.

Lynne Munson
President and Executive Director
Common Core
Washington, DC
October 25, 2013

Common Core's K-5 Math Staff

Scott Baldridge, Lead Mathematician and Writer
Robin Ramos, Lead Writer, PreKindergarten-5
Jill Diniz, Lead Writer, 6-12
Ben McCarty, Mathematician

Nell McAnelly, Project Director
Tiah Alphonso, Associate Director
Jennifer Loftin, Associate Director
Catriona Anderson, Curriculum Manager, PreKindergarten-5

Sherri Adler, PreKindergarten
Debbie Andorka-Aceves, PreKindergarten

Kate McGill Austin, Kindergarten
Nancy Diorio, Kindergarten
Lacy Endo-Peery, Kindergarten
Melanie Gutierrez, Kindergarten
Nuhad Jamal, Kindergarten
Cecilia Rudzitis, Kindergarten
Shelly Snow, Kindergarten

Beth Barnes, First Grade
Lily Cavanaugh, First Grade
Ana Estela, First Grade
Kelley Isinger, First Grade
Kelly Spinks, First Grade
Marianne Strayton, First Grade
Hae Jung Yang, First Grade

Wendy Keehfus-Jones, Second Grade
Susan Midlarsky, Second Grade
Jenny Petrosino, Second Grade
Colleen Sheeron, Second Grade
Nancy Sommer, Second Grade
Lisa Watts-Lawton, Second Grade
MaryJo Wieland, Second Grade
Jessa Woods, Second Grade

Eric Angel, Third Grade
Greg Gorman, Third Grade
Susan Lee, Third Grade
Cristina Metcalf, Third Grade
Ann Rose Santoro, Third Grade
Kevin Tougher, Third Grade
Victoria Peacock, Third Grade
Saffron VanGalder, Third Grade

Katrina Abdussalaam, Fourth Grade
Kelly Alsup, Fourth Grade
Patti Dieck, Fourth Grade
Mary Jones, Fourth Grade
Soojin Lu, Fourth Grade
Tricia Salerno, Fourth Grade
Gail Smith, Fourth Grade
Eric Welch, Fourth Grade
Sam Wertheim, Fourth Grade
Erin Wheeler, Fourth Grade

Leslie Arceneaux, Fifth Grade
Adam Baker, Fifth Grade
Janice Fan, Fifth Grade
Peggy Golden, Fifth Grade
Halle Kananak, Fifth Grade
Shauntina Kerrison, Fifth Grade
Pat Mohr, Fifth Grade
Chris Sarlo, Fifth Grade

Additional Writers

Bill Davidson, Fluency Specialist
Robin Hecht, UDL Specialist
Simon Pfeil, Mathematician

Document Management Team

Tam Le, Document Manager
Jennifer Merchan, Copy Editor

Table of Contents

GRADE K • MODULE 4

Number Pairs, Addition and Subtraction to 10

Module Overview i

Topic A: Compositions and Decompositions of 2, 3, 4, and 5 ....4.A.1

Topic B: Decompositions of 6, 7, and 8 into Number Pairs.....................................4.B.1

Topic C: Addition with Totals of 6, 7, and 8..4.C.1

Topic D: Subtraction from Numbers to 8 ....4.D.1

Topic E: Decompositions of 9 and 10 into Number Pairs.......................................4.E.1

Topic F: Addition with Totals of 9 and 10 ....4.F.1

Topic G: Subtraction from 9 and 10 ....4.G.1

Topic H: Patterns with Adding 0 and 1 and Making 10...4.H.1

Module Assessments 4.S.1

Grade K • Module 4
Number Pairs, Addition and Subtraction to 10

OVERVIEW

Module 4 marks the next exciting step in math for kindergartners, addition and subtraction! They begin to harness their practiced counting abilities, knowledge of the value of numbers, and work with embedded numbers to reason about and solve addition and subtraction expressions and equations (**K.OA.1**, **K.OA.2**).

In Topic A, decompositions and compositions of numbers to 5 are revisited to reinforce how a whole can be broken into two parts and how two parts can be joined to make a whole. Decomposition and composition are taught simultaneously using the number bond model so that students begin to understand the relationship between parts and wholes before adding and subtracting, formally addressed in Topics C and D.

Topic B continues with decomposing and composing 6, 7, and 8 using the number bond model. Students systematically work with each quantity, finding all possible number pairs using story situations, objects, sets, arrays, 5 + n patterns,[1] and numerals (**K.OA.3**).

Topic C introduces addition to totals of 6, 7, and 8 within concrete and pictorial settings, first generating number sentences without unknowns (e.g., 5 + 2 = 7) to develop an understanding of the addition symbol and the referent of each number within the equation. Next, students graduate to working within the addition word problem types taught in kindergarten, *add to with result unknown* (A + B = ___), *put together with total unknown* (A + B = ___), and *both addends unknown* (C = ___ + ___) (**K.OA.2**). Students draw a box around the total to track the unknown.

Topic D introduces subtraction with 6, 7, and 8 with no unknown. The lessons in Topic D build from the concrete level of students acting out, crossing out objects in a set, and breaking and hiding parts to more formal representations of decomposition recorded as or matched to equations (C – B = ___).

Topics E, F, and G parallel the first half of the module with the numbers 9 and 10. Topic E explores composition, decomposition, and number pairs using the number bond model (**K.OA.3**). It is essential that students build deep understanding and skill with identifying the number pairs of 6 through 10 as this is foundational to Grade 1's fluency with sums and differences within 10 and Grade 2's fluency with sums and differences to 20. Topics F and G deal with addition and subtraction, respectively. Students are refocused on representing larger numbers by drawing the 5 + n pattern to bridge efficiently from seeing the embedded five to representing that as addition.

---

[1] Operations and Algebraic Thinking progression document, p. 10.

After addition and subtraction have been introduced, Topic H explores the behavior of zero: the additive identity. Students learn that adding or subtracting zero does not change the original quantity. Students will also begin to see patterns when adding 1 more and the inverse relationship between addition and subtraction (8 + 2 = 10, and 10 – 2 = 8). Finally, students will begin to formally study and explore partners to 10 (**K.OA.4**), though this essential work has been supported throughout Module 4 during Fluency Practice.

The culminating task of this module asks students to demonstrate their understanding of addition as *putting together* and *adding to,* and subtraction as *taking apart* and *taking from*. Students use mathematical models and equations to teach a small group of students, administrators, family members, or community partners about a decomposition of 10.

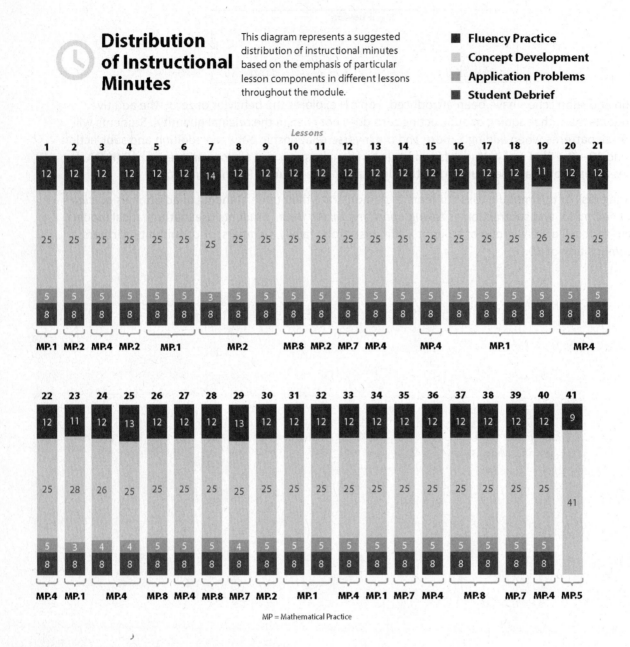

Distribution of Instructional Minutes

This diagram represents a suggested distribution of instructional minutes based on the emphasis of particular lesson components in different lessons throughout the module.

■ **Fluency Practice**
  Concept Development
■ **Application Problems**
■ **Student Debrief**

Lessons

	1	2	3	4	5	6	7	8	9	10	11	12	13	14	15	16	17	18	19	20	21
	12	12	12	12	12	12	14	12	12	12	12	12	12	12	12	12	12	12	11	12	12
	25	25	25	25	25	25	25	25	25	25	25	25	25	25	25	25	25	25	26	25	25
	5	5	5	5	5	5	3	5	5	5	5	5	5	5	5	5	5	5	5	5	5
	8	8	8	8	8	8		8	8	8	8	8	8	8	8	8	8	8	8	8	8

MP.1 MP.2 MP.4 MP.2 MP.1 MP.2 MP.8 MP.2 MP.7 MP.4 MP.4 MP.1 MP.4

	22	23	24	25	26	27	28	29	30	31	32	33	34	35	36	37	38	39	40	41
	12	11	12	13	12	12	12	13	12	12	12	12	12	12	12	12	12	12	12	9
	25	28	26	25	25	25	25	25	25	25	25	25	25	25	25	25	25	25	25	41
	5	3	4	4	5	5	5	4	5	5	5	5	5	5	5	5	5	5	5	
	8	8	8	8	8	8	8	8	8	8	8	8	8	8	8	8	8	8	8	

MP.4 MP.1 MP.4 MP.8 MP.4 MP.8 MP.7 MP.2 MP.1 MP.4 MP.1 MP.7 MP.4 MP.8 MP.7 MP.4 MP.5

MP = Mathematical Practice

Focus Grade Level Standards

Understand addition as putting together and adding to, and understand subtraction as taking apart and taking from.

K.OA.1 Represent addition and subtraction with objects, fingers, mental images, drawings, sounds (e.g., claps), acting out situations, verbal explanations, expressions, or equations. (Drawings need not show details, but should show the mathematics in the problem. This applies wherever drawings are mentioned in the Standards.)

Module 4: Number Pairs, Addition and Subtraction to 10
Date: 11/12/13

iv

K.OA.2   Solve addition and subtraction word problems, and add and subtract within 10, e.g., by using objects or drawings to represent the problem.

K.OA.3   Decompose numbers less than or equal to 10 into pairs in more than one way, e.g., by using objects or drawings, and record each decomposition by a drawing or equation (e.g., 5 = 2 + 3 and 5 = 4 + 1).

K.OA.4   For any number from 1 to 9, find the number that makes 10 when added to the given number, e.g., by using objects or drawings, and record the answer with a drawing or equation.

K.OA.5   Fluently add and subtract within 5.

Foundational Standards

PK.OA.1   Demonstrate an understanding of addition and subtraction by using objects, fingers, and responding to practical situation (e.g., If we have 3 apples and add two more, how many apples do we have all together?).

PK.OA.2   Duplicate and extend (e.g., What comes next?) simple patterns using concrete objects.

Focus Standards for Mathematical Practice

MP.1   **Make sense of problems and persevere in solving them.** Students identify story problems as addition or subtraction situations and find the unknown. Students will demonstrate with drawings and verbal explanations the referent of each number in a given problem type.

MP.2   **Reason abstractly and quantitatively.** Students reason about the relationships between numbers in composition and decomposition situations. They can show, using the number bond mat, and explain that 6 and 4 make 10 and that 10 can be broken into 6 and 4.

MP.4   **Model with mathematics.** Students use number bonds and addition and subtraction equations to model composition and decomposition. Students will tell story problems using drawings, numbers, and symbols.

MP.5   **Use appropriate tools strategically.** Students select and use tools such as drawings, number bonds, and the number path to solve problems.

MP.7   **Look for and make use of structure.** Students draw the 5 + n pattern to reason about numbers within 10.

MP.8   **Look for and express regularity in repeated reasoning.** Students add and subtract 0 to get the same number. They also use linking cubes to add and subtract 1 to reason about 1 more and 1 less than with numbers to 10.

Overview of Module Topics and Lesson Objectives

Standards		Topics and Objectives	Days
K.OA.1 **K.OA.3** **K.OA.5**	A	**Compositions and Decompositions of 2, 3, 4, and 5**	6
		Lesson 1: Model composition and decomposition of numbers to 5 using actions, objects, and drawings.	
		Lesson 2: Model composition and decomposition of numbers to 5 using fingers and linking cube sticks.	
		Lesson 3: Represent composition story situations with drawings using numeric number bonds.	
		Lesson 4: Represent decomposition story situations with drawings using numeric number bonds.	
		Lesson 5: Represent composition and decomposition of numbers to 5 using pictorial and numeric number bonds.	
		Lesson 6: Represent number bonds with composition and decomposition story situations.	
K.OA.3 K.OA.1 K.OA.4	B	**Decompositions of 6, 7, and 8 into Number Pairs**	6
		Lesson 7: Model decompositions of 6 using a story situation, objects, and number bonds.	
		Lesson 8: Model decompositions of 7 using a story situation, sets, and number bonds.	
		Lesson 9: Model decompositions of 8 using a story situation, arrays, and number bonds.	
		Lesson 10: Model decompositions of 6–8 using linking cube sticks to see patterns.	
		Lesson 11: Represent decompositions for 6–8 using horizontal and vertical number bonds.	
		Lesson 12: Use 5-groups to represent the 5 + n pattern to 8.	
K.OA.1 **K.OA.2** K.OA.3 K.OA.4	C	**Addition with Totals of 6, 7, and 8**	6
		Lesson 13: Represent decomposition and composition addition stories to 6 with drawings and equations with no unknown.	
		Lesson 14: Represent decomposition and composition addition stories to 7 with drawings and equations with no unknown.	
		Lesson 15: Represent decomposition and composition addition stories to 8 with drawings and equations with no unknown.	

➡

Module 4:	Number Pairs, Addition and Subtraction to 10
Date:	11/12/13

vi

Standards		Topics and Objectives	Days
		Lesson 16: Solve *add to with result unknown* word problems to 8 with equations. Box the unknown.	
		Lesson 17: Solve *put together with total unknown* word problems to 8 using objects and drawings.	
		Lesson 18: Solve *both addends unknown* word problems to 8 to find addition patterns in number pairs.	
K.OA.1 K.OA.2 K.OA.3	D	**Subtraction from Numbers to 8**	6
		Lesson 19: Use objects and drawings to find *how many are left*.	
		Lesson 20: Solve *take from with result unknown* expressions and equations using the minus sign with no unknown.	
		Lesson 21: Represent subtraction story problems using objects, drawings, expressions, and equations.	
		Lesson 22: Decompose the number 6 using 5-group drawings by breaking off or removing a part, and record each decomposition with a drawing and subtraction equation.	
		Lesson 23: Decompose the number 7 using 5-group drawings by hiding a part, and record each decomposition with a drawing and subtraction equation.	
		Lesson 24: Decompose the number 8 using 5-group drawings and crossing off a part, and record each decomposition with a drawing and subtraction equation.	
		Mid-Module Assessment: Topics A–D	3
K.OA.3	E	**Decompositions of 9 and 10 into Number Pairs**	4
		Lesson 25: Model decompositions of 9 using a story situation, objects, and number bonds.	
		Lesson 26: Model decompositions of 9 using fingers, linking cubes, and number bonds.	
		Lesson 27: Model decompositions of 10 using a story situation, objects, and number bonds.	
		Lesson 28: Model decompositions of 10 using fingers, sets, linking cubes, and number bonds.	
K.OA.2	F	**Addition with Totals of 9 and 10**	4
		Lesson 29: Represent pictorial decomposition and composition addition stories to 9 with 5-group drawings and equations with no	

Standards		Topics and Objectives	Days
		unknown.	
		Lesson 30: Represent pictorial decomposition and composition addition stories to 10 with 5-group drawings and equations with no unknown.	
		Lesson 31: Solve *add to with total unknown* and *put together with total unknown* problems with totals of 9 and 10.	
		Lesson 32: Solve *both addends unknown* word problems with totals of 9 and 10 using 5-group drawings.	
K.OA.1 K.OA.2 K.OA.3	G	**Subtraction from 9 and 10**	4
		Lesson 33: Solve *take from* equations with no unknown using numbers to 10.	
		Lesson 34: Represent subtraction story problems by breaking off, crossing out, and hiding a part.	
		Lesson 35: Decompose the number 9 using 5-group drawings, and record each decomposition with a subtraction equation.	
		Lesson 36: Decompose the number 10 using 5-group drawings, and record each decomposition with a subtraction equation.	
K.OA.1 K.OA.2 K.OA.4	H	**Patterns with Adding 0 and 1 and Making 10**	5
		Lesson 37: Add or subtract 0 to get the same number and relate to word problems wherein the same quantity that joins a set, separates.	
		Lesson 38: Add 1 to numbers 1–9 to see the pattern of *the next number* using 5-group drawings and equations.	
		Lesson 39: Find the number that makes 10 for numbers 1–9, and record each with a 5-group drawing.	
		Lesson 40: Find the number that makes 10 for numbers 1–9, and record each with an addition equation.	
		Lesson 41: Culminating task—choose tools strategically to model and represent a stick of 10 cubes broken into two parts.	
		End-of-Module Assessment: Topics E–H	3
Total Number of Instructional Days			**47**

Module 4:   Number Pairs, Addition and Subtraction to 10
Date: 11/12/13

viii

Terminology

New or Recently Introduced Terms

- Addition (specifically using *add to with result unknown, put together with total unknown, put together with both addends unknown*)
- Addition and Subtraction sentences (equations)
- Make 10 (combine two numbers from 1–9 that add up to 10)
- Minus (−)
- Number bond (mathematical model)
- Number pairs or partners (embedded numbers)
- Part (addend or embedded number)
- Put together (add)
- Subtraction (specifically using *take from with result unknown*)
- Take apart (decompose)
- Take away (subtract)
- Whole (total)

Number Bond

Familiar Terms and Symbols[2]

- 5-group
- Equals (=)
- Hidden partners (embedded numbers)
- Number sentence (3 = 2 + 1)
- Number story (stories with *add to* or *take from* situations)
- Numbers 0–10
- Plus (+)

		5 + n **pattern**		
6 = 5 + 1	7 = 5 + 2	8 = 5 + 3	9 = 5 + 4	10 = 5 + 5

5-groups highlight the 5 + n pattern

Suggested Tools and Representations

- 5-group dot cards
- Linking cubes
- Number bonds
- Number path
- Number towers
- Sets of objects
- Showing fingers the Math way

1	2	3	4	5	6	7	8	9	10

Number Path

---

[2] These are terms and symbols students have seen previously.

Scaffolds[3]

The scaffolds integrated into *A Story of Units* give alternatives for how students access information as well as express and demonstrate their learning. Strategically placed margin notes are provided within each lesson elaborating on the use of specific scaffolds at applicable times. They address many needs presented by English language learners, students with disabilities, students performing above grade level, and students performing below grade level. Many of the suggestions are organized by Universal Design for Learning (UDL) principles and are applicable to more than one population. To read more about the approach to differentiated instruction in *A Story of Units,* please refer to "How to Implement *A Story of Units.*"

Assessment Summary

Type	Administered	Format	Standards Addressed
Mid-Module Assessment Task	After Topic D	Constructed response with rubric	K.OA.1 K.OA.2 K.OA.3 K.OA.5
End-of-Module Assessment Task	After Topic H	Constructed response with rubric	K.OA.1 K.OA.2 K.OA.3 K.OA.4
Culminating Task	Lesson 41	Demonstration of understanding of part–whole relationships and corresponding equations	K.OA.1 K.OA.2 K.OA.4

---

[3] Students with disabilities may require Braille, large print, audio, or special digital files. Please visit the website, www.p12.nysed.gov/specialed/aim, for specific information on how to obtain student materials that satisfy the National Instructional Materials Accessibility Standard (NIMAS) format.

Module 4:	Number Pairs, Addition and Subtraction to 10
Date:	11/12/13

x

Topic A

Compositions and Decompositions of 2, 3, 4, and 5

K.OA.1, K.OA.3, K.OA.5

Focus Standard:	K.OA.1	Represent addition and subtraction with objects, fingers, mental images, drawings, sounds (e.g., claps), acting out situations, verbal explanations, expressions, or equations. (Drawings need not show details, but should show the mathematics in the problem.)
	K.OA.3	Decompose numbers less than or equal to 10 into pairs in more than one way, e.g., by using objects or drawings, and record each decomposition by a drawing or equation (e.g., 5 = 2 + 3 and 5 = 4 + 1).
	K.OA.5	Fluently add and subtract within 5.
Instructional Days:	6	
Coherence -Links from:	GPK–M5	Numerals to 5, Addition and Subtraction Stories, Counting to 20
-Links to:	G1–M1	Sums and Differences to 10

In Module 1, students found embedded numbers and experienced decomposition by finding hidden partners. Topic A formally teaches composition and decomposition using number bonds as students explore the relationships between numbers to set the foundation for addition and subtraction.

In the first two lessons, students play with composition (3 and 2 make 5) by talking about the number of birds, fingers, and cubes together and decomposition (5 is 3 and 2) by finding embedded numbers in a group. They learn to record the relationships between quantities by drawing pictures in the number bond model.

In Lesson 3, students explore composing number pairs and record their findings using drawings and numerals in the number bond model.

Lesson 4 then has students consider decomposition as a whole separated into number pairs and record their findings using drawings and numerals in the number bond model.

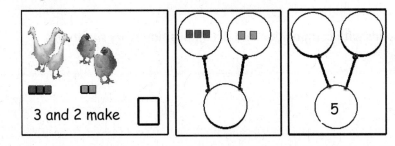

Lesson 5 allows students to use the number bond model as a tool to help them model composition and decomposition. The end goal of this topic is for students to be flexible with the number bond model oriented in various ways and be able to understand the part–part–whole components. By the end of the module, they will understand the number bond's relationship to the accompanying expression or equation.

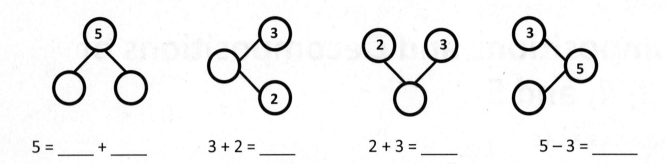

5 = ____ + ____   3 + 2 = ____   2 + 3 = ____   5 − 3 = ____

The final lesson of the topic gives students opportunities to move from abstract to concrete by acting out and creating stories based on a given number bond. Throughout Topic A, a fluid movement between composition and decomposition provides a firm foundation for understanding the relationship between addition and subtraction.

A Teaching Sequence Towards Mastery of Compositions and Decompositions of 2, 3, 4, and 5
Objective 1: Model composition and decomposition of numbers to 5 using actions, objects, and drawings.   (Lesson 1)
Objective 2: Model composition and decomposition of numbers to 5 using fingers and linking cube sticks.   (Lesson 2)
Objective 3: Represent composition story situations with drawings using numeric number bonds.   (Lesson 3)
Objective 4: Represent decomposition story situations with drawings using numeric number bonds.   (Lesson 4)
Objective 5: Represent composition and decomposition of numbers to 5 using pictorial and numeric number bonds.   (Lesson 5)
Objective 6: Represent number bonds with composition and decomposition story situations.   (Lesson 6)

Lesson 1

Objective: Model composition and decomposition of numbers to 5 using actions, objects, and drawings.

Suggested Lesson Structure

■ Fluency Practice	(12 minutes)
■ Application Problem	(5 minutes)
■ Concept Development	(25 minutes)
■ Student Debrief	(8 minutes)
Total Time	**(50 minutes)**

Fluency Practice (12 minutes)

- 5-Frames: Counting Dots and Spaces **K.OA.5**   (3 minutes)
- Making 3, 4, and 5 Finger Combinations **K.OA.3**   (4 minutes)
- Make 5 Matching Game **K.OA.5**   (5 minutes)

Note: The following fluency activities review hidden partners of 3–5. This will help students recall familiar relationships between numbers 1–5, preparing them to explore those relationships using the number bond model.

5-Frames: Counting Dots and Spaces (3 minutes)

Materials: (T) Large 5-frame cards (Fluency Template A)

T: Raise your hand when you have counted the dots, then wait for the snap to say the number. How many dots? (Show 4 dot card. Wait until all hands are raised, and then give the signal.)

S: 4.

T: How many empty spaces? (Wait until all hands are raised, and then give the signal.)

S: 1.

Continue to show cards, exploring all of the decompositions of 5.

Making 3, 4, and 5 Finger Combinations (4 minutes)

T: I'll show you some fingers. I want to make 3. Show me what is needed to make 3. (Show 2 fingers.)

Lesson 1:	Model composition and decomposition of numbers to 5 using actions, objects, and drawings.	
Date:	11/12/13	4.A.3

S: (Show 1 finger.)

T: Raise your hand when you can say the number sentence. Start with my number.

S: 2 and 1 make 3.

Continue with number pairs for 3, 4, and 5. Once students understand the game, let them play with a partner, rapidly and energetically.

Make 5 Matching Game (5 minutes)

Materials: (S) Fluency Template B cards with quantities of 0, 1, 2, 3, 4, 5 (use only dots, dice, and fingers) per pair

1. Shuffle and place the cards face down in two equal rows.

2. Partner A turns over two cards.

3. If the total of the numbers on both cards is 5, then she collects both cards. If not, then Partner A turns them back over in their original place facedown.

4. Repeat for Partner B.

Variation: Provide each partner with a stick of 5 cubes to help them determine the missing part. For example, a student turns over 4, then breaks off 4 cubes, revealing 1 as the missing part, that way he knows to look for the card with the number 1.

A NOTE ON
MULTIPLE MEANS OF
ENGAGEMENT:

For students with processing or memory issues, place cards face up to play the game. Students can match partners of 5 without the added memory requirement.

Application Problem (5 minutes)

MP.1

Julia went to the beach and found 3 seashells. Her sister Megan found 2 seashells. Draw the seashells the girls found. How many did they find in all? Talk to your partner about how you know!

Note: This problem anticipates the composition of numbers to 5 in today's lesson.

NOTES ON
MULTIPLE MEANS OF
ACTION AND
EXPRESSION:

Scaffold the Application Problem for your below level students by giving them linking cubes to use in solving the problem. Once students are comfortable solving problems with manipulatives, you can transition them to the pictorial strategy of drawing a representation of the problem.

Concept Development (25 minutes)

Materials: (T) 3 hula hoops, colorful masking tape, template graphic of birds (S) Number bond template and 5 cubes

Before the lesson begins, prepare a large number bond template on the classroom floor using hula hoops and tape, and place the template graphic of birds on the board.

T: We are going to play a game today! Student A, please come and stand in this hula hoop. (Direct the student to stand in one part of the "number bond.") Students B and C, please come stand in this

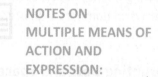

COMMON CORE

Lesson 1:

Date:

Model composition and decomposition of numbers to 5 using actions, objects, and drawings.
11/12/13

4.A.4

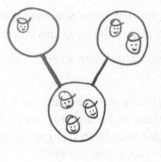

hula hoop. (Direct students to stand in the other part.) What do you notice?

S: There are two students in one hoop and one in the other.
→ There are three students standing up. → One hoop is still empty. → There are some lines on the floor, too!

T: Yes, there are some special paths on the floor connecting our hoops. I am going to make a picture to show our friends right now. (Construct visual of the number bond on the board showing two students in one part and one in the other.)

T: Let's pretend the students are all going to a party. Please walk along the tape paths to get to the party. Don't fall off the path! What do you notice now?

S: Now all three of them are in one hoop!

T: So we started with one student in one hoop and two in the other. Now we have all three students in one hoop! Let me put that in my picture. (Complete the pictorial number bond on the board.) 1 student and 2 students together makes…

S: 3 students!

Repeat game three times with other students and combinations for 3, 4 and 5, recording the results in the pictorial number bond on the board each time.

T: Look at the picture of the birds on the board. What do you notice?

S: I see some geese. There are chickens, too.

T: How many birds are there?

S: 5.

T: How many geese? (3) How many hens? (2) So we have five birds. There are 3 geese and 2 hens. Repeat after me: 3 and 2 make 5. (Write the number sentence on the board.)

S: 3 and 2 make 5.

T: I can show that in a hoop picture like we did before! We call this sort of picture a **number bond**. It takes a long time to draw ducks and hens, so I will just draw squares instead.

T: In my picture, I have 3 pretend geese and 2 pretend hens. I have 5 pretend birds in all. Look at my picture to see how this is like what we did with our students in the hoops. (Demonstrate and guide students to see that 3 and 2 make 5 in the number bond.)

T: In both stories two groups were **put together**. One is about students going to a party, and one is about geese and chickens, but the number bond is the same!

T: Turn and talk to your partner. Partner A, tell a put together story about apples and bananas that

A NOTE ON MULTIPLE MEANS OF REPRESENTATION:

After you have introduced *number bonds* to the class, create a visual of a number bond and put it on your math word wall. Be sure that your visual shows number bonds in all orientations. The visual will help your English language learners remember what the term means and enable them to use it in partner talks.

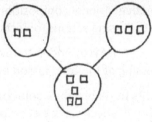

COMMON CORE™

Lesson 1:   Model composition and decomposition of numbers to 5 using
actions, objects, and drawings.
Date: 11/12/13

4.A.5

matches the same number bond. (Wait for Partner A to share.) Now, Partner B, tell a put together story about monkeys and lizards to match the number bond.

Listen as the students share their compostion stories with each other, and give new ideas if they need more practice.

T: Great job putting bananas and apples together, putting the monkeys and lizards together. Now let's start with all the birds and put them into two groups. Look at the picture of the 5 birds. What would you tell me?

S: There are two different kinds of birds. → There are 5 birds in the picture, 3 are geese and 2 are hens!

T: Yes, I could take my 5 birds and show that we have 3 geese and 2 hens. The number bond shows that, too, but I am going to switch it around! (Demonstrate with the bond on the board, this time putting the total on the top.)

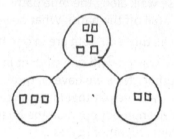

T: Let's tell **take apart** stories to match the number bond, too. Turn and talk to your partner. Partner A, tell a take apart story about 5 animals in two groups: snakes and turtles. (Wait for Partner A to share.) Partner B, tell a take apart story about 5 balls in two groups: basketballs and tennis balls.

T: We're going to practice this some more in our Problem Set. You will get a chance to draw some put together and take apart number bond pictures yourself.

Problem Set (10 minutes)

Students should do their personal best to complete the Problem Set within the allotted 10 minutes.

Student Debrief (8 minutes)

Lesson Objective: Model composition and decomposition of numbers to 5 using actions, objects, and drawings.

The Student Debrief is intended to invite reflection and active processing of the total lesson experience.

Invite students to review their solutions for the Problem Set. They should check work by comparing answers with a partner before going over answers as a class. Look for misconceptions or misunderstandings that can be addressed in the Debrief. Guide students in a conversation to debrief the Problem Set and process the lesson.

You may choose to use any combination of the questions below to lead the discussion.

- What new type of drawing did we use today? (**Number bond**.)

- In the Problem Set, which story was about putting together and which story was about taking apart?

- Did you notice that the number bond was different for the butterflies and cats? Why do you think I drew the number bond differently?

- Look at the butterflies on your Problem Set. Why did we draw all the butterflies in the bottom circle?

- We drew circles in the last number bond on our Problem Set. What do the three circles represent?

- What do the two circles you drew represent? How does drawing little circles instead of cats help us in math?

- What happened when we played the games with the hula hoops?

- How did you know what we should write in each of the hoops in our number bonds?

- Did our number bond look different when we worked backwards, starting with the whole group of birds?

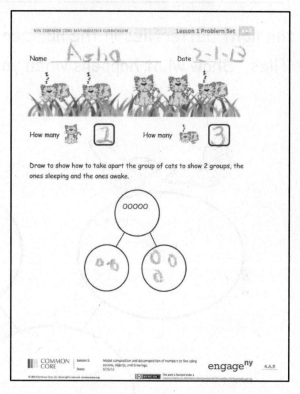

Lesson 1:   Model composition and decomposition of numbers to 5 using actions, objects, and drawings.

Date: 11/12/13

4.A.7

Name _____   Date _____

Draw the light butterflies in the number bond. Then draw the dark butterflies. Show what happens when you put the butterflies together.

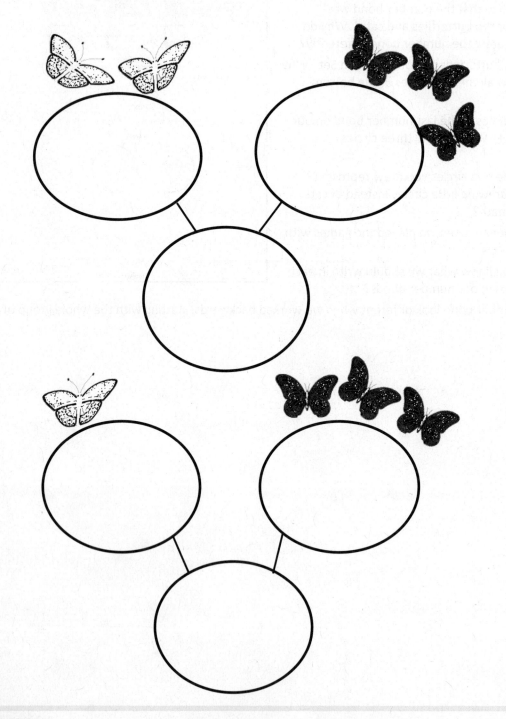

Lesson 1:   Model composition and decomposition of numbers to 5 using actions, objects, and drawings.
Date: 11/12/13

4.A.8

Name _____   Date _____

How many  ? ☐   How many  ? ☐

Draw to show how to take apart the group of cats to show 2 groups, the ones sleeping and the ones awake.

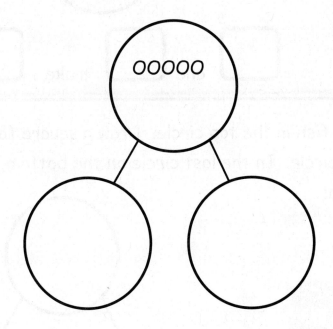

 Lesson 1: Model composition and decomposition of numbers to 5 using actions, objects, and drawings.

Date: 11/12/13

4.A.9

Name _____   Date _____

Draw the blue fish in the first circle on top. Draw the orange fish in the next circle on top. Draw all the fish in the bottom circle.

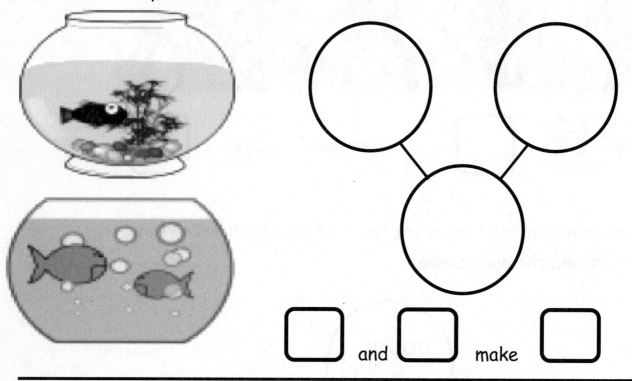

Draw a square for each fish in the top circle. Draw a square for each goldfish in the bottom circle. In the last circle on the bottom, draw a cube for each spiny fish.

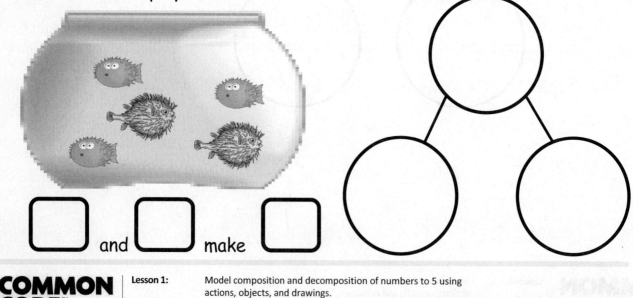

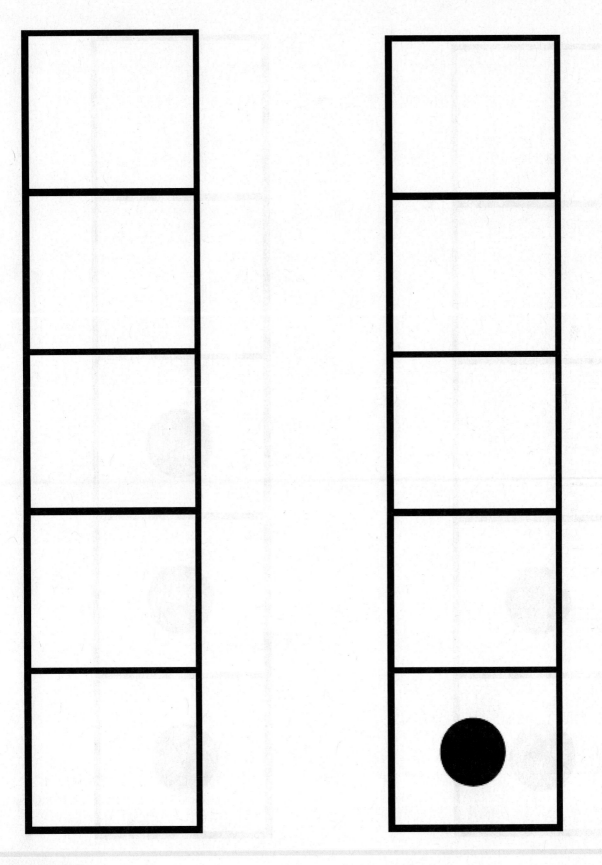

COMMON CORE™   Lesson 1:   Model composition and decomposition of numbers to 5 using
                                    actions, objects, and drawings.
                     Date: 11/12/13   4.A.11

© 2013 Common Core, Inc. All rights reserved. **commoncore.org**

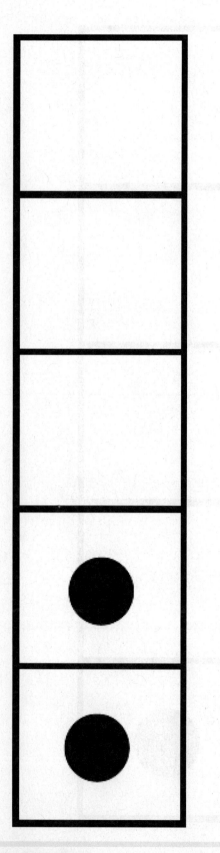
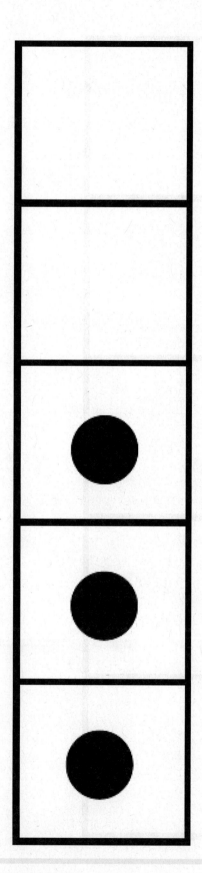

COMMON CORE™

Lesson 1:   Model composition and decomposition of numbers to 5 using actions, objects, and drawings.

Date: 11/12/13

4.A.12

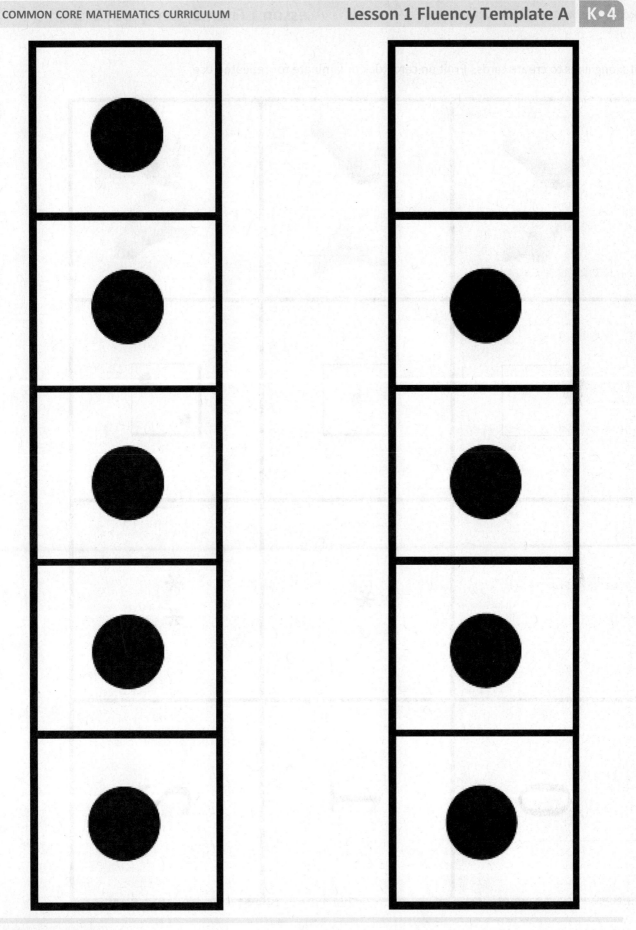

COMMON CORE™   Lesson 1:   Model composition and decomposition of numbers to 5 using
actions, objects, and drawings.   4.A.13
            Date: 11/12/13

© 2013 Common Core, Inc. All rights reserved. commoncore.org

Cut along lines to create cards. Print on cardstock or laminate for repeated use.

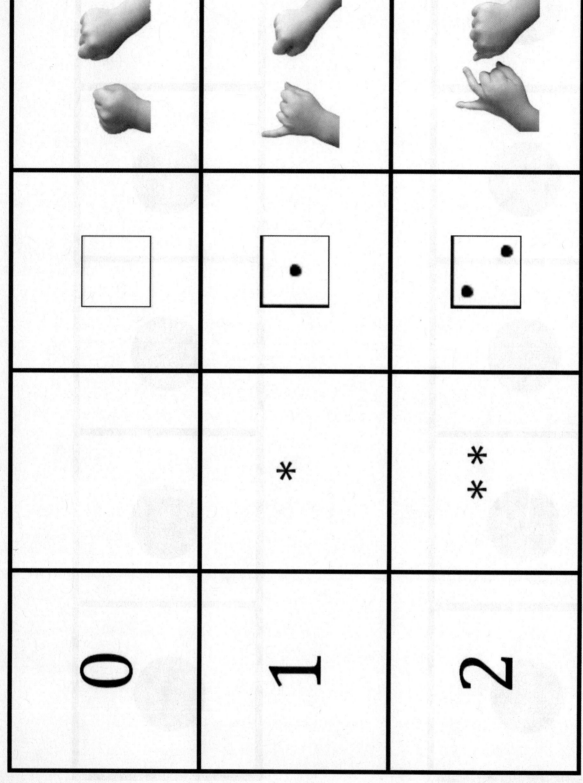

COMMON CORE™

Lesson 1: Model composition and decomposition of numbers to 5 using actions, objects, and drawings.
Date: 11/12/13

4.A.14

* * *	* * * *	* * * * *
3	4	5

Lesson 1:

Date:

Model composition and decomposition of numbers to 5 using actions, objects, and drawings.

11/12/13

4.A.15

Lesson 1:   Model composition and decomposition of numbers to 5 using
Date: actions, objects, and drawings.
             11/12/13

4.A.16

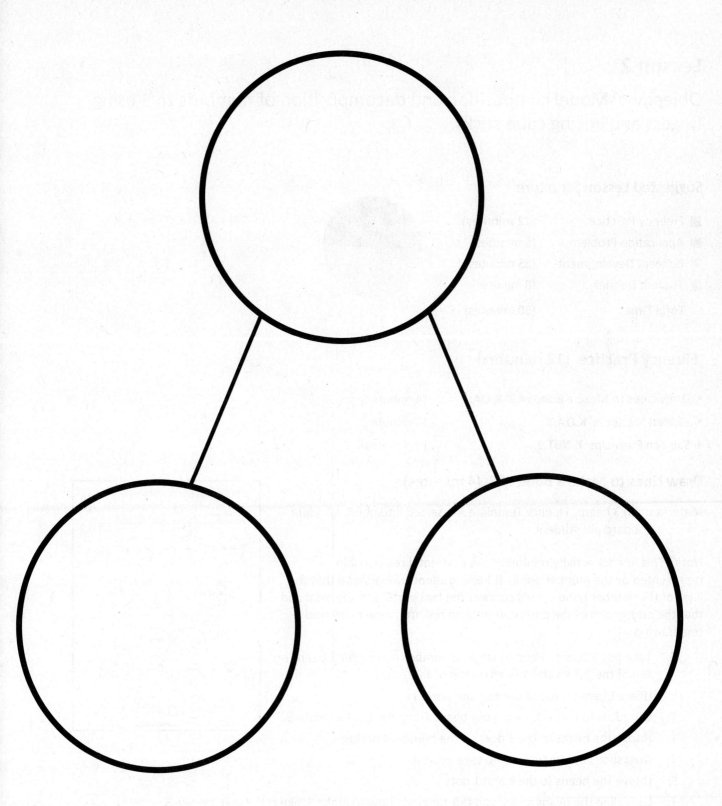

COMMON CORE™

Lesson 1:   Model composition and decomposition of numbers to 5 using
             actions, objects, and drawings.
Date: 11/12/13

4.A.17

Lesson 2

Objective: Model composition and decomposition of numbers to 5 using fingers and linking cube sticks.

Suggested Lesson Structure

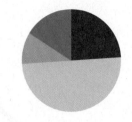

■ Fluency Practice   (12 minutes)

■ Application Problem   (5 minutes)

■ Concept Development   (25 minutes)

■ Student Debrief   (8 minutes)

   Total Time   **(50 minutes)**

Fluency Practice (12 minutes)

- Draw Lines to Make a Bond of 3 **K.OA.1**   (4 minutes)
- Hidden Numbers **K.OA.3**   (4 minutes)
- Say Ten Push-Ups **K.NBT.1**   (4 minutes)

Draw Lines to Make a Bond of 3 (4 minutes)

Materials: (S) 3 beans, Fluency Template A inserted into personal white board per student

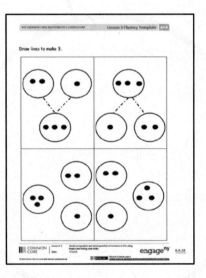

Note: This fluency activity reinforces the part–total relationship represented by the number bond. It helps students understand that the lines of the number bond should connect the two parts with the total and that the orientation of the parts and total do not affect the numerical relationship.

  T: Take out 3 beans. Point to the first number bond. Put 2 beans on top of the 2 dots and 1 bean on top of the 1 dot.

  S: (Place beans on top of the number bond.)

  T: Our job is to make 3. Slide your beans along the lines to make 3.

  S: (Move the beans to the 3 dots on the number bond.)

  T: Now slide your beans back to take apart 3.

  S: (Move the beans to the 2 and 1 dots.)

  T: Let's slide the beans again, and this time, tell how to make 3, like this 2 and 1 make 3.

  S: 2 and 1 make 3 (move the beans to the 3 dots).

Lesson 2:	Model composition and decomposition of numbers to 5 using fingers and linking cube sticks.
Date:	11/12/13

4.A.18

T: Take them apart again.

S: (Move the beans to the 2 and 1 dots.)

T: This time we'll flip it: 1 and 2 make 3.

S: 1 and 2 make 3 (move the beans to the 3 dots).

T: Great. Now leave your beans there. Draw (or trace) the lines to show how to make 3.

Continue guiding students through the process as necessary, and then allow them to complete the remainder of the template independently. Circulate to ensure that they are saying the compositions aloud.

As a variation, have students state the decomposition (i.e., 3 is 2 and 1, 3 is 1 and 2).

Hidden Numbers (5 as the Whole) (4 minutes)

Materials: (S) Fluency Template B inserted into personal white boards

Note: Finding embedded numbers anticipates the work of this module by developing part–whole thinking.

T: Touch and count the fish on your mat. Raise your hand when you know how many (wait for all hands to go up, and then give the signal). Ready?

S: 10.

T: 10 what?

S: 10 fish!

T: Put X's on 5 of the fish. Pretend they swam away!

S: (Cross out 5 fish.)

T: How many fish are left?

S: 5 fish.

T: Circle a group of 4 of the fish who didn't swim away. Pretend they swam away, too.

T: How many fish are left now?

S: 1 fish.

T: Let's circle that 1 fish. How many did you circle all together?

S: 5.

Repeat the process. This time, have 5 fish swim away again but circle 3 fish, then another 2 fish and ask how many are circled. Repeat with other combinations equal to 5. Continue this procedure looking for hidden numbers within groups of 3, 4, and 5. Pause occasionally to allow students to explain efficient ways of locating the groups.

Say Ten Push-Ups (4 minutes)

Note: This activity reviews students' understanding of numbers to 10 for the work of this module and extends to teen numbers in anticipation of Module 5.

T: We are going to do Say Ten Push-Ups. First, let's get ready to push up by counting to 10 the Math

Lesson 2:   Model composition and decomposition of numbers to 5 using fingers and linking cube sticks.

Date: 11/12/13

4.A.19

Way.

S: 1, 2, 3, 4, 5, 6, 7, 8, 9, 10. (Students should start counting with 1 on the left pinky and continue to 10 on the right pinky.)

T: Great! Now that we have 10, we can continue counting with ten (push out both hands as if doing a push-up exercise in the air, then pause with closed fists close to body), 1 (push out the left hand, pinky finger). Repeat please.

S: Ten (push out both hands as if doing a push-up exercise in the air, then pause with closed fists close to body), 1 (push out the left hand, pinky finger).

T: Keep going with me. Ten (repeating push-up), 2 (push out the left hand pinky and ring finger).

Continue to 20 (2 ten or 10 and 10).

Application Problem (5 minutes)

Materials: (S) Set of 5 pennies per student

Margaret and Caleb discovered that if they put their money together, they would have the 5 pennies they needed to buy some gum. Yum!

Put 5 pennies in the middle of your desk. Now slide some to one side of your desk to show how much money Margaret might have had. Put the other coins on the other side of the desk to show how much money Caleb might have had.

Check with your friend to see how he showed Margaret and Caleb's coins. What do you notice?

Slide the coins together again to make sure you have enough for the gum. Now act out the story again. Could you divide the pennies in a different way?

NOTES ON MULTIPLE MEANS OF ENGAGEMENT:

Scaffold the directions to the Application Problem for your English language learners by modeling what you want them to do. Slide the pennies together as you give the direction to slide the pennies together.

Note: The practice in making different compositions for 5 serves as the anticipatory set for today's lesson.

Concept Development (25 minutes)

Materials: (T) 3 hula hoops; colorful masking tape (S) Number bond template on cardstock in a sheet protector, linking cube 5-stick

Prepare a large number bond template on the classroom floor using the hula hoops and tape.

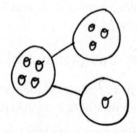

T: It's time for another party game! Students A, B, C, and D, would you please come stand in our hula hoop? (Direct students to stand in the "whole" of the model.) What do you notice?

S: There are four students standing up! → Two of the hoops are empty.

COMMON CORE

Lesson 2:   Model composition and decomposition of numbers to 5 using fingers and linking cube sticks.
Date: 11/12/13

4.A.2

→ We have the paths on the floor.

T: The students have had a wonderful time at the party and now it is time to go home. Student A, please take this path to your hoop home. Students B, C, and D, take the other path to your hoop home. Don't forget—stay on the path! What do you see now?

S: There are 3 in one hoop and 1 in the other! → There are still 4 students.

T: Let's draw what happened on the board. We had 4 students, but we made our 4 into 3 and 1. (Demonstrate by creating the pictorial number bond on the board. Practice the decomposition and number bond recording several times with groups of 2, 3, 4, and 5 students until students seem confident and familiar with the material.)

T: (Hand out number bond templates in the personal white boards). Let's play our party game some more using our linking cubes. Put your 5-stick in the place where the paths come together to show the students at the party. (Circulate to ensure accuracy.) Now let's pretend it is time for the students to go home. Break your 5-stick into two pieces and send each piece home on one of the paths. Put them in your hoops. What do you have now?

| MP.2 |

S: I have a 1 and a 4 in my hoops! → I have a 2 and a 3. → I have 4 and 1.

T: We can make number bonds to show what you have! Tell me your stories. I will draw how many students were at the party and then what happened when they went home. (Demonstrate several student examples using linking cube sketches in the bonds.)

T: In the first picture, I can see that 5 students is the same as 1 student and 4 students. Could we show this with our fingers? Show me 1 on your left hand and 4 on your right hand. How many fingers are you showing me in all?

S: 5!

T: What do you see in the other number bonds? Could you show me each of these with your fingers, too? (Allow time for discussion.) Let's practice more of this in our Problem Set.

Problem Set (10 minutes)

Students should do their personal best to complete the Problem Set within the allotted 10 minutes.

> **NOTES ON MULTIPLE MEANS OF ACTION AND EXPRESSION:**
>
> Extend the lesson for students who are above grade level by asking them to help the teacher by writing down all the decomposition possibilities for numbers 2 to 5. Challenge them to find the 0 and number combination if they do not come up with it on their own.

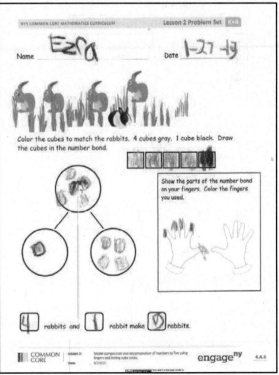

COMMON CORE™ | Lesson 2: Model composition and decomposition of numbers to 5 using fingers and linking cube sticks.
Date: 11/12/13

4.A.21

Student Debrief (8 minutes)

Lesson Objective: Model composition and decomposition of numbers to 5 using fingers and linking cube sticks.

The Student Debrief is intended to invite reflection and active processing of the total lesson experience.

Invite students to review their solutions for the Problem Set. They should check work by comparing answers with a partner before going over answers as a class. Look for misconceptions or misunderstandings that can be addressed in the Debrief. Guide students in a conversation to debrief the Problem Set and process the lesson.

You may choose to use any combination of the questions below to lead the discussion.

- What happened in our number bond when we decided to send the students home from the party?
- Did the whole number of students change when they went home in different groups?
- How did we make our stories into number bonds?
- What did you think about when you were deciding how to break apart your 5-stick?
- How did you show me the number bonds with your fingers?

COMMON CORE™

Lesson 2:   Model composition and decomposition of numbers to 5 using fingers and linking cube sticks.

Date: 11/12/13

4.A.2

Name _____   Date _____

Color the cube stick to match the rabbits. 4 cubes gray. 1 cube black.
Draw the cubes in the number bond.

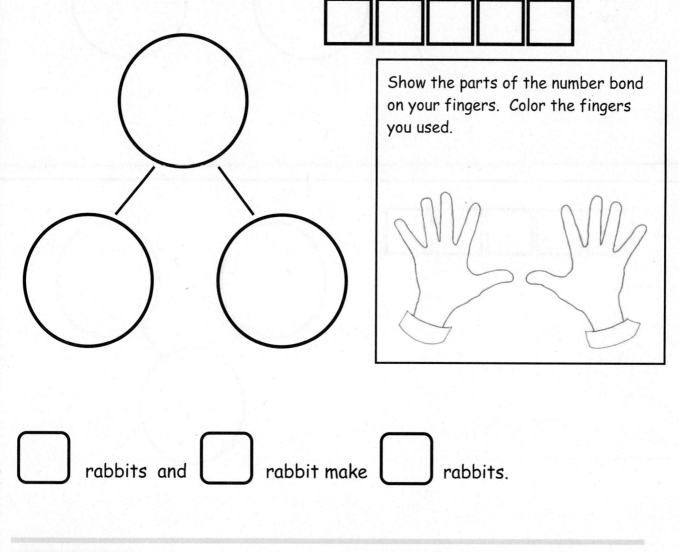

Show the parts of the number bond on your fingers. Color the fingers you used.

☐ rabbits and ☐ rabbit make ☐ rabbits.

COMMON CORE™ | Lesson 2:   Model composition and decomposition of numbers to 5 using fingers
                     and linking cube sticks.   4.A.23
                   | Date: 11/12/13

Name _____   Date _____

In each cube stick, color some cubes blue and the rest of the cubes red.
Draw the cubes you colored in the number bond. Show the hidden partners
on your fingers to an adult. Color the fingers you showed.

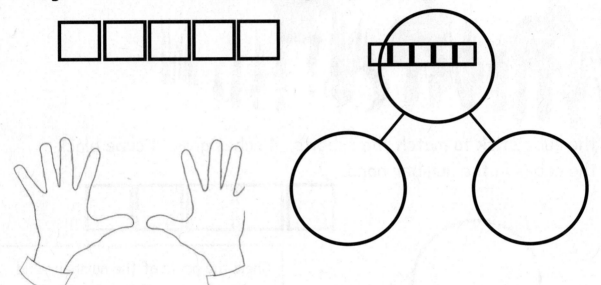

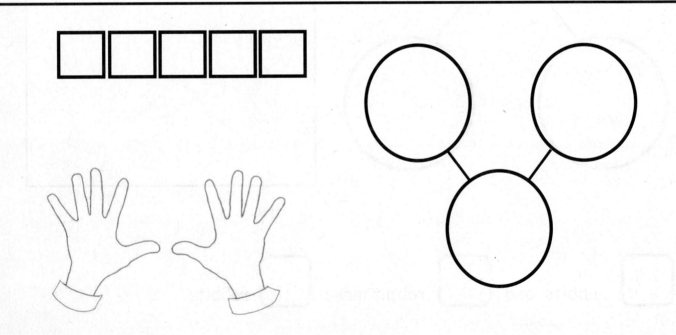

 | **Lesson 2:**

Date: Model composition and decomposition of numbers to 5 using fingers
and linking cube sticks.

11/12/13

4.A.2

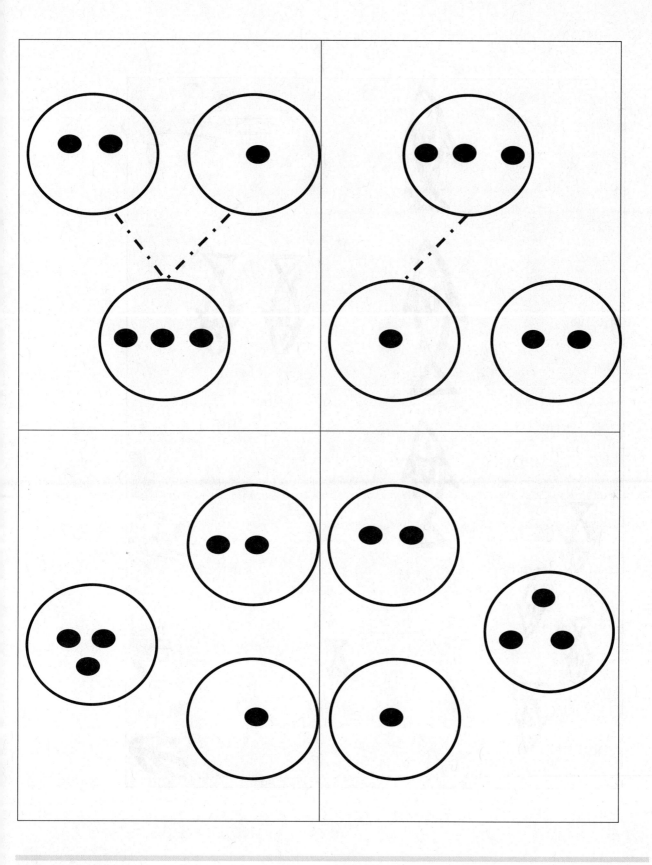

COMMON CORE™

Lesson 2: Model composition and decomposition of numbers to 5 using fingers and linking cube sticks.

Date: 11/12/13

4.A.25

Lesson 2: Model composition and decomposition of numbers to 5 using fingers and linking cube sticks.

Date: 11/12/13

4.A.2

Lesson 3

Objective: Represent composition story situations with drawings using numeric number bonds.

Suggested Lesson Structure

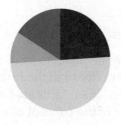

■ Fluency Practice   (12 minutes)
■ Application Problem   (5 minutes)
■ Concept Development   (25 minutes)
■ Student Debrief   (8 minutes)
    Total Time   **(50 minutes)**

Fluency Practice (12 minutes)

▪ Sprint: Number Order to 5 **K.CC.2**   (12 minutes)

Sprint: Number Order to 5 (12 minutes)

Materials: (S) 2 copies of Number Order to 5 Sprint per student

Note: Students grow more comfortable with the Sprint routine while completing a task that involves relatively simple concepts. This will continue to build confidence and enthusiasm for Sprints.

T: It's time for a Sprint! (Briefly recall previous Sprint preparation activities, and distribute Sprints facedown.) Take out your pencil and one crayon, any color.

T: (Distribute the first set of Sprint papers facedown.) For this Sprint, using your pencil, you are going to fill in the missing number. On your mark, get set, go!

T: (Ring the bell or give another signal for students to stop.) Pencils up!

T: Pencils down, crayons up!

T: It's time to check answers. What do you do if the answer is right?

S: Circle it. (Circling correct answers instead of crossing out wrong ones avoids stigmatization.)

T: What do you say?

S: Yes.

T: We'll begin at the top. Ready? 5.

S: Yes!

Continue checking the remaining answers, then have students count how many correct and write the number at the top. Keep the mood celebratory.

T: Before we try again, let's get our mind and body ready to work hard with an exercise. Stand up and push in your chairs. Let's touch our toes while counting to 10. Ready?

S: 1, 2, 3, …10 (touch toes at every count).

T: Hands on your hips, twist slowly, counting down from 10. Ready? (While students exercise, distribute the second set of Sprints, which is the same as the first.)

S: 10, 9, 8, …1 (while twisting).

T: Have a seat. Pencils up. Do you remember the number you got the first time?

S: Yes.

T: See if you can beat your score! Race against yourself! On your mark, get set, go!

Students work on the Sprint for a second time. Give the signal to stop, reiterating that is ok not to finish. Continue to emphasize that the goal is simply to do better than the first time. Proceed through the checking answers procedure with more enthusiasm than ever. Then, facilitate a comparison of Sprint A to Sprint B. Because students are still developing understanding of the concept of more, it may be necessary to circulate and facilitate the comparison, either visually, or numerically.

T: Stand up if you beat your score.

T: Let's celebrate (e.g., congratulate each other, give three pats on the back, shake hands, have a parade, etc.).

Variation: Allow students to finish, but provide an early finisher activity to do on the back.

Application Problem (5 minutes)

Materials: (S) Set of 5 linking cubes per student, number bond template in personal white boards

Chris had 3 baseball cards. Use your cubes to show his cards. Katharine had 2 baseball cards. Show her cards with your cubes. Now, with your cubes, show how many cards they have together.

Make a picture on your personal board to show the story. Can you make a number bond picture about your story? Talk about your work with your partner.

Note: This problem sets the stage for compositions of numbers to 5 in today's lesson and is the first time students are making a number bond drawing without a template.

A NOTE ON
MULTIPLE MEANS OF
REPRESENTATION:

Scaffold the Application Problem for your students who are below grade level by modeling your directions step by step, "Let's show 3 baseball cards. Count with me, 1, 2, 3. Now let's show Katharine's 2 baseball cards. 1, 2," until students are able to work on their own.

Lesson 3:	Represent composition story situations with drawings using numeric number bonds.
Date:	11/12/13

4.A.28

Concept Development (25 minutes)

Materials: (S) Number bond template in personal white board

T: Close your eyes and imagine this story. Two squirrels were playing in the park. Two more squirrels came to join them. Now, open your eyes. In one of your hoops, one of the **parts**, draw squares to show the squirrels that were first playing in the park. (Demonstrate.) In another hoop, the other **part**, draw squares to show the squirrels that joined them. (Demonstrate.) Where would we draw the squares to show all of the squirrels together? (Allow time for discussion.)

S: In the hoop with two paths! → We would draw 4 squares there.

T: Yes, we would draw cubes for all of the squirrels together in the **whole** (demonstrate). Finish your number bond on your personal board and hold it up.

T: What would happen if we turned our number bond around so that the whole is on the left? Try it. Does it change our story?

S: No. → It just looks different. → The squirrels are the same. → To me, it makes the story start with the 4 squirrels. I saw 4 squirrels. 2 were in the park and 2 more came to play.

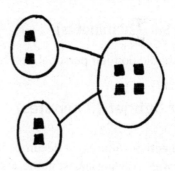

T: Sometimes I get so tired of drawing squares! Would it be fair to use a secret shortcut? How many squares are in this part?

S: 2.

T: Can we erase the squares in that part and write a 2 instead? Would that be fair?

S: Yes! You could put a number for the squares! → You could use numbers instead of the pictures.

T: Let me replace my squares with numbers. (Demonstrate.) Have I changed anything about the story?

S: No. It just looks different. → You just used numbers instead.

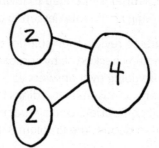

T: Count the squares in each of your hoops, erase them, and write the numbers instead. Turn and talk to your partner about the secret shortcut. (Allow time for discussion.)

T: Erase your personal boards. Listen to my next story and draw a picture on your personal board to show what happens.

T: John read 3 picture books one night. Draw his books. (Pause to allow time for drawing.) The next night, he read 2 more picture books. Draw his new books. (Pause to allow time for drawing.) How many books did John read?

T: Hold up your personal board to show me John's books. (Circulate to ensure accuracy.)

MP.4

T: Great! Let's use our secret shortcut to make a number bond for this story. How many books did John read the first night?

S: 3.

T: Write the number 3 in this part of the number bond. (Demonstrate). How many books did he read the second night?

S: 2.

T: Write the number 2 in this part of the number bond. Now, turn and talk to your partner to find out how many books John read in all. (Allow time for discussion.) How many?

S: 5!

T: Write the number 5 in the whole part of the number bond. We did it! Hold up your personal board! (Circulate to ensure accuracy.)

Use other combinations to create additional number bonds. For example, "What if John had read only 1 book the first night and 4 the second? How would that change our number bond? Could you write the number bonds using only numbers?" Let students practice writing the bonds without demonstrating on the board.

Problem Set (10 minutes)

Students should do their personal best to complete the Problem Set within the allotted 10 minutes.

Student Debrief (8 minutes)

Lesson Objective: Represent decomposition story situations with drawings using numeric number bonds.

The Student Debrief is intended to invite reflection and active processing of the total lesson experience.

Invite students to review their solutions for the Problem Set. They should check work by comparing answers with a partner before going over answers as a class. Look for misconceptions or misunderstandings that can be addressed in the Debrief. Guide students in a conversation to debrief the Problem Set and process the lesson.

You may choose to use any combination of the questions below to lead the discussion.

- What is a **part**? What is the **whole**? How do they work together?

- Does it matter if we use pictures or numbers to show a story? Does it matter if we use pictures or numbers in our number bond? Why or why not?

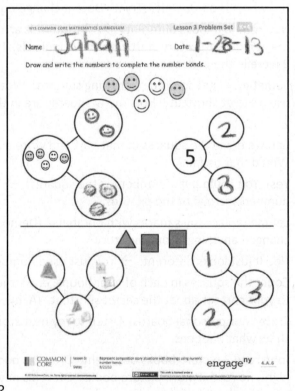

Lesson 3:   Represent composition story situations with drawings using numeric
Date: number bonds.
                 11/12/13

4.A.30

- Look at the smiley faces on your Problem Set. Did your neighbor put the yellow (gray) faces and the white faces in the same parts as you did? Does it matter where we draw the smiley faces that are in the parts?

- What is the fastest way to tell about the triangles and squares in a number bond? Drawing the shapes or writing the numbers?

- Does it make a difference where I write the numbers in the number bond?

NYS COMMON CORE MATHEMATICS CURRICULUM   Lesson 3 Problem Set K•4

Write numbers to complete the number bond. Put the dogs in one part and the balls in the other part.

Look at the picture. Tell a story about the birds going home to your neighbor. Draw a number bond and write numbers that match your story.

COMMON CORE | Lesson 3: Represent composition story situations with drawings using numeric number bonds.
4.A.7

engage^ny

COMMON CORE™

Lesson 3:
Date: 11/12/13

Represent composition story situations with drawings using numeric number bonds.

4.A.31

Fill in the missing number.

0, 1, 2, 3, 4, _____	_____, 4, 3, 2, 1, 0
0, 1, 2, 3, _____, 5	5, _____, 3, 2, 1, 0
0, 1, 2, _____, 4, 5	5, 4, _____, 2, 1, 0
0, 1, _____, 3, 4, 5	5, 4, 3, _____, 1, 0
0, _____, 2, 3, 4, 5	5, 4, 3, 2, _____, 0
_____, 1, 2, 3, 4, 5	5, 4, 3, 2, 1, _____
0, _____, 2, 3, 4, 5	0, 1, 2, 3, _____, 5
0, 1, _____, 3, 4, 5	5, 4, _____, 2, 1, 0
0, 1, 2, _____, 4, 5	0, 1, _____, 3, 4, 5
0, 1, 2, 3, _____, 5	_____, 1, 2, 3, 4, 5

Lesson 3:   Represent composition story situations with drawings using numeric number bonds.

Date: 11/12/13

4.A.32

Name _____   Date _____

Draw and write the numbers to complete the number bonds.

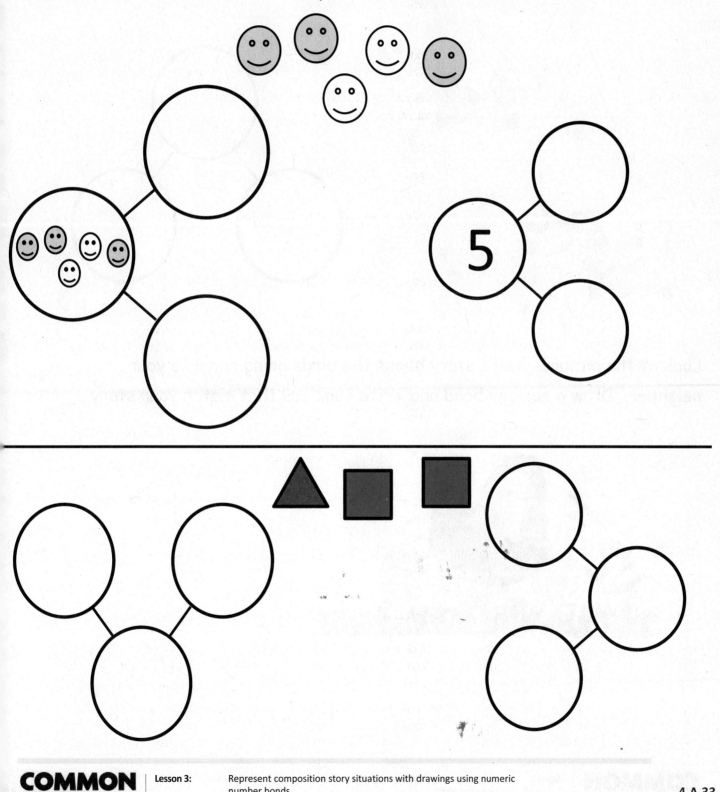

Write numbers to complete the number bond. Put the dogs in one part and the balls in the other part.

Look at the picture. Tell a story about the birds going home to your neighbor. Draw a number bond and write numbers that match your story.

Lesson 3:   Represent composition story situations with drawings using numeric
number bonds.
Date: 11/12/13

4.A.34

Name _____   Date _____

Fill in the number bond to match the domino.

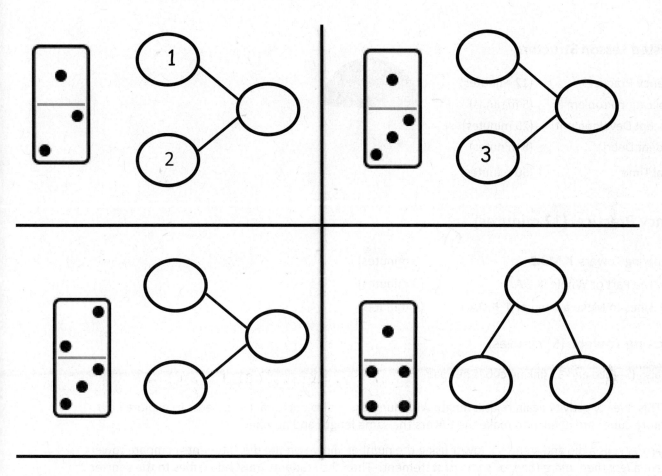

Fill in the domino with dots and fill in the number bond to match.

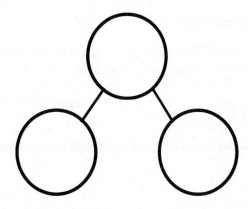

Lesson 3:   Represent composition story situations with drawings lesing numeric number bonds.
Date: 11/12/13

4.A.35

Lesson 4

Objective: Represent decomposition story situations with drawings using numeric number bonds.

Suggested Lesson Structure

■ Fluency Practice   (12 minutes)
■ Application Problem   (5 minutes)
■ Concept Development   (25 minutes)
■ Student Debrief   (8 minutes)

   Total Time   **(50 minutes)**

Fluency Practice (12 minutes)

- Comparing Towers **K.MD.2**   (5 minutes)
- Show Me Part or Whole **K.OA.1**   (3 minutes)
- Draw Lines to Make a Bond of 4 **K.OA.1**   (4 minutes)

Comparing Towers (5 minutes)

Materials: (S) Dice and 12 linking cubes per pair

Note: This fluency activity again relates length with number. It also encourages students to explore how many more cubes are needed to make the towers the same length and number.

Each partner rolls a die and creates a tower using the number shown on the die. Students compare towers and make a *less than*, *more than,* or *same as* statement. Then the students must add cubes to the shorter tower so it is the same height as the longer tower. Consider providing cubes of different colors so that students can easily count how many more cubes they added to make the towers the same length.

Show Me Part or Whole (3 minutes)

Materials: (T) Familiar objects that exemplify the part–whole relationship such as a whole apple and an apple slice or a whole banana and a banana peel

   T: Show me the sign for *whole*. (Model two hands clasped together).
   S: (Hold two hands clasped together.)
   T: Let's use our math muscles and take it apart (exaggerate with facial expression, as if straining to pull the two hands apart).
   S: (Pull two hands apart.)

Lesson 4:   Represent decomposition story situations with drawings using
            numeric number bonds.
Date: 11/12/13

4.A.36

T: Show me whole.

S: (Hold two hands clasped together.)

T: Show me parts.

S: (Pull two hands apart.)

T: Whole, part, whole, part, part, part, whole, whole, part….

S: (Show hand gestures as indicated.)

T: Now, I'll show you some objects, and I want you to decide if it's the whole thing (reinforce with hand gestures), or just part of something (emphasize with gesture). (Hold up an apple slice.) Is this the whole apple, or part of the apple? Think (pause). Now show me.

S: (Hold hands apart, as before.)

T: Now tell me. Is it whole (gesture) or part (gesture)?

S: Part!

T: Very good. Look at what I have now (show a whole apple). Whole or part? Think (pause). Now show me.

S: (Hands clasped together to indicate *whole*.)

T: Raise your hand when you know the math word. (Wait for all hands to go up, then signal.)

S: Whole!

Repeat with a few more objects, being careful to avoid a predictable pattern. Increase the pace, and reduce scaffolding as students demonstrate mastery.

Note: This activity prepares students for today's lesson by linking mathematical vocabulary to kinesthetic movement, and seeing the part-whole relationship in familiar objects.

Draw Lines to Make a Bond of 4 (4 minutes)

Materials: (S) 4 beans, fluency template inserted into personal white board per student

Note: This fluency activity reinforces the part–total relationship represented by the number bond. It helps students understand that the lines of the number bond should connect the two parts with the total and that the orientation of the parts and total do not affect the numerical relationship.

Conduct activity as outlined in GK–M4–Lesson 2. As a variation, have students write the numerals into the parts and wholes (on top of the dots) and then state the decomposition (e.g., 4 is 2 and 2).

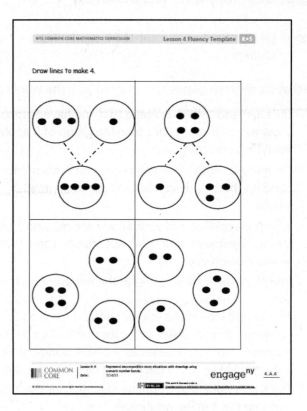

Lesson 4:   Represent decomposition story situations with drawings using
             numeric number bonds.   4.A.37
Date: 11/12/13

Application Problem (5 minutes)

Materials: (S) Small piece of clay, paper, and pencil

NOTES ON
MULTIPLE MEANS OF
ENGAGEMENT:

Chunk the Application Problem into
small pieces for students with
disabilities. Give a direction, and then
watch as the students carry it out
before moving on with the next one.
For example, "Make 5 bananas with
your clay. (Pause.) Draw two plates on
your paper. (Pause.) Put the bananas
on the plates to show one way to share
the bananas."

Anthony had 5 bananas. Make the 5 bananas with your clay.

He wanted to share the bananas with one of his friends. Draw two plates on your paper. Put the bananas on the plates to show one way he could share the bananas with his friend. Draw a number bond to show how he shared his 5 bananas.

Turn and talk with your partner. Did she do it the same way? How many different ways can you find to share the bananas? What if there were only 4 bananas?

Note: The Application Problem will encourage the students to explore different configurations of 5 in preparation for today's lesson on decomposition.

Concept Development (25 minutes)

Materials: (S) Number bond template from prior lessons, two linking cube 5-sticks (all of the same color) per student

Ensure that student templates are oriented with the whole on the top and the parts on the bottom.

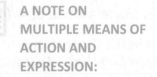

T: Let's pretend today! Pretend that you have 5 apples. Show me with your cubes how the group of 5 apples would look on your mat.

T: I'm going to draw the linking cubes into this number bond on the board, just like you put them in your whole.

T: Now pretend that 3 of your apples are red and 2 are green. Show with your other set of cubes how that would look on your mat.

MP.2

A NOTE ON
MULTIPLE MEANS OF
ACTION AND
EXPRESSION:

Using cubes of one color to represent
the apples pushes students to think
abstractly about the problem. If it is
necessary to start with different color
cubes to support a student who is
struggling with decomposition, do so,
but repeat the problem with cubes of
one color to help the student move
toward more abstract thinking.

T: Good! I'll draw those cubes in the number bond, too. Look carefully at your groups of cubes. Let's show how they would look in the number bond if we used numbers instead. Take your cubes off and write the numbers with your marker as we have done before. Who would like to tell me how to fill in our numbers?

S: The 5 is in this circle, in the whole. → I put the 2 in this part and the 3 in the other part.

T: Great job! You separated the 5 cubes as a set of 2 cubes and a set of 3 cubes. 5 is the same as 2 and 3 together. Did anyone do it a different way? (Allow time for discussion.)

Lesson 4: Represent decomposition story situations with drawings using numeric number bonds.
Date: 11/12/13

4.A.38

T: Put your cubes away. Let's make a different number bond. This time, I want to pretend I have 4 balls. 1 is blue and 3 are orange. How could I show this in my number bond picture? (Allow students to guide you in creating the pictorial number bond.) Make this number bond picture on your mat, too.

T: Now erase the pictures in your number bond and write the numbers instead. Did we change our story?

S: No! We just wrote it in a different way.

T: Let's make another story about 3 things. Let's draw 3 circles for 3 things in the place for our whole. Does anyone have an idea for a story that could give us the parts of a number bond for this 3?

S: I have 3 toy cars. 1 is red and 2 are blue.

T: Hmmm... 1 red car and 2 blue cars. How would I show that in the number bond? (Allow time for discussion and creation of the new pictorial number bond.) Now, show me how it would look with numbers instead. Hold up your white boards!

> **A NOTE ON MULTIPLE MEANS OF ACTION AND EXPRESSION:**
>
> Encourage English language learners to reach for experiences from their culture to tell you a story about their number bond. Use the students' prior knowledge to encourage them to participate in class and use the language they are learning.

Repeat the exercise several times with wholes of 3, 4, and 5. This time, encourage students to only use numbers in the bonds.

Sample further decomposition stories:

- 4 rabbits were hopping through the forest. When they heard a noise, 1 went under a tree, and 3 found a little cave to hide in.
- Marta's father bought 5 bananas. 2 were eaten on Monday and 3 were eaten on Tuesday.
- Mama robin had 3 eggs. 2 eggs hatched in the morning. 1 egg hatched in the afternoon.

T: Let's do some more of this in our Problem Sets.

Problem Set (10 minutes)

Students should do their personal best to complete the Problem Set within the allotted 10 minutes.

Student Debrief (8 minutes)

Lesson Objective: Represent decomposition story situations with drawings using numeric number bonds.

The Student Debrief is intended to invite reflection and active processing of the total lesson experience.

Invite students to review their solutions for the Problem Set. They should check work by comparing answers with a partner before going over answers as a class. Look for misconceptions or misunderstandings that can be addressed in the Debrief. Guide students in a conversation to debrief the Problem Set and process the lesson.

COMMON CORE | Lesson 4:   Represent decomposition story situations with drawings using
                    numeric number bonds.   4.A.39
              Date: 11/12/13

You may choose to use any combination of the questions below to lead the discussion.

- Share with your neighbor the number bond you drew on your Problem Set. How are they the same? How are they different?

- Yesterday, we started with the parts and found the whole. When we started with the parts, could we figure out what the whole had to be?

- Today we started with the whole and found the parts. When we start with the whole can we figure out what the parts have to be, or do we need to be told more of the story? If we just know the whole, can we still figure out what the parts in our story *might* be?

- When we start with the whole, it makes sense to me to put the whole on top so it's as if the parts are falling down. When we start with the parts, I like to put them on top. Then it's as if they are falling down and landing in the same spot. It doesn't have to be like that but do you understand my thinking? Can you explain my thinking to your partner? (It is also valid to think of the story progressing from left to right. Explaining this orientation supports the pattern of reading text from left to right.)

- When you drew your bananas in the number bond, did your number bond look exactly like your partner's? How were they different? (Focus in on orientation of the number bond.) Does it really matter where we put the parts and the whole?

- How do we know where to write each number in a number bond?

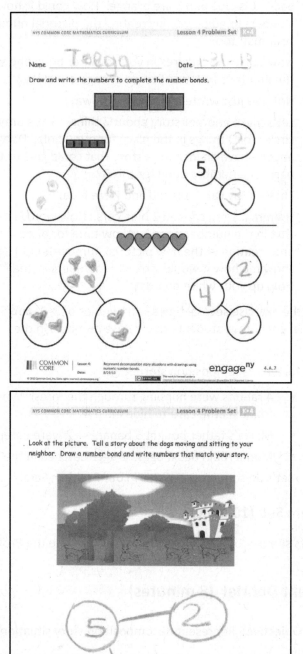

COMMON CORE™

Lesson 4:   Represent decomposition story situations with drawings using numeric number bonds.
Date: 11/12/13

4.A.40

© 2013 Common Core, Inc. All rights reserved. commoncore.org

Draw lines to make a bond of 4.

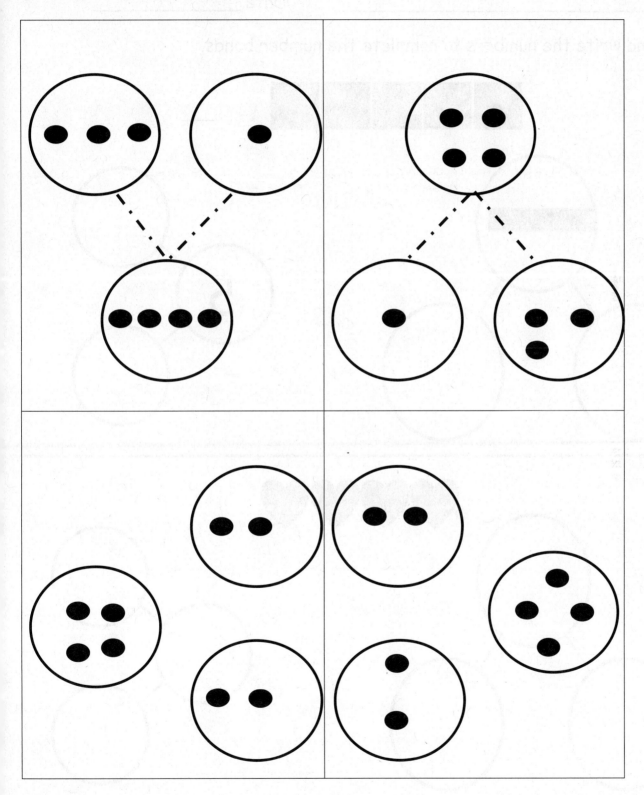

Name _____   Date _____

Draw and write the numbers to complete the number bonds.

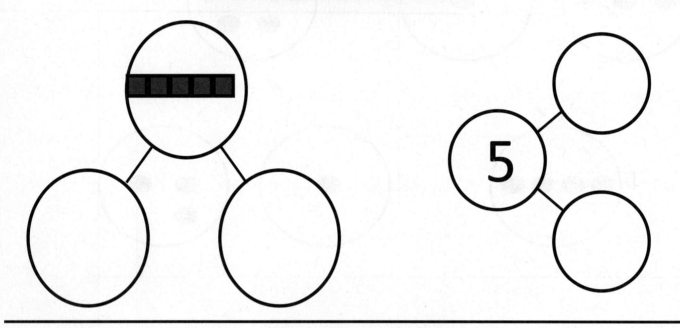

COMMON CORE™

Lesson 4:   Represent decomposition story situations with drawings using
              numeric number bonds.
Date: 11/12/13

© 2013 Common Core, Inc. All rights reserved. commoncore.org

4.A.42

Look at the picture. Tell your neighbor a story about the dogs moving and sitting. Draw a number bond and write numbers that match your story.

Lesson 4: Represent decomposition story situations with drawings using numeric number bonds.
Date: 11/12/13

4.A.43

Name _____   Date _____

Finish the number bonds.   Finish the sentence.

3   is   ☐   and   ☐   2   1

☐   is   ☐   and   ☐   4

Tell an adult a story about the
animals and then make a number
sentence and number bond about it.

☐   is   ☐   and   ☐

Lesson 5

Objective: Represent composition and decomposition of numbers to 5 using pictorial and numeric number bonds.

Suggested Lesson Structure

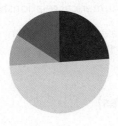

■ Fluency Practice   (12 minutes)
■ Application Problem   (5 minutes)
□ Concept Development   (25 minutes)
■ Student Debrief   (8 minutes)
   Total Time   **(50 minutes)**

Fluency Practice (12 minutes)

- Counting the Say Ten Way with the Rekenrek **K.NBT.1**   (4 minutes)
- Draw Lines to Make a Bond of 5 **K.OA.1**   (4 minutes)
- Making 4 with Squares and Beans **K.OA.3**   (4 minutes)

Counting the Say Ten Way with the Rekenrek (4 minutes)

Materials: (T) 20-bead Rekenrek

Note: This activity is an extension of students' previous work with the Rekenrek, and anticipates working with teen numbers.

   T: We can count with the Rekenrek the same way we do our Say Ten push-ups. (Keep the screen on
        the right side of the Rekenrek to cover beads that are not being counted. Slide over all of the beads
        on the top row.) How many do you see?
   S: 10.
   T: Here's 1 more (slide over 1 bead on the bottom row). How many do you see?
   S: Ten 1.
   T: (Slide 1 more bead over on the bottom row.) How many do you see?
   S: Ten 2.
   T: (Slide 1 more bead over on the bottom row.) How many do you see?
   S: Ten 3.

Continue counting forward and backward. Here is a suggested sequence: ten 1, ten 2, ten 3, ten 2, ten 3,
ten 4, ten 5, ten 4, ten 3, ten 4, ten 3, ten 2, ten 1, etc.

COMMON CORE™ | Lesson 5:   Represent composition and decomposition of numbers to 5 using   4.A.45
                     | pictorial and numeric number bonds.
                     | Date: 11/12/13

Draw Lines to Make a Bond of 5 (4 minutes)

Materials: (S) 5 beans, fluency template inserted into personal white board
              per student

Note: This fluency activity reinforces the part–total relationship represented by the number bond. It helps students understand that the lines of the number bond should connect the two parts with the total and that the orientation of the parts and total do not affect the numerical relationship.

Conduct activity as outlined in GK–M4–Lesson 2. Have students add numerals to the first two bonds if needed to help them move from pictorial to abstract thinking.

Making 4 with Squares and Beans (4 minutes)

Materials: (S) 4 beans, paper or foam squares

Note: This fluency activity is a familiar way for students to practice decompositions of 4 while reviewing geometric properties of squares (4 corners). Students will take what they know about this activity and apply it to number bonds.

- T: Touch and count the corners of the square.
- S: 1, 2, 3, 4.
- T: Touch and count your beans.
- S: 1, 2, 3, 4.
- T: Our job is to make 4. Use 3 beans to mark 3 of the square's corners. Keep the other one in your hand. How many beans on your square?
- S: 3.
- T: How many beans in your hand?
- S: 1.
- T: We can tell how to make 4 like this: 3 and 1 make 4. Echo me, please.
- S: 3 and 1 make 4.

Have students record this on a number bond. Continue with all of the number combinations, including 4 and 0.

Application Problem (5 minutes)

Windsor the puppy had 5 juicy bones. He buried some of them in the yard and put some of them by his dish. Draw his bones. Compare your picture to your friend's. Did you make your pictures the same way? Talk to your friend about how your pictures are alike and how they are different. Make a number

A NOTE ON
MULTIPLE MEANS OF
REPRESENTATION:

Scaffold the Application Problem for English language learners by explaining what you want them to do at each step. Explain that when a dog buries a bone, we cannot see it because it is hidden. Help them draw their 5 bones with some in the dish and some not.

COMMON CORE™ | Lesson 5:   Represent composition and decomposition of numbers to 5 using
              | pictorial and numeric number bonds.
              | Date: 11/12/13

4.A.46

bond about your problem!

Note: In this problem, the students work with and discuss different decompositions of 5 in preparation for today's lesson.

Concept Development (25 minutes)

Materials: (T) White board and various color markers (S) Personal white boards

Draw 4 triangles on the board. Draw a blank number bond.

- T: What do you notice on the board?
- S: There are 4 triangles! → There are some empty number bonds.
- T: I wonder if we could use these triangles to help me make a number bond? Do you remember some ways we learned to sort shapes earlier this year? Let's color 2 red and 2 blue. What would I do now?
- S: We could sort them by color!
- T: Could we put the total number of triangles somewhere in my number bond? In which circle should I draw the whole group of 4 triangles? (Allow time for discussion.)
- S: In the place where you put the whole thing!
- T: I will draw them in the whole. Now, where could I draw my set of 2 red triangles?
- S: In one of the parts.
- T: And the blue ones?
- S: In the other part!
- T: You are right! Please draw these groups on your number bond mat.
- T: You showed me how I can take my 4 triangles and make them into 2 groups of 2! 4 is the same as 2 and 2.

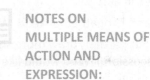

NOTES ON
MULTIPLE MEANS OF
ACTION AND
EXPRESSION:

Ask students who above grade level to explain (either orally or in writing) how they know which circle to draw the total number of triangles in. Ask them to explain why they should not draw the total number of triangles in one of the circles with just one path to it. If other students are confused about where to draw their triangles, ask the advanced students to help.

- T: Help me write the triangle story with numbers in the number bond. (Allow students to assist in writing the numerical number bond and to copy this onto their number bond mat.) We can write what we did in a special **number sentence**:
  4 = 2 + 2. (Say as you write, "4 is the same as 2 and 2.")
- T: Let's try another one. I'm going to make a new number bond and put another shape surprise on the board. (Draw a red circle and create a new number bond template in a different orientation.)
- T: Draw your number bond like mine. How could I use all of my shapes to make a new number bond? How could we sort them?
- S: Some are triangles and one is a circle! → We can sort them by shape.
- T: What would my number bond look like?

Lesson 5:   Represent composition and decomposition of numbers to 5 using
            pictorial and numeric number bonds.
Date: 11/12/13

4.A.47

S: You would draw a circle in one part. → Draw the triangles in the other part.

T: Good. Please draw this picture in your number bond. (Demonstrate.) So, we have 1 shape in this part and four in the other. How many shapes do we have in all?

S: 5!

T: Yes, 1 shape and 4 shapes make 5 shapes altogether. Please draw the whole group of shapes in your number bond.

T: Now, let's write the numbers instead to show our story. Replace the shapes with numbers! (Demonstrate.) 1 and 4 make…

S: 5!

T: I can write it like this: 1 + 4 = 5. (Say as you write, "1 and 4 make 5.") Is there another way we could sort our shapes?

S: We could sort them by color again. → 2 are blue and 3 are red.

T: (Guide students to help you create pictorial and numerical number bonds for the new situation, having them write the number bonds on their mat.) Are we putting the groups together or taking them apart?

S: We are putting the shapes together.

T: When we put them together, where do we put the number for our whole?

S: We put the 5 in the place where the parts come together.

T: You are right. 2 blue shapes and 3 red shapes make…

S: 5 shapes in all!!

T: Yes, 2 and 3 together make 5! We could write that like this: 2 + 3 = 5. Great job!

T: With your partner, draw more shapes and make you own number bonds! (Allow time for drawing and discussion.) Who would like to share their number bonds with the class?

Problem Set (10 minutes)

Students should do their personal best to complete the Problem Set within the allotted 10 minutes. Since this worksheet is single sided, ask early finishers to draw a picture of a story about tomatoes and carrots that either brings the vegetables together or separates them. Ask them to make a number bond to match.

Student Debrief (8 minutes)

Lesson Objective: Represent composition and decomposition of numbers to 5 using pictorial and numeric number bonds.

The Student Debrief is intended to invite reflection and active processing of the total lesson experience.

Invite students to review their solutions for the Problem Set. They should check work by comparing answers with a partner before going over answers as a class. Look for misconceptions or misunderstandings that can be addressed in the Debrief. Guide students in a conversation to debrief the Problem Set and process the lesson.

You may choose to use any combination of the questions below to lead the discussion.

Lesson 5:	Represent composition and decomposition of numbers to 5 using pictorial and numeric number bonds.
Date:	11/12/13

4.A.48

- Look at the cats in the Problem Set. How many cats are there in each problem? (5.) Are they the same or different? Why?
- What ways did we sort our shapes on the board?
- How did we know which number to write in which circle?
- Today we put some things together. Can anyone think of something we put together? How did we use the number bond to show putting together?
- We also took things apart. What did we take apart? How did we use the number bond to show taking apart?

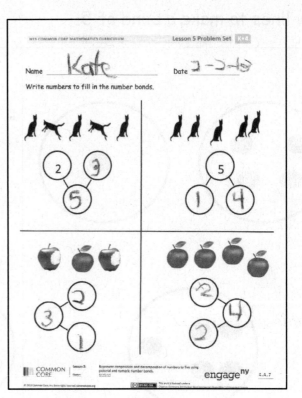

Draw lines to make a bond of 5.

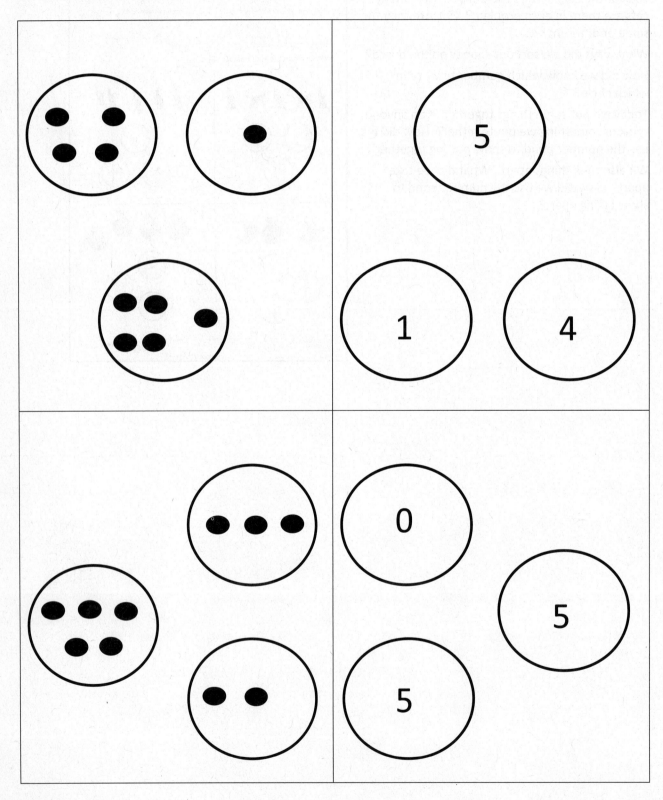

| Lesson 5: | Represent composition and decomposition of numbers to 5 using pictorial and numeric number bonds. |
| Date: | 11/12/13 |

4.A.50

Name _____   Date _____

Write numbers to fill in the number bonds.

COMMON CORE™ | Lesson 5: | Represent composition and decomposition of numbers to 5 using pictorial and numeric number bonds.
Date: | 11/12/13

4.A.51

Name _____   Date _____

There were 2 pandas in a tree. Two more were walking on the ground.
How many pandas were there? Fill in the number bond and the
sentence.

☐ and ☐ make ☐

Tell a story about the penguins. Fill in the number bond to match your story.

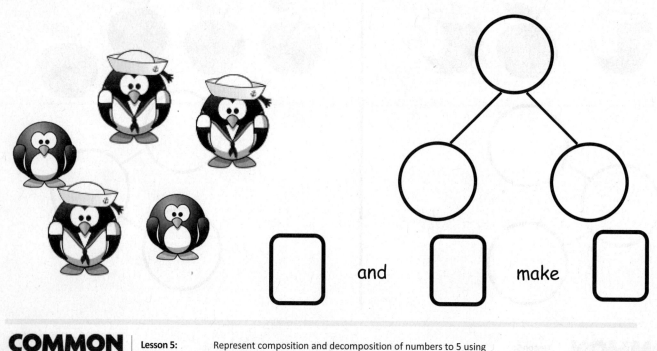

☐ and ☐ make ☐

COMMON CORE™

Lesson 5:   Represent composition and decomposition of numbers to 5 using
               pictorial and numeric number bonds.
Date: 11/12/13

4.A.52

Lesson 6

Objective: Represent number bonds with composition and decomposition story situations.

Suggested Lesson Structure

- ■ Fluency Practice   (12 minutes)
- ■ Application Problem   (5 minutes)
- ☐ Concept Development   (25 minutes)
- ■ Student Debrief   (8 minutes)

   Total Time   **(50 minutes)**

Fluency Practice (12 minutes)

- Sprint: Make 5 **K.OA.5**   (12 minutes)

Sprint: Make 5 (12 minutes)

Materials: (S) 2 copies of the Make 5 Sprint per student

Note: This Sprint focuses on composing 5 in anticipation of the Concept Development. Students grow more comfortable with the Sprint routine while completing a task that involves relatively simple concepts. This will continue to build confidence and enthusiasm for Sprints.

T: It's time for a Sprint! (Briefly recall previous Sprint preparation activities, and distribute Sprints facedown.) Take out your pencil and one crayon, any color. For this Sprint, you are going to circle the number that will make 5. (Demonstrate the first problem as needed.)

Continue to follow the Sprint procedure as outlined in GK–M4–Lesson 3. Have students work on the Sprint for a second time (they will soon work on two different Sprints in a single day). Continue to emphasize that the goal is simply to do better than the first time and celebrate improvement.

Application Problem (5 minutes)

Materials: (S) 5-stick of linking cubes per student, pencil, paper.

Play a game called Snap with your friend! Show him your 5-stick. Now, put your linking cube stick behind your back. When he says, "Snap!" quickly break your linking stick into two parts. Show him one of the parts. Can he guess the other one? If not, show him. Draw a number bond to show what you did with your cubes. Then, it is his turn! If you have time, play it with a 4-stick, a 3-stick, and a 2-stick!

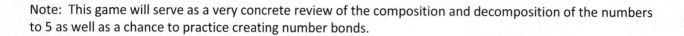
Note: This game will serve as a very concrete review of the composition and decomposition of the numbers to 5 as well as a chance to practice creating number bonds.

Concept Development (25 minutes)

Materials: (T) White board and markers (S) 5-stick per student

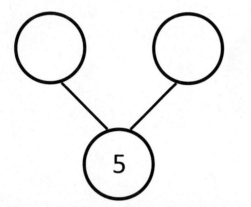

NOTES ON MULTIPLE MEANS OF REPRESENTATION:

To help English language learners ask them to repeat the term *number sentence*, and post it on your math word wall so that you can point to it as you teach. Ask them to give an example of a number sentence and ask them to tell you what we call "2 + 3 = 5." With practice, students will feel more confident to participate in the lessons.

MP.1

T: (Draw the number bond on the white board.) Oh, no! I have a number bond and no story! Who could help me? Use your 5-sticks to help me make up a story. Think about the missing numbers and let's talk about a story to go with your picture. Does anyone have an idea?

S: There were 5 red and green balls. 2 were red. 3 were green. → There was 1 horse sleeping and 4 horses came running up. Then there were 5 horses. → (Various answers which might move from part to whole or whole to part. Accept all responses. We are not encouraging a rigid interpretation of the number bond but rather want students to think flexibly. What matters is that within their stories the sum of the parts equals the whole, though not using those terms.)

T: That's a great story! Let's fill in the number bond. (Demonstrate.) You are right. 5 is the same as 2 and 3 together! We can also write the story in a number sentence like this: 5 = 2 + 3.

T: Let's try one more. (Draw the number bond to the right on the board.)

T: Oh, no! We have another number bond with empty circles! Could you use your linking cubes to help us solve the problem? Could one of my friends help me make up a story to go with this picture?

S: There were 2 sleeping cats and 2 awake cats. How many cats were there in all? → There were 4 cats sleeping. 2 woke up and 2 were still sleeping.

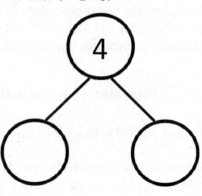

T: Yes! 2 sleeping cats and 2 awake cats make 4 cats in all. Let's fill in our number bond. (Demonstrate.) We could also write it in a number sentence like this: 2 + 2 = 4.

COMMON CORE™	Lesson 6:	Represent number bonds with composition and decomposition story situations.	4.A.54
	Date:	11/12/13	

Repeat exercise for several more number bonds for 5, 4, 3, and 2 before proceeding to the Problem Set. Allow students to share and discuss their stories. Model the associated number sentences in a casual manner, but do not focus on them. Students will begin formal work with expressions (e.g., 3 + 4) and equations (e.g., 3 + 4 = 7) in Topic C.

Problem Set (10 minutes)

Students should do their personal best to complete the Problem Set within the allotted 10 minutes.

Student Debrief (8 minutes)

Lesson Objective: Represent number bonds with composition and decomposition story situations.

The Student Debrief is intended to invite reflection and active processing of the total lesson experience.

Invite students to review their solutions for the Problem Set. They should check work by comparing answers with a partner before going over answers as a class. Look for misconceptions or misunderstandings that can be addressed in the Debrief. Guide students in a conversation to debrief the Problem Set and process the lesson.

You may choose to use any combination of the questions below to lead the discussion.

- How did you decide what numbers to use for your number story?
- Do your stories and the number bonds tell the same thing?
- How were your number stories different from your friends'?
- How did the Snap game connect to today's lesson?
- Look at the Problem Set with the cubes. Look at the first two sticks. How many cubes are in each stick? (5.) Look at the matching number bond. Are the numbers the same in each bond? There are 5 cubes in each stick, so why are the parts different?

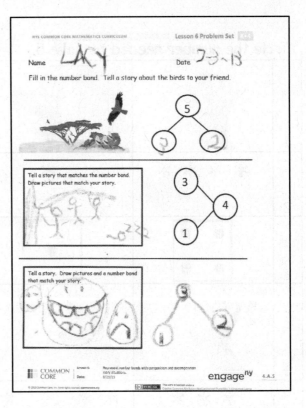

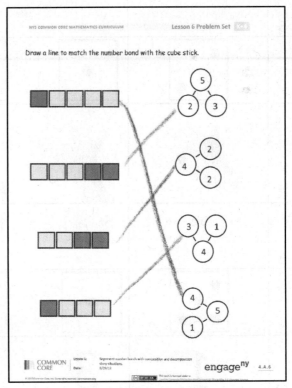

COMMON CORE | Lesson 6:   Represent number bonds with composition and decomposition story situations.
| Date: 11/12/13

4.A.55

Circle the number needed to make 5.

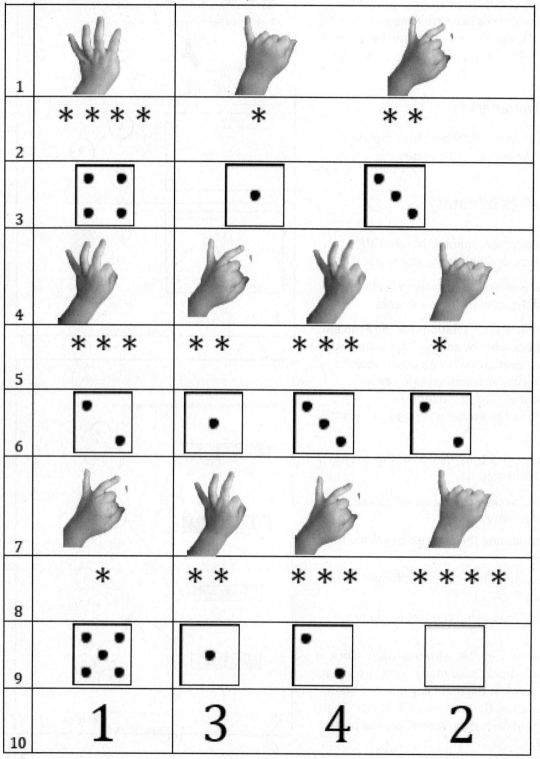

Lesson 6:	Represent number bonds with composition and decomposition
Date:	story situations.
	11/12/13

4.A.56

© 2013 Common Core, Inc. All rights reserved. commoncore.org

Name _____ Date _____

Fill in the number bond. Tell a story about the birds to your friend.

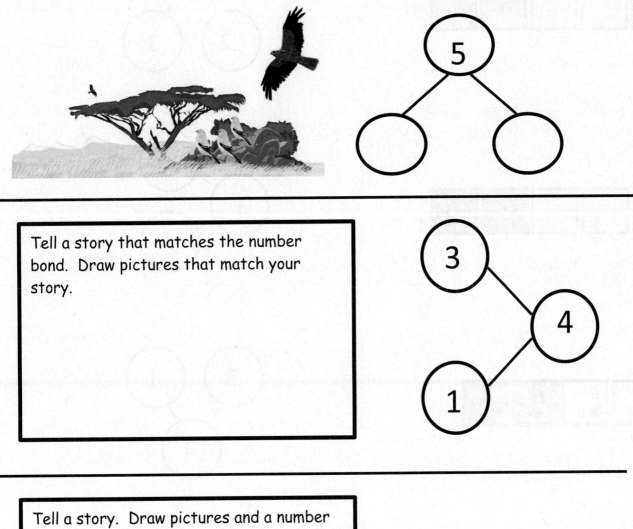

Tell a story that matches the number bond. Draw pictures that match your story.

Tell a story. Draw pictures and a number bond that match your story.

Lesson 6:   Represent number bonds with composition and decomposition story situations.
Date: 11/12/13

4.A.57

Draw a line to match the number bond to the cube stick.

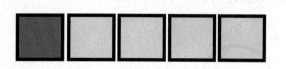

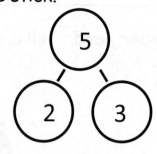

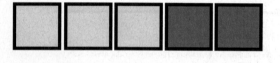

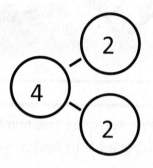

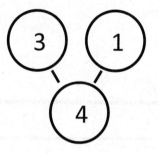

Lesson 6:   Represent number bonds with composition and decomposition
Date: 11/12/13   story situations.

4.A.58

Name _____   Date _____

Tell a story. Complete the number bonds. Draw pictures that match your story and number bonds.

Draw some balls for your story.

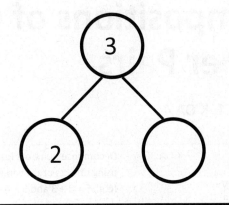

Draw some crayons for your story.

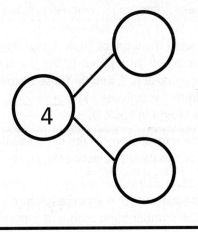

Draw some shapes for your story.

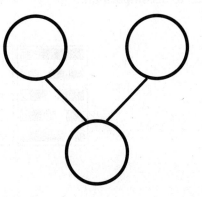

On the back of your paper, draw a picture and make a number bond to match it.

COMMON CORE™   Lesson 6:   Represent number bonds with composition and decomposition
                                  story situations.   4.A.59
                     Date: 11/12/13

Mathematics Curriculum

Topic B

Decompositions of 6, 7, and 8 into Number Pairs

K.OA.3, K.OA.1, K.OA.4

Focus Standard:	K.OA.3	Decompose numbers less than or equal to 10 into pairs in more than one way, e.g., by using objects or drawings, and record each decomposition by a drawing or equation (e.g., 5 = 2 + 3 and 5 = 4 + 1).
Instructional Days:	6	
Coherence -Links from:	GPK–M5	Numerals to 5, Addition and Subtraction Stories, Counting to 20

Topic B carries forward the work of Topic A, building students' skill with number pairs for 6, 7, and 8, which is cultivated and maintained throughout Topics B and C during Fluency Practice. In the first three lessons of this topic, students decompose 6, 7, and 8. These decompositions are modeled as *put together* situations and represented as addition expressions (C = ___+ ___), as opposed to the *take from* decomposition type (C – B = ___), which will be taught in Topic D.

Lessons 7–9 provide intensive work with decomposing 6, 7, and 8 into number pairs. Students identify all of the pairs using story situations, objects, sets, arrays, and numerals.

In Lessons 10 and 11, students use linking cube sticks to again model the decompositions of 6, 7, and 8 in order to explore the patterns that emerge (pictured below). Throughout, they work with different configurations of the number bond model to support flexible thinking moving from part to whole and whole to part, composition to decomposition.

▓▓▓▓▓ □	6 is 5 and 1.
▓▓▓▓ ▓	6 is 4 and 2.
▓▓▓ ▓▓	6 is 3 and 3.
▓▓ ▓▓▓	6 is 2 and 4.
▓ ▓▓▓▓	6 is 1 and 5.

Lesson 12 explores the important 5 + n pattern in 5-groups for 6, 7, and 8 (pictured below). Understanding and usage of the 5-group is foundational for students moving from Level 1 (counting all) to Level 2 (counting on) addition and subtraction strategies.

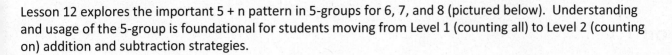

By the end of this topic, students should have a solid understanding of the relationships between numbers 1–8 and be ready for more formal work with addition and subtraction. Due to the length of this module, there is the option to take a day and a half to administer Topics A and B of the mid-module assessment at the end of Lesson 12. This will identify students who may need more support and allow more time to re-assess these students throughout the module.

A Teaching Sequence Towards Mastery of Decompositions of 6, 7, and 8 into Number Pairs
Objective 1: Model decompositions of 6 using a story situation, objects, and number bonds. (Lesson 7)
Objective 2: Model decompositions of 7 using a story situation, sets, and number bonds. (Lesson 8)
Objective 3: Model decompositions of 8 using a story situation, arrays, and number bonds. (Lesson 9)
Objective 4: Model decompositions of 6–8 using linking cube sticks to see patterns. (Lesson 10)
Objective 5: Represent decompositions for 6–8 using horizontal and vertical number bonds. (Lesson 11)
Objective 6: Use 5-groups to represent the 5 + n pattern to 8. (Lesson 12)

Lesson 7

Objective: Model decompositions of 6 using a story situation, objects, and number bonds.

Suggested Lesson Structure

■ Fluency Practice   (14 minutes)
■ Application Problem   (3 minutes)
□ Concept Development   (25 minutes)
■ Student Debrief   (8 minutes)

Total Time   **(50 minutes)**

Fluency Practice (14 minutes)

▪ Number Bond Flash **K.OA.5**   (5 minutes)
▪ 5-Group on the Dot Path **K.CC.2**   (4 minutes)
▪ Make 6 Matching Game **K.OA.1**   (5 minutes)

Number Bond Flash (5 minutes)

Materials: (T) Magnetic shapes or dry erase markers (S) Personal white boards

Note: This is a maintenance activity to support fluent understanding of the relationships between numbers to 5 through number bonds.

T: (Show 3 red squares and 1 yellow square.) How many squares do I have?
S: 4 squares.
T: How many are yellow?
S: 1.
T: How many are red?
S: 3.
T: 1 and 3 are the parts. 4 is the whole. Draw a number bond to tell about my squares. Lift up your board when you are done.
S: (Write number bonds using drawings or numerals. Lift board to signal completion.)
T: Nice job.

Repeat with 2 + 2, 4 + 1, 2 + 3. As students show mastery, stop naming the parts and whole before they draw.

Lesson 7:   Model decompositions of 6 using a story situation, objects, and number bonds.
Date: 11/12/13

4.B.3

5-Group on the Dot Path (4 minutes)

Materials: (S) Dot path placed inside a personal white board

Dot Path

Note: This activity helps students gain flexibility in grouping 5 and starting to count on from 5 pictorially. This will help students think about 6 as 5 and 1 more in preparation for the day's lesson.

- T: Touch and count the dots on your dot path.
- S: 1, 2, 3, …10.
- T: What do you notice about the dot path?
- S: There are 10 dots. → There are two different colors of dots. → The color changes after 5.
- T: Yes. I'm going to ask you to circle a group of dots. Use the color change after 5 to count and circle them as fast as you can. Ready? Circle 5.
- S: (Circle a group of 5 dots.)
- T: How did you do that so fast?
- S: I just circled all the light ones, and I knew it was 5.
- T: Erase. Get ready for your next number. Circle 6.
- S: (Circle a group of 6 dots.)
- T: How did you count 6?
- S: I counted all of the dots until I got to 6. → I counted 1 more than 5.

If students are starting to count on, let them share their thinking with the class. Continue the process with numbers to 10. Deviate from a predictable pattern as students show mastery.

NOTES ON MULTIPLE MEANS OF REPRESENTATION:

Counting on is a Level 2 method for solving single-digit addition and subtraction problems. Students are not expected to use this method until first grade. Advanced kindergarteners may be ready to count on in this simplified context. If students are starting to count on, invite them to talk or write about their thinking.

Make 6 Matching Game (5 minutes)

Materials: (S) Picture cards 0–6 (1 picture of each quantity) per pair (use Fluency Template B and the cards from GK–M4–Lesson 1)

Note: Reviewing the hidden partners of 6 will help students recall familiar relationships between numbers 1–6, preparing them to depict those relationships using the number bond model.

1.   Shuffle and place the cards face up from 0 to 6 in one equal row.

2.   Partner A chooses 2 cards that make 6.

3.   If the total of the numbers on both cards is 6, then she collects both cards. If not, then Partner A puts them back in their place.

4.   Repeat for Partner B

Have early finishers repeat the game, but this time put the cards in order from 0 to 6 to see if they notice that they can take the cards from either end, 0 and 6, 1 and 5, etc.

Lesson 7:   Model decompositions of 6 using a story situation, objects, and number bonds.
Date: 11/12/13

4.B.4

Application Problem (3 minutes)

Materials: (T) Bell or other gentle noisemaker or instrument

Close your eyes and count each time that I clap. (Clap 5 times; pause, and then clap 1 more time.) Open your eyes. How many claps did you hear? (Allow time for students to answer.) Let's do it 1 more time. (Repeat.) How many claps did you hear? What is 1 more than 5?

Repeat this exercise several times, using claps and instrument sound parts of 4 and 2, 3 and 3, 2 and 4, and 1 and 5.

Now, try the game with your partner! Take turns clapping different **number partners** for 6.

Note: This exercise will help the students to focus on the decomposition of 6 in preparation for today's lesson.

Concept Development (25 minutes)

Materials: (S) Linking cube 5-stick, loose cubes, personal white
            boards

Put the loose cubes in between students so that there are enough for each student to choose 1 additional cube.

Draw a blank number bond on the board in any configuration.

A NOTE ON MULTIPLE MEANS OF REPRESENTATION:

To help English language learners follow the story and lesson, show them pictures of a squirrel and nuts with the words *squirrel* and *nuts* on it. This will allow them to follow along and respond to questions.

- T: I'm going to tell you a story. Show me the story with your cubes as I go.
- T: A squirrel collected 6 nuts for the fall. With your cubes, show me a linking cube stick as long as her 6 nuts. Begin with your 5-stick.
- T: She buried 4 nuts in the ground and stored the other 2 nuts in a tree. Break your stick and hold up the piece that shows me how many nuts were in the ground. How many?
- S: (Hold up a 4-stick.) 4!
- T: Hold up the stick that shows how many nuts were stored in the tree.
- S: (Hold up a 2-stick.) 2!
- T: Yes! She took her 6 nuts and made sets of 4 and 2. Let's show what the squirrel did in this number bond. (Guide students to help you place the numbers representing the whole and the parts in the number bond.) Our number bond shows us that 6 is the same as…
- S: 4 and 2!
- T: (Write 6 = 4 + 2.) 6 is 4 and 2.

Lesson 7:   Model decompositions of 6 using a story situation, objects, and
Date: number bonds.
              11/12/13

4.B.5

MP.2

T: Put your 6-sticks back together. Does anyone know another way the squirrel can divide her nuts?

S: She can put 3 in the tree and bury the other 3!

T: Show me with your linking cube sticks what that looks like. Hold them up! (Check for understanding.)

T: Help me to make a new number bond for the new story. (Create a new blank number bond in a different orientation.) Do we still put the 6 in the place for the whole?

S: Yes. She still has 6 nuts all together.

T: What did change?

S: The parts in the other circles. We have to change the 4 and the 2 for the 3's.

T: (Demonstrating.) Thank you! You are right. I'll write it the special math way, too. (Write $6 = 3 + 3$ underneath the number bond.) 6 is the same as 3 and 3. Is there another way she could have split up her nuts?

Continue exercise several times with other partners for 6, each time asking the students to model the decomposition with the linking cubes, and creating new number bonds and corresponding equations each time.

T: Now draw the 6 nuts on your personal board. With your partner, take turns deciding how the squirrel should store her nuts. Circle the nuts that she will bury, and draw a box around the nuts that she will hide in the tree. Draw a number bond to show how the squirrel stored them each time.

$$6 = 5 + 1$$
$$6 = 4 + 2$$
$$6 = 3 + 3$$
$$6 = 2 + 4$$
$$6 = 1 + 5$$

T: Wow! You found a lot of different ways to make 6! The squirrel will be happy. How many different ways will you discover? (Allow time for discussion.) Let's review them and then do some more work with 6 in our problem set. (Review the different number bonds, using the language "6 is…." We can omit the partners including zero from the written list to keep the list more manageable.)

Problem Set (10 minutes)

Students should do their personal best to complete the Problem Set within the allotted 10 minutes.

Note: Encourage students to find many decompositions of 6 in the birds: 1 facing left and 4 facing right, 2 finches and 4 ducks, 3 white and 3 shaded, 4 big and 2 small, or, for advanced students, 2 big ducks, 2 small ducks, and 2 big finches. Add a part to the number bond if students see a combination with three parts.

Student Debrief (8 minutes)

Lesson Objective: Model decompositions of 6 using a story situation, objects, and number bonds.

The Student Debrief is intended to invite reflection and active processing of the total lesson experience.

Invite students to review their solutions for the Problem Set. They should check work by comparing answers with a partner before going over answers as a class. Look for misconceptions or misunderstandings that can be addressed in the Debrief. Guide students in a conversation to debrief the Problem Set and process the lesson.

Lesson 7:   Model decompositions of 6 using a story situation, objects, and
number bonds.
Date: 11/12/13   4.B.6

You may choose to use any combination of the questions below to lead the discussion.

- Share with a partner how you sorted the birds. Did your partner do it differently than you?

- Look with a partner at the numbers you put in both of your number bonds. Which numbers are the same? Why? Which numbers are different? Why?

- When I told my story, how did you know which number to put in which circle in the first number bond?

- How did it change when you split up the squirrel's nuts in different ways?

- Did the total number of nuts ever change?

- What are some of the ways you found to make 6?

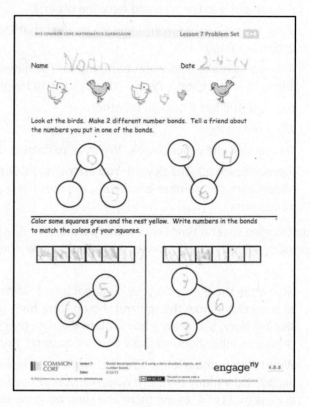

Lesson 7:   Model decompositions of 6 using a story situation, objects, and
            number bonds.
Date: 11/12/13

4.B.7

© 2013 Common Core, Inc. All rights reserved. commoncore.org

Name _____   Date _____

Look at the birds. Make 2 different number bonds. Tell a friend about the numbers you put in one of the bonds.

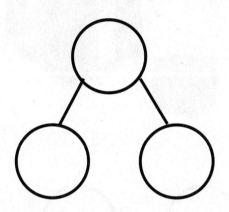 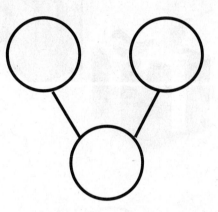

Color some squares green and the rest yellow. Write numbers in the bonds to match the colors of your squares.

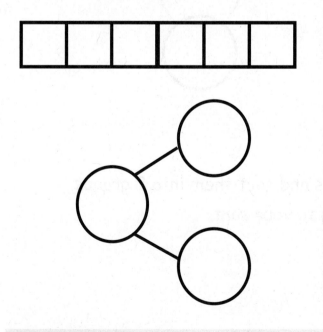 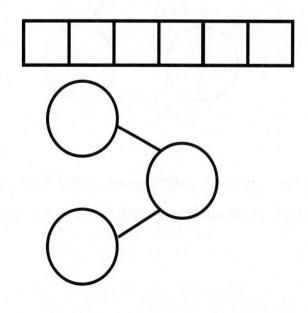

Name _____   Date _____

Look at the presents. Make 2 different number bonds. Tell an adult about the numbers you put in the number bonds.

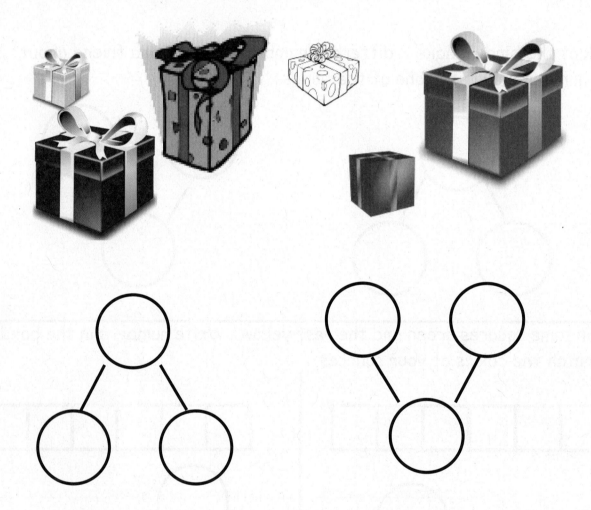

On the back of your paper, draw 6 presents and sort them into 2 groups. Make a number bond and fill it in according to your sort.

Lesson 7:   Model decompositions of 6 using a story situation, objects, and
            number bonds.
Date: 11/12/13

4.B.9

© 2013 Common Core, Inc. All rights reserved. commoncore.org

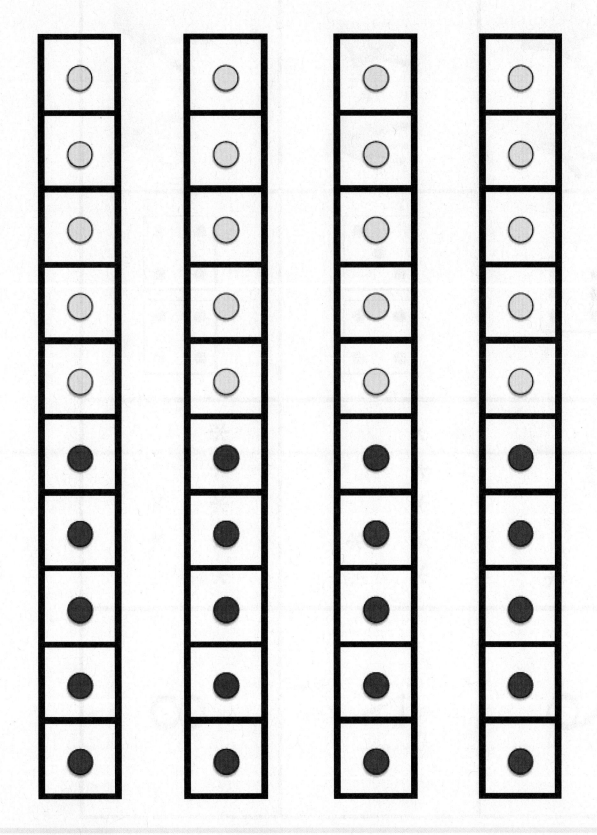

Lesson 7:

Date:

Model decompositions of 6 using a story situation, objects, and
number bonds.

11/12/13

4.B.10

© 2013 Common Core, Inc. All rights reserved. **commoncore.org**

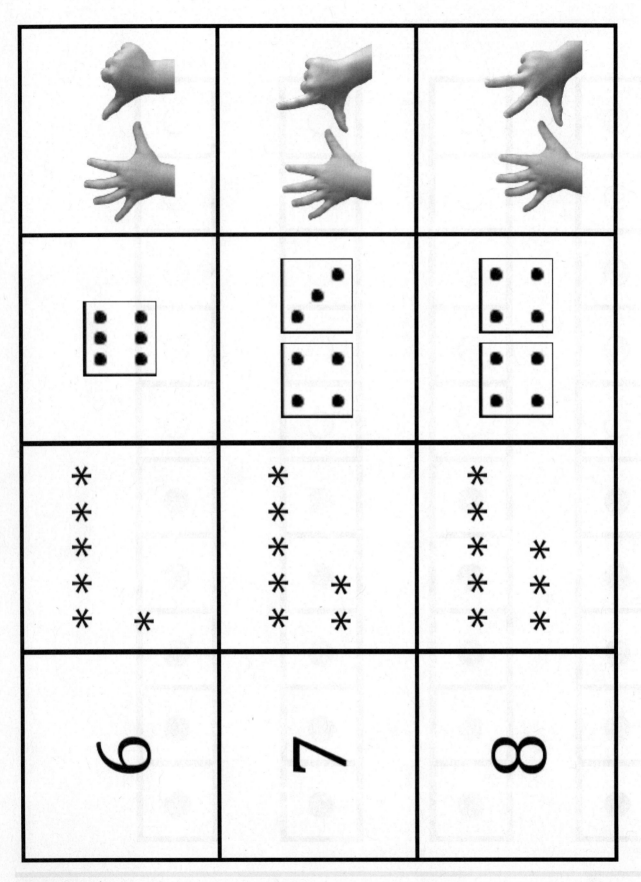

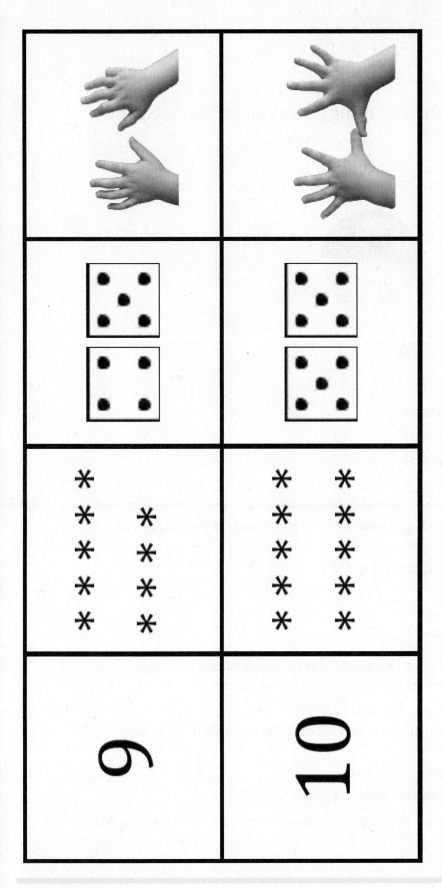

Lesson 7: Model decompositions of 6 using a story situation, objects, and
number bonds.

Date: 11/12/13

4.B.12

© 2013 Common Core, Inc. All rights reserved. commoncore.org

Lesson 8

Objective: Model decompositions of 7 using a story situation, sets, and number bonds.

Suggested Lesson Structure

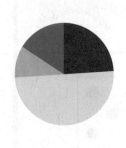

- ■ Fluency Practice   (12 minutes)
- ■ Application Problem   (5 minutes)
- ■ Concept Development   (25 minutes)
- ■ Student Debrief   (8 minutes)

   Total Time   **(50 minutes)**

Fluency Practice (12 minutes)

- ▪ Say Ten Push-Ups **K.NBT.1**   (3 minutes)
- ▪ Snap **K.OA.3**   (5 minutes)
- ▪ Comparing Towers **K.MD.2**   (4 minutes)

Say Ten Push-Ups (3 minutes)

Note: This activity reviews students' understanding of numbers to 10 for the work of this module and extends to teen numbers in anticipation of Module 5.

Conduct activity as outlined in GK–M4–Lesson 2, continuing to 20.

Snap (5 minutes)

Materials: (S) 5-stick of linking cubes per student

Note: This fast-paced game will serve as a very concrete review of the composition and decomposition of numbers to 5. It also supports the part–whole thinking needed in the upcoming lesson.

1. Partner A shows Partner B her 5-stick, and then puts it behind her back.
2. When Partner B says, "Snap!" Partner A quickly breaks her stick into two parts.
3. Partner A shows Partner B one part.
4. Partner B tries to guess the hidden part.
5. Partner A shows the hidden part and checks Partner B's guess.

Partners take turns, continuing with the 5-stick. If time permits, students can also play with a 4-stick, 3-stick, etc.

Lesson 8:	Model decompositions of 7 using a story situation, sets, and number bonds.
Date:	11/12/13

4.B.13

Comparing Towers (4 minutes)

Materials: (S) Die and 14 linking cubes per pair

Note: This fluency activity again relates length with number. It also encourages students to explore how many fewer cubes are needed to make the towers the same length and number. The focus is on decompositions of 7 to prepare for the Concept Development.

Continue play like in GK–M4–Lesson 4, except that one partner starts with a 7-stick. The other partner rolls a die and creates a tower using the number shown on the die. Students compare towers and make a *less than* or *more* than statement. Then the students take cubes from the 7-stick so it is the same height as the shorter tower.

Application Problem (5 minutes)

Materials: (S) Small ball of clay

Ming had 5 raisins. Represent her raisins with the clay.   Dan had 2 raisins. Represent his raisins, too. How many raisins are there in all?

- Put Ming's raisins into a 5-group. Now, put Dan's raisins in a row underneath Ming's raisins like this. Do you still have 7 raisins?
- Hide the bottom two raisins. How many raisins do you see now?
- Talk about the raisins with your friend.
- (If time allows, include the following.) Draw a number bond to represent Ming and Dan's raisins.

Note: Representing 7 as 5 and 2 will serve as the anticipatory set for today's lesson.

Concept Development (25 minutes)

Materials: (S) Personal white boards, 1 bucket of shapes with multiple variations of squares, triangles, hexagons and circles per table (construction paper cutouts can be used, if desired)

T: Find 4 shapes with three straight sides and three corners and put them in front of you. You have a set of 4…

S: Triangles!

T: Now find 3 shapes with no corners and put them in front of you. You have a set of 3…

S: Circles!

T: Push both of your sets together. How many shapes are in front of you?

NOTES ON MULTIPLE MEANS OF REPRESENTATION:

So much of this lesson depends on students understanding that circles and triangles are examples of shapes. Remind students, especially English language learners, what qualifies as a shape. Ask, "Who can name a shape they know?" Be sure to point to the words on your word wall as students practice naming the shapes they know.

| Lesson 8: | Model decompositions of 7 using a story situation, sets, and number bonds. |
| Date: | 11/12/13 |

4.B.14

S: 7.

T: You have 7 shapes. Let's count them together to be sure.

S: 1, 2, 3, 4, 5, 6, 7.

T: Sort your shapes into two sets again. (Draw number bond template on the board.) Let's make a number bond about what you just did. Point to where I should put the number that tells the total number of shapes. As you point, loudly say "whole!"

S: (Students point and speak. You might playfully point to the wrong one so they can correct you.)

T: Point to where I should write the numbers that tell how many triangles and squares. As you point, whisper "two parts!"

S: (Students point and speak.)

T: Write the number bond on your personal board.

T: Great job! You took your 7 shapes and sorted them into 3 circles and 4 triangles. You made two parts! Read with me while I write the number sentence: 7 = 3 + 4.

S: 7 is the same as 3 and 4.

T: Put your shapes back in the bucket. Now find 1 shape with six sides and put it in front of you. What do you see?

S: A hexagon!

T: Find 6 shapes with four straight sides and put them in front of you. What do you see?

S: I see 6 squares.

T: Make a set of all of your shapes. How many do you have all together? Let's count.

S: 1, 2, 3, 4, 5, 6, 7.

T: You have 7 shapes. Sort them into two groups again. How many are in each of your new groups?

S: There are 6 squares and 1 hexagon.

T: Let's make a new number bond for our new sets. (Draw a new number bond in a different configuration.) Where should I put the 7? Where should I put the number of squares and the number of hexagons? (Allow students to guide you in creating the new number bond.) Draw your new number bond on your white board.

T: We can't forget our number sentence—say it with me. (Write 7 = 6 + 1.)

NOTES ON MULTIPLE MEANS OF ACTION AND REPRESENTATION:

Challenge above grade level students during the lesson by giving them individual boards and asking them to respond to your challenges by filling in a number bond and equation to show how many ways they can think of to make a 7. Give them a recording sheet to keep track of the pairs they come up with.

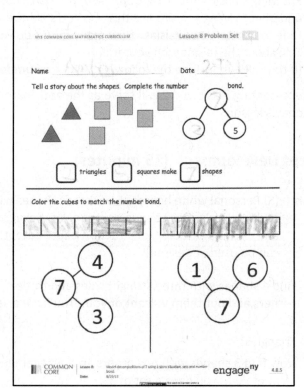

 Lesson 8: Model decompositions of 7 using a story situation, sets, and number bonds.

Date: 11/12/13

4.B.1

S: 7 is the same as 6 and 1.

P.2

T: Put your attribute blocks back. I wonder if there are any other ways to make a 7?

S: You can use 4 squares and 3 triangles. → You could use 2 circles and 5 hexagons.

T: Great ideas. Let's make your sets and then make the number bonds and sentences to go with them. I'm going to give you some time to work on this with your partner. Take turns finding different sets of shapes to make 7. Each time that you do, write the new number bond on your white board.

Problem Set (10 minutes)

Students should do their personal best to complete the Problem Set within the allotted 10 minutes.

Student Debrief (8 minutes)

Lesson Objective: Model decompositions of 7 using a story situation, sets, and number bonds.

The Student Debrief is intended to invite reflection and active processing of the total lesson experience.

Invite students to review their solutions for the Problem Set. They should check work by comparing answers with a partner before going over answers as a class. Look for misconceptions or misunderstandings that can be addressed in the Debrief. Guide students in a conversation to debrief the Problem Set and process the lesson.

You may choose to use any combination of the questions below to lead the discussion.

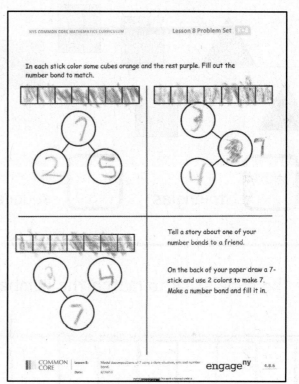

- What are some of the ways you found to make a 7? Let's put them in a list!

- How did you find all of those different ways? How did you know that you had found a way to make 7?

- In the Problem Set, what does the number 5 represent? How about the number 2? And the number 7?

- Did the story you and your partner told match the amount you put in each circle of the number bond?

- Why do we have to color all the cubes in the stick in the Problem Set?

$$7 = 6 + 1$$
$$7 = 5 + 2$$
$$7 = 4 + 3$$
$$7 = 3 + 4$$
$$7 = 2 + 5$$
$$7 = 1 + 6$$

COMMON CORE™

Lesson 8:   Model decompositions of 7 using a story situation, sets, and number bonds.
Date: 11/12/13

4.B.16

Name _____   Date _____

Tell a story about the shapes. Complete the number bond.

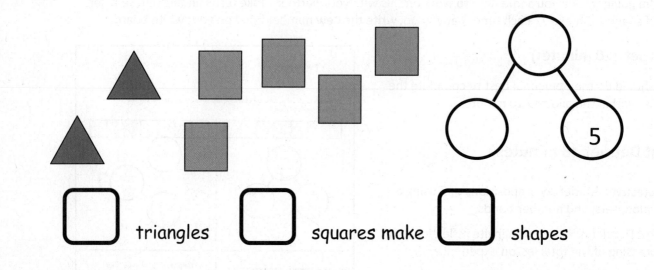

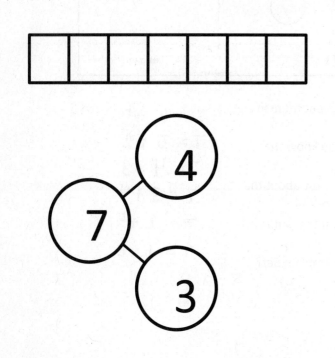

Color the cube stick to match the number bond.

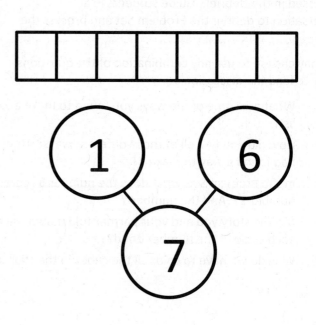

COMMON CORE™ | **Lesson 8:**   Model decompositions of 7 using a story situation, sets, and number bonds.

                 Date: 11/12/13

4.B.1

In each stick, color some cubes orange and the rest purple. Fill out the number bond to match. Tell a story about one of your number bonds to a friend.

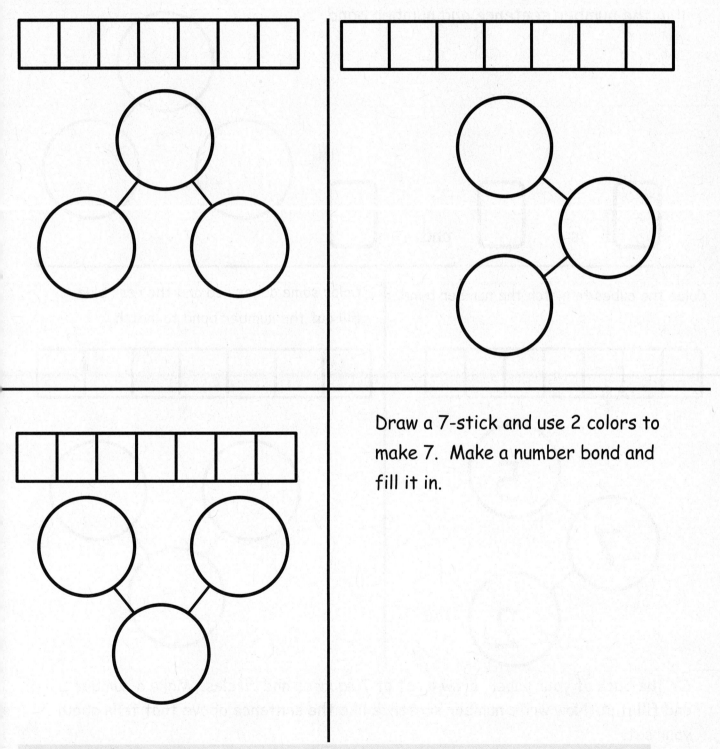

Draw a 7-stick and use 2 colors to make 7. Make a number bond and fill it in.

 | Lesson 8: Model decompositions of 7 using a story situation, sets, and number bonds.

Date: 11/12/13

4.B.18

© 2013 Common Core, Inc. All rights reserved. commoncore.org

Name _____   Date _____

Draw a set of 4 circles and 3 triangles. How many shapes do you have?

Fill in the number sentence and number bond.

☐   is   ☐   and   ☐

Color the cubes to match the number bond.

☐☐☐☐☐☐☐

7 — 5 / 2

Color some cubes red and the rest blue.
Fill out the number bond to match.

☐☐☐☐☐☐☐

On the back of your paper, draw a set of 7 squares and circles. Make a number bond and fill it in. Now write number sentence like the sentence above that tells about your set.

COMMON CORE | Lesson 8: Model decompositions of 7 using a story situation, sets, and number bonds.

Date: 11/12/13

4.B.1

Lesson 9

Objective: Model decompositions of 8 using a story situation, arrays, and number bonds.

Suggested Lesson Structure

▪ Fluency Practice	(12 minutes)
▪ Application Problem	(5 minutes)
▪ Concept Development	(25 minutes)
▪ Student Debrief	(8 minutes)
Total Time	**(50 minutes)**

Fluency Practice (12 minutes)

- Making 8 with Squares and Beans **K.OA.3**   (6 minutes)
- Hidden Numbers **K.OA.3**   (6 minutes)

Making 8 with Squares and Beans (6 minutes)

Materials: (S) 8 beans, 2 paper or foam squares per student

Note: This fluency activity extends students' familiarity with squares and the number 4 and applies it to the number 8. This activity also anticipates the use of arrays in the day's lesson.

T: Let's put one bean on each corner of our squares. Count each bean as you put it down.

S: 1, 2, 3, 4, 5, 6, 7, 8.

T: How many beans did you count?

S: 8 beans!

T: Let's count the corners of the squares. As you count each corner, move the bean a little off the corner so you can remember which ones you already counted.

S: 1, 2, 3, 4, 5, 6, 7, 8.

T: Our job is to make 8. Move 7 beans on the corners of your squares. Leave the other one where it is. Count how many beans are on your corners. Wait for the signal to tell me. (Allow time to count, then signal.)

S: 7.

T: How many beans are not on a corner?

S: 1.

NOTES ON
MULTIPLE MEANS OF
REPRESENTATION:

Some advanced students may not need to count the corners again. They may know that there are 8 corners because they matched 1 bean to each corner. If this happens, ask the students to explain how they knew there were 8 corners without counting.

	Lesson 9:	Model decompositions of 8 using a story situation, arrays, and number bonds.	
	Date:	11/12/13	

4.B.20

Continue with all of the number combinations, including 8 and 0.

Hidden Numbers (6 minutes)

Materials: (S) Fluency template from GK–M4–Lesson 2 inserted into
personal white boards

Note: Finding embedded numbers continues the work of this module by developing part–whole thinking.

- T: Touch and count the fish on your mat. Raise your hand when you know how many. (Wait for all hands to go up, and then give the signal.) Ready?
- S: 10.
- T: Put X's on 2 of the fish. Pretend they swam away!
- S: (Cross out 2 fish.)
- T: Circle a group of 7 from the fish who didn't swim away.
- T: How many fish are left?
- S: 1.
- T: Let's circle that 1. How many did you circle all together?
- S: 8.

Repeat the process. This time, have 2 fish swim away again but circle 5 fish, then another 3 fish, and ask how many are circled. Repeat with other combinations equal to 8 as time allows. Pause occasionally to allow students to explain efficient ways of locating the groups.

Application Problem (5 minutes)

Materials: (S) Two linking cube 5-sticks, 1 each of 2 colors

Take one of your 5-sticks. Add 1 more cube. How many cubes are in your stick now? (6.) Add 1 more cube. How many are in your stick now? (7.) Add another cube. Now how many cubes are in your stick? (8.) Take your 8-stick apart. Work with your partner to make two rows of cubes out of your stick. Make sure you have the same number of cubes in each row. How many cubes are in each row? (4.) Yes, you took your 8 and made 2 rows of 4!

Now take your cubes and make a tiny row of 2. Make another tiny row of 2 underneath. Keep going until all of your cubes are used up. How many cubes are in each row? (2) How many tiny rows do you have? (4). You made your 8 into 4 rows of 2! You made your 8 into 2 columns. Talk to your partner about the ways you made your 8 look.

Note: Reviewing the array formations of 8 from GK–Module 1 will serve as an anticipatory set for the decomposition work with 8 in today's lesson.

COMMON CORE

Lesson 9:	Model decompositions of 8 using a story situation, arrays, and number bonds.
Date:	11/12/13

4.B.2

© 2013 Common Core, Inc. All rights reserved. commoncore.org

Concept Development (25 minutes)

Materials: (S) Personal white boards

NOTES ON
MULTIPLE MEANS OF
REPRESENTATION:

If you have below grade level students who are still confused about where to place the whole and the parts of decomposed numbers, have them practice the activity introduced in Lesson 1 of this module where students begin in a hoop representing the whole and have to walk along the path to arrive at different hoops representing the parts. Continue practicing until students understand the relationship represented between the whole and the parts in the number

T: Draw a row of 8 crackers on your personal board. (Demonstrate.) Let's pretend you want to share them between two friends. How many crackers should we give your first friend?

S: (Example.) Let's give her 3!

T: O.K., we will give her 3. Let's draw a line after the first three crackers to show the ones she will get. Draw the line on your white board like this. (Demonstrate.)

T: I'm going to put an empty number bond on the board. Who can help me fill in the numbers that would tell

about your drawing?

MP.2

S: There are 8 crackers, so put that in the whole. → There are 3 for one friend and 5 for the other friend. → Put 3 and 5 in the parts.

T: You took your 8 crackers and divided them into groups of 3 and 5. Help me with the number sentence: (write) 8 = 3 + 5.

S: 8 is the same as 3 and 5.

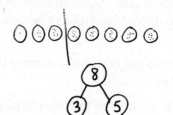

T: Could we share your crackers another way?

S: (Example) I want to give them all away except 1 for me!

T: Draw another row of 8 crackers and draw a line in the row to show that idea. (Demonstrate.) Let's make another number bond to show that story. (Guide students to assist in the creation of the new number bond.) This time you took your 8 crackers and made groups of 7 and 1. Let's write the number sentence: (write) 8 = 7 + 1.

S: 8 is the same as 7 and 1!

T: Does anyone have other ideas? Work with your partner to make other number bonds equal to eight.

Encourage students to draw and experiment with several different partners for 8, always following up with a number bond and a number sentence. Make sure that the number bonds are shown in a variety of configurations.

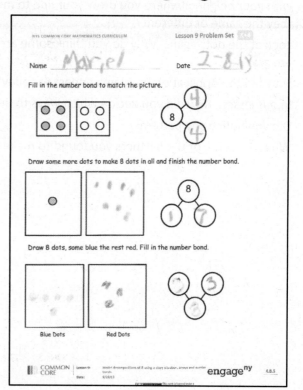

COMMON CORE™

Lesson 9:   Model decompositions of 8 using a story situation, arrays, and
              number bonds.
Date: 11/12/13

4.B.22

Problem Set (10 minutes)

Students should do their personal best to complete the Problem Set within the allotted 10 minutes.

Student Debrief (8 minutes)

Lesson Objective: Model decompositions of 8 using a story situation, arrays, and number bonds.

The Student Debrief is intended to invite reflection and active processing of the total lesson experience.

Invite students to review their solutions for the Problem Set. They should check work by comparing answers with a partner before going over answers as a class. Look for misconceptions or misunderstandings that can be addressed in the Debrief. Guide students in a conversation to debrief the Problem Set and process the lesson.

You may choose to use any combination of the questions below to lead the discussion.

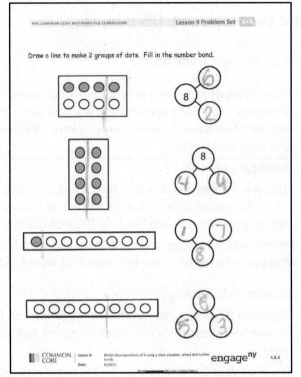

- Look at the dots on the second page of the Problem Set. Compare with your neighbor where you drew your line to make two parts. Are they the same or different?
- Look at the dots again. Why do you think some are white and some are gray?
- How did the Application Problem connect to today's lesson?
- In our lesson, how did you decide which ways to divide the crackers?
- Did you notice any patterns?
- What are some of the partners you found to make 8?

$$8 = 7 + 1$$
$$8 = 6 + 2$$
$$8 = 5 + 3$$
$$8 = 4 + 4$$
$$8 = 3 + 5$$
$$8 = 2 + 6$$
$$8 = 1 + 7$$

Lesson 9:	Model decompositions of 8 using a story situation, arrays, and number bonds.
Date:	11/12/13

4.B.2

Name _____   Date _____

Fill in the number bond to match the picture.

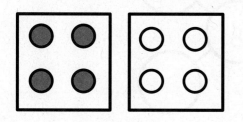   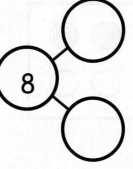

Draw some more dots to make 8 dots in all and finish the number bond.

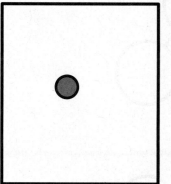   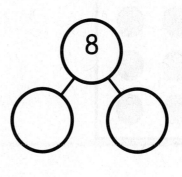

Draw 8 dots, some blue the rest red. Fill in the number bond.

      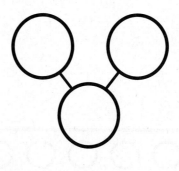

Blue Dots   Red Dots

Draw a line to make 2 groups of dots. Fill in the number bond.

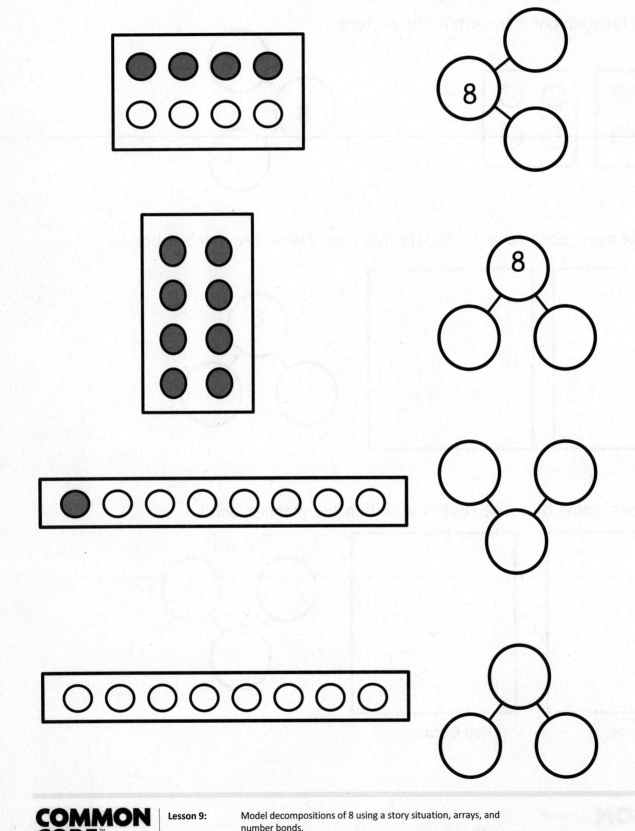

COMMON CORE™ | **Lesson 9:**   Model decompositions of 8 using a story situation, arrays, and
                                    number bonds.
                  | **Date:**   11/12/13

4.B.2

Name _____ Date _____

Complete the number bond to match the dot picture.

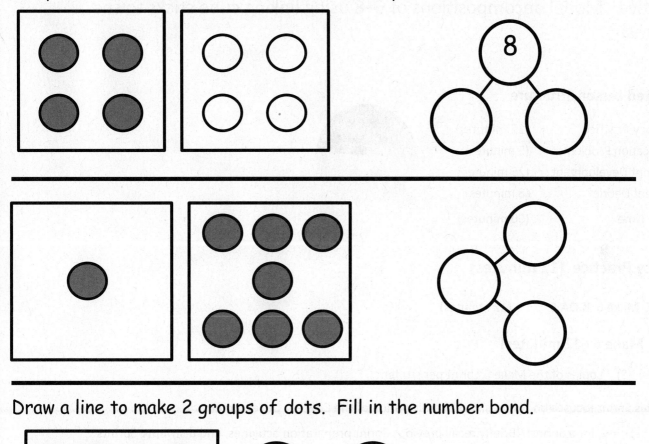

Draw a line to make 2 groups of dots. Fill in the number bond.

On the back of your paper:

- Draw a number bond for 4. Fill in the number bond.
- Draw a number bond for 5. Fill in the number bond.
- Draw a number bond for 6. Fill in the number bond.
- Draw a number bond for 7. Fill in the number bond.

Lesson 9:   Model decompositions of 8 using a story situation, arrays, and number bonds.
Date: 11/12/13

4.B.26

Lesson 10

Objective: Model decompositions of 6–8 using linking cube sticks to see patterns.

Suggested Lesson Structure

■ Fluency Practice   (12 minutes)
■ Application Problem   (5 minutes)
■ Concept Development   (25 minutes)
■ Student Debrief   (8 minutes)
    Total Time   **(50 minutes)**

Fluency Practice (12 minutes)

▪ Sprint: Make 6 **K.OA.5**   (12 minutes)

Sprint: Make 6 (12 minutes)

Materials: (S) 2 copies of the Make 6 Sprint per student

Note: This Sprint focuses on composing 6 in anticipation of the Content Development.

   T: It's time for a Sprint! (Briefly recall previous Sprint preparation activities, and distribute Sprints facedown.) Take out your pencil and one crayon, any color. For this Sprint, you are going to circle the number that will make 6. (Demonstrate the first problem as needed.)

Continue to follow the Sprint procedure as outlined in GK–M4–Lesson 3. Have students work on the Sprint for a second time (they will soon work on two different Sprints on a single day). Continue to emphasize that the goal is simply to do better than the first time and celebrate improvement.

Application Problem (5 minutes)

Materials: (S) 6-stick of linking cubes per pair of students,
            personal white boards

Time for a game of Snap! Hold your 6-stick behind your back. When your partner says, "Snap!" break your 6-stick into two parts. Show your friend one of the parts and see if she can guess the other part. If she can't guess, show her the missing piece. On your white board, draw the number bond about your game. Then

NOTES ON MULTIPLE MEANS OF ENGAGEMENT:

Encourage students, especially your English language learners, to use the math vocabulary you have taught them by extending the game, asking them to tell their partner, e.g., "8 is 7 and 1," after they have guessed the missing part at every turn.

COMMON CORE™   Lesson 10:   Model decompositions of 6–8 using linking cube sticks to see patterns.
            Date: 11/12/13   4.B.27

© 2013 Common Core, Inc. All rights reserved. commoncore.org

it will be your turn. Try it again with a 7-stick and then a 8-stick!

Note: The Application Problem today will serve as a review for today's lesson.

Concept Development (25 minutes)

Materials: (S) Linking cube 5-stick and 5 loose linking cubes of another color

T: Add one cube to the end of your 5-stick.
     How many cubes are in your stick now?

S: 6.

T: Take off 1 cube and put it on the table.
     Tell me what the partners are right now.

S: 5 and 1.

T: (Write 6 = 5 + 1.) Say the number
     sentence with me. Rather than saying
     "is the same as" let's say "**equals**."

S: 6 equals 5 and 1.

T: Take off another cube and add it to the
     cube on the table to make a 2-stick. What are the partners now?

S: 4 and 2.

T: (Write 6 = 4 + 2 underneath the first equation.) Say it
     with me.

S: 6 equals 4 and 2!

Continue with the exercise until the students are left holding
only one cube.

S: 6 equals 1 and 5!

T: Did anyone notice any patterns?

MP.8 S: The 6 is always the same. → The number in the middle
     is getting one smaller each time. → The number on
     the end gets one bigger every time.

T: You are right! There is a pattern. Let's put our 6-stick
     back together and then add one more cube. How
     many are in our stick now?

S: 7.

T: Play the same game with your partner but with 7 cubes! Move a cube from one stick to the other so
     that one stick has 1 less, and the other has 1 more. Each time use your words, 7 equals 6 and 1, for
     example.

Repeat the process with 8 cubes, too. Students who need it might be in a small group with you to support
them in the use of the language and the systematic movement of 1 cube.

**NOTES ON
MULTIPLE MEANS OF
ENGAGEMENT:**

Give students with disabilities and
below grade level students a chance to
get extra practice finding partners of 6,
7, and 8 using interactive technology
such as the one found at
http://www.ictgames.com/save_the_w
hale_v4.html.

Lesson 10:   Model decompositions of 6–8 using linking cube sticks to see
               patterns.
Date: 11/12/13

4.B.28

Problem Set (10 minutes)

Students should do their personal best to complete the Problem Set within the allotted 10 minutes.

Student Debrief (8 minutes)

Lesson Objective: Model decompositions of 6–8 using linking cube sticks to see patterns.

The Student Debrief is intended to invite reflection and active processing of the total lesson experience.

Invite students to review their solutions for the Problem Set. They should check work by comparing answers with a partner before going over answers as a class. Look for misconceptions or misunderstandings that can be addressed in the Debrief. Guide students in a conversation to debrief the Problem Set and process the lesson.

You may choose to use any combination of the questions below to lead the discussion.

- In the Problem Set, when you were counting the pineapples and the oranges, were there any sets that you could count faster than the others? Why or why not?
- What was the difference when you were filling in the parts of the number bonds for the fruit and the faces? (Parts are divided for you with the fruit. There is a *1 more* pattern with the fruit.)
- What patterns did you notice when we were working with your 6-stick?
- What did you notice about the patterns with the 7- and 8-sticks? Were the patterns similar?
- If we were to play the game with a 5-stick, do you think the pattern would still be similar?

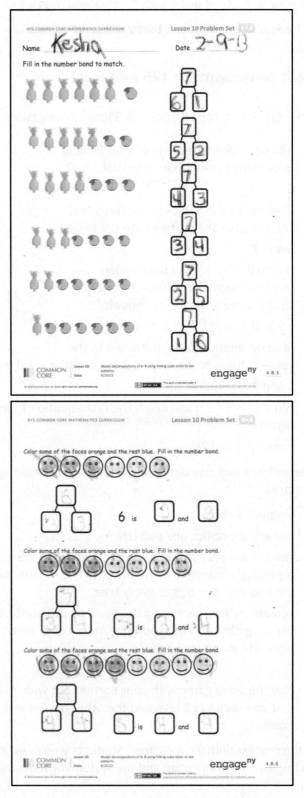

 | Lesson 10: | Model decompositions of 6–8 using linking cube sticks to see patterns.
Date: | 11/12/13

4.B.29

© 2013 Common Core, Inc. All rights reserved. commoncore.org

Circle the number to make 6.

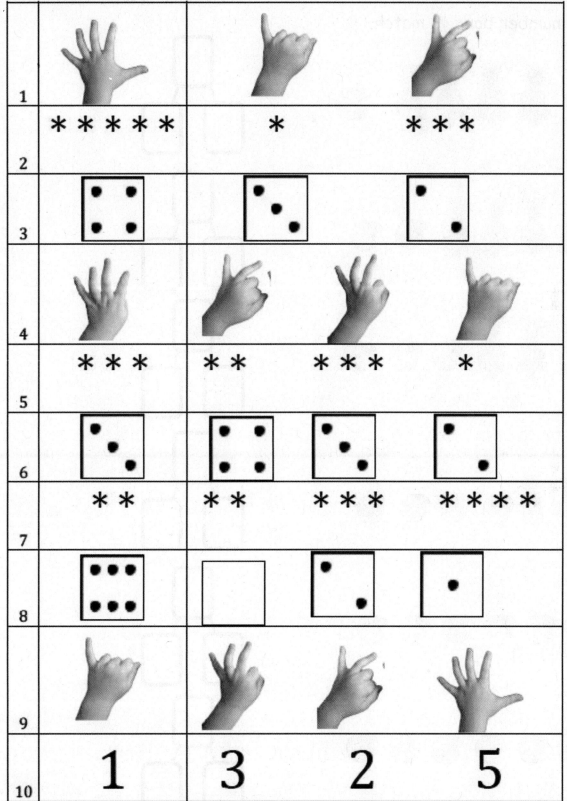

COMMON CORE™ | **Lesson 10:** Model decompositions of 6–8 using linking cube sticks to see patterns.
Date: 11/12/13

4.B.30

© 2013 Common Core, Inc. All rights reserved. **commoncore.org**

Name _____   Date _____

Fill in the number bond to match.

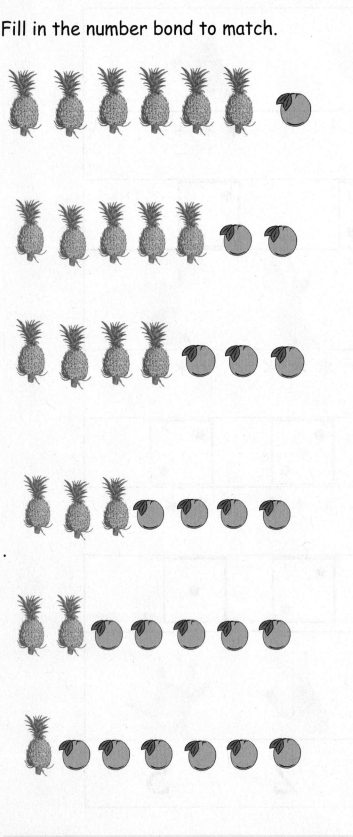

Color some of the faces orange and the rest blue. Fill in the number bond.

6 equals ☐ and ☐

Color some of the faces orange and the rest blue. Fill in the number bond.

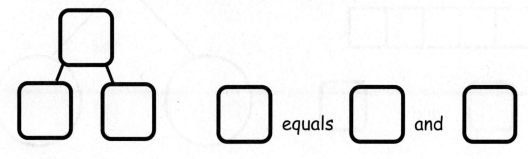

☐ equals ☐ and ☐

Color some of the faces orange and the rest blue. Fill in the number bond.

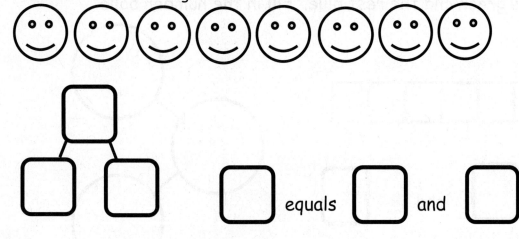

☐ equals ☐ and ☐

COMMON CORE™

Lesson 10: Model decompositions of 6–8 using linking cube sticks to see patterns.

Date: 11/12/13

4.B.32

Name _____   Date _____

Color 7 cubes green and 1 blue. Fill in the number bond.

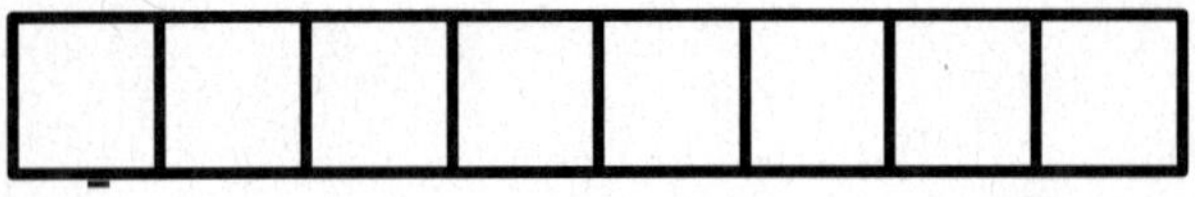

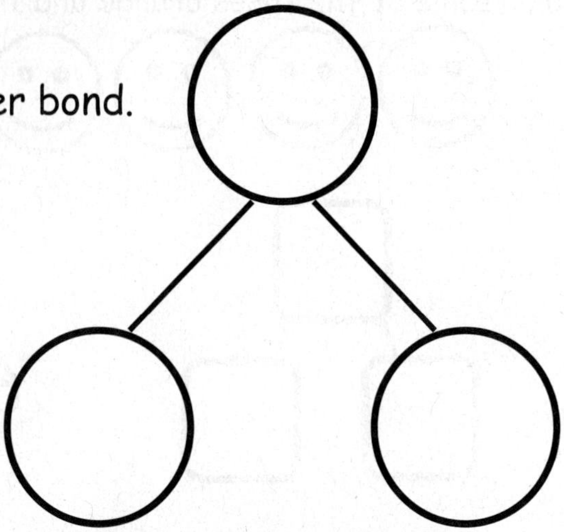

equals   and

_____

Color 6 cubes green and 2 blue. Fill in the number bond.

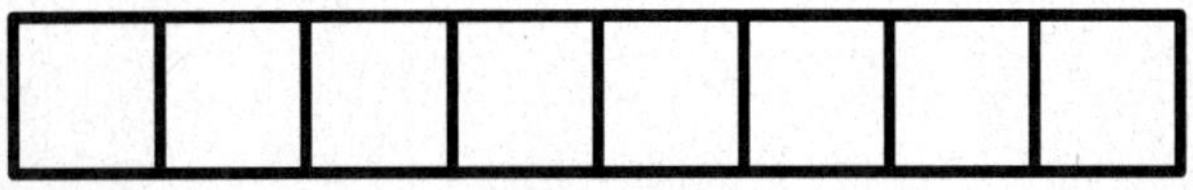

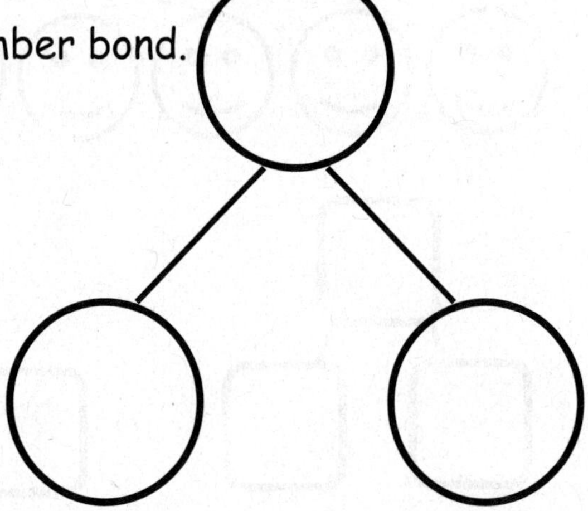

equals   and

_____

Color some cubes green and the rest blue. Fill in the number bond.

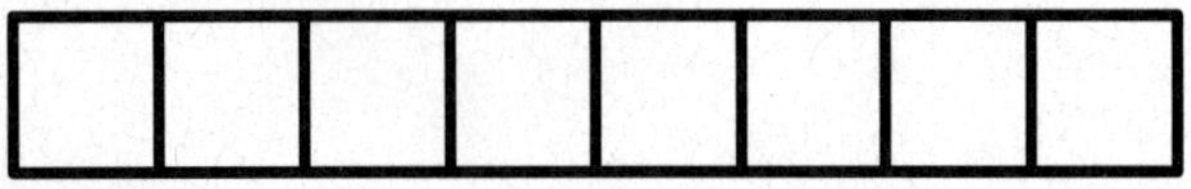

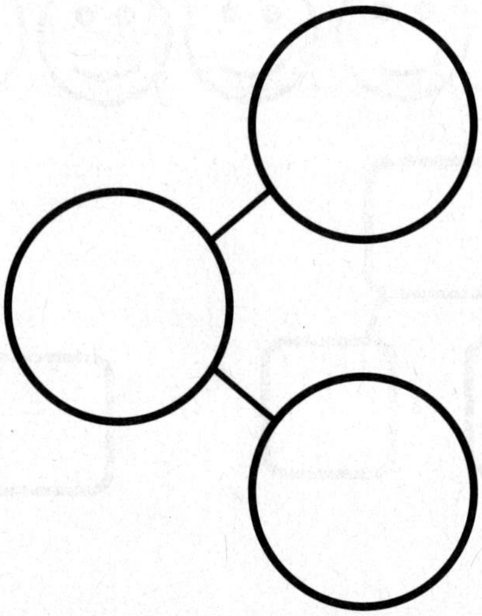

equals   and

COMMON CORE™   **Lesson 10:**   Model decompositions of 6–8 using linking cube sticks to see
                                      patterns.
                Date: 11/12/13

© 2013 Common Core, Inc. All rights reserved. **commoncore.org**

4.B.33

Color 4 cubes green and 4 blue. Fill in the number bond.

⬚ equals ⬚ and ⬚

Color 3 cubes green and 5 blue. Fill in the number bond.

⬚ equals ⬚ and ⬚

Color some cubes green and the rest blue. Fill in the number bond.

⬚ equals ⬚ and ⬚

Lesson 11

Objective: Represent decompositions for 6–8 using horizontal and vertical number bonds.

Suggested Lesson Structure

- ■ Fluency Practice   (12 minutes)
- ■ Application Problem   (5 minutes)
- ■ Concept Development   (25 minutes)
- ■ Student Debrief   (8 minutes)
  - **Total Time**   **(50 minutes)**

Fluency Practice (12 minutes)

- ▪ Take Apart Groups of Circles **K.OA.1**   (4 minutes)
- ▪ Finger Number Pairs **K.OA.3**   (3 minutes)
- ▪ Make 7 Matching Game **K.OA.1**   (5 minutes)

Take Apart Groups of Circles (4 minutes)

Materials: (S) Personal white boards

Note: This activity anticipates the day's work with decomposition.

T: Draw three circles on your board. (Wait for students to do this.) Put X's on two of them. How many circles have X's?

S: 2.

T: How many circles do not have an X?

S: 1.

T: How many circles are on your board?

S: 3.

T: Raise your hand when you can say the number sentence starting with 2 (wait for all students to raise hands, and then signal). Ready?

S: 2 plus 1 equals 3.

T: Very good. Let's go a little faster now. Erase. Draw 4 circles on your board. (Wait for students to do this.) Put X's on 3 of them. (Wait.) How many do not have an X?

S: 1.

Lesson 11:   Represent decompositions for 6–8 using horizontal and vertical
number bonds.
Date: 11/12/13

4.B.3

T: Raise your hand when you can say the number sentence starting with 3. (Wait for all students to raise hands and then signal.) Ready?

S: 3 plus 1 equals 4.

Continue working through problems with totals of 1–5. The following is a suggested sequence: 4 +1, 2 + 2, 3 + 2, 2 + 3, 1 + 1, 1 + 2, 1 + 3, and 1 + 4.

Finger Number Pairs (3 minutes)

Note: This activity gives students an opportunity to decompose numbers in more than one way, anticipating the work of the lesson. It also serves as an active practice for the Make 7 Matching Game.

T: You've gotten very good at showing fingers the Math way. I want to challenge you to think of other ways to show numbers on your fingers. Hint… you can use two hands! First I'll ask you to show me fingers the Math way. Then, I'll ask you to show me the number another way. Ready? Show me 5!

S: (Hold up all the fingers of the left hand.)

T: Now show me another way to make 5, using two hands.

S: (Show 3 fingers on one hand and 2 on the other. → Show 1 finger on one hand and 4 on the other.)

T: How we can be sure that we're still showing 5?

S: Count the fingers on both hands.

Continue the process with 6–8. For numbers where more than one combination is possible, have students try each other's combinations.

Make 7 Matching Game (5 minutes)

Materials: (S) Picture cards 0–7 (1 picture of each quantity) per pair

Note: Students will find the hidden partners of 7 in support of the day's work with composition and decomposition.

Conduct activity as outlined in GK–M4–Lesson 7, but now have students find partners of 7.

Application Problem (5 minutes)

Materials: (S) Personal white boards

Nesim had 5 toy cars. Draw Nesim's cars.

Awate had 3 toy cars. Draw a picture to show his cars, too. How many cars did they have together? Can you show the number bond to go with the story? Talk with your partner about your work.

Note: Composition of the number 8 will serve as an anticipatory set for this lesson.

NOTES ON MULTIPLE MEANS OF ACTION AND EXPRESSION:

Scaffold the Application Problem for students with disabilities and below grade level students who are having difficulty using the number bond by providing them with a number bond that has one of the parts (5 or 3) already filled out.

Concept Development (25 minutes)

Materials: (S) Linking cube 5-stick, 5 additional loose linking cubes (all of one color or with color change at 5), number bond template inserted into personal white board

T: Starting with your 5-stick, make an 8-stick with your linking cubes. How many more cubes did you add?

S: 3!

T: When I say, "Snap!" break your 8-stick into two smaller sticks. *Snap!* What numbers did you find hiding inside the 8?

S: I have a 2 and a 6!

MP.2

T: Great! You found a 2 and a 6 inside your 8! How would I show that in a number bond? (Allow students to guide you in creating the number bond on the board.) Make this number bond on your white board, too. (Allow students time to create the number bond.) Did anyone do it a different way?

S: I found a 5 and a 3. → I have a 1 and a 7! (Allow students to share other partners for 8, modeling it in the number bond format each time.

> **NOTES ON MULTIPLE MEANS OF REPRESENTATION:**
>
> Scaffold the lesson for your English language learning students by keeping a record of the number partners students find in their 8, 7, and 6 linking cubes. You can use the format: 8 is 7 and 1, 8 is 5 and 3, etc. This will help all students to keep track of the various number combinations.

T: Put your stick back together. You have 8 cubes. Please take one off and put it aside. How many cubes are in your stick now?

S: There are 7.

T: Let's play the game again... but first, please erase your white boards and turn them upside down. Could we still make a number bond this way?

S: Yes! It doesn't matter which way it faces.

T: All right... *snap!* What partners to make 7 did you find?

S: I have a 2 and a 5.

T: Let's write this in a number bond, too. (Guide students to help you create a number bond in a different orientation. After they copy it onto their personal boards, ask for other partners for 7.)

Ask students to repeat the activity with a partner using a cube stick of 6. Students who need support might be in a small group with you for assistance in using the language or identifying multiple decompositions of 6.

Problem Set (10 minutes)

Students should do their personal best to complete the Problem Set within the allotted 10 minutes.

Lesson 11:	Represent decompositions for 6–8 using horizontal and vertical number bonds.
Date:	11/12/13

4.B.37

Student Debrief (8 minutes)

Lesson Objective: Represent decompositions for 6–8 using horizontal and vertical number bonds.

The Student Debrief is intended to invite reflection and active processing of the total lesson experience.

Invite students to review their solutions for the Problem Set. They should check work by comparing answers with a partner before going over answers as a class. Look for misconceptions or misunderstandings that can be addressed in the Debrief. Guide students in a conversation to debrief the Problem Set and process the lesson.

You may choose to use any combination of the questions below to lead the discussion.

- Look at the stick with 6 cubes in the Problem Set. Share with a partner where you drew a line to break the stick. Do you have the same parts?

- When you broke apart your 8-stick, did your number bond have the same numbers as everyone else? Why?

- When you turned the number bond, what did you notice?

- Does the number bond change when it faces different directions?

- With your partner, talk about how many different ways you could break the 6-stick. The 7-stick. The 8-stick.

Lesson 11:   Represent decompositions for 6–8 using horizontal and vertical
number bonds.

Date: 11/12/13

4.B.38

© 2013 Common Core, Inc. All rights reserved. **commoncore.org**

Name _____   Date _____

Draw a line to break the stick into 2 parts. Complete the number bond and number sentence.

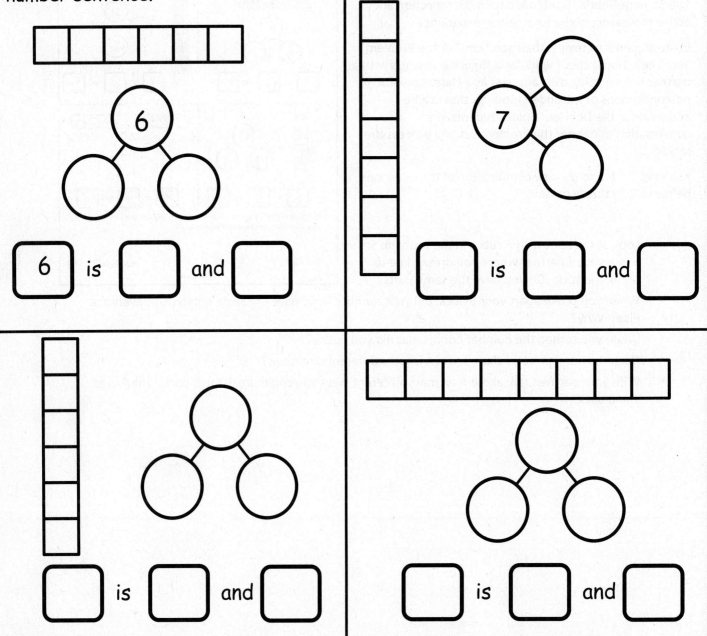

6 is ___ and ___

___ is ___ and ___

___ is ___ and ___

___ is ___ and ___

On the back of your paper, draw a cube stick with some red cubes and some blue cubes. Draw a number bond to match.

Name _____   Date _____

Color 5 cubes green and 1 blue. Fill in the number bond.

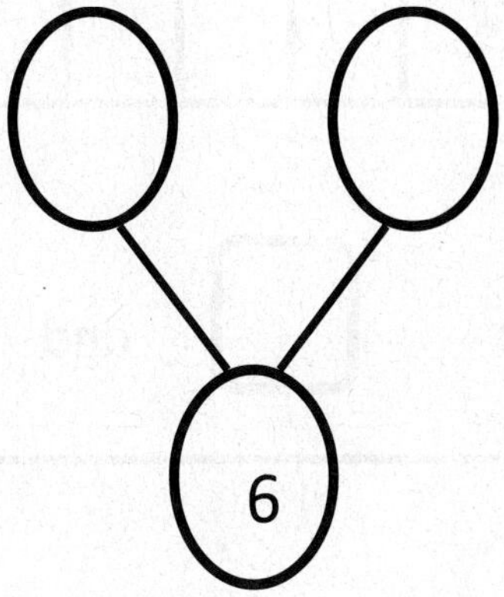

6 is ☐ and ☐

Color 5 cubes green and 2 blue. Fill in the number bond.

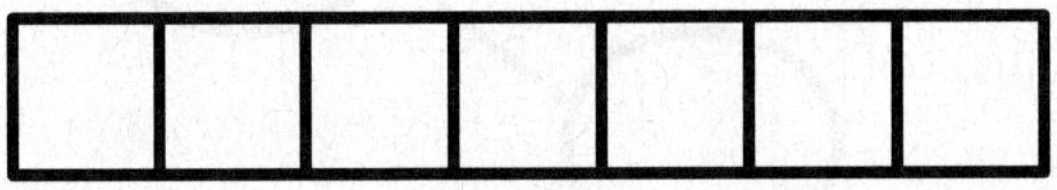

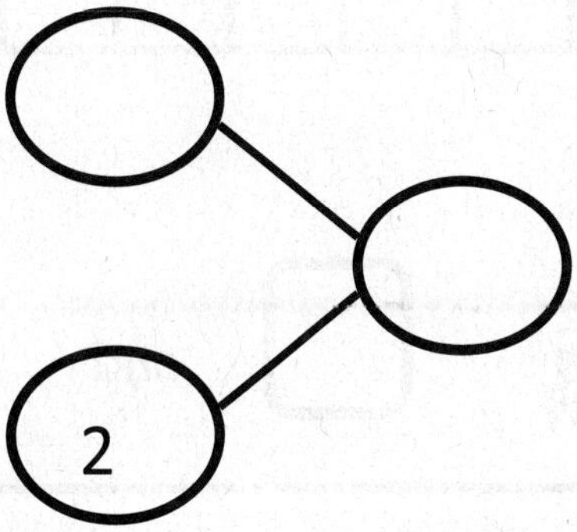

☐ is ☐ and ☐

2

Color 4 cubes green and 3 blue. Fill in the number bond.

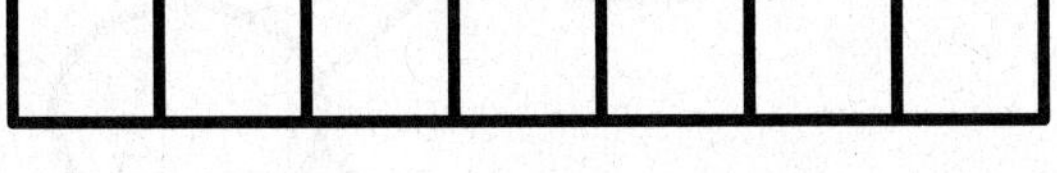

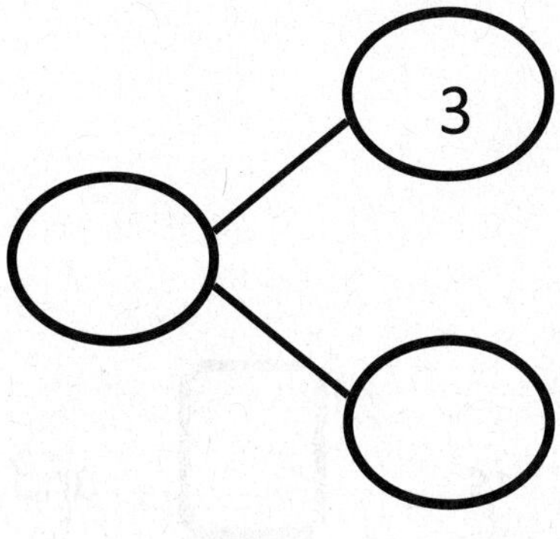

3

☐ is ☐ and ☐

COMMON CORE

Lesson 11:   Represent decompositions for 6–8 using horizontal lend vertical
number bonds.
Date: 11/12/13

4.B.40

© 2013 Common Core, Inc. All rights reserved. commoncore.org

Color 4 cubes green and 4 blue. Fill in the number bond.

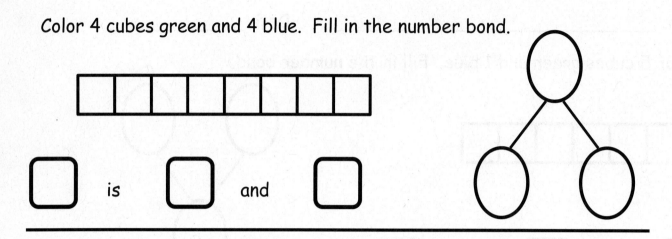

is   and

Color 3 cubes green and 5 blue. Fill in the number bond.

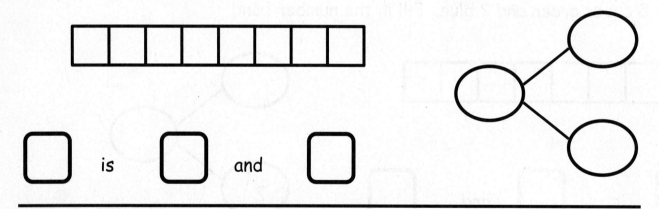

is   and

Color 2 cubes green and 6 blue. Fill in the number bond.

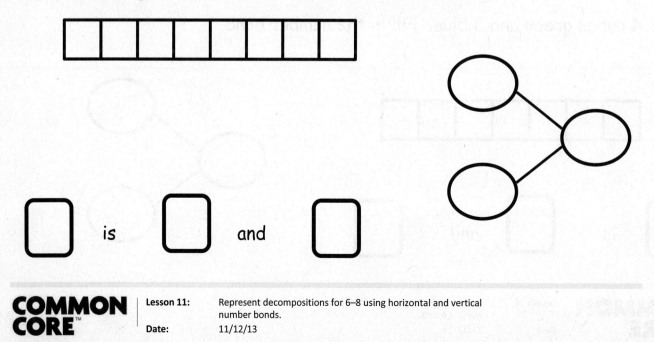

is   and

COMMON CORE™   Lesson 11:   Represent decompositions for 6–8 using horizontal land vertical
                                      number bonds.
                     Date: 11/12/13

4.B.41

Lesson 12

Objective: Use the 5-groups to represent the 5 + n pattern to 8.

Suggested Lesson Structure

■ Fluency Practice	(12 minutes)
■ Application Problem	(5 minutes)
■ Concept Development	(25 minutes)
■ Student Debrief	(8 minutes)
Total Time	**(50 minutes)**

Fluency Practice (12 minutes)

- Draw More to Make 5 **K.OA.3**   (5 minutes)
- 5-Group Hands **K.CC.2**   (3 minutes)
- 5-Group on the Dot Path **K.CC.2**   (4 minutes)

Draw More to Make 5 (5 minutes)

Materials: (S) Fluency Problem Set

Note: This activity focuses students on the number 5 in order to prepare students to explore the 5 + n pattern.

After giving clear instructions and completing the first few problems together, allow students time to work independently. Encourage them to do as many problems as they can within a given timeframe. Go over the answers and direct students to energetically shout, "Yes!" for each correct answer.

5-Group Hands (3 minutes)

Materials: (T) Large 5-group cards (5–10)

Note: This activity helps to solidify students' understanding of numbers to 10 in relationship to the five, an important understanding as students deepen their work with 6–10.

A student demonstrates 7 as 5 on top and 2 on the bottom.

T: (Show the 6 dot card.) Raise your hand when you know how many dots are on top. (Wait until all hands are raised, then signal.) Ready?

S: 5.

T: Bottom?

S: 1.

T: We can show this 5-group on our hands. 5 on top, 1 on the bottom, like this. (Demonstrate on hands, one above the other.)

S: (Show 5 and 1 on hands, one above the other.)

T: Push your hands out as you count on from 5, like this. 5 (extend the top hand forward), 6 (extend the bottom hand forward). Try it with me.

S: 5 (extend the top hand forward), 6 (extend the bottom hand forward).

Continue to 10, steadily decreasing guidance, until students can show the 5-groups on their hands with ease. Variation: Complete this activity without using the 5-group cards as support.

5-Group on the Dot Path (4 minutes)

Materials: (S) Dot path placed inside of personal white board

Note: This activity helps students gain flexibility in grouping 5 and understanding the 5 + n pattern for numbers 6–10.

Conduct activity as outline in GK–M4–Lesson 7.

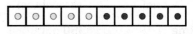

Dot Path

Application Problem (5 minutes)

Materials: (S) Personal white boards

5 bees were buzzing around a tasty flower. Draw the flower and the bees. 2 more bees came to join them. Draw the new hungry bees.

We had 5 bees. Now we have 2 more bees! Use your picture to show how many bees are enjoying the flower together. Talk to your partner about the picture. Can you write a number bond to go with the story?

Note: The *5 and some more* language of the story will serve as an anticipatory set for today's lesson.

A NOTE ON MULTIPLE MEANS OF ACTION AND EXPRESSION:

Challenge your above grade level students by asking them to write their own word problem expressing the *5 and some more* pattern. If there is more than one early finisher, have them trade problems from each other to solve.

Concept Development (25 minutes)

Materials: (S) Two 5-group mats (template found at end of lesson) or template drawn on paper, 1 linking cube 5-stick, 5 loose linking cubes, personal white boards

T: Place your 5-group mats in front of you. Find your 5-stick. Let's take it apart and put one cube in each square of the top 5-group mat. What do you notice?

S: We have a cube in each square. → The top mat is full.

T: You have 5 cubes. Take another cube from your bag. Put it in the next 5-group mat. Now, how many cubes do you have?

S: Now there are 5 and 1 more. → There are 6 cubes.

T: Yes! We now have 6 cubes. We could write what you did as a number bond. (Demonstrate). We have a 5 in one of the parts and a 1 in the other. Our whole is 6. We can also write it this way (write 5 + 1 = 6): 5 and 1 equals 6. Let's take another cube and add it to our picture. What do you notice now?

S: Now we have 5 and 2! → We have 7 cubes.

T: Let's write that in a number bond, too. We have 5 in one part and 2 in the other. Our whole is 7. (Demonstrate.) We can also write it this way (write 5 +2 = 7): 5 and 2 equals 7. Add 1 more cube. Now how many?

S: Now there are 8 cubes.

T: Let's write it in a number bond. We have 5 in 1 part and 3 in the other. Our whole is 8. (Demonstrate.) Here is the number sentence (write 5 + 3 = 8): 5 and 3 equals 8. Does anyone see a pattern? What if we added another cube? (Allow time for discussion, encouraging the students to notice the 5 + n pattern.)

T: Take off all of the cubes. Let's try to do it quickly. Make 6. How did you do it?

S: 5 and 1 more!

MP.7 T: Make 7. How did you do it?

S: 5 and 2 more.

T: Please make 8. How did you do it?

S: 5 and 3 more!

T: Take a few minutes to work with your partner. Practice making all of the numbers to 8 starting with a 5. Use your fingers or linking cubes to show your ideas. Draw the number bond each time.

T: Are there other number bonds that have 5 in one of the parts? (Allow time for sharing and discussion.)

T: Who would like to share one of their number bonds with the class? I wonder how many number bonds have 5 as a part. Let's put as many as we can on the board! (Just be playful. See what your students come up with!)

NOTES ON MULTIPLE MEANS OF REPRESENTATION:

Encourage English language learners' use of the language by writing out the phrases *5 and n is 6* and *5 plus n = 6* and asking students to say it after you as you point to the phrases on your word wall. ELLs will become familiar with the phrases and will be more likely to use them appropriately.

Problem Set (10 minutes)

Students should do their personal best to complete the Problem Set within the allotted 10 minutes.

Student Debrief (8 minutes)

Lesson Objective: Use the 5-groups to represent the 5 + n pattern to 8.

The Student Debrief is intended to invite reflection and active processing of the total lesson experience.

Lesson 12:   Use the 5-groups to represent the 5 + n pattern to 8.
Date: 11/12/13

4.B.44

Invite students to review their solutions for the Problem Set. They should check work by comparing answers with a partner before going over answers as a class. Look for misconceptions or misunderstandings that can be addressed in the Debrief. Guide students in a conversation to debrief the Problem Set and process the lesson.

You may choose to use any combination of the questions below to lead the discussion.

- Look at your Problem Set. Why do we color all the cubes in one 5-group mat before coloring the cubes in the next 5-group mat?

- Look at the last problem where you colored 8 cubes. Compare with your neighbor's. Did you color the same cubes? Did you color 5 cubes in the top row or did you color 8 a different way? (Discuss advantages and disadvantages to the different coloring combinations.)

- When you used your 5-group mat, was it easy to know how many cubes you had?

- Did you have to count them all each time to know how many you had?

- What patterns did you see in the number bonds today?

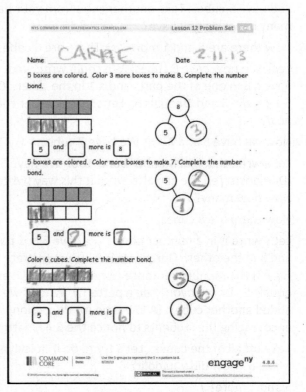

Draw more to make 5.

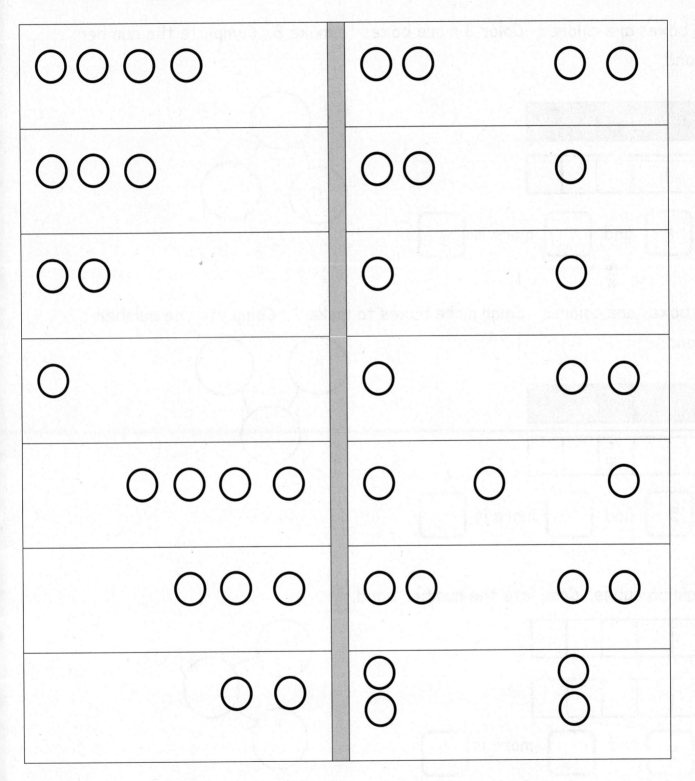

Name _____   Date _____

5 boxes are colored. Color 3 more boxes to make 8. Complete the number bond.

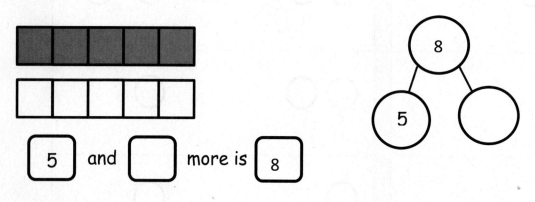

5 and ____ more is 8

5 boxes are colored. Color more boxes to make 7. Complete the number bond.

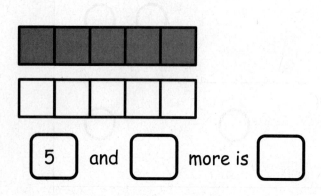
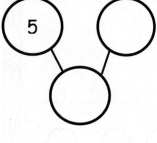

5 and ____ more is ____

Color 6 cubes. Complete the number bond.

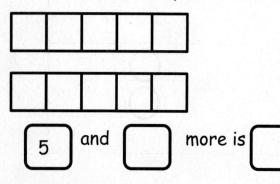
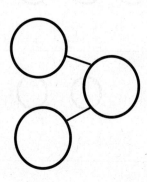

5 and ____ more is ____

Draw more to make 6. Complete the number bond.

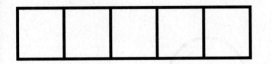

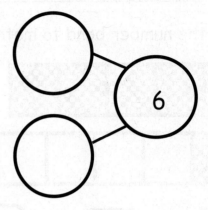

Draw more to make 7. Complete the number bond.

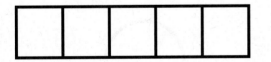

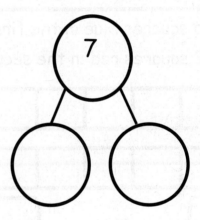

Draw more to make 8. Complete the number bond.

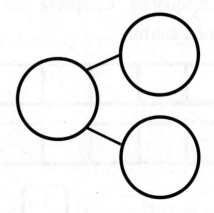

Name _____   Date _____

Fill in the number bond to match the squares.

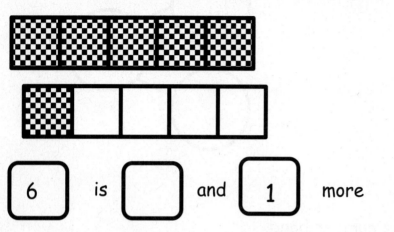

6   is   [ ]   and   1   more

Color 5 squares blue in the first row.

Color 2 squares red in the second row.

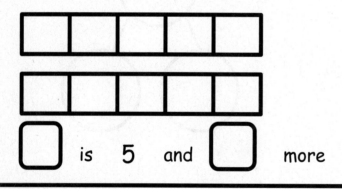

[ ]   is   5   and   [ ]   more

Color 8 squares. Complete the number
bond and sentence.

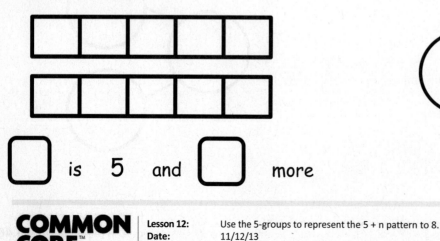

[ ]   is   5   and   [ ]   more

Color the sticks to match the number bond.

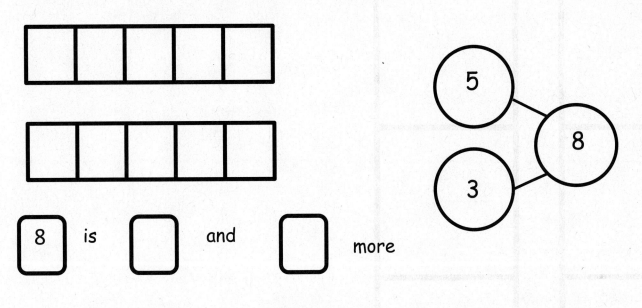

8 is ☐ and ☐ more

Color the sticks to match the number bond.

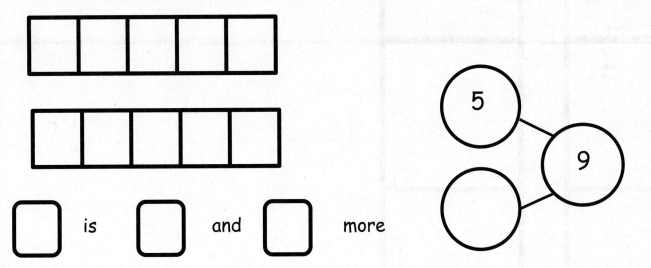

☐ is ☐ and ☐ more

Lesson 12: Use the 5-groups to represent the 5 + n pattern to 8.
Date: 11/12/13

4.B.51

Topic C

Addition with Totals of 6, 7, and 8

K.OA.1, K.OA.2, K.OA.3, K.OA.4

Focus Standard:	K.OA.1	Represent addition and subtraction with objects, fingers, mental images, drawings, sounds (e.g., claps), acting out situations, verbal explanations, expressions, or equations. (Drawings need not show details, but should show the mathematics in the problem. This applies wherever drawings are mentioned in the Standards.)
	K.OA.2	Solve addition and subtraction word problems, and add and subtract within 10, e.g., by using objects or drawings to represent the problem.
Instructional Days:	6	
Coherence -Links from:	GPK–M5	Numerals to 5, Addition and Subtraction Stories, Counting to 20
-Links to:	G1–M1	Sums and Differences to 10

Topic C introduces formal addition concepts including writing and solving expressions and equations. The first three lessons ask students to represent addition story problems involving decomposition and composition, modeled by A + B = C and C = A + B. In these first formal addition lessons the stories are told with no unknown. "There are 7 apples in the bowl. Five of them are red and 2 of them are green." Students write addition sentences and identify the referent of each number within the problem. Lessons 13–15 work with 6, 7, and 8 respectively, representing such addition stories with pictures, numbers, and equations.

In Lesson 16, students solve *add to with result unknown* (A + B = ___) word problems within 8. "There were 5 birds in the tree. Three more birds flew to the tree. How many birds are in the tree now?" Students learn to put a box around the equation's unknown.

Lesson 17 teaches *put together total unknown* (also A + B = ___) word problems. On the surface these problems appear similar those of Lesson 16, but lack the embedded *action* of the previous problems. Instead, they focus on a set of objects and part–whole relationships. "There are 4 red toy cars and 3 blue toy cars on the table. How many toy cars are on the table?"

Lesson 18 deals with the last type of addition situation in kindergarten, *both addends unknown* (C = ___+___). Note that this *take apart* situation is modeled with an addition equation. Students are given a total and are asked to find a number pair in the context of an addition story. "There were 8 toy cars. Some are on a shelf and the rest are in a toy box. Write an addition sentence to show how many could be in each place."

For examples of all problem types, refer to the Operations and Algebraic Thinking progression document, page 9.

A Teaching Sequence Towards Mastery of Addition with Totals of 6, 7, and 8

Objective 1: Represent decomposition and composition addition stories to 6 with drawings and equations with no unknown.
  (Lesson 13)

Objective 2: Represent decomposition and composition addition stories to 7 with drawings and equations with no unknown.
  (Lesson 14)

Objective 3: Represent decomposition and composition addition stories to 8 with drawings and equations with no unknown.
  (Lesson 15)

Objective 4: Solve *add to with result unknown* word problems to 8 with equations. Box the unknown.
  (Lesson 16)

Objective 5: Solve *put together with total unknown* word problems to 8 using objects and drawings.
  (Lesson 17)

Objective 6: Solve *both addends unknown* word problems to 8 to find addition patterns in number pairs.
  (Lesson 18)

Lesson 13

Objective: Represent decomposition and composition addition stories to 6 with drawings and equations with no unknown.

Suggested Lesson Structure

■ Fluency Practice   (12 minutes)
■ Application Problem   (5 minutes)
■ Concept Development   (25 minutes)
■ Student Debrief   (8 minutes)
    Total Time   **(50 minutes)**

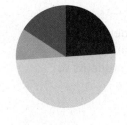

Fluency Practice (12 minutes)

- Counting the Say Ten Way with the Rekenrek **K.NBT.1**   (3 minutes)
- Dot Cards of 6 **K.OA.3**   (3 minutes)
- Draw More to Make 6 **K.CC.2**   (6 minutes)

Counting the Say Ten Way with the Rekenrek (3 minutes)

Materials: (T) 20-bead Rekenrek

Note: This activity is an extension of students' previous work with the Rekenrek, and anticipates working with teen numbers.

Conduct activity as written in GK–M4–Lesson 5.

Dot Cards of 6 (3 minutes)

Materials: (T/S) Varied dot cards of 6 (card template from GK–M3–Lesson 13)

Note: This activity deepens students' knowledge of embedded numbers and develops part–whole thinking.

    T: (Show card.) How many do you see?
    S: 6.
    T: How did you see them in two parts?
    S: (Possible answers.) 5 on this side and 1 on that side. → 2 down and 4 up.
         → 3 up and 3 down.

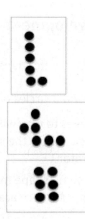

	Lesson 13:	Represent decomposition and composition addition stories to 6 with drawings and equations with no unknown.	
	Date:	11/12/13	**4.C.3**

Continue with other cards of 6. Distribute the cards to the students for partner sharing time. Have them pass on the card at a signal and repeat with a new card.

Draw More to Make 6 (6 minutes)

Materials: (S) Fluency Problem Set

Note: This activity further develops students' understanding of the decompositions of 6.

After giving clear instructions and completing the first few problems together, allow students time to work independently. Encourage them to do as many problems as they can within a given time frame. Go over the answers, and direct students to energetically shout, "Yes!" for each correct answer.

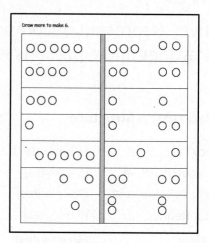

Application Problem (5 minutes)

Materials: (S) Personal white board, 6 linking cubes per student

Four silly seals were splashing in the water. Show the silly seals with your linking cubes. Two more silly seals came to splash. Show the new seals. How many silly seals are splashing in the water now?

Use your cubes and talk to your partner about the seals. Can you write about the silly seals in a number bond?

Note: Composition of the number 6 serves as an anticipatory set for today's lesson, providing students an opportunity to work with concrete materials before moving into the pictorial stage in today's lesson.

NOTES ON MULTIPLE MEANS OF ENGAGEMENT:

Scaffold the Application Problem for English language learners by providing sentence starters such as "__ seals, and ____ seals is ___ seals" and "___ + ____ = ." This will support their oral response to the problem's prompt.

Concept Development (25 minutes)

Materials: (T) Magnetic shapes (optional) (S) Personal white boards

Draw 2 squares and 3 circles on the board.

- T: Noah loves to play with magnets on his refrigerator. He has these magnets. (Show the shapes on the board.) What does Noah have on his refrigerator?
- S: He has some shape magnets. → There are some circles and some squares. → There are 5 magnets in all.

Lesson 13: Represent decomposition and composition addition stories to 6 with drawings and equations with no unknown.
Date: 11/12/13

4.C.4

MP.4

T: Copy these shape magnets onto your personal board. Hmmm. We've practiced making number bonds from shape pictures before. Can anyone help me make a number bond about our picture? (Allow students to guide you in the creation of a number bond on the board starting with the total and then designating the parts.)

T: I want to write about this in the special math way in a number sentence. (Write 5 = 3 + 2 under the number bond.)

T: What does this 5 tell us about?

S: The 5 tells how many shape magnets Noah has in all.

T: I showed the parts of our picture like this: 3 + 2. Where does the 3 come from?

S: The circles!

T: Where does the 2 come from?

S: The squares!

T: Yes, there are 5 shape magnets on Noah's refrigerator. 2 are squares and 3 are circles. 5 equals 2 and 3 together! Write the number sentence on your board. (Circulate to ensure understanding.)

T: Erase your personal boards. Noah's friend gave him another circle magnet. I'll draw it on the board. Copy all of the shapes onto your own board. What do you notice?

S: Now we have 4 circles! → We have 2 squares and 4 circles!

T: Count the sets of shapes and write the numbers underneath your pictures. Let's make a number bond about our new picture. (Allow students to guide you in creation of the number bond.) Who can tell me about the number sentence?

S: 4 shapes and 2 more shapes make 6 in all.

T: Yes! We can write it like this: 4 + 2 = 6.

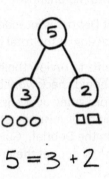

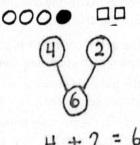

Talk students through the referents once again as was done with 5 = 3 + 2 (a referent is the thing that the numerals represent). Switch the order of the addends and lead them through the referents again. Have them notice which number bond might better show the total amount made into parts and which might better show the parts put together to make the total.

Lead students in more examples with totals of 6 as time allows. Release them to work in pairs as they show independence.

NOTES ON MULTIPLE MEANS OF ACTION AND EXPRESSION:

Ask your above grade level students to explain to you why they think that 5 = 2 + 3 can also be written as 2 + 3 = 5 without changing the picture of the 3 squares and 2 circles on the board. Encourage them to use their math words.

Problem Set (10 minutes)

Students should do their personal best to complete the Problem Set within the allotted 10 minutes.

Note: The final question asks students to write a number sentence. This is not a mastered skill, but this question provides an opportunity for students who are ready to write number sentences independently.

Lesson 13: Represent decomposition and composition addition stories to 6 with drawings and equations with no unknown.
Date: 11/12/13

4.C.5

Student Debrief (8 minutes)

Lesson Objective: Represent decomposition and composition addition stories to 6 with drawings and equations with no unknown.

The Student Debrief is intended to invite reflection and active processing of the total lesson experience.

Invite students to review their solutions for the Problem Set. They should check work by comparing answers with a partner before going over answers as a class. Look for misconceptions or misunderstandings that can be addressed in the Debrief. Guide students in a conversation to debrief the Problem Set and process the lesson.

You may choose to use any combination of the questions below to lead the discussion.

- Look at the corn stalk problem. Did your number bond match your neighbors'?

- How did your drawings help you to make your number sentences?

- How did the number bond help you to make your number sentence? How are number bonds and number sentences alike, or similar?

- Does it matter if you put the parts first or the whole first in a number sentence?

- Did you notice anything special about the parts in the gecko problem? (The parts were the same.) How do you know which part shows the spotted geckos? Does it matter?

- Think back to our silly seals. Can you think of a number sentence to describe them?

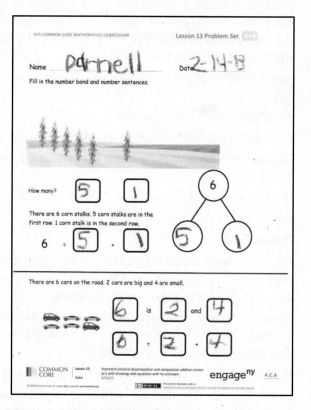

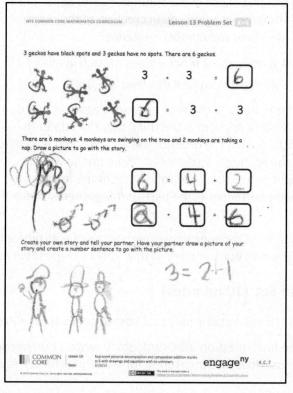

COMMON CORE™   Lesson 13:   Represent decomposition and composition addition stories to 6 with drawings and equations with no unknown.   4.C.6

Date: 11/12/13

Draw more to make 6.

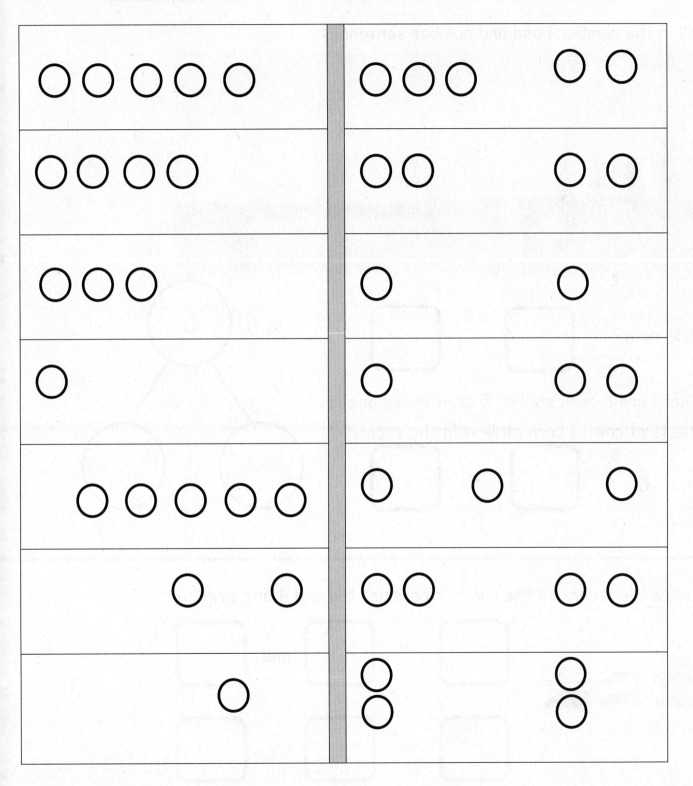

Lesson 13:   Represent decomposition and composition addition stories to 6
             with drawings and equations with no unknown.
Date: 11/12/13

4.C.7

© 2013 Common Core, Inc. All rights reserved. commoncore.org

Name _____   Date _____

Fill in the number bond and number sentences.

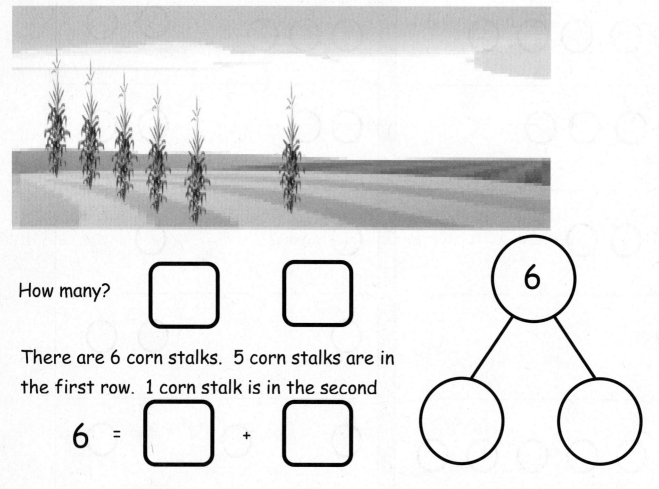

How many? ☐ ☐

There are 6 corn stalks. 5 corn stalks are in the first row. 1 corn stalk is in the second

6 = ☐ + ☐

There are 6 cars on the road. 2 cars are big and 4 are small.

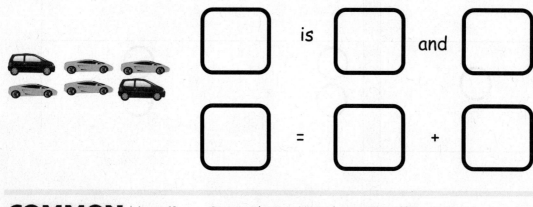

☐ is ☐ and ☐

☐ = ☐ + ☐

3 geckos have black spots and 3 geckos have no spots. There are 6 geckos.

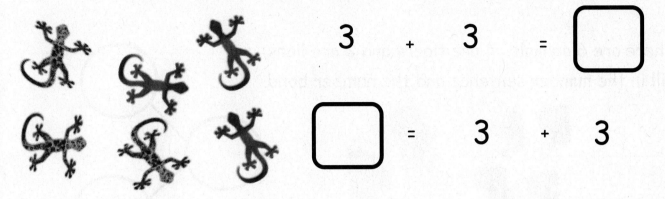

There are 6 monkeys. 4 monkeys are swinging on the tree, and 2 monkeys are taking a nap. Draw a picture to go with the story.

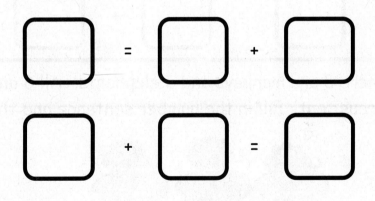

Create your own story and tell your partner. Have your partner draw a picture of your story and create a number sentence to go with the picture.

Lesson 13:	Represent decomposition and composition addition stories to 6 with drawings and equations with no unknown.
Date:	11/12/13

4.C.9

Name _____   Date _____

There are 6 animals. 4 are tigers and 2 are lions.
Fill in the number sentence and the number bond.

☐   is   ☐   and   ☐

☐   =   ☐   +   ☐

There 3 are monkeys and 3 elephants. All 6 animals are going into the circus tent. Fill in the number sentence and the number bond.

☐   and   ☐   is   ☐

☐   +   ☐   =   ☐

On the back of your paper, draw some animals. Make a number bond to match your picture.

COMMON CORE™   Lesson 13:   Represent decomposition and composition addition stories to 6
with drawings and equations with no unknown.
Date: 11/12/13

4.C.10

Lesson 14

Objective: Represent decomposition and composition addition stories to 7 with drawings and equations with no unknown.

Suggested Lesson Structure

■ Fluency Practice   (12 minutes)
■ Application Problem   (5 minutes)
■ Concept Development   (25 minutes)
■ Student Debrief   (8 minutes)
   Total Time   **(50 minutes)**

Fluency Practice (12 minutes)

- Sprint: Make 7 **K.OA.3**   (12 minutes)

Sprint: Make 7 (12 minutes)

Materials   (S) 2 copies of the Make 7 Sprint per student

Note: This Sprint continues to support students' understanding of part–total relationships. The addition of numerals to the end of the Sprint gives students who are comfortable with the partners of 7 an opportunity to move from pictorial to more abstract thinking.

   T: It's time for a Sprint! (Briefly recall previous Sprint preparation activities, and distribute Sprints facedown.) Take out your pencil and one crayon, any color. For this Sprint, you are going to circle the number that will make 7. (Demonstrate the first problem as needed.)

Continue to follow the Sprint procedure as outlined in GK–M4– Lesson 3. Have students work on the Sprint for a second time (they will soon work on two different Sprints in a single day). Continue to emphasize that the goal is simply to do better than the first time and celebrate improvement.

> **NOTES ON MULTIPLE MEANS OF ENGAGEMENT:**
>
> Push above grade level students' thinking by asking them to solve another Application Problem, but with an unknown, such as, "The train is now pulling some cars. Two of the cars are empty and 3 are full." Ask the students to draw a number bond and a number sentence of the situation.

Application Problem (5 minutes)

Materials: (S) Personal white boards

Larry the train is pulling 7 cars. Three cars are full and 4 cars are empty.

Draw the train and make a number bond about your picture. Discuss your work with your partner.
Extension: Can you make a number sentence to go with your picture?

Note: Decomposition and composition of the number 7 serves as an anticipatory set for today's lesson.

Concept Development (25 minutes)

Materials: (S) Linking cube 7-sticks, train template inserted in personal white boards

T: You learned a lot about how to write number sentences yesterday! We will practice this more today using our 7-sticks. Let's pretend each cube is a train car. How many cars on your train?

S: 7 cars!

T: Record that on your personal board and put your cars on the train track.

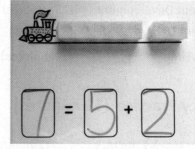

T: Snap your train into 2 groups to show 5 cars and 2 cars on your train track.

T: 7 cars is the same as…?

S: 5 cars and 2 cars.

T: We write 7 = 5 + 2. Write the number sentence that tells about what we did.

S: (Write 7 = 5 + 2.)

T: Now, we will put the parts together again. How many are in the longer part of the train?

S: 5 cars.

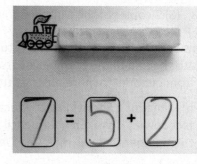

T: In the shorter part of the train?

S: 2 cars.

T: Let's write 5 + 2. Put your cars together on the track. What number equals 5 + 2?

S: 7!

T: Let's look at our number sentence. What does the 5 tell us about?

S: The longer part of the train.

MP.2 T: The 2?

S: The shorter part of the train.

T: The 7?

S: The **total** number of cars on the track.

T: Turn and talk to your partner about your cars on the track. What if we broke your group of 7 train cars into a part with 3 and a part with 4? Show the cars on your track and write a number sentence to tell about the new story. (Allow time for sharing and discussion. Circulate to ensure that the parts of the equation are being accurately represented.)

T: With your partner, you are going to play several games of Snap with the train cars (see GK–M4– Lesson 11 for Snap instructions). Each time that you play, work together to show the cars on the

Lesson 14: Represent decomposition and composition addition stories to 7 with drawings and equations with no unknown.

Date: 11/12/13

4.C.1

track and to write a number sentence that shows what happened. Hmm... I wonder how many different number sentences our class can find about seven? (Circulate to observe accuracy and understanding, listening for correct vocabulary and rich mathematical discussion.)

T: It's time to show and share how many number sentences you found! Hold up your personal boards. What were some of your discoveries? Use your math words and your number sentences to tell me. (Create a list on the board as the students share.)

S: 7 = 6 + 1. → 3 + 4 = 7, too. → 2 + 5 = 7! → 7 = 5 + 2.

T: How did you know where the numbers would go in your number sentences? Tell me how you decided to write them.

Problem Set (10 minutes)

Students should do their personal best to complete the Problem Set within the allotted 10 minutes.

Student Debrief (8 minutes)

Lesson Objective: Represent decomposition and composition addition stories to 7 with drawings and equations with no unknown.

The Student Debrief is intended to invite reflection and active processing of the total lesson experience.

Invite students to review their solutions for the Problem Set. They should check work by comparing answers with a partner before going over answers as a class. Look for misconceptions or misunderstandings that can be addressed in the Debrief. Guide students in a conversation to debrief the Problem Set and process the lesson.

You may choose to use any combination of the questions below to lead the discussion.

- Look at the bears on the Problem Set. How did you know where to put the 6? The 1? The 7? Does it matter where you write the numbers for

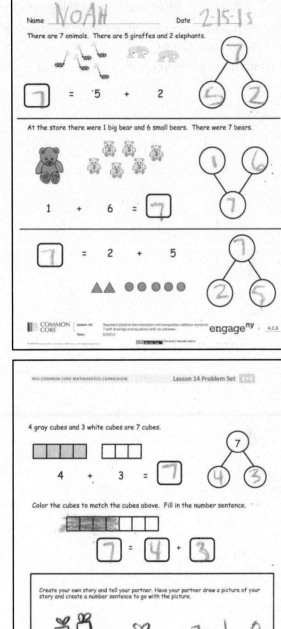

Lesson 14: Represent decomposition and composition addition stories to 7 with drawings and equations with no unknown.
Date: 11/12/13

4.C.13

the big bear and the little bears in the number bond?

- Look at the gray and white cubes. Is there a difference between the broken stick and the whole stick? What is the difference? What things are the same about the sticks?

- Why do you think you and your classmates were able to find so many different number sentences for 7 in the Snap game?

- What happens when you turn around one of the addition number sentences like I did on the board?

Lesson 14:   Represent decomposition and composition addition stories to 7 with drawings and equations with no unknown.

Date: 11/12/13

4.C.1

Circle the number to make 7.

1	(die showing 6)	(square with 1 dot)	(square with 2 dots)
2	(hand)	(hand)	(hand)
3	* * * * *	* *	* * *
4	(die showing 5)	(die showing 3)	(die showing 2)
5	(hand)	(hand)	(hand) (hand)
6	* * *	* * *	* * * * * *
7	(die showing 3)	(die showing 4)	(die showing 3) (die showing 2)
8	(hand)	(hand)	(hand) (hand)
9	* *	* *	* * * * * * * * *
10	2	2	5 4
11	(hand)	(hand)	(hand) (hand) (hand)
12	(square with 1 dot)	(square with 2 dots)	(die showing 6) (die showing 5)
13	1	2	6 5

Lesson 14: Represent decomposition and composition addition stories to 7 with drawings and equations with no unknown.

Date: 11/12/13

4.C.15

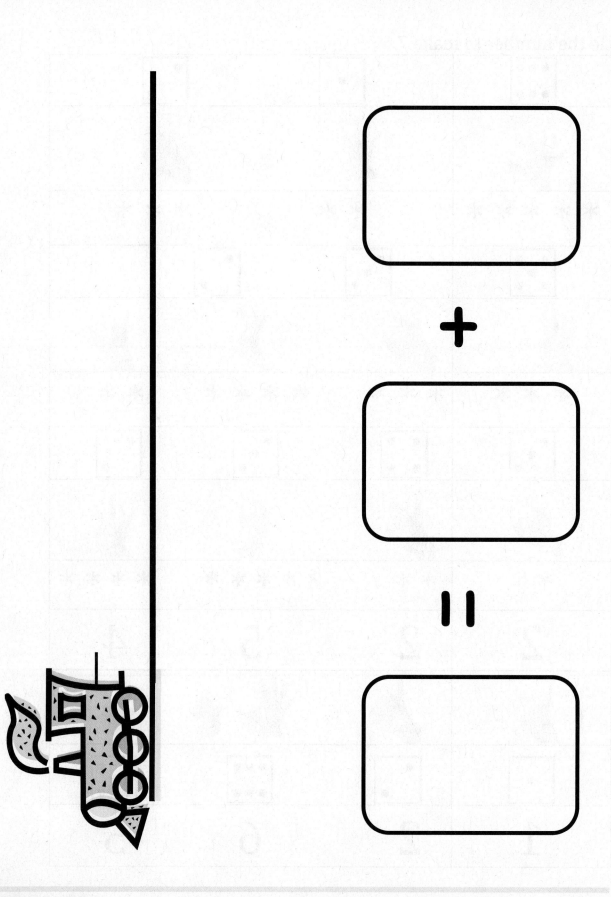

Lesson 14: Represent decomposition and composition addition stories to 7 with drawings and equations with no unknown.

Date: 11/12/13

4.C.1

Name _____   Date _____

There are 7 animals. There are 5 giraffes and 2 elephants.

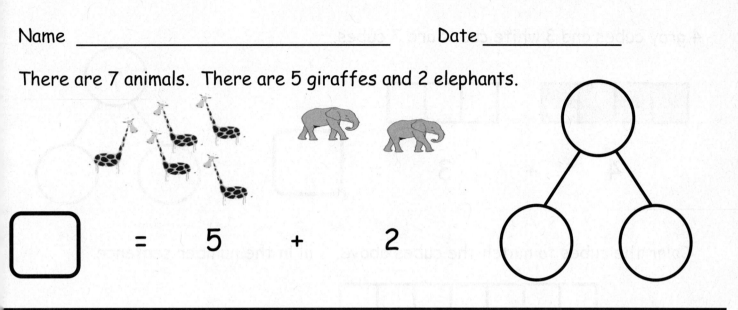

☐ = 5 + 2

At the store there were 1 big bear and 6 small bears. There were 7 bears.

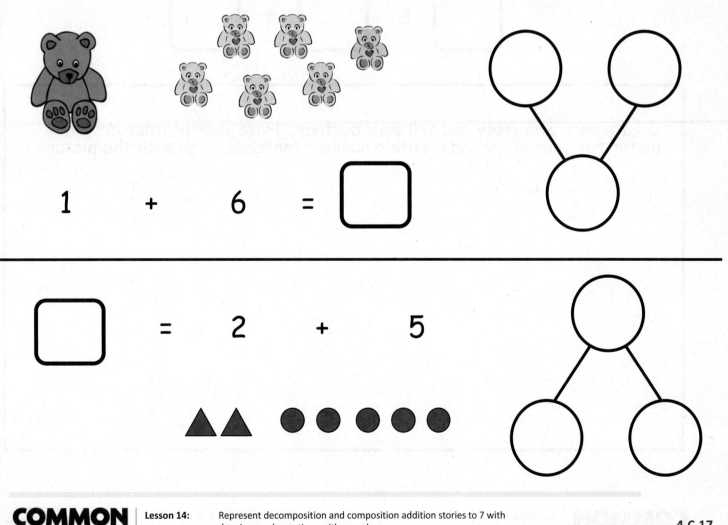

1 + 6 = ☐

☐ = 2 + 5

COMMON CORE™

Lesson 14:   Represent decomposition and composition addition stories to 7 with
drawings and equations with no unknown.

Date: 11/12/13

4.C.17

4 gray cubes and 3 white cubes are 7 cubes.

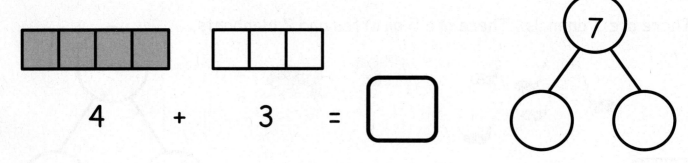

$$4 \quad + \quad 3 \quad = \quad \boxed{}$$

Color the cubes to match the cubes above. Fill in the number sentence.

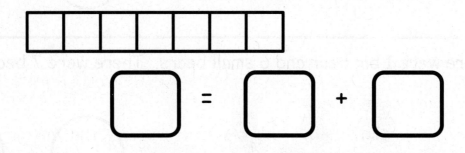

$$\boxed{} = \boxed{} + \boxed{}$$

Create your own story and tell your partner. Have your partner draw a picture of your story and create a number sentence to go with the picture.

COMMON CORE™ | **Lesson 14:** Represent decomposition and composition addition stories to 7 with drawings and equations with no unknown.
Date: 11/12/13

4.C.1

Name _____   Date _____

There are 7 bears. 3 bears have bowties. 4 bears have a heart. Fill in the number sentences and the number bond.

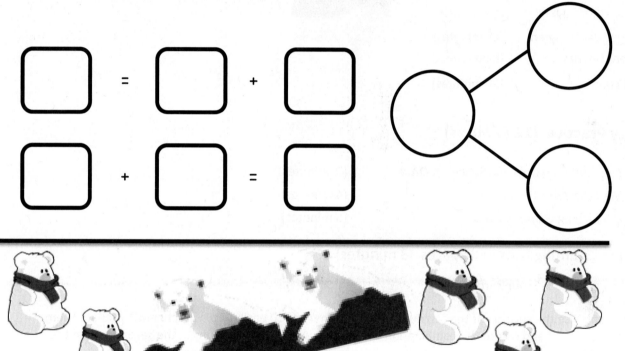

□ = □ + □

□ + □ = □

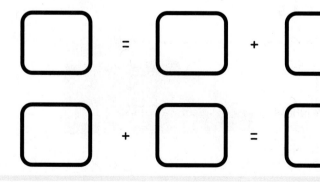

5 bears have scarves on and 2 do not. There are 7 bears.

Write a number sentence that tells about the bears.

□ = □ + □

□ + □ = □

On the back of your paper, draw a picture about the 7 bears. Write a number sentence and make a number bond to go with it.

COMMON CORE™   Lesson 14:   Represent decomposition and composition addition stories to 7 with drawings and equations with no unknown.   4.C.19

Date: 11/12/13

Lesson 15

Objective: Represent decomposition and composition addition stories to 8 with drawings and equations with no unknown.

Suggested Lesson Structure

■ Fluency Practice   (12 minutes)
■ Application Problem   (5 minutes)
□ Concept Development   (25 minutes)
■ Student Debrief   (8 minutes)
   Total Time   **(50 minutes)**

Fluency Practice (12 minutes)

- 5-Groups: Counting Dots and Spaces **K.OA.4**   (3 minutes)
- Show Me Taller/Shorter **K.MD.2**   (4 minutes)
- Make 8 Matching Game **K.OA.3**   (5 minutes)

5-Groups: Counting Dots and Spaces (3 minutes)

Materials: (T) Large 5-Group cards

Note: Students use the support of the 5-groups to find partners of 10 easily. This practice will prepare them to find partners of 10 and record the combination through drawings and equations in the second half of the module.

> T: Raise your hand when you know the number of dots, then wait for the snap to say the number. How many dots? (Show 9 dots.)
> S: 9.
> T: How many spaces?
> S: 1.

Continue to show cards. A possible sequence is 9, 1, 8, 2, 7, 3, 6, 4, 5.

Show Me Taller/Shorter (4 minutes)

Materials: (T) Number towers 1–10 showing color change at 5

Note: This is a maintenance activity to keep students sharp on length comparisons and to reiterate the relationship between length and

Lesson 15:   Represent decomposition and composition addition stories to 8
                 with drawings and equations with no unknown.
Date: 11/12/13

4.C.20

number. Having the color change at 5 will reinforce students' work with the 5 + n pattern throughout this module.

- T: Do you remember how we use our hands to show taller and shorter? Show me taller.
- S: (Hold one hand above head.)
- T: Good memories. Now show me shorter.
- S: (Hold hand lower than before, indicating less height.)
- T: Nice. I want you to help me compare the height of my number towers. (Hold the 5 and 8 number towers in your hand so it looks like the 5-stick is taller.) Do we know which one is taller?
- S: No! → We can't see all of the tower. → You need to line them up!
- T: Okay, I'll line up the endpoints. (Show the 8-stick and the 5-stick with endpoints aligned.) Is my 5-stick taller or shorter than my 8-stick?
- S: The 5-stick is shorter than the 8-stick.

Continue, using the following sequence: 2 and 6, 9 and 4, 4 and 6, 2 and 3, 8 and 6, 7 and 6, 6 and 5. Starting with numbers that are far apart makes it easier to compare. Make sure to set up your question so that the answer fluctuates between taller and shorter.

Make 8 Matching Game (5 minutes)

Materials: (S) Cards with quantities of 0–8 (use only dots, dice, and fingers) per pair (use cards from GK–M4– Lessons 1 and 7)

Note: Students will find the hidden partners of 8 in support of the day's work with composition and decomposition.

Conduct activity as outlined in GK–M4–Lesson 2, but now have students find partners of 8.

Application Problem (5 minutes)

Materials: (S) Personal white boards

You are having a party! You get 8 presents. Two presents have stripes, and 6 presents have polka dots. Draw the presents, and write the number sentences two different ways on your personal board.

Note: Decomposition and composition of the number 8 serves as an anticipatory story context for this lesson.

Concept Development (25 minutes)

Materials: (T) Cup containing 8 loose linking cubes or other small manipulatives (S) Personal white boards

Stretch a line of tape or chalk down the middle of the rug, table, or desk.

T: We are going to play the gravity game today! Let's pretend my cubes are space rocks. Help me count how many rocks I am putting into my cup.

S: 1, 2, 3, 4, 5, 6, 7, 8.

T: I have 8 space rocks in my cup. This side of the tape is the land (point) and this side is the ocean (point). I will use gravity and my magic tape line to help me find some number sentences about 8. How many space rocks landed, and how many fell into the ocean? Let me shake it 8 times, and then I will pour it out to see what happens! (Demonstrate and pour the cubes onto the surface.) What happened?

S: There are some on that side of the line and some on this side. → There are 6 on that side and 2 on this one!

T: Can we make a number sentence about our picture?

MP.4 S: We had 8 rocks, but they broke into a 2 and a 6. → 8 = 2 + 6. → 2 + 6 = 8! (Other varying responses.)

T: Write the number sentence on your personal board.

T: Did anyone think of a different number sentence that tells how our cubes look right now? (Allow time for sharing and discussion.)

T: Let's try it again and see if gravity can help us make another sentence! Student B, would you like to try? I wonder how many different number sentences we can find about 8?

NOTES ON MULTIPLE MEANS OF ENGAGEMENT:

Allow your students with disabilities or who might be below grade level who might still need the scaffold to engage in the lesson by continuing to use number bonds to show what happened when you poured out the cubes. Encourage them to write the number sentences underneath.

Allow several more iterations of the game, directing the students to represent the equations for the situation each time. List the equations on the board to help students appreciate all of their new names for 8! Ensure that the students are confident as to the placement of the addends and the total in their number sentences.

Problem Set (10 minutes)

Students should do their personal best to complete the Problem Set within the allotted 10 minutes.

Student Debrief (8 minutes)

Lesson Objective: Represent decomposition and composition addition stories to 8 with drawings and equations with no unknown.

The Student Debrief is intended to invite reflection and active processing of the total lesson experience.

Invite students to review their solutions for the Problem Set. They should check work by comparing answers with a partner before going over answers as a class. Look for misconceptions or misunderstandings that can be addressed in the Debrief. Guide students in a conversation to debrief the Problem Set and process the lesson.

You may choose to use any combination of the questions below to lead the discussion.

Lesson 15:   Represent decomposition and composition addition stories to 8
             with drawings and equations with no unknown.
Date: 11/12/13

4.C.22

- In the Problem Set, how many yellow and red flowers did you draw? What did your number sentence look like?

- Look for a partner whose flowers look different from yours. Talk about how they are different.

- How many different partners did we find to make 8 today? (Count equations on the board. If students try to count equations like 6 + 2 = 8 and 2 + 6 = 8 twice, talk about how one set of partners can make two different equations.)

- How do the number sentences on the board look similar?

- How are they different?

- What if we would have played the gravity game with only 7 cubes?

COMMON CORE | Lesson 15:   Represent decomposition and composition addition stories to 8
              Date: with drawings and equations with no unknown.
                           11/12/13   4.C.23

Name _____   Date _____

Fill in the number sentences.

There are 8 fish. There are 4 striped fish and 4 goldfish.

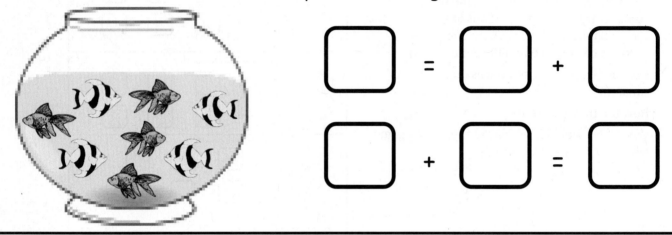

There are 8 shapes. There are 5 triangles and 3 diamonds.

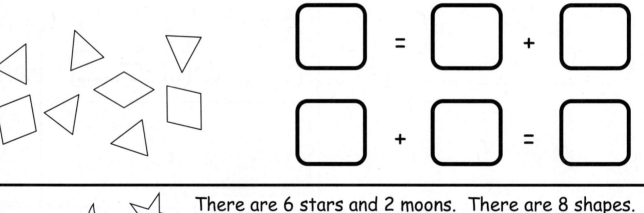

There are 6 stars and 2 moons. There are 8 shapes.

COMMON CORE™

Lesson 15:   Represent decomposition and composition addition stories to 8
             with drawings and equations with no unknown.
Date: 11/12/13

4.C.24

There are 8 shapes. Count and circle the squares. Count and circle the triangle.

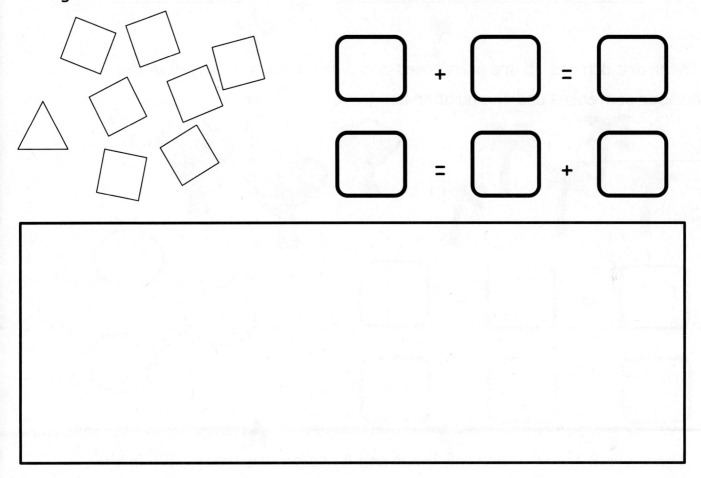

There are 8 flowers. Some flowers are yellow and some flowers are red. Draw a picture to go with the story.

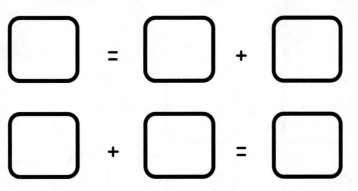

Create your own story and tell your partner. Have your partner draw a picture of your story and create a number sentence to go with the picture.

 | Lesson 15: | Represent decomposition and composition addition stories to 8 with drawings and equations with no unknown. | 4.C.25

Date: 11/12/13

Name _____   Date _____

There are 8 trees. 5 are palm trees and 3 are apple trees. Fill in the
number sentences and the number bond.

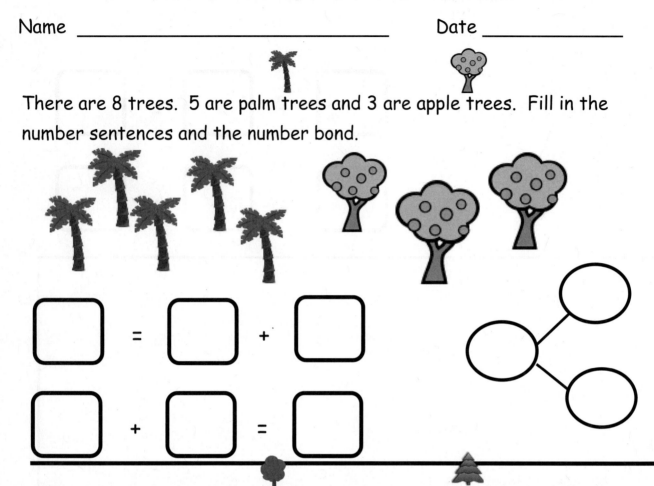

□ = □ + □

□ + □ = □

There are 8 trees. 4 are oak trees and 4 are spruce trees.   Fill in the
number sentences and the number bond.

□ = □ + □

□ + □ = □

Lesson 16

Objective: Solve *add to with result unknown* word problems to 8 with equations. Box the unknown.

Suggested Lesson Structure

■ Fluency Practice   (12 minutes)
■ Application Problem   (5 minutes)
□ Concept Development   (25 minutes)
■ Student Debrief   (8 minutes)
  Total Time   **(50 minutes)**

Fluency Practice (12 minutes)

▪ Sprint: Count Up to 8 **K.CC.2**   (12 minutes)

Sprint: Count Up to 8 (12 minutes)

Materials: (S) 2 copies of the Count Up to 8 Sprint

Note: This Sprint focuses on composing 8 using both pictures and numerals to support students' work with equations in the day's lesson.

> T: It's time for a Sprint! (Briefly recall previous Sprint preparation activities, and distribute Sprints facedown.) Take out your pencil and one crayon, any color. For this Sprint, you are going to circle the number that means you count up to exactly 8. (Demonstrate the first problem as needed, both by counting all and counting on.)

Continue to follow the Sprint procedure as outlined in GK–M4–Lesson 3. Have students work on the Sprint for a second time (they will soon work on two different Sprints on a single day). Continue to emphasize that the goal is simply to do better than the first time and celebrate improvement.

Application Problem (5 minutes)

Materials: (S) 10 linking cubes per student

Note: A set of 10 linking cubes for each student deliberately gives the students more cubes than necessary to model the story so that they can select those needed from the larger set.

Three airplanes were flying in the air. Use your cubes to show the planes. Three more airplanes came to join

A NOTE ON CLASSROOM ORGANIZATION FOR LESSONS 16, 17, AND 18:

Because Lessons 16, 17, and 18 involve word problems that must be read aloud to the majority of kindergarten students, it is suggested that additional adult support be sought for these instructional days. Kindergarten students draw and write at very different rates. Small groups of students organized to address these differences will allow for better management and greater engagement. It is very important that students begin their experience of word problems in a positive way. Support might be found in the parent community, in upper grade classes, or within the school community's personnel.

Lesson 16:   Solve *add to with result unknown* word problems to 8 with equations.
              Box the unknown.
Date: 11/12/13

4.C.27

the flying fun. Show the airplanes with your cubes.

Now, with your cubes, show how many airplanes were flying in the air. Talk to your partner about what the number sentence would look like.

Note: This problem sets the stage for solve *add to with result unknown* word problems in today's lesson.

Concept Development (25 minutes)

 NOTES ON
MULTIPLE MEANS OF
REPRESENTATION:

Help students, especially English language learners, to have meaningful conversations with each other by teaching them to ask questions such as, "Do you agree?" and "Why did you do that?" Teaching students to ask meaningful questions of each other extends their sharing and holds them accountable for sharing their thinking.

Materials: (S) Personal white boards

T: We are going to do some imagining today. I'm going to tell you a story, but I want you to close your eyes and just think about the picture in your mind. Then, I will let you draw the picture on your personal board. Ready?

T: Five kittens were playing in the yard. Two more kittens came over to join their game. How many kittens are in the yard now? Raise your hand when you have a picture in your mind. (Wait.) Ok, you may open your eyes. Who were the characters in our story?

S: Kittens!

T: How many were in the yard at first?

S: 5.

T: How many other kittens came to play?

S: 2 more.

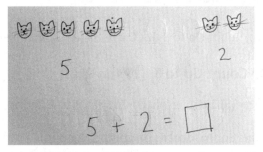

T: Good listening! Draw the kittens on your personal board. (Allow time for drawing. Depending on the abilities of the students, another option would be to have the students act out the situation with linking cubes rather than drawing the animals.)

T: Hold up your personal boards so I can see your cute kittens. I'll put mine on the board, too. (Demonstrate.) Now, write a number to show the kittens who were there at first. How many?

S: 5.

T: Write a number to show the kittens who came later to play. How many?

S: 2.

T: Great job! We have 5 + 2 kittens. We don't know how many there are yet, though. Let me finish my number sentence with mystery box, and when we find the answer, we can write it in the box. Write

NOTES ON
MULTIPLE MEANS OF
ENGAGEMENT:

Teach below grade level students by chunking the tasks for them a step at a time. "Draw the 5 kittens and show me. Now draw the 2 kittens who came after. Write the number of the kittens," etc. Continue to practice a step at a time until students feel confident and can continue on their own.

MP.1

 **COMMON CORE** | Lesson 16:   Solve *add to with result unknown* word problems to 8 with equations.
Box the unknown.
Date: 11/12/13

4.C.2

the number sentence on your board like mine. (Demonstrate.) How can we find out how many kittens there are in the yard?

S: We can count them all! → We could use our fingers. → I started at 5 and counted 2 more.

T: Talk with your partner about how you can find out the number that belongs in the box. (Allow time for sharing and discussion.) Who would like to share their answer?

S: 7!

T: What if 3 kittens had come to play instead of 2? Could you change your picture and make a new number sentence?

Continue with additional "imagining" situations to 8, encouraging the students to listen with their eyes closed and draw the pictures. They should then write the equations and box the unknowns on their personal boards. Encourage Level 1 and 2 problem solving strategies, as in the Sprint, but do not require students to use Level 2 strategies.

Problem Set (10 minutes)

Students should do their personal best to complete the Problem Set within the allotted 10 minutes.

Please see the note at the beginning of this lesson. The adults should read each problem aloud to their groups and watch to ensure understanding during the completion of the exercise.

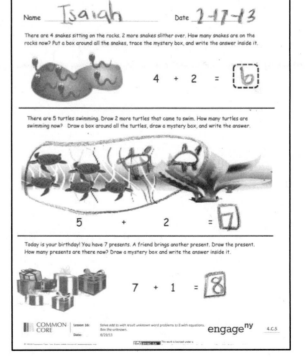

Student Debrief (8 minutes)

Lesson Objective: Solve *add to with result unknown* word problems to 8 with equations. Box the unknown.

The Student Debrief is intended to invite reflection and active processing of the total lesson experience.

Invite students to review their solutions for the Problem Set. They should check work by comparing answers with a partner before going over answers as a class. Look for misconceptions or misunderstandings that can be addressed in the Debrief. Guide students in a conversation to debrief the Problem Set and process the lesson.

You may choose to use any combination of the questions below to lead the discussion.

- Look at the snakes in the Problem Set. What is the same about the snakes and the number you

Lesson 16:	Solve *add to with result unknown* word problems to 8 with equations. Box the unknown.	4.C.29
Date:	11/12/13	

wrote in the mystery box? How about the turtles and the presents?

- In the Problem Set, how many friends were playing soccer? What did you do to find out how many there were?
- How did you decide what number should go in the mystery box?
- Did your friend do the same thing?
- How did your drawings help you with your work?

Lesson 16: Solve *add to with result unknown* word problems to 8 with equations. Box the unknown.

Date: 11/12/13

4.C.3

Circle the number to make 8.

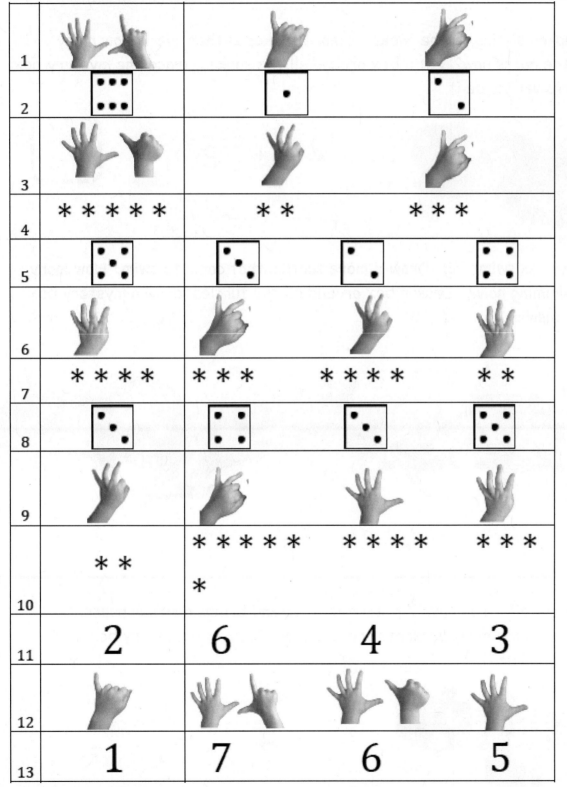

Lesson 16: Solve *add to with result unknown* word problems to 8 with equations. Box the unknown.

Date: 11/12/13

4.C.31

Name _____   Date _____

There are 4 snakes sitting on the rocks. 2 more snakes slither over. How many snakes are on the rocks now? Put a box around all the snakes, trace the mystery box, and write the answer inside it.

4   +   2   =

There are 5 turtles swimming. Draw 2 more turtles that came to swim. How many turtles are swimming now?   Draw a box around all the turtles, draw a mystery box, and write the answer.

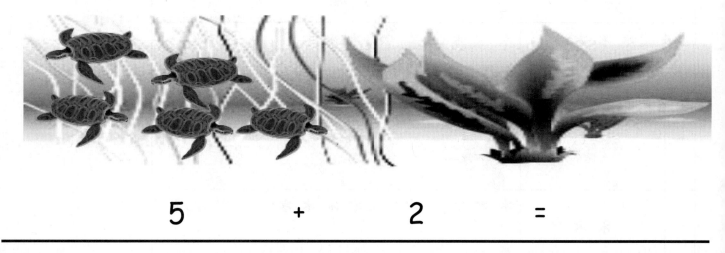

5   +   2   =

Today is your birthday! You have 7 presents. A friend brings another present. Draw the present. How many presents are there now? Draw a mystery box and write the answer inside it.

7   +   1   =

COMMON CORE™ | **Lesson 16:**   Solve *add to with result unknown* word problems to 8 with equations.
Box the unknown.
Date: 11/12/13

4.C.3

Listen and draw. There were 6 girls playing soccer. A boy came to play. How many children were playing soccer now? Draw a box around all the children.

6   +   1   =   [ ]

Listen and draw. There were 3 frogs on a log. 5 more frogs hopped onto the log. How many frogs were on the log now? Draw a box around the frogs and box the answer.

3   +   5   =

COMMON CORE™   **Lesson 16:** Solve *add to with result unknown* word problems to 8 with equations.
Box the unknown.
Date: 11/12/13

4.C.33

Name _____   Date _____

There are 3 penguins on the ice. 4 more penguins are coming. How many penguins are there?

$$3 \quad + \quad 4 \quad = \quad \boxed{}$$

There is 1 mama bear. 5 baby bears are following her. How many bears are there? Draw a box for the answer.

$$1 \quad + \quad 5 \quad =$$

Draw 7 balls in the ball box. Draw a girl putting 1 more ball in the ball box. Circle all the balls and draw a box for the answer. Write your answer.

$$7 \quad + \quad 1 \quad =$$

Lesson 16:   Solve *add to with result unknown* word problems to 8 with equations.
             Box the unknown.
Date: 11/12/13

4.C.3

Lesson 17

Objective: Solve *put together with total unknown* word problems to 8 using objects and drawings.

Suggested Lesson Structure

■ Fluency Practice   (12 minutes)
■ Application Problem   (5 minutes)
■ Concept Development   (25 minutes)
■ Student Debrief   (8 minutes)
    Total Time   **(50 minutes)**

A NOTE ON CLASSROOM ORGANIZATION FOR LESSONS 16, 17, AND 18:

Because Lessons 16, 17, and 18 involve word problems that must be read aloud to the majority of kindergarten students, it is suggested that additional adult support be sought for these instructional days. (See the more extensive note in Lesson 16.)

Fluency Practice (12 minutes)

▪ How Many? **K.OA.1**   (7 minutes)
▪ Partners of 5 **K.OA.3**   (5 minutes)

How Many? (7 minutes)

Materials: (S) Bags of red and white beans, number bond work mat, blank paper or personal white board, dice (with the 6 side covered on both dice or the 5 and 6 covered on one die)

Note: This fluency focuses on composition in preparation for the day's work. Students use the familiar number bond model to refresh their understanding of part–total relationships before working with equations in this lesson.

1. Partner A rolls a die and places that many beans in one of the part circles in the number bond.
2. Partner B rolls a die and places that many beans on the other part circle.
3. The partners move their beans to the total circle and count the total number of beans.
4. Both partners record the number bond using pictures or numerals.

Circulate to observe and provide support.

Partners of 5 (5 minutes)

Materials: (S) Personal white boards

Note: Students write number bonds and number sentences to 5 using fingers and the more abstract numerals.

    T: Write your numbers 1, 2, 3, and 4. (Pause as students do so.)

Lesson 17:   Solve *put together with total unknown* word problems to 8 using objects and drawings.
Date: 11/12/13

4.C.35

T: (Draw a number bond with a 5 as the whole.) You are going to write number bonds that have 5 as the total. Use only these numbers as parts. You can use your fingers if that will help you.

Encourage students to write at least two number bonds. Ask early finishers to write addition number sentences to match their bonds.

Application Problem (5 minutes)

Materials: (S) Personal white boards

Marissa is creating designs with shapes. She has 5 triangles and 2 circles. Draw the shapes, and write a number sentence. Talk to your partner about your picture and number sentence.

Note: Solving a *put together with total unknown* story will serve as an anticipatory set for this lesson.

Concept Development (25 minutes)

Materials: (S) 8 attribute blocks for each pair or small group of students (4 circles, 4 triangles), personal white boards, template

T: In your container, you have a block with three sides. What is it called?

S: A triangle!

T: With your partner, find 3 of them and put them on your desk.

T: Do you have a block with no straight sides? What is it called?

S: A circle!

T: Put three circles in front of you, too. What do you notice about the blocks in front of you?

S: There are 3 circles and 3 triangles! → We have a lot of shapes.

T: Draw your shapes on your personal white board. We want to make a number sentence about all of our shapes. We already have two clues for our number sentence! We have 3 circles and 3 triangles. Write a 3 under your set of circles and another 3 under your set of triangles to show how many. On your personal board, show me how we could use these numbers to help us make a number sentence.

S: 3 + 3.

T: Let's add our equal sign. Now put a mystery box at the end of your number sentence like we did yesterday so that we have a place to show how many shapes there are in all. How could we figure

MP.1

NOTES ON MULTIPLE MEANS OF ACTION AND EXPRESSION:

Provide students with disabilities and below grade level students with pattern blocks to represent the problem concretely before asking them to draw the problem and write a number sentence. Make manipulatives available to students who still need them.

NOTES ON MULTIPLE MEANS OF REPRESENTATION:

To assist English language learners, refer students to your word wall and have them point to the shapes (triangles, circles, etc.) as they respond to your prompts. Students can refer back to the visuals of the shapes as they complete the tasks of the lesson.

COMMON CORE™   **Lesson 17:**   Solve *put together with total unknown* word problems to 8 using objects and drawings.
      Date: 11/12/13

4.C.3

out our total number of shapes?

S: We could count them. → We could start from 3 and count 3 more.

T: You are right! Those are good ideas. Let's count the shapes. Help me finish the number sentence. 3 + 3 is...?

MP.1

S: 6!

T: Let's write it together: 3 + 3 = 6. Show your partner how you wrote your number sentence! (Circulate to ensure accuracy and understanding.)

T: Erase your board. Turn it over so you can see the tree and sun. Let's pretend our shapes are robins. How many robins do you have?

S: 6 robins!

T: Put those robins in the tree. Now let's pretend that 2 more robins are flying.

T: On your mat, use your attribute blocks to show what that would look like.

T: How many robins are there in all?

S: 8 robins!

T: Now let's just draw. Take off your blocks and draw a circle for each robin, like this (demonstrate).

S: (Draw.)

T: How many robins do you have now?

S: 8 robins.

T: Erase your boards. Listen to the story. Four of the robins are flying through the air. Draw the robins flying through the air. (Students do so.) Four robins are on the ground, eating worms. Draw the robins on the ground. (Students do so.)

T: Let's write a number sentence about our robins. The robins will give us clues for our number sentence. How many robins are flying?

S: 4 robins.

T: Let's start with the number 4. (Write 4 + on the board). What should we add to find out how many robins we have in all?

S: The robins on the ground. → The rest of the robins!

T: How many robins are on the ground?

S: 4 robins.

T: (Write the second 4 in the expression). 4 + 4. Let's write the equal sign. (Write =.) We want to find the total. (Draw a mystery box next to the equal sign to designate the unknown.) Now, work with your partner to find the rest of the number sentence. 4 + 4 is...?

S: 8!

T: Yes, 4 robins and 4 robins equal 8 robins all together. 4 + 4 = 8.

Have students continue to play with the robin story in partners. Partners should take turns telling a story about the bird while the other draws the story on the board and writes a number sentence.

Lesson 17:   Solve *put together with total unknown* word problems to 8 using
              objects and drawings.

Date: 11/12/13

4.C.37

Problem Set (10 minutes)

Students should do their personal best to complete the Problem Set within the allotted 10 minutes.

Please see the note at the beginning of this lesson. The adults should read each problem aloud to their group and watch to ensure understanding during the completion of the exercise.

Student Debrief (8 minutes)

Lesson Objective: Solve *put together with total unknown word* problems to 8 using objects and drawings.

The Student Debrief is intended to invite reflection and active processing of the total lesson experience.

Invite students to review their solutions for the Problem Set. They should check work by comparing answers with a partner before going over answers as a class. Look for misconceptions or misunderstandings that can be addressed in the Debrief. Guide students in a conversation to debrief the Problem Set and process the lesson.

You may choose to use any combination of the questions below to lead the discussion.

- Look at the Problem Set. Talk to your neighbor about the balloons. Tell your neighbor what each number in your number sentences is talking about.

- Look at the Problem Set. Sometimes the mystery box is at the beginning and sometimes it is at the end. Does it matter? (Lead a discussion that the mystery box tells "what you are trying to figure out" no matter where it is.)

- How did you and your partner find out how many shapes you had together?

- How are the number sentences you wrote today different from the ones we worked on before?

- Is there another way you could have written the number sentence?

Lesson 17:   Solve *put together with total unknown* word problems to 8 using
               objects and drawings.
Date: 11/12/13

4.C.3

© 2013 Common Core, Inc. All rights reserved. **common**core.org

Name _____   Date _____

There are 4 green balloons and 3 orange balloons in the air. How many balloons are in the air? Color the balloons to match the story, and fill in the number sentences.

$$\square + \square = \square$$

$$\square = \square + \square$$

Dominic has 6 yellow star stickers and 2 blue star stickers. How many stickers does Dominic have? Color the stars to match the story, and fill in the number sentences.

$$\square + \square = \square$$

$$\square = \square + \square$$

There are 5 big robots and 1 little robot. How many robots are there? Fill in the number sentences.

$$\square + \square = \square$$

$$\square = \square + \square$$

Lesson 17:	Solve *put together with total unknown* word problems to 8 using objects and drawings.
Date:	11/12/13

4.C.39

Listen and draw. Charlotte is playing with pattern blocks. She has 3 squares and 3 triangles. How many shapes does Charlotte have?

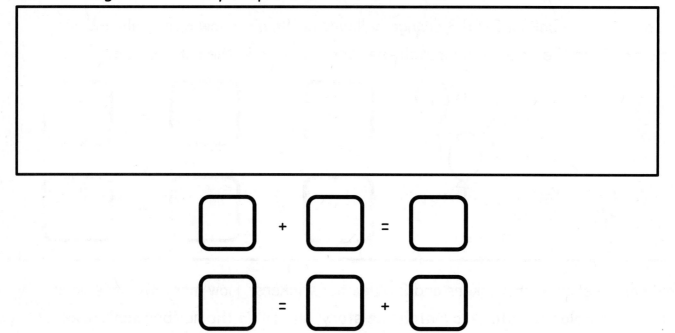

Listen and draw. Gavin is making a tower with linking cubes. He has 5 purple and 3 orange cubes. How many linking cubes does Gavin have?

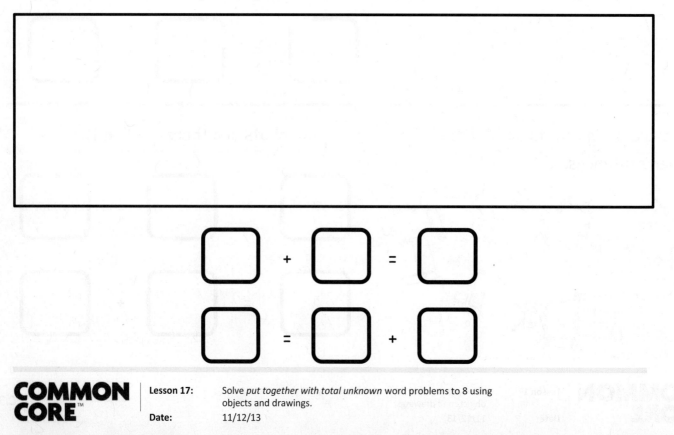

COMMON CORE™   **Lesson 17:**   Solve *put together with total unknown* word problems to 8 using
                                         objects and drawings.   4.C.4(

                     Date: 11/12/13

Name _____ Date _____

There are 5 hexagons and 2 triangles. How many shapes are there?

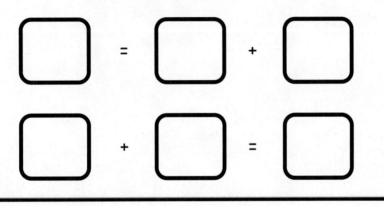

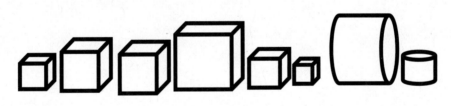

There are 6 cubes and 2 cylinders. How many shapes are there?

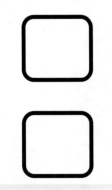 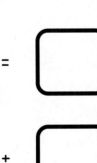 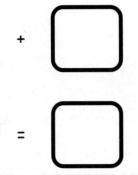

On the back of your paper, draw some shapes, and make a number sentence to match.

COMMON CORE™

Lesson 17: Solve *put together with total unknown* word problems to 8 using objects and drawings.

Date: 11/12/13

4.C.41

COMMON CORE™

Lesson 17: Solve *put together with total unknown* word problems to 8 using objects and drawings.
Date: 11/12/13

4.C.42

Lesson 18

Objective: Solve *both addends unknown* word problems to 8 to find addition patterns in number pairs.

Suggested Lesson Structure

■ Fluency Practice   (12 minutes)
■ Application Problem   (5 minutes)
□ Concept Development   (25 minutes)
■ Student Debrief   (8 minutes)
   Total Time   **(50 minutes)**

> **A NOTE ON CLASSROOM ORGANIZATION FOR LESSONS 16, 17, AND 18:**
>
> Because Lessons 16, 17, and 18 involve word problems that must be read aloud to the majority of kindergarten students, it is suggested that additional adult support be sought for these instructional days. (See a more extensive note in Lesson 16)

Fluency Practice (12 minutes)

• Sprint: Make 5 **K.OA.5**   (12 minutes)

Sprint: Make 5 (12 minutes)

Materials: (S) 2 copies of the Make 5 Sprint

Note: This Sprint extends the work that students did in Topic A with pictures to include numerals. Students are moving toward a more abstract understanding of the relationships between numbers to 5, though they may continue to rely on the support of pictures and objects throughout kindergarten.

   T: It's time for a Sprint! (Briefly recall previous Sprint preparation activities, and distribute Sprints facedown.) Take out your pencil and one crayon, any color. For this Sprint, you are going to circle the number that will make 5. (Demonstrate the first problem as needed.)

Continue to follow the Sprint procedure as outlined in GK–M4– Lesson 3. Have students work on the Sprint for a second time (they will soon work on two different Sprints in a single day). Continue to emphasize that the goal is simply to do better than the first time and celebrate improvement.

> **NOTES ON MULTIPLE MEANS OF REPRESENTATION:**
>
> Because the Application Problem depends heavily on English language learners being able to understand that apples and oranges are fruits, use visuals of apples and oranges to count pieces of fruit: "Let's see how many pieces of fruit we have. Count with me, 1 apple, 2 apples, 1 orange, 2 oranges, etc. How many pieces of fruit in all did we count?"

Application Problem (5 minutes)

Sam brought 8 pieces of fruit at the farmer's market. He loves apples and oranges, so he bought some of each. Draw a plate and show his fruit on the plate. Don't lose any!

Show your work to your friend. Does her plate look the same? Can you make a number bond and number sentence about your picture?

Note: This story introduces the thinking for the *put together with both addends unknown* problem structure in today's lesson.

Concept Development (25 minutes)

Materials: (T) Large foam die or substitute (S) Personal white boards, dry erase markers in black, red, and green (if not available, use paper and crayons)

T: Listen to my silly story: The students were playing with 7 balls on the playground. They accidently kicked some of the balls into a big puddle and now some are muddy! What is one way the balls might look now? Turn and talk to your partner about your ideas. (Allow time for discussion.)

● ● ● ○ ○ ○ ○
$7 = 3 + 4$

T: Let's make a math problem about my silly story. Draw 7 balls on your personal board. (Demonstrate drawing empty circles.) Make some muddy. (Do not draw mud on any of your circles. Let students develop partners of their own.) Student A, show us your drawing. How many of your balls got muddy?

● ● ● ● ● ○ ○
$7 = 5 + 2$

S: 3!

T: (Fill in 3 circles on your drawing.) Could we make a number sentence for Student A's picture?

● ● ● ● ● ● ○
$7 = 6 + 1$

T: How many balls in all?

S: 7.

● ● ○ ○ ○ ○ ○
$7 = 2 + 5$

T: How many were muddy?

S: 3!

T: How many were clean?

● ○ ○ ○ ○ ○ ○
$7 = 1 + 6$

S: 4.

T: Read the number sentence with me: $7 = 3 + 4$. Write the number sentence on your board, too! (Circulate to ensure understanding.)

● ● ● ● ○ ○ ○
$7 = 4 + 3$

T: Did anyone have a different picture of the balls?

S: I do! I drew 6 muddy balls and 1 clean ball. → I have 2 muddy balls. (Other varied answers.)

T: Go ahead and write a number sentence to match your picture. Start with the 7. (Circulate to ensure understanding.) If you finish early, figure out another way the balls might have looked and write another number sentence to match that.

After students have worked, quickly represent all the combinations. Write each one on a separate paper so that you can sequence them in the Debrief.

COMMON CORE™ | Lesson 18: Solve *both addends unknown* word problems to 8 to find addition patterns in number pairs.
Date: 11/12/13

4.C.44

MP.1

T: Erase your boards and listen to my next little story. Close your eyes while you listen and think, and then I will have you draw your picture on your personal board.

T: Cora went to a birthday party. At the party, she saw a dish of 8 jellybeans. Some were red and some were green. Open your eyes and draw a picture of the jelly beans. (Allow time for drawing.) Who would like to share their picture with the class first? Go ahead, Student A.

S: I drew 1 red jellybean and 7 green ones.

T: Let's use your idea to write our number sentence. How would I complete the first one? How many jellybeans did Cora have in all?

S: 8.

T: (Fill in equation template). How many were red? (1.) How many were green? (7.) Read with me: 8 = 1 + 7.

T: What if I put the number of green jelly beans first instead, like this: 7 + 1 = 8 (demonstrate). Would that be fair?

S: Yes! It doesn't matter which color you put first. →There are still the same number of beans in the dish.

T: Thank you for sharing your idea, Student A! Look carefully at your own pictures now and see if you can make some number sentences that show your own idea. Turn and talk to your partner about your work when you are done. Do your jellybeans look the same? (Allow time for sharing and discussion.)

T: Who would like to share another picture and idea with the class? If your picture was different, could it still be true? (Allow time for sharing and discussion.)

$$7 = 1 + 6$$

$$7 = 2 + 5$$

$$7 = 3 + 4$$

$$7 = 4 + 3$$

$$7 = 5 + 2$$

$$7 = 6 + 1$$

NOTES ON MULTIPLE MEANS OF ACTION AND EXPRESSION:

For students who are below grade level, repeat the lesson with numbers to 5. Watch students as you ask them to solve a put together with addends unknown problem and guide them through it step by step: "5 red and green crayons on the desk. Draw and color crayons using green and red markers. Now let's fill in the number sentence."

Problem Set (10 minutes)

Students should do their personal best to complete the Problem Set within the allotted 10 minutes.

Please see the note at the beginning of this lesson. The adults should read each problem aloud to their group and watch to ensure understanding during the completion of the exercise.

Note: Allow students to use concrete objects if needed.

Lesson 18:   Solve *both addends unknown* word problems to 8 to find addition patterns in number pairs.

Date: 11/12/13

4.C.45

Student Debrief (8 minutes)

Lesson Objective: Solve *both addends unknown* word problems to 8 to find addition patterns in number pairs.

The Student Debrief is intended to invite reflection and active processing of the total lesson experience.

Invite students to review their solutions for the Problem Set. They should check work by comparing answers with a partner before going over answers as a class. Look for misconceptions or misunderstandings that can be addressed in the Debrief. Guide students in a conversation to debrief the Problem Set and process the lesson.

You may choose to use any combination of the questions below to lead the discussion.

- Talk about the pencils on your paper. Did you and your neighbor put the same amount in the desk and the pencil box?

- How did the cubes help you to think about Shania's necklaces?

- What was the difference between the two types of number sentences we made for each picture on the board?

- When we were drawing our jellybean number sentences, did it matter which color we wrote about first?

- Could different pictures about the 8 jelly beans still be true? Why?

- Let's put our muddy ball number sentences and pictures in order. I'll put the first ones, 7 = 1 + 6. Next comes 7 = 2 + 5 (move the cards). Talk to your partner, which number sentence will come next in our pattern?

- Talk to your partner. What patterns do you notice?

- What was the same about all of our problems today? (There was more than one way to solve and write the problem.)

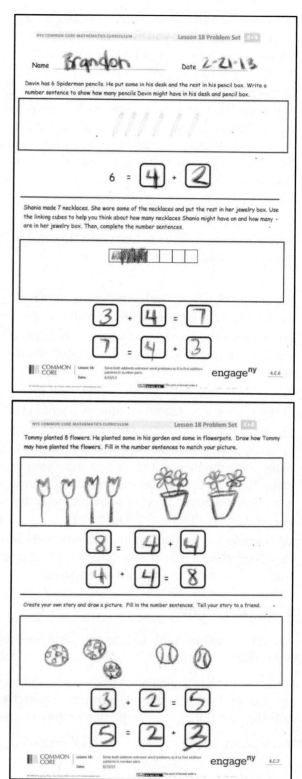

COMMON CORE™ | Lesson 18: Solve *both addends unknown* word problems to 8 to find addition patterns in number pairs.
Date: 11/12/13

4.C.46

Circle the number to make 5.

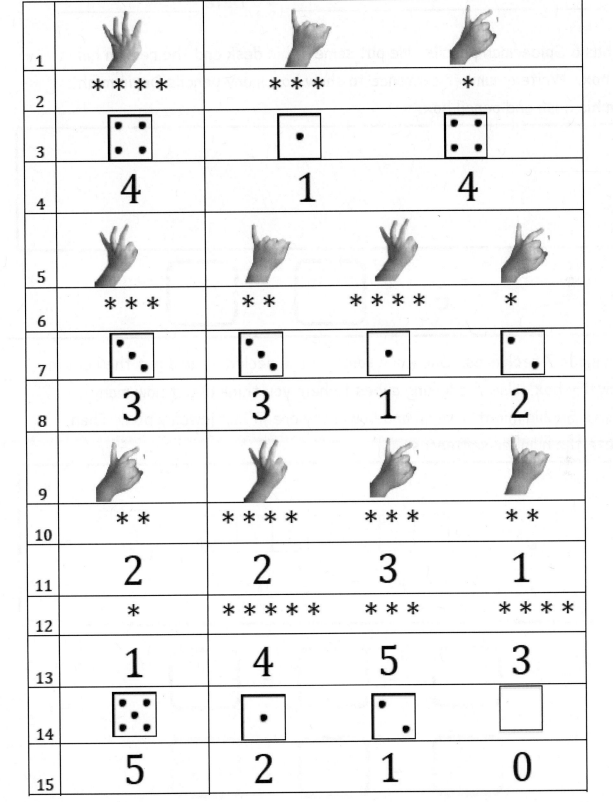

COMMON CORE™ | Lesson 18: | Solve *both addends unknown* word problems to 8 to find addition patterns in number pairs. | **4.C.47**

Date: 11/12/13

Name _____   Date _____

Devin has 6 Spiderman pencils. He put some in his desk and the rest in his pencil box. Write a number sentence to show how many pencils Devin might have in his desk and pencil box.

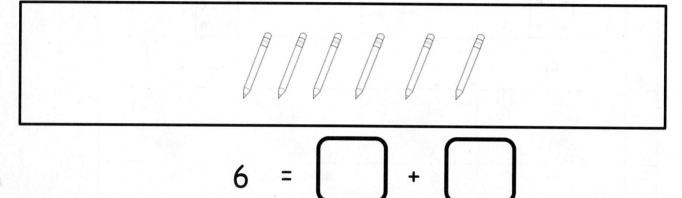

6 = ☐ + ☐

Shania made 7 necklaces. She wore some of the necklaces and put the rest in her jewelry box. Use the linking cubes to help you think about how many necklaces Shania might have on and how many are in her jewelry box. Then, complete the number sentences.

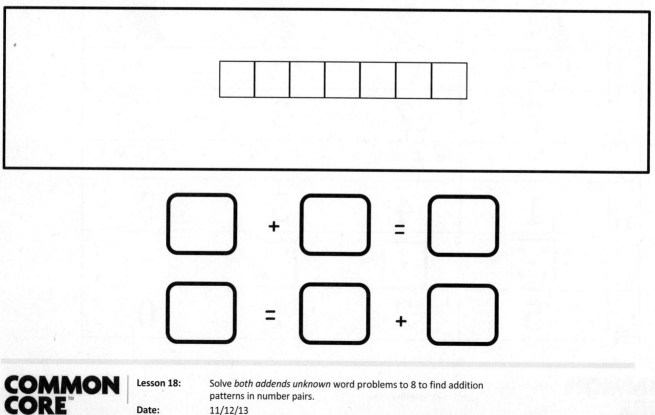

☐ + ☐ = ☐

☐ = ☐ + ☐

Lesson 18:   Solve *both addends unknown* word problems to 8 to find addition patterns in number pairs.

Date: 11/12/13

4.C.48

Tommy planted 8 flowers. He planted some in his garden and some in flowerpots. Draw how Tommy may have planted the flowers. Fill in the number sentences to match your picture.

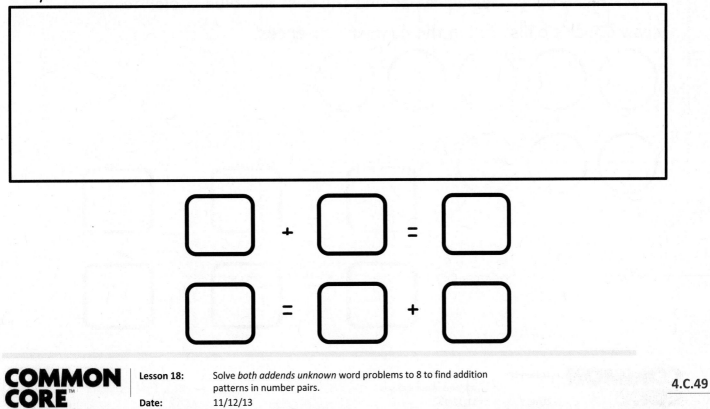

☐ = ☐ + ☐

☐ + ☐ = ☐

Create your own story and draw a picture. Fill in the number sentences. Tell your story to a friend.

☐ + ☐ = ☐

☐ = ☐ + ☐

Lesson 18: Solve *both addends unknown* word problems to 8 to find addition patterns in number pairs.

Date: 11/12/13

4.C.49

Name _____   Date _____

Ted has 7 toy cars. Color some cars red and the rest blue. Write a number sentence that shows how many are red and how many are blue.

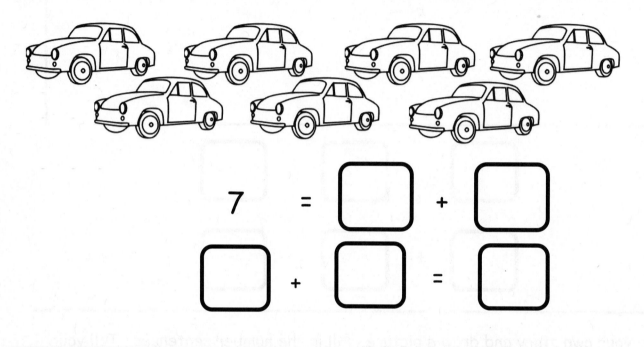

7 = ☐ + ☐

☐ + ☐ = ☐

Chuck has 8 balls. Some are red and the rest are blue. Color to show Chuck's balls. Fill in the number sentences.

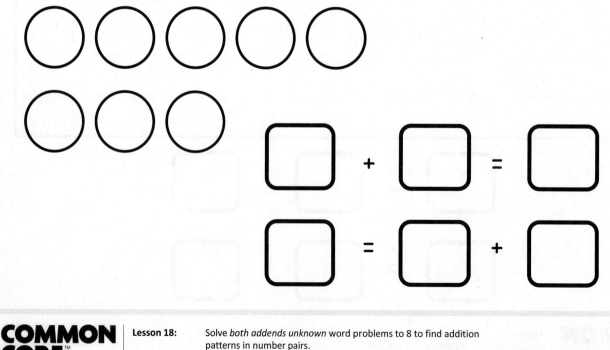

☐ + ☐ = ☐

☐ = ☐ + ☐

COMMON CORE™

Lesson 18: Solve *both addends unknown* word problems to 8 to find addition patterns in number pairs.

Date: 11/12/13

4.C.5C

Topic D

Subtraction from Numbers to 8

K.OA.1, K.OA.2, K.OA.3

Focus Standard:	K.OA.1	Represent addition and subtraction with objects, fingers, mental images, drawings, sounds (e.g., claps), acting out situations, verbal explanations, expressions, or equations. (Drawings need not show details, but should show the mathematics in the problem. This applies wherever drawings are mentioned in the Standards.)
	K.OA.2	Solve addition and subtraction word problems, and add and subtract within 10, e.g., by using objects or drawings to represent the problem.
	K.OA.3	Decompose numbers less than or equal to 10 into pairs in more than one way, e.g., by using objects or drawings, and record each decomposition by a drawing or equation (e.g., 5 = 2 + 3 and 5 = 4 + 1).
Instructional Days:	6	
Coherence -Links from:	GPK–M5	Numerals to 5, Addition and Subtraction Stories, Counting to 20
-Links to:	G1–M1	Sums and Differences to 10

Topic D introduces formal subtraction concepts including writing and solving expressions and equations. Lesson 19 begins at the concrete level with students acting out *take away* stories and working at the pictorial level crossing off to see what remains.

In Lesson 20, the concrete objects and pictorial representations are tied to or matched to the representative subtraction expression or equation using the minus sign with no unknown. As in Topic C, this progression helps students move from concrete processes to reasoning abstractly and quantitatively (**MP.2**).

In Lesson 21, students solve subtraction story problems using concrete and pictorial representations and write the corresponding equation. As with addition, it is important that students understand what each numeral in the equation represents from the story situation.

Lessons 22–24 focus on decompositions of 6, 7, and 8, which are recorded as equations. These equations are described in the progressions as *take from with result unknown* (C – B = ___) situations. These three lessons explore the decompositions of 6, 7, and 8 by breaking off a part, hiding a part, and crossing off a part. "There were 7 bears sleeping in a cave. Four bears left to go fishing. How many bears are still in the cave?"

A Teaching Sequence Towards Mastery of Subtraction from Numbers to 8

Objective 1: Use objects and drawings to find *how many are left*.
(Lesson 19)

Objective 2: Solve *take from with result unknown* expressions and equations using the minus sign with no unknown.
(Lesson 20)

Objective 3: Represent subtraction story problems using objects, drawings, expressions, and equations.
(Lesson 21)

Objective 4: Decompose the number 6 using 5-group drawings by breaking off or removing a part, and record each decomposition with a drawing and subtraction equation.
(Lesson 22)

Objective 5: Decompose the number 7 using 5-group drawings by hiding a part, and record each decomposition with a drawing and subtraction equation.
(Lesson 23)

Objective 6: Decompose the number 8 using 5-group drawings and crossing off a part, and record each decomposition with a drawing and subtraction equation.
(Lesson 24)

Lesson 19

Objective: Use objects and drawings to find *how many are left*.

Suggested Lesson Structure

■ Fluency Practice	(11 minutes)
■ Application Problem	(5 minutes)
■ Concept Development	(26 minutes)
■ Student Debrief	(8 minutes)
Total Time	**(50 minutes)**

Fluency Practice (11 minutes)

- Happy Counting **K.CC.2**   (3 minutes)
- Building *1 More* and *1 Less* Towers **K.CC.4c**   (4 minutes)
- Make It Equal **K.CC.6**   (4 minutes)

Happy Counting (3 minutes)

Note: This activity helps students internalize the whole number counting sequence and become comfortable changing directions in their count.

   T: Let's play Happy Counting! Remember, when I hold my hand like this (two fingers pointing up), I want you to count up. If I put my hand like this (two fingers pointing down), I want you to count down. If I do this (closed fist) that means stop, but try hard to remember the last number you said. Ready?

   S: (Teacher's fingers up) 1, 2, 3, 4, 5 (closed fist, fingers pointing down), 4, 3, 2, 1 (closed fist, fingers up), 2, 3 (closed fist, fingers down), 2, 1 (closed fist, fingers up), 2, 3, 4, 5 (closed fist, fingers down), 4, 3 (closed fist, fingers up), 4, 5, 6 (closed fist, fingers down), 5, 4 (closed fist, fingers up), 5, 6, 7, 8 (closed fist, fingers down).

Continue Happy Counting to ten 3 (i.e., 13), increasing the numbers as students demonstrate mastery.

Building *1 More* and *1 Less* Towers (4 minutes)

Materials: (S) 10 linking cubes per student

Note: This helps students transition from addition to subtraction operations in preparation for today's lesson.

Guide students through the process of building a tower while stating the pattern as *1 more*. Maintain consistency in the language: 1. 1 more is 2. 2. 1 more is 3. 3. 1 more is 4. (Continue to 10.)

Disassemble the tower while stating the pattern as *1 less*. Again, the language is crucial to students' conceptual understanding: 10. 1 less is 9. 9. 1 less is 8. 8. 1 less is 7. (Continue to 0.)

If students are ready for the challenge, begin constructing the towers again but stop the *1 more* sequence at 5. Change directions, using the *1 less* sequence. Continue moving up and down according to teacher directions, like Happy Counting.

Make It Equal (4 minutes)

Materials: (S) Bags of cubes, laminated paper or foam work mat, dice per pair

Note: Students add and take away objects in this fluency activity, helping to solidify the shared numerical relationships underlying both addition and subtraction.

1. The teacher introduces the term *equal* as meaning *the same number*.
2. Both partners roll dice, and put that many cubes on their mat.
3. Partner A has to make her cubes equal to her partner's by taking off or putting on more cubes.
4. Partner B counts to verify.
5. Switch roles and play again.

Application Problem (5 minutes)

Materials: (S) Small ball of clay

The mice are hungry today! Make 5 little pieces of cheese out of your clay and put them on your desk. Pretend that a pair of little mice came to your desk (a pair means 2 mice!), and that each of them stole a piece of cheese. Take away their pieces to show that they ate them. How many pieces are left?

Now, start with 4 morsels of cheese and act out the story again. How many are left?

Talk about the mice and the cheese with your partner. Did she have the same number of pieces left each time? What do you think would happen if you had only 3 pieces of cheese before they came?

Note: This concrete application of *how many are left* serves as the anticipatory set for today's lesson. Circulate during the activity to observe which students might need extra support with concrete materials during this topic.

NOTES ON
MULTIPLE MEANS OF
REPRESENTATION:

Introduce the term *pair* to English language learners prior to the lesson by showing them lots of pictures of pairs of things, e.g., eyes, arms, legs, etc. Have the students practice saying the word, and ask them to give you examples of pairs of things they can think of. Have them use two fingers to represent the pair of mice and act out the story. Once they have learned the word, they will be able to solve the Application Problem.

Lesson 19:   Use objects and drawings to find *how many are left*.
Date: 11/12/13

4.D.4

Concept Development (26 minutes)

Materials: (S) Personal white boards

T: Who knows the song "Five Little Monkeys Jumping on the Bed"?

S: Me! Me!

T: We are going to sing it today. Let's pretend your fingers are the monkeys. Show me 5 monkeys the Math way. (Demonstrate.) Show me your monkeys jumping! (Waving hand and wiggling fingers in the air, sing....)

T/S: *5 little monkeys jumping on the bed; one fell off and bumped his head. Mama called the doctor and the doctor said, "NO MORE MONKEYS JUMPING ON THE BED!"*

T: Oh no! One of our monkeys fell off! We had 5, but we need to **take** one **away**. How many monkeys are left?

S: 4!

T: Yes. 5 take away 1 is 4. Show me your 4 monkeys!

Repeat until all monkeys have fallen.

T: How many monkeys are left?

S: None!

T: Let's make a picture about the song we just sang. Draw circles on your personal white board to show your 5 monkeys. Let's pretend the first monkey just fell. What can we do to the picture to show that one monkey fell?

MP.1 S: Cross off the monkey.

T: Yes! Let's cross off a circle to show that he fell. (Demonstrate.) **How many are left** on the bed? Use a complete sentence.

S: There are 4 left on the bed.

T: 5 monkeys take away 1 monkey is...

S: 4 monkeys!

T: Now, the next monkey fell. Cross off another circle. You had 5 monkeys in the beginning. 2 monkeys have fallen. How many are left on the bed now?

S: Now there are 3 left on the bed.

T: 5 take away 2 is...

S: 3!

NOTES ON MULTIPLE MEANS OF ACTION AND EXPRESSION:

Scaffold the lesson for below grade level students and for those who seem unsure during the "monkeys jumping on the bed" portion of the lesson by providing them with manipulatives to aid them in making their drawings. Pair students who need the extra support to make the task more meaningful and manageable.

Repeat the exercise with the same pattern until all monkeys are crossed out, each time emphasizing the language of *take away* and *how many are left*. Circulate during discussion to see which students might benefit from using linking cubes or other counters to support their drawings.

T: Erase your boards. Let's pretend each monkey had a banana. Draw 5 bananas. (Allow time for drawing.)

T: During the song, 2 bananas were squished. Cross off 2 bananas to show the ones that were squished. (Demonstrate.) How many are left?

S: There are 3 left.

T: 5 take away 2 is…

S: 3!

T: Erase your boards. Let's pretend the monkeys liked to eat strawberries instead. Draw a strawberry for each monkey. How many strawberries did you draw?

S: 5.

T: During their game, 4 of the strawberries rolled onto the floor. Cross off 4 strawberries to show the ones that rolled. (Demonstrate.) How many are left?

S: There is only 1 left!

T: 5 take away 4 is…

S: 1!

Problem Set (10 minutes)

Students should do their personal best to complete the Problem Set within the allotted 10 minutes.

Student Debrief (8 minutes)

Lesson Objective: Use objects and drawings to find "how many are left."

The Student Debrief is intended to invite reflection and active processing of the total lesson experience.

Invite students to review their solutions for the Problem Set. They should check work by comparing answers with a partner before going over answers as a class. Look for misconceptions or misunderstandings that can be addressed in the Debrief. Guide students in a conversation to debrief the Problem Set and process the lesson.

You may choose to use any combination of the questions below to lead the discussion.

- Look at the things you crossed out on your Problem Set. Compare your Problem Set with your neighbor's. Did you cross out the same things? Does it matter which things you crossed out?

- Is the number you wrote in the box the same as your neighbor even though you might have crossed out different things?
- What happened when a monkey fell off the bed in our song? What did you have to do with your fingers?
- How did we use our math words to talk about what happened in the song?
- How did your drawings help you solve the other stories in our lesson? What did the crossed-off parts show?

Name _____   Date _____

The cat ate 3 mice. Cross out 3 mice. Write how many mice are left.

The fish ate 2 worms. Cross out 2 worms. Write how many worms are left.

The frog ate 5 flies. Cross out 5 flies. Write how many flies are left.

The monkey ate 4 bananas. Cross out 4 bananas. Write how many bananas are left.

Draw 6 balls. The boy kicked 3 balls down the hill. How many balls does he have left?

There are 5 butterflies flying around the flower. Draw them. 1 of the butterflies flew away, so cross it out. How many butterflies are left?

Name _____ Date _____

1 train drove away. Cross out 1. Write how many were left. □

2 horses were bought. Cross out 2. How many were left at the store? □

4 ducks swam away. Cross out 4. Write how many are left. □

There are 7 apples in the tree. Draw them. A bird ate 1 of them, so cross it out. How many apples are left?

Lesson 20

Objective: Solve *take from with result unknown* expressions and equations using the minus sign with no unknown.

Suggested Lesson Structure

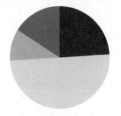

■ Fluency Practice   (12 minutes)
▦ Application Problem   (5 minutes)
▢ Concept Development   (25 minutes)
■ Student Debrief   (8 minutes)
   Total Time   **(50 minutes)**

Fluency Practice (12 minutes)

  Sprint: Cross 1 Out and Write How Many **K.CC.4c**   (12 minutes)

Sprint: Cross 1 Out and Write How Many (12 minutes)

Materials: (S) 2 copies of the Cross 1 Out and Write How Many Sprint per student

Note: This Sprint supports the learning of this topic, giving students experience with taking away and determining how many are left within the familiar context of *1 less*.

   T: It's time for a Sprint! (Briefly recall previous Sprint preparation activities, and distribute Sprints facedown.) Take out your pencil and one crayon, any color. For this Sprint, you are going to cross 1 out and write how many. (Demonstrate the first problem as needed.)

Continue to follow the Sprint procedure as outlined in GK–M4–Lesson 3. Have students work on the Sprint for a second time (they will soon work on two different Sprints in a single day). Continue to emphasize that the goal is simply to do better than the first time and celebrate improvement.

NOTES ON MULTIPLE MEANS OF ENGAGEMENT:

Support English language learners' oral responses by providing sentence starters like "I drew ___ monkeys. I took away ___monkeys, and I have ___ monkeys left," to facilitate their partner share and provide them with a review of the *take away* language they need for the lesson.

Application Problem (5 minutes)

Materials: (S) Paper and pencil or personal white boards

Draw the 5 monkeys from yesterday's song on your paper. Decide how many monkeys were sensible and stayed on the bed, and cross off the monkeys who fell off and bumped their

---

COMMON CORE™ | Lesson 20:   Solve *take from with result unknown* expressions and equations using
                     the minus sign with no unknown.

                   Date: 11/12/13

4.D.11

© 2013 Common Core, Inc. All rights reserved. **commoncore.org**

heads.

With your math words, think about how you would tell the story. How many did you start with? How many did you take away? How many were left?

Share your picture with your partner and use your math words to tell your story. Did your partner do it the same way? How are your number stories different?

Note: A review of the math language from yesterday's lesson and a chance for the students to articulate their knowledge serve as a gateway to today's more abstract presentation of the subtraction concept.

Concept Development (25 minutes)

Materials: (S) 5 linking cubes per student, personal white boards

T: Place your linking cubes on the table in front of you. Count them. How many?

S: There are 5.

T: Put 3 linking cubes in your hand and take them away. How many are left on the table?

S: 2.

T: Yes, 5 take away 3 is 2. There is a special math way to write what we just did. We had 5 cubes. I will write the number 5 to show all of the cubes together. (Demonstrate.) There is a special sign that we can use when we want to show that we are removing some cubes. It looks like this (write the **minus** sign). How many did we take away?

S: 3.

T: I write the 3 here. (Demonstrate.) You know the next part already! Our sign for *is the same as* or *equals*. (Write the equal sign.) How many were left on the table?

S: 2.

T: I will write that here: 2. Read with me: 5 take away 3 equals 2.

S: 5 take away 3 equals 2!

T: Let's do another one. This time, let's make a picture on our boards about the cubes. Draw your 5 cubes. Now, we want to take away 4. How should we show that we are taking them away?

S: Cross them out.

T: Cross out 4 cubes. How many cubes do you have left?

S: 1.

T: Let's write the number sentence together. I will write it on the class board while you write it on your personal white board. 5 cubes take away 4 cubes is 1 cube. 5 − 4 = 1. Read it with me.

S: 5 take away 4 is 1.

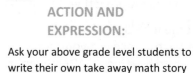

NOTES ON
MULTIPLE MEANS OF
ACTION AND
EXPRESSION:

Ask your above grade level students to write their own take away math story for you and show their solution in writing. Ask early finishers to share their new stories with each other and encourage them to solve as many stories as they come up with.

At times we use *equals* and sometimes *is* or *is the same as*. These multiple means of expression keep the meaning of the symbol fresh.

Lesson 20:   Solve *take from with result unknown* expressions and equations using the minus sign with no unknown.

Date: 11/12/13

T: Erase your boards. I have a story for you! 5 students were playing on the slide. Draw a circle for each student on your board. 2 of the students left to go to the swings. In your drawing, cross out the students who went to the swings. How many students were left at the slide?

S: 3.

T: Help me write the number sentence, and write it on your board, too. How many students were there at first?

S: 5.

T: 5 minus…. How many students went to the swings?

S: 2.

T: 5 – 2 equals?

S: 3!

T: Let's read it all together: 5 – 2 = 3.

S: 5 – 2 = 3!

T: On your personal board, draw pictures to make up a take away story of your own. Share your picture with your friend. Can you write the number sentence that tells your story? (Allow time for writing and discussion.)

T: Who would like to share their story and picture with the class?

Problem Set (10 minutes)

Students should do their personal best to complete the Problem Set within the allotted 10 minutes.

Student Debrief (8 minutes)

Lesson Objective: Solve *take from with result unknown* expressions and equations using the minus sign with no unknown.

The Student Debrief is intended to invite reflection and active processing of the total lesson experience.

Invite students to review their solutions for the Problem Set. They should check work by comparing answers with a partner before going over answers as a class. Look for misconceptions or misunderstandings that can be addressed in the Debrief. Guide students in a conversation to debrief the Problem Set and process the lesson.

You may choose to use any combination of the questions below to lead the discussion.

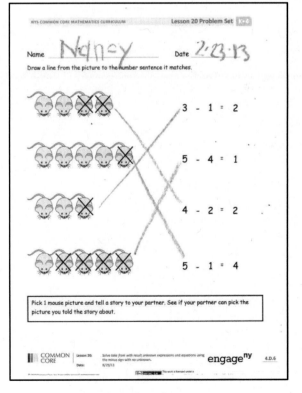

- Look at the mice. What numbers did you use in the number sentence to find the matching mice?

Lesson 20:   Solve *take from with result unknown* expressions and equations using
            the minus sign with no unknown.
Date: 11/12/13

4.D.13

- Look at the 4 mice, how many have an X? Tell your neighbor what number in the matching number sentence would have an X on it.

- Look at the bears you crossed out. Compare with your partner, did you cross out the same bears as your partner? Does it make a difference which bears you cross out?

- When we write a number sentence about taking away, what number do we write first?

- If we want to show that a number is being *taken away* what symbol do we use? Draw it in the air with your finger.

- Which number do we write next?

- What number do we write after our symbol for *is*?

NYS COMMON CORE MATHEMATICS CURRICULUM   Lesson 20 Fluency Practice

Cross out the bears to match the number sentences.

6 - 1 = 5   7 - 2 = 5

6 - 4 = 2   7 - 3 = 4

8 - 1 = 7   8 - 2 = 6

Lesson 20: Solve *take from with result unknown* expressions and equations using the minus sign with no unknown.

Date: 11/12/13

4.D.1

Cross 1 out and write how many.

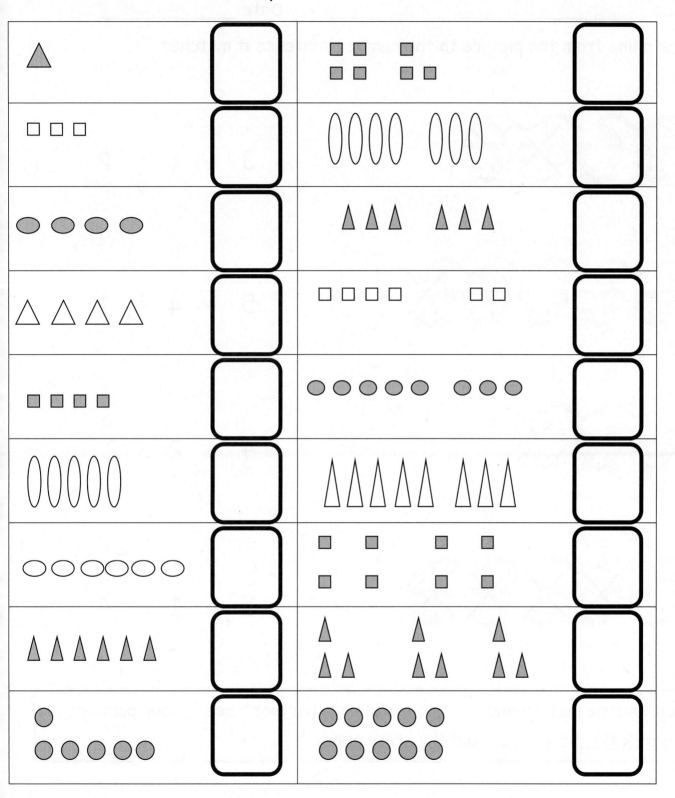

COMMON CORE™ | **Lesson 20:** | Solve *take from with result unknown* expressions and equations using the minus sign with no unknown.
Date: 11/12/13

4.D.15

© 2013 Common Core, Inc. All rights reserved. **commoncore.org**

Name _____   Date _____

Draw a line from the picture to the number sentence it matches.

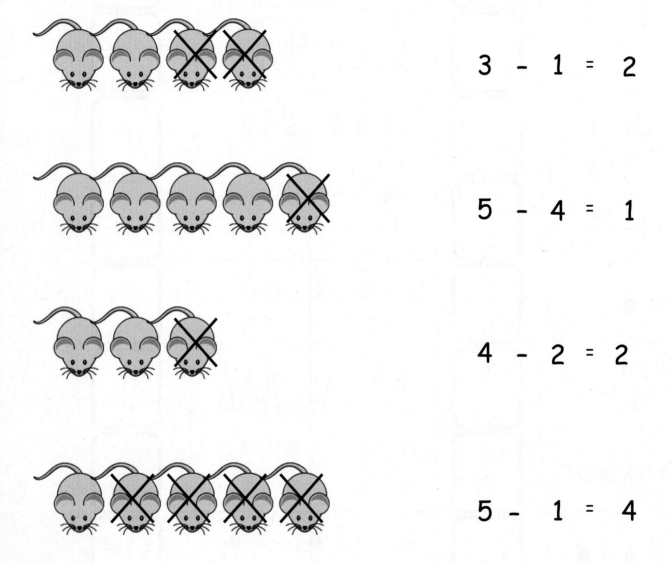

$3 - 1 = 2$

$5 - 4 = 1$

$4 - 2 = 2$

$5 - 1 = 4$

Pick 1 mouse picture and tell a story to your partner. See if your partner can pick the picture you told the story about.

 **COMMON CORE**™

Lesson 20:   Solve *take from with result unknown* expressions and equations using the minus sign with no unknown.

Date: 11/12/13

4.D.1

Cross out the bears to match the number sentences.

6 - 1 = 5

7 - 2 = 5

6 - 4 = 2

7 - 3 = 4

8 - 1 = 7

8 - 2 = 6

Lesson 20:   Solve *take from with result unknown* expressions and equations using
the minus sign with no unknown.

Date: 11/12/13

Name _____ Date _____

Match the cube stick to the number sentence.

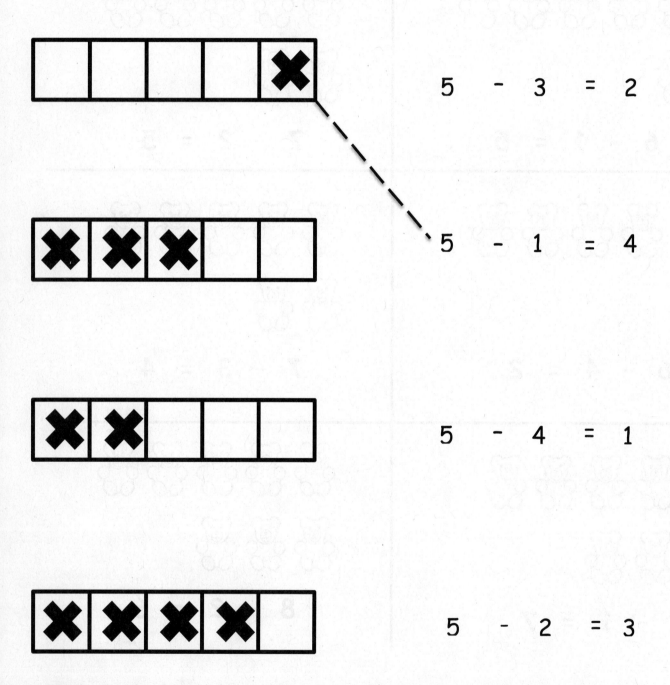

5   –   3   =   2

5   –   1   =   4

5   –   4   =   1

5   –   2   =   3

On the back of the paper draw a 5-stick, cross out some cubes and write a number sentence.

Lesson 20:	Solve *take from with result unknown* expressions and equations using the minus sign with no unknown.
Date:	11/12/13

4.D.18

Lesson 21

Objective: Represent subtraction story problems using objects, drawings, expressions, and equations.

Suggested Lesson Structure

■ Fluency Practice   (12 minutes)
■ Application Problem   (5 minutes)
□ Concept Development   (25 minutes)
■ Student Debrief   (8 minutes)

   Total Time   **(50 minutes)**

Fluency Practice (12 minutes)

- Take Away 1 **K.OA.1**   (3 minutes)
- Roll and Show 1 Less **K.CC.4c**   (4 minutes)
- Hide and See **K.OA.1**   (5 minutes)

Take Away 1 (3 minutes)

Note: Students begin to use subtraction sentences and their new *take away* language in the familiar context of *1 less*.

   T: Show me 3 fingers, the Math way.
   S: (Hold up the left pinky, left ring finger, and the left middle finger, to show 3 fingers the Math way.)
   T: Now take away 1.
   S: (Put down the left middle finger, so that only the left pinky and left ring finger remain, showing 2 the Math way.)
   T: How many fingers are you showing me now?
   S: 2.
   T: Say the number sentence after me. 3 take away 1 is 2.

Continue to take away 1 from numbers 1–5 (show 0 as a closed fist). Avoid showing the finger combinations yourself. Some students may still need to count all of the fingers each time. Allow time to do so, but invite students to share more efficient strategies.

	Lesson 21:	Represent subtraction story problems using objects, drawings,	
	Date:	expressions, and equations.	4.D.19
		11/12/13	

Roll and Show 1 Less (4 minutes)

Materials: (S) Dice (with the 6 dot side covered as a scaffold, or uncovered as an extension)

Note: Students begin to use subtraction sentences and their new *take away* language in the familiar context of *1 less*.

1. Partner A rolls the die (or dice).
2. Both partners count the dots.
3. Partner B takes away 1 and shows that many fingers, the Math way and says, "4 take away 1 is 3."
4. Partner A verifies that the number is 1 less.
5. Switch roles and play again.

Remind students that if they should roll a 1, they can show 1 less by indicating 0 as a closed fist. As students get more comfortable with subtraction sentences, they can try to tell about their fingers.

Hide and See (5 minutes)

Materials: (S) 5 linking cubes

T: Show me 2 cubes.
S: 1, 2.
T: Hide 1 behind your back. How many can you see?
S: 1.
T: Put them back together. How many cubes do you have?
S: 2.
T: Say the number sentence with me. 2 take away 1 is 1.

Repeat using the following possible sequence: $3 - 1, 4 - 1, 5 - 1, 5 - 2, 4 - 2, 3 - 2, 4 - 3, 5 - 3, 5 - 4$.

Application Problem (5 minutes)

Materials: (S) Personal white boards or pencil and paper

Five little green frogs were sitting on the side of the pond. Draw the frogs.

It was so hot that two of the froggies decided to go for a swim! Cross out the frogs in your picture to show the ones who hopped into the pond. How many frogs were still by the side of the pond?

Talk to your partner about the story. How can you write about your story in a number sentence?

**NOTES ON
MULTIPLE MEANS OF
REPRESENTATION:**

Provide below grade level students who are still having difficulty solving take away problems with independent practice time using interactive technology.

Lesson 21:   Represent subtraction story problems using objects, drawings, expressions, and equations.
Date: 11/12/13

4.D.20

Note: Talking with a partner about the work from yesterday and thinking about representing stories with numbers serves as an anticipatory set for today's lesson. Again, circulate to see which students might benefit from more extensive work with manipulatives during this topic.

Concept Development (25 minutes)

Materials: (S) 5 linking cubes or other counters, personal white boards

T: Take out your linking cubes. Let's pretend that your cubes are all little frogs sitting by the edge of a pond just like you did in your picture earlier. Show 5 frogs. Now, take 2 of the cubes away to show the frogs that decided to take a swim. How many frogs are left?

S: 3.

T: Let's write our story as a take away number sentence like we did yesterday. Which number should I write first?

S: 5. → You need to tell first about how many frogs you started with.

T: So, I will write 5. I will write − (demonstrate) to show that we are taking something away. What should I write next?

S: 2! You need to show how many went away!

T: Ok. 5 − 2. Now what do I do?

S: Now you write how many are left at the end. → You need to show the 3 that are left. → Don't forget the "equals"!

T: (Demonstrate) 5 − 2 = 3. Read the number sentence with me.

S: 5 take away 2 equals 3.

NOTES ON
MULTIPLE MEANS OF
REPRESENTATION:

Support English language students by providing a visual for the math they need to learn and use. Post a visual that combines the "5 take away 2 is 3" with "5 − 2 = 3" right under it with a picture of 5 cubes with 2 crossed out. Point to the visual as you teach. This will help students bridge the language gap and follow lesson.

Repeat exercise and translation into an equation several times using the cubes and different subtrahends.

T: Put your cubes away now. It is time to draw. Listen to my story and make a picture.

T: There were 4 butterflies on a flower. Two of the butterflies left to go to another flower. How many butterflies were left? Draw the four butterflies. (Allow time for drawing.) How should we show that 2 butterflies went away?

S: Cross them out.

T: How many butterflies are still on the flower? Count the butterflies that are left in your picture.

S: There are still 2.

T: Tell me how to write the number sentence about our story. Let's write it together.

$$4 - 2 = 2$$

COMMON CORE™ | Lesson 21: | Represent subtraction story problems using objects, drawings, expressions, and equations.   **4.D.21**

Date: 11/12/13

S: 4 butterflies take away 2 butterflies leaves 2 butterflies. 4 – 2 = 2!

T: Hold up your boards so I can see your number sentences. (Check for understanding.)

T: Erase your boards. Listen to my next story.

T: Five children were playing in the park. One child had to go home for dinner. How many children were still playing in the park?

T: This time, I want you to draw the children and show what happened on your own. Write the number sentence. (Allow time for drawing.) Talk to your partner about your picture and your number sentence.

MP.4

Allow time for discussion. Circulate to ensure understanding, and encourage use of the cubes as a concrete aid for those students who might need additional support to model the story.

T: Would anyone like to share their number sentence with the class so that I may write it on the board?

S: 5 – 1 = 4! (Write sentence on the board.)

T: Did anyone do it in a different way?

Allow time for discussion to ensure that students understand the correct placements of the minuend, subtrahend, and difference. Guide them to see that, unlike with the addition number sentences, there is less flexibility with subtraction. If a student should write
4 = 5 – 1, acknowledge the correct equation.

T: Great job! Let's do some more of this in our Problem Set.

Problem Set (10 minutes)

Students should do their personal best to complete the Problem Set within the allotted 10 minutes.

Student Debrief (8 minutes)

Lesson Objective: Represent subtraction story problems using objects, drawings, expressions, and equations.

The Student Debrief is intended to invite reflection and active processing of the total lesson experience.

Invite students to review their solutions for the Problem Set. They should check work by comparing answers with a partner before going over answers as a class. Look for misconceptions or misunderstandings that can be addressed in the Debrief. Guide students in a conversation to debrief the Problem Set and process the lesson.

COMMON CORE™ | Lesson 21: | Represent subtraction story problems using objects, drawings, expressions, and equations. | 4.D.22
Date: | 11/12/13

© 2013 Common Core, Inc. All rights reserved. commoncore.org

You may choose to use any combination of the questions below to lead the discussion.

- How did you know which number to write first in your number sentences today?
- How did you know what to write next?
- How did you find the last number in your number sentence?
- How did your pictures help you to write your number sentences?
- Were there different ways to write the number sentences about your stories?

NYS COMMON CORE MATHEMATICS CURRICULUM   Lesson 21 Problem Set

Anthony had 5 erasers in his pencil box. He dropped his pencil box and 4 erasers fell on the floor. How many erasers are in Anthony's pencil box now? Draw the erasers and fill in the number sentence.

$$5 - 4 = \boxed{1}$$

Tanisha had 5 grapes. She gave 3 grapes to a friend. How many grapes does Tanisha have now? Draw the grapes and fill in the number sentence.

$$\boxed{5} - \boxed{3} = \boxed{2}$$

COMMON CORE   Lesson 21:   Represent subtraction story problems using objects, drawings, expressions, and equations.

engage^ny   4.D.6

Lesson 21:   Represent subtraction story problems using objects, drawings, expressions, and equations.
Date: 11/12/13

4.D.23

Name _____ Date _____

Tyler bought a cone with 4 scoops. He ate 1 scoop. Cross out 1 scoop.
How many scoops were left?

4 - 1 = ☐

Eva ate ice cream too. She ate 2 scoops. How many scoops were left?

4 - 2 = ☐

There were 4 bottles. 3 of them broke. How many were left?

4 - 3 = ☐

COMMON CORE™

Lesson 21:   Represent subtraction story problems using objects, drawings,
                  expressions, and equations.
Date: 11/12/13

4.D.24

Anthony had 5 erasers in his pencil box. He dropped his pencil box and 4 erasers fell on the floor. How many erasers are in Anthony's pencil box now? Draw the erasers and fill in the number sentence.

5 – 4 = ☐

Tanisha had 5 grapes. She gave 3 grapes to a friend. How many grapes does Tanisha have now? Draw the grapes and fill in the number sentence.

☐ – ☐ = ☐

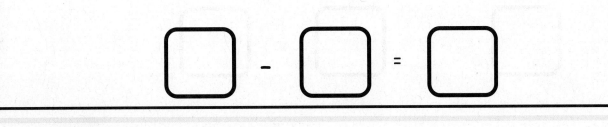

Lesson 21:
Date: 11/12/13

Represent subtraction story problems using objects, drawings, expressions, and equations.

4.D.25

Name _____   Date _____

There were 5 apples. Bill ate 1. Cross out the apple he ate. How many apples were left? Fill in the boxes.

5   take   away   1   is   ☐

5   –   1   =   ☐

There were 5 oranges. Pat took 2. Draw the oranges. Cross out the 2 she took. How many oranges were left? Fill in the boxes.

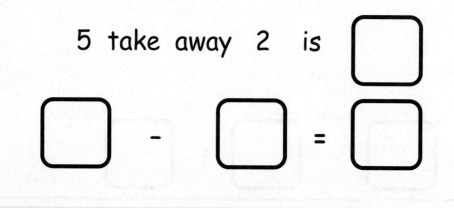

5   take   away   2   is   ☐

☐   –   ☐   =   ☐

4.D.26

Lesson 22

Objective: Decompose the number 6 using 5-group drawings by breaking off or removing a part, and record each decomposition with a drawing and subtraction equation.

Suggested Lesson Structure

■ Fluency Practice   (12 minutes)
■ Application Problem   (5 minutes)
■ Concept Development   (25 minutes)
■ Student Debrief   (8 minutes)
   Total Time   **(50 minutes)**

Fluency Practice (12 minutes)

▪ Sprint: Complete the Number Bond **K.OA.1**   (12 minutes)

Sprint: Complete the Number Bond (12 minutes)

Materials: (S) 1 copy of each Complete the Number Bond Sprint per student

Note: This Sprint focuses on part–whole relationships for numbers to 6 in anticipation of the Content Development.

T: It's time for a Sprint! (Briefly recall previous Sprint preparation activities, and distribute Sprints facedown.) Take out your pencil and one crayon, any color. For this Sprint, you are going to complete the number bond. You can use drawings or numbers. (Demonstrate the first problem as needed.)

Continue to follow the Sprint procedure as outlined in GK–M4–Lesson 3. Today students will work on two different Sprints. Continue to emphasize that the goal is simply to do better than the first time and celebrate improvement.

NOTES ON MULTIPLE MEANS OF ENGAGEMENT:

Scaffold the Application Problem for English language learners by providing sentence starters to use during the game. "You have __ cubes behind your back." Encourage students to say, "You have __ cubes behind your back because __ take away __ is __." Students will learn the mathematical language as they use it regularly.

Application Problem (5 minutes)

Materials: (S) Linking cube 6-stick per pair, personal white boards

T: Let's play a game of Snap! Count the cubes in your stick. How many are you starting with?

COMMON CORE™

Lesson 22:

Date:

Decompose the number 6 using 5-group drawings by breaking off or removing a part, and record each decomposition with a drawing and subtraction equation.
11/12/13

4.D.27

T: Put the stick behind your back. When your partner says, "Snap!" break your stick. Show him how many cubes you have left.

T: Can he figure out how many are still behind your back? If not, show him.

T: Make a number bond about your snap on your personal board.

T: Can you and your partner think of a take away number sentence to tell about the snap?

Note: Re-introduction of this game and reviewing the number bond helps students to contemplate the relationships between addition and subtraction. Focusing on the decomposition of 6 will serve as an additional anticipatory set for this lesson.

Concept Development (25 minutes)

Materials: (T) Large foam die   (S) Linking cube 6-sticks, personal white boards, 1 die per pair

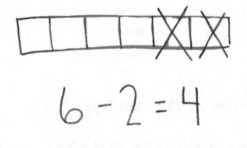

$$6 - 2 = 4$$

T: Count the number of cubes in your stick. How many?

S: 6!

T: Break 2 cubes off the end of your stick and put them in your lap. How many cubes do you still have left in your hand?

S: 4.

T: Tell me a number sentence about what you just did.

S: 6 take away 2 equals 4!

T: Draw a picture to show what you did. Draw your 6 cubes. Now, cross off 2 to show the ones you broke off. Count the ones that are left. Write a number sentence to tell about your cubes. (Allow time for drawing and creation of the number sentence. Circulate to assist students who still need additional help.) Would anyone like to share their number sentence with the class?

S: $6 - 2 = 4$.

T: Put your stick back together and we will make a number bond about what we just did. You had 2 cubes and 4 cubes. How many together?

S: 6.

T: (Demonstrate number bond on board.) Then, you took 2 away. (Cover part of the number bond.) How many were left?

S: 4!

NOTES ON MULTIPLE MEANS OF ENGAGEMENT:

For students with disabilities consider breaking down the steps of the lesson while they work: "Draw your 6 cubes. Now cross out 2. Let's count what's left, 1, 2, 3, 4. Show me how you write the number sentence." Practice with more problems until student feels confident enough to work independently.

Lesson 22:   Decompose the number 6 using 5-group drawings by breaking off or removing a part, and record each decomposition with a drawing and subtraction equation.

Date: 11/12/13

4.D.28

T: Write the number bond on your personal board, too. You can cross out the part of 2 to show what you did.

Repeat exercise several times with varying subtrahends, each time allowing students to record the action, the number bond, and the number sentence each time on their personal white boards.

T: Put your cubes away. We learned another way to show 6 this year with our 5-groups. Does anyone remember how we could draw 6 the 5-group way? (Allow students to guide you in the creation of the representation on the board.)

T: Let's roll the die to see how many we should take away from our 6. (Demonstrate.) How many?

S: 3!

T: I will cross off 3 to show the ones we are taking away. (Demonstrate.) How many are left?

S: 3!

T: What would my number sentence be?

S: $6 - 3 = 3$!

T: How could we make a number bond about our picture, and then show that we are taking part away? (Allow time for discussion and demonstration.)

T: On your personal board, draw the 5-group for the number 6. With your partner, take turns rolling the die to find out how many you should take away each time. When you roll, cross off the number and work with your partner to write the number bond and the number sentence. Let's see how many different number sentences we can find! (Circulate during the activity to ensure understanding and correct representation of the 5-group situations, number bonds, and equations.)

T: Who would like to share one of their number sentences with the class? I will list them on the board.

S: $6 - 2 = 4$! → We got $6 - 5 = 1$. → What about $6 - 1 = 5$? → We found $6 - 3 = 3$ again.

MP.4

$$6 - 3 = 3$$

$$6 - 1 = 5$$
$$6 - 2 = 4$$
$$6 - 3 = 3$$
$$6 - 4 = 2$$
$$6 - 5 = 1$$

Problem Set (10 minutes)

Students should do their personal best to complete the Problem Set within the allotted 10 minutes.

COMMON CORE™   Lesson 22:   Decompose the number 6 using 5-group drawings by breaking off or removing a part, and record each decomposition with a drawing and subtraction equation.   4.D.29

Date: 11/12/13

© 2013 Common Core, Inc. All rights reserved. commoncore.org

Student Debrief (8 minutes)

Lesson Objective: Decompose the number 6 using 5-group drawings by breaking off or removing a part, and record each decomposition with a drawing and subtraction equation.

The Student Debrief is intended to invite reflection and active processing of the total lesson experience.

Invite students to review their solutions for the Problem Set. They should check work by comparing answers with a partner before going over answers as a class. Look for misconceptions or misunderstandings that can be addressed in the Debrief. Guide students in a conversation to debrief the Problem Set and process the lesson.

You may choose to use any combination of the questions below to lead the discussion.

- In the Problem Set, what did your number bond and number sentence look like with the hats? Did your partner's number bond and number sentence look the same as yours?

- Look at the snowflakes. Show a partner which snowflakes you crossed out. Can you tell your partner which snowflakes the other numbers in the number sentence are talking about?

- Did drawing the 5-group help you to cross out the objects and easily count how many were left? Why?

- What are some of the take away number sentences you found about 6?

- How do these make you think about the ways we made 6 in our number bonds before?

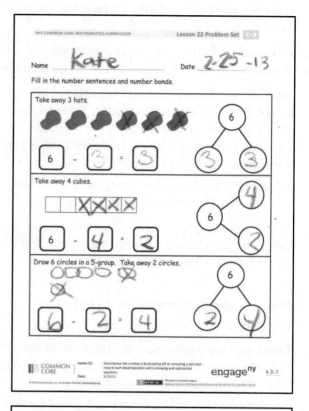

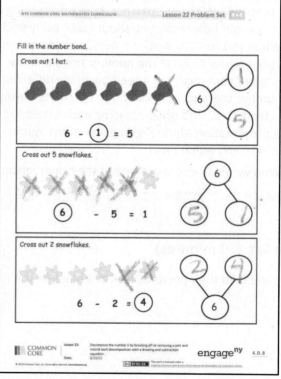

Lesson 22:

Date:

Decompose the number 6 using 5-group drawings by breaking off or removing a part, and record each decomposition with a drawing and subtraction equation.

11/12/13

4.D.30

Complete the number bond.

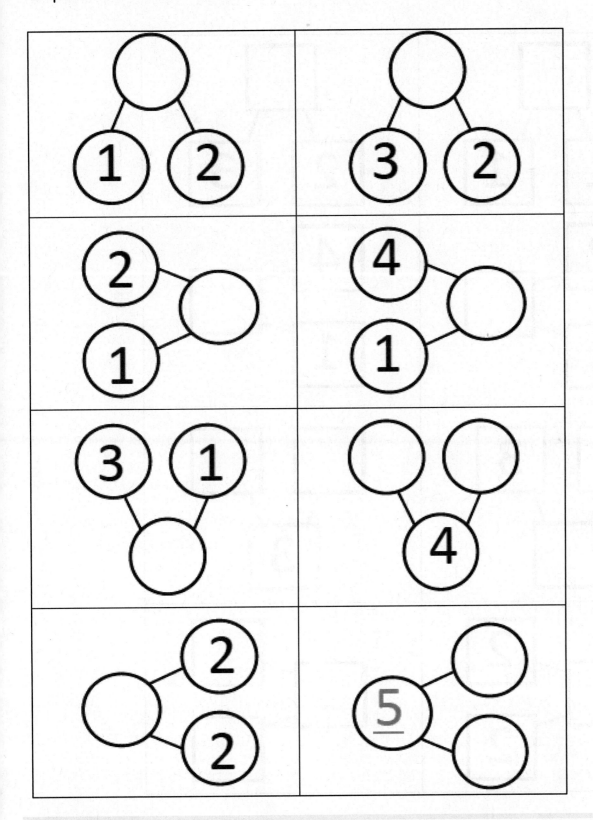

COMMON CORE™ | **Lesson 22:**   Decompose the number 6 using 5-group drawings by breaking off or removing a part, and record each decomposition with a drawing and subtraction equation.   **4.D.31**

Date: 11/12/13

© 2013 Common Core, Inc. All rights reserved. commoncore.org

Complete the number bond.

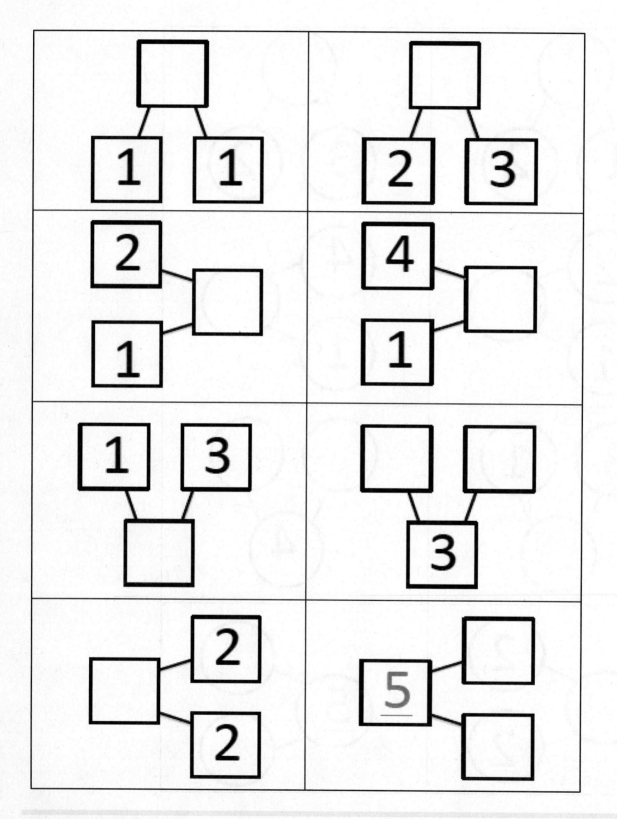

Lesson 22: Decompose the number 6 using 5-group drawings by breaking off or removing a part, and record each decomposition with a drawing and subtraction equation.

Date: 11/12/13

4.D.32

Name _____   Date _____

Fill in the number sentences and number bonds.

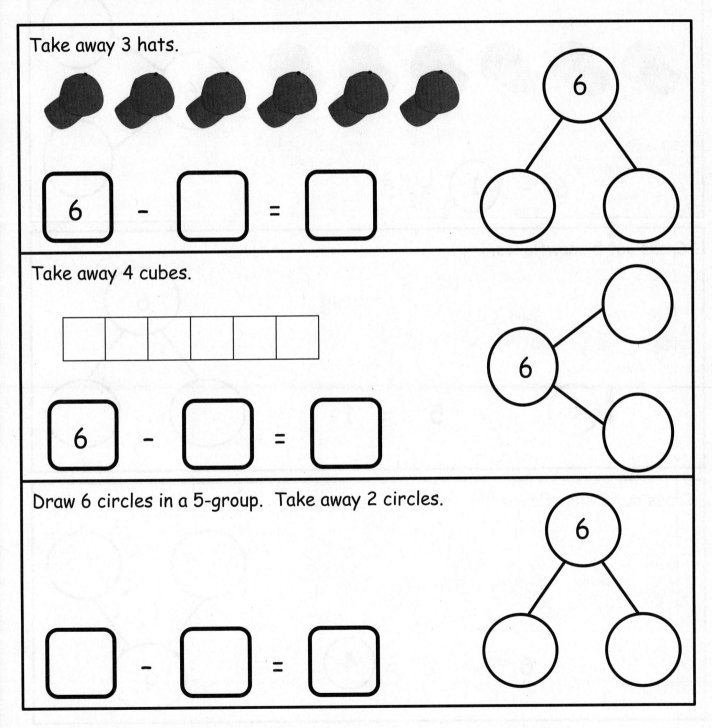

Take away 3 hats.

6 $-$ ☐ $=$ ☐

Take away 4 cubes.

6 $-$ ☐ $=$ ☐

Draw 6 circles in a 5-group. Take away 2 circles.

☐ $-$ ☐ $=$ ☐

COMMON CORE™

Lesson 22:   Decompose the number 6 using 5-group drawings by breaking off or
             removing a part, and record each decomposition with a drawing and
Date: subtraction equation.
             11/12/13

4.D.33

Fill in the number bond.

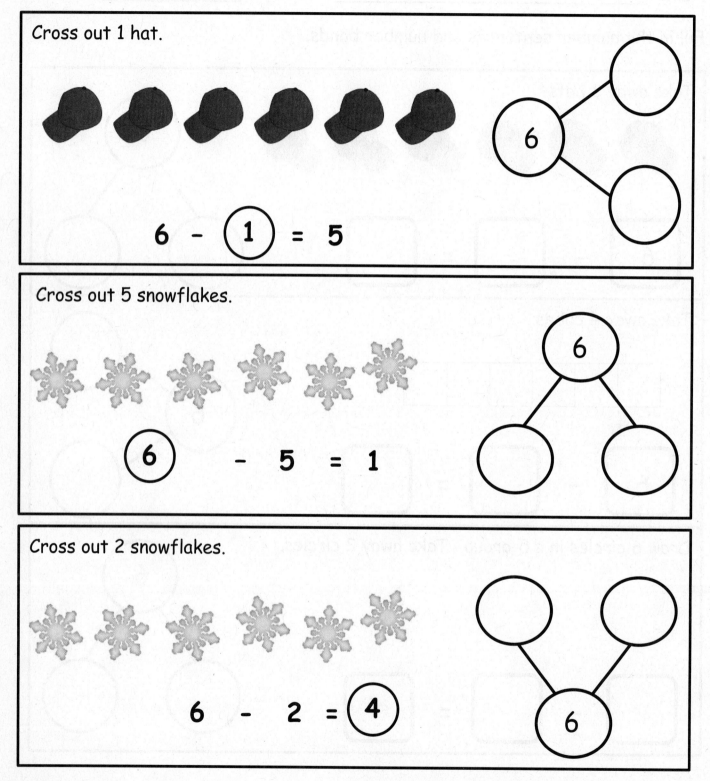

Cross out 1 hat.

6 – (1) = 5

Cross out 5 snowflakes.

(6) – 5 = 1

Cross out 2 snowflakes.

6 – 2 = (4)

COMMON CORE™

Lesson 22: Decompose the number 6 using 5-group drawings by breaking off or removing a part, and record each decomposition with a drawing and subtraction equation.

Date: 11/12/13

4.D.34

Name _____   Date _____

Here are 6 books. Cross out 2. How many are left? Fill in the number bond and the number sentence.

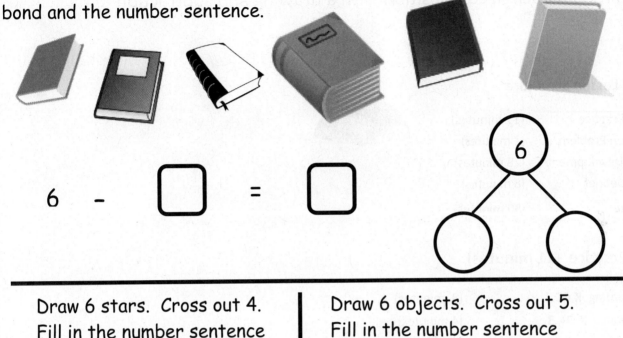

6 - ☐ = ☐

Draw 6 stars. Cross out 4. Fill in the number sentence and the number bond.	Draw 6 objects. Cross out 5. Fill in the number sentence and the number bond.
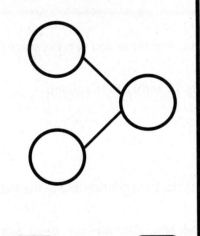	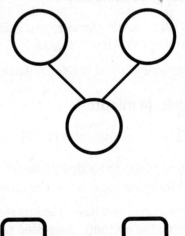
☐ − ☐ = ☐	☐ − ☐ = ☐

On the back of your paper, draw 6 triangles. Cross out 1. Write a number sentence and draw a number bond to match.

COMMON CORE™

Lesson 22:

Date: 11/12/13

Decompose the number 6 using 5-group drawings by breaking off or removing a part, and record each decomposition with a drawing and subtraction equation.

4.D.35

Lesson 23

Objective: Decompose the number 7 using 5-group drawings by hiding a part, and record each decomposition with a drawing and subtraction equation.

Suggested Lesson Structure

- ■ Fluency Practice   (11 minutes)
- ■ Application Problem   (3 minutes)
- □ Concept Development   (28 minutes)
- ■ Student Debrief   (8 minutes)

  Total Time   **(50 minutes)**

Fluency Practice (11 minutes)

- ▪ Happy Counting **K.CC.2**   (3 minutes)
- ▪ 5-Group Hands **K.OA.3**   (4 minutes)
- ▪ Take Away Fingers **K.OA.1**   (4 minutes)

Happy Counting (3 minutes)

Note: Fluidity with counting forward and backward builds students' number sense and sets the stage for counting on strategies used in first grade.

Conduct activity as described in GK–M4–Lesson 19. As a variation, add 11 and 12 to the count.

5-Group Hands (4 minutes)

Materials: (T) Large 5-group cards (1–10)

Note: This activity helps to solidify students' understanding of numbers to 10 in relationship to the five and prepares them for using 5-groups with subtraction operations.

Show the 5-group cards and have students show the 5-group using their hands (for numbers 6–10, 5 on top and some ones on the bottom). Suggested sequence: 4, 5, 6, 2, 3, 7, 8, 1, 9, 10. Repeat without using the 5-group cards as support.

Take Away Fingers (4 minutes)

Note: This fluency activity provides additional practice with subtraction using fingers, a set of manipulatives always available to students. Some kindergarteners will need to count all of their fingers to determine how

COMMON CORE™	Lesson 23:	Decompose the number 7 using 5-group drawings by hiding a part, and record each decomposition with a drawing and subtraction equation.	4.D.36
	Date:	11/12/13	

many fingers are left, but when working within 5, many have the ability to subitize, especially after much practice counting the Math way.

- T: Show me 3 fingers the Math way.
- S: (Hold up the pinky, ring, and middle fingers of the left hand.)
- T: Take away 1 finger. (Students put down middle finger.) How many fingers are left?
- S: 2!
- T: Say the number sentence with me: 3 minus 1 equals 2.

Continue with the following suggested progression: $3 - 2, 2 - 1, 4 - 1, 4 - 3, 4 - 2, 5 - 1, 5 - 4, 5 - 2, 5 - 3$. Stop saying the number sentence along with the students after two or three examples. Listen to determine who has gained mastery.

Application Problem (3 minutes)

Materials: (S) Personal white boards

Noah had 7 red balloons. Two balloons popped as he and his kitties played with them.

Draw Noah's balloons. How would you show that 2 of them popped in the picture? Can you make a number sentence about your story? Try to draw a number bond to go with it!

Note: This problem introduces work with the number 7 for today's decomposition lesson.

NOTES ON MULTIPLE MEANS OF ENGAGEMENT:

Scaffold the Application Problem for students with disabilities who might still need support by providing linking cubes to model the problem before drawing on their personal white boards.

Concept Development (28 minutes)

Materials: (T) Large foam die (S) Linking cube 7-sticks, personal white boards, 1 die per pair

- T: Count the number of cubes in your stick. How many?
- S: There are 7.
- T: Break 2 cubes off the end of your stick and hide them in your lap. How many cubes do you still have left in your hand?
- S: 5.
- T: Tell me a number sentence about what you just did.
- S: 7 take away 2 is 5!
- T: Yes! You took your 7 and made it into a 2 and a 5! Draw the cubes on your personal board and cross off the ones you hid. Now, let's make a number bond about what we just did. You have 2 cubes hiding in your lap and 5 cubes in your hand. How many together?

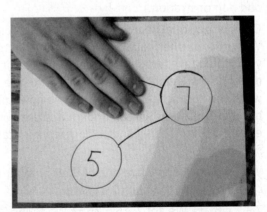

COMMON CORE™   Lesson 23:   Decompose the number 7 using 5-group drawings by hiding a part, and record each decomposition with a drawing and subtraction equation.   **4.D.37**

Date: 11/12/13

S: 7.

T: (Demonstrate the number bond on board.) Then, you took 2 away. I will hide the part, 2. (Cover part of the number bond.) How many were left?

S: 5!

T: Write the number bond on your personal board, too. You can cross out the part, 2, to show what you did. How would we write our number sentence? (Demonstrate 7 – 2 = 5.)

S: 7 take away 2 is 5!

Repeat exercise several times with varying subtrahends, each time allowing students to record the action, the number bond, and the number sentence on their personal boards.

T: Put your cubes away and erase your personal boards. Does anyone remember how we could draw 7 the 5-group way? (Allow students to guide you in the creation of the representation on the board.) Let's roll the die to see how many we should take away from our 7. (Demonstrate.) How many?

S: 4!

T: I will cross off 4 to show the ones we are taking away. (Demonstrate.) How many are left?

S: There are still 3 left.

T: What would my number sentence be?

S: 7 – 4 = 3!

T: How could we make a number bond about our picture, and then show that we are taking part away? (Allow time for discussion and demonstration.)

T: On your personal board, draw the 5-group for the number 7. With your partner, take turns rolling the die to find out how many you should take away each time. When you roll, cross off the dots and work with your partner to make the number bond and write the number sentence. Let's see how many different number sentences we can find! (Circulate during the activity to ensure understanding and correct representation of the 5-group situations.)

T: Who would like to share one of their number sentences with the class? I will list them on the board.

S: 7 – 1 = 6. → We got 7 – 5 = 2! → We found 7 – 3 = 4.

NOTES ON MULTIPLE MEANS OF REPRESENTATION:

Scaffold the lesson for English language learners by pointing to visuals on your word wall as you talk about *number bond*s and the *5-group way*. Model the use of the math vocabulary you want them to use with their partners (e.g., "I rolled a 3; 7 take away 3 leaves 4").

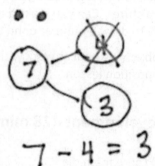

$$7 - 1 = 6$$
$$7 - 2 = 5$$
$$7 - 3 = 4$$
$$7 - 4 = 3$$
$$7 - 5 = 2$$
$$7 - 6 = 1$$

Problem Set (10 minutes)

Students should do their personal best to complete the Problem Set within the allotted 10 minutes.

Lesson 23:	Decompose the number 7 using 5-group drawings by hiding a part, and record each decomposition with a drawing and subtraction equation.	**4.D.38**
Date:	11/12/13	

Student Debrief (8 minutes)

Lesson Objective: Decompose the number 7 using 5-group drawings by hiding a part, and record each decomposition with a drawing and subtraction equation.

The Student Debrief is intended to invite reflection and active processing of the total lesson experience.

Invite students to review their solutions for the Problem Set. They should check work by comparing answers with a partner before going over answers as a class. Look for misconceptions or misunderstandings that can be addressed in the Debrief. Guide students in a conversation to debrief the Problem Set and process the lesson.

You may choose to use any combination of the questions below to lead the discussion.

- Look at the Problem Set. Why is there a 7 at the top of each number bond? Where is the 7 in the number sentence?

- Which dots is the number seven talking about?

- Compare with your neighbor the dots you put an X on. Did you put the X on the same dots as your neighbor? Did it change how many dots were left?

- How can the number bond help you when you are taking away part of a number?

- How do the number bonds and number sentences go together?

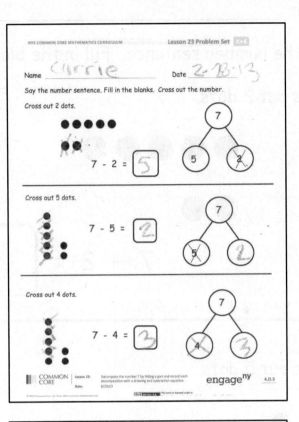

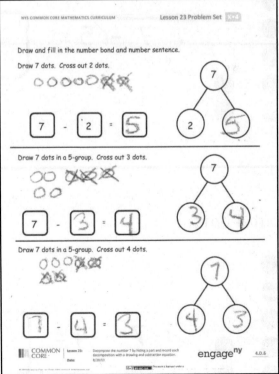

Lesson 23:
Date:

Decompose the number 7 using 5-group drawings by hiding a part, and record each decomposition with a drawing and subtraction equation.
11/12/13

4.D.39

© 2013 Common Core, Inc. All rights reserved. commoncore.org

Name _____   Date _____

Say the number sentence. Fill in the blanks. Cross out the number.

Cross out 2 dots.

Cross out 5 dots.

Cross out 4 dots.

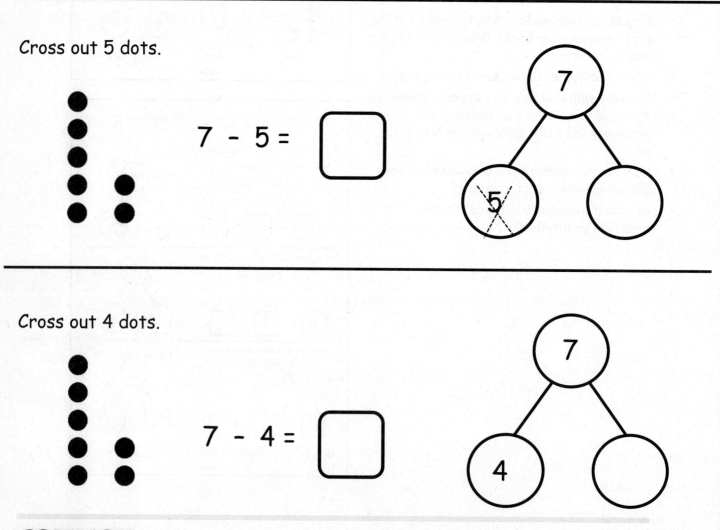

7 – 2 =

7 – 5 =

7 – 4 =

COMMON CORE™   Lesson 23:   Decompose the number 7 using 5-group drawings by hiding a part, and record each decomposition with a drawing and subtraction equation.   **4.D.40**

Date: 11/12/13

Draw and fill in the number bond and number sentence.

Draw 7 dots. Cross out 2 dots.

7 − 2 = ☐

7

2

Draw 7 dots in a 5-group. Cross out 3 dots.

7 − ☐ = ☐

7

Draw 7 dots in a 5-group. Cross out 4 dots.

☐ − ☐ = ☐

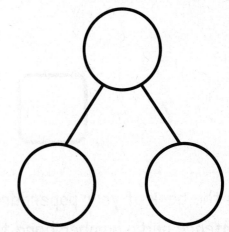

COMMON CORE™ | **Lesson 23:**   Decompose the number 7 using 5-group drawings by hiding a part, and
record each decomposition with a drawing and subtraction equation.   **4.D.41**

Date: 11/12/13

Name _____   Date _____

Fill in the number sentence and number bond. Cross out 5 dots.

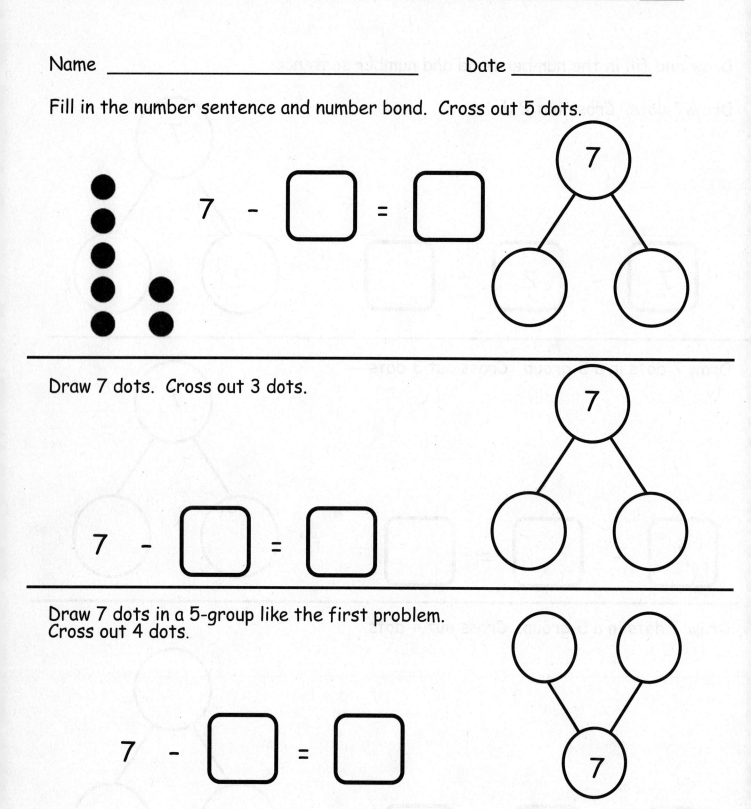

Draw 7 dots. Cross out 3 dots.

Draw 7 dots in a 5-group like the first problem.
Cross out 4 dots.

On the back of your paper, draw 7 dots. Cross out some, and write a number
sentence and a number bond to match.

COMMON CORE™   Lesson 23:   Decompose the number 7 using 5-group drawings by hiding a part, and record each decomposition with a drawing and subtraction equation.

Date: 11/12/13   4.D.42

Lesson 24

Objective: Decompose the number 8 using 5-group drawings and crossing off a part, and record each decomposition with a drawing and subtraction equation.

Suggested Lesson Structure

- ■ Fluency Practice   (12 minutes)
- ■ Application Problem   (4 minutes)
- ■ Concept Development   (26 minutes)
- ■ Student Debrief   (8 minutes)
- **Total Time**   **(50 minutes)**

Fluency Practice (12 minutes)

- Happy Counting **K.CC.2**   (3 minutes)
- Roll and Draw 5-Groups **K.OA.3**   (5 minutes)
- Take Apart Groups of Circles **K.OA.1**   (4 minutes)

Happy Counting (3 minutes)

Note: Fluidity with counting forward and backward builds students' number sense and sets the stage for counting on strategies used in first grade.

Conduct activity as described in GK–M4–Lesson 19, but continue count to 20.

Roll and Draw 5-Groups (5 minutes)

Materials: (S) Pair of dice (with the 6 sides covered) per student, personal white boards

Note: This activity helps students see numbers in relationship to the five and prepares them for using 5-groups with subtraction operations.

Have students roll the dice, count the dots, and then draw the number as a 5-group. Observe to see which students erase completely and begin each time from one rather than draw more or erase some to adjust to the new number.

Take Apart Groups of Circles (4 minutes)

Materials: (S) Personal white boards

Lesson 24:   Decompose the number 8 using 5-group drawings and crossing off a part, and record each decomposition with a drawing and subtraction equation.
Date: 11/12/13

4.D.43

Note: This activity anticipates the day's work with decomposition and subtraction equations.

T: Draw 4 circles on your board. (Wait for students to do this.) Put X's on two of them. How many circles have X's?

S: 2.

T: How many circles do not have an X?

S: 2.

T: Raise your hand when you can say the **subtraction** number sentence starting with 4. (Wait for all students to raise hands and then signal). Ready?

S: 4 minus 2 is 2.

Continue working through problems with minuends of $2 - 7$. The following is a suggested sequence: $5 - 2$, $6 - 2$, $7 - 2$, $3 - 2$, $4 - 3$, $5 - 4$, $6 - 5$, and $7 - 6$.

Application Problem (4 minutes)

Robin had 8 cats in her house. Three of the cats went outside to play in the sunshine. Draw her cats. Use your picture to help you draw a number bond about the cats. How many cats were still in the house? Can you make a number sentence to tell how many cats were still inside?

Share your work with your partner. Did he do it the same way?

Note: Practice in exploring the relationships among representational drawings, number bonds, and number sentences will serve as the anticipatory set for today's lesson with 8.

NOTES ON MULTIPLE MEANS OF REPRESENTATION:

Scaffold the Application Problem for students with disabilities by providing a black-line master insert of a number bond and the outline for writing number sentence. This will enable them to focus on the mathematics and build their conceptual understanding. The inserts can also be used as a mat for use with linking cubes to show the problem.

Concept Development (26 minutes)

Materials: (T) Large foam die (S) Linking cube 8-sticks, personal white boards, 1 die per pair

T: Count the number of cubes in your stick. How many?

S: There are 8.

T: Break 1 cube off the end of your stick and put it on your desk. How many cubes do you still have left in your hand?

S: 7.

T: Tell me a number sentence about what you just did.

S: We took 1 away. → 8 take away 1 is 7!

T: Draw the cubes on your personal board and cross off the one you took off. Now, let's make a number bond about your picture. You have 1 cube on your desk and 7 cubes in your hand. Help me draw the number bond. What is the whole? (8.) What are your parts? (1 and 7.) (Demonstrate

Lesson 24:   Decompose the number 8 using 5-group drawings and crossing off a part, and record each decomposition with a drawing and subtraction equation.

Date: 11/12/13

4.D.44

number bond on the board.) You took 1 away. (Cover part of the number bond.) How many were left?

S: 7!

T: Write the number bond on your board, too. You can cross out the part of 1 to show what you did when you took the cube away. How would we write our number sentence? (Demonstrate 8 – 1 = 7.)

S: 8 take away 1 is 7.

T: Great! Put your 8-stick back together. This time, take 2 cubes off the end. Draw the picture on your personal board. What would our number bond look like this time?

Repeat exercise several times, each time increasing the subtrahend by 1 until you have 8 – 7 = 1. In each situation, demonstrate and allow students to record a picture of the action, the number bond, and the number sentence on their personal white boards. Show how hiding a part in the number bond is a representation of the *take away* concept.

8 take away 5 leaves 3!

T: Put your cubes away and erase your boards. Does anyone remember how we could draw 8 the 5-group way? (Allow students to guide you in the creation of the representation on the board.) Let's roll the die to see how many we should take away from our 8. (Demonstrate.) How many?

S: 2!

T: I will cross off 2 to show the ones we are taking away. (Demonstrate.) How many are left?

S: There are 6 left.

T: What would my number sentence be?

S: 8 – 2 = 6.

T: How could we make a number bond about our picture, and then show that we are taking part away? (Allow time for discussion and demonstration.)

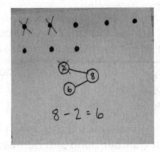

8 – 2 = 6

T: On your board, draw the 5-group for the number 8. With your partner, take turns rolling the die to find out how many you should take away each time. When you roll, cross off the dots and work with your partner to make the number bond and write the number sentence. Let's see how many different number sentences we can find! (Circulate during the activity to ensure understanding and correct representation of the 5-group situations.)

MP.4

T: Who would like to share one of their number sentences with the class? I will list them on the board.

S: 8 – 1 = 7. → 8 – 4 = 4! → We found 8 – 2 = 6.

NOTES ON MULTIPLE MEANS OF ACTION AND EXPRESSION:

Scaffold the lesson for English language learners by pointing to images on the board (or word wall) that correspond to your words. For example, point to a number sentence while asking, "What would my number sentence be?"

Lesson 24:   Decompose the number 8 using 5-group drawings and crossing off a part, and record each decomposition with a drawing and subtraction equation.

Date: 11/12/13

4.D.45

Problem Set (10 minutes)

Students should do their personal best to complete the Problem Set within the allotted 10 minutes.

Student Debrief (8 minutes)

Lesson Objective: Decompose the number 8 using 5-group drawings and crossing off a part, and record each decomposition with a drawing and subtraction equation.

The Student Debrief is intended to invite reflection and active processing of the total lesson experience.

Invite students to review their solutions for the Problem Set. They should check work by comparing answers with a partner before going over answers as a class. Look for misconceptions or misunderstandings that can be addressed in the Debrief. Guide students in a conversation to debrief the Problem Set and process the lesson.

You may choose to use any combination of the questions below to lead the discussion.

- In the Problem Set, did the 5-group dots make it easier to see how many dots were left? Why?
- In the last problem, how many dots did you put an X on? What did your number sentence and number bond look like?
- Look at the first problem. Tell me all the numbers in your number bond and number sentence.
    - Show me which dots the 8 is talking about.
    - Show me which dots the 3 is talking about.
    - Show me which dots the 5 is talking about.
- What number is the same in all of the number bonds and all of the number sentences. Why is 8 in all of them?
- How did the number bonds and the number sentences help one another in our lesson?

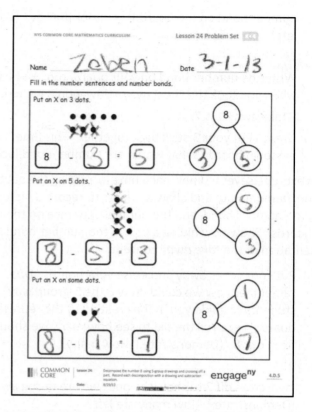

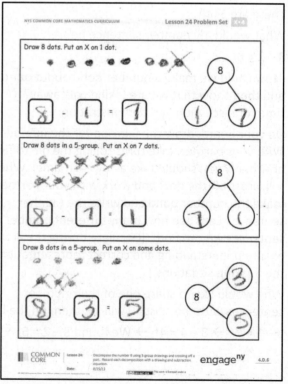

COMMON CORE

Lesson 24:   Decompose the number 8 using 5-group drawings and crossing off a part, and record each decomposition with a drawing and subtraction equation.

Date: 11/12/13

4.D.46

Name _____   Date _____

Fill in the number sentences and number bonds.

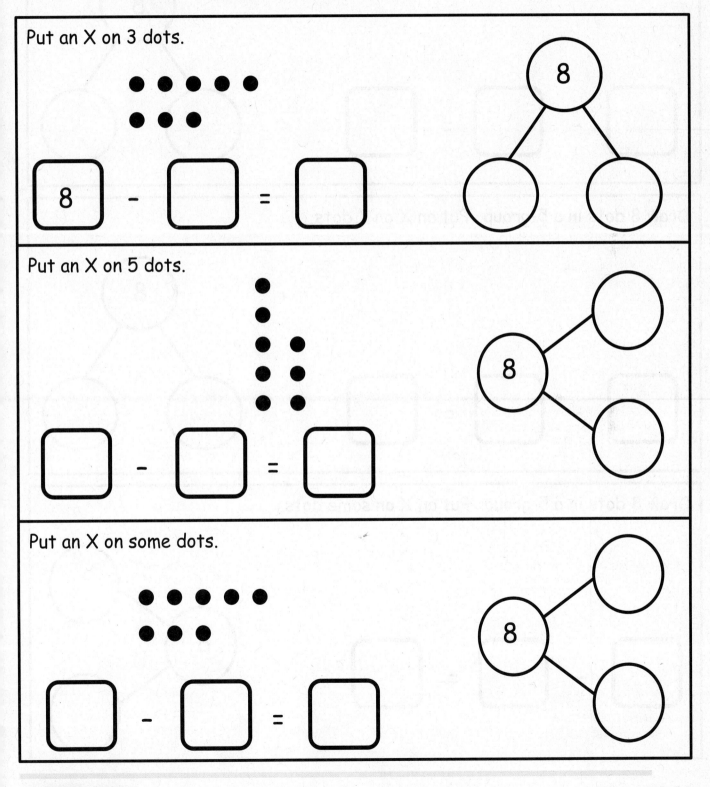

Put an X on 3 dots.

8 - ☐ = ☐

Put an X on 5 dots.

☐ - ☐ = ☐

Put an X on some dots.

☐ - ☐ = ☐

COMMON CORE™   Lesson 24:   Decompose the number 8 using 5-group drawings and crossing off a part, and record each decomposition with a drawing and subtraction equation.   **4.D.47**

Date: 11/12/13

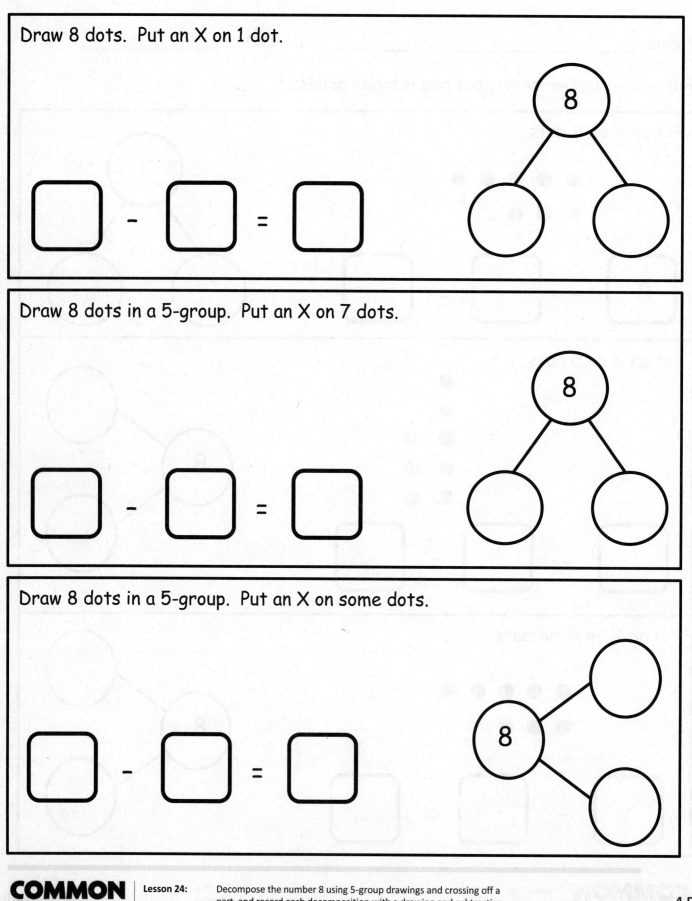

Draw 8 dots. Put an X on 1 dot.

☐ - ☐ = ☐

8

Draw 8 dots in a 5-group. Put an X on 7 dots.

☐ - ☐ = ☐

8

Draw 8 dots in a 5-group. Put an X on some dots.

☐ - ☐ = ☐

8

COMMON CORE™ | **Lesson 24:**   Decompose the number 8 using 5-group drawings lend crossing off a part, and record each decomposition with a drawing and subtraction equation.

Date: 11/12/13

4.D.4

Name _____   Date _____

Here is 8 the 5-group way. Put an X on 2 cubes. How many are left?

Fill in the number sentence and number bond.

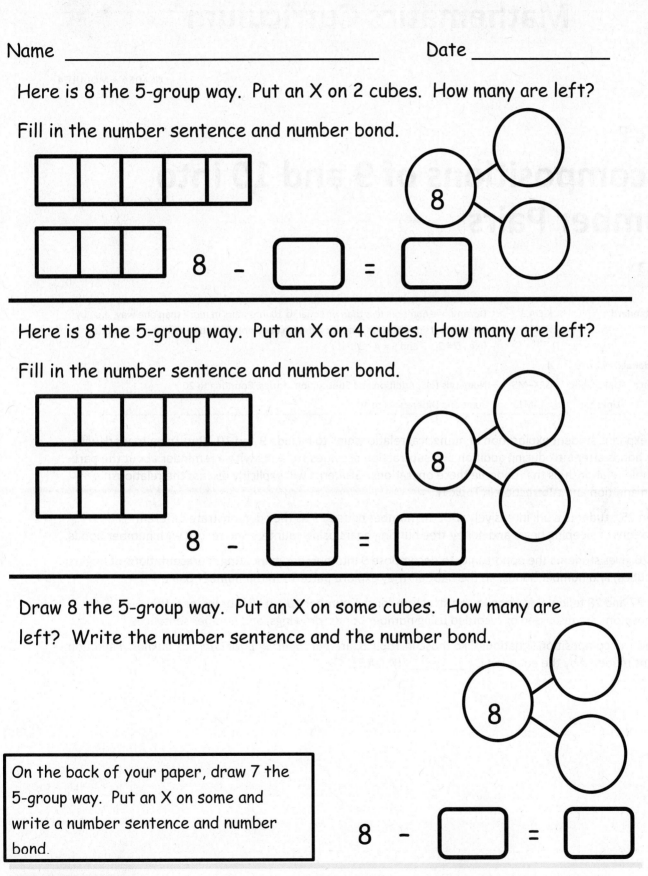

8 - ☐ = ☐

Here is 8 the 5-group way. Put an X on 4 cubes. How many are left?

Fill in the number sentence and number bond.

8 - ☐ = ☐

Draw 8 the 5-group way. Put an X on some cubes. How many are left? Write the number sentence and the number bond.

On the back of your paper, draw 7 the 5-group way. Put an X on some and write a number sentence and number bond.

8 - ☐ = ☐

COMMON CORE™ | Lesson 24: Decompose the number 8 using 5-group drawings and crossing off a part, and record each decomposition with a drawing and subtraction equation.
Date: 11/12/13

4.D.49

Topic E

Decompositions of 9 and 10 into Number Pairs

K.OA.3

Focus Standard:	K.OA.3	Decompose numbers less than or equal to 10 into pairs in more than one way, e.g., by using objects or drawings, and record each decomposition by a drawing or equation (e.g., 5 = 2 + 3 and 5 = 4 + 1).
Instructional Days:	4	
Coherence -Links from:	GPK–M5	Numerals to 5, Addition and Subtraction Stories, Counting to 20
-Links to:	G1–M1	Sums and Differences to 10

Topic E expands student exploration of numerical relationships to include 9 and 10. Returning to work with number bonds after introducing addition and subtraction provides students with a reminder about the part–part–whole relationships that underlie these operations. Students will explicitly discuss the relationship between addition and subtraction in Topic H.

In Lesson 25, students work intensively with the number pairs of 9 as they demonstrate different combinations of sleeping bears and honey-tree hunting bears using counters and record with number bonds.

Lesson 26 gives students the opportunity to decompose 9 into number pairs using representations of fingers, linking cubes, and number bonds. In the Debrief, they explore patterns in the number pairs.

Lessons 27 and 28 follow this same lesson structure for the number 10. In all four lessons, the decompositions are discussed or recorded using number bonds, drawings, and number sentences.

This topic's decomposition situations, like those in Topic B, are *put together both addends unknown* addition equations modeled by the equation C = ___ + ___ **(K.OA.3)**.

A Teaching Sequence Towards Mastery of Decompositions of 9 and 10 into Number Pairs

Objective 1: Model decompositions of 9 using a story situation, objects, and number bonds.
(Lesson 25)

Objective 2: Model decompositions of 9 using fingers, linking cubes, and number bonds.
(Lesson 26)

Objective 3: Model decompositions of 10 using a story situation, objects, and number bonds.
(Lesson 27)

Objective 4: Model decompositions of 10 using fingers, sets, linking cubes, and number bonds.
(Lesson 28)

Lesson 25

Objective: Model decompositions of 9 using a story situation, objects, and number bonds.

Suggested Lesson Structure

■ Fluency Practice   (13 minutes)
■ Application Problem   (4 minutes)
■ Concept Development   (25 minutes)
■ Student Debrief   (8 minutes)

Total Time   **(50 minutes)**

Fluency Practice (13 minutes)

- Rekenrek Wave **K.NBT.1**   (3 minutes)
- 5-Group Flashes **K.OA.5**   (5 minutes)
- Take Apart the Array **K.OA.3**   (5 minutes)

Rekenrek Wave (3 minutes)

Materials: (T) 20-bead Rekenrek

T: You've become very good at counting with the Rekenrek the Say Ten way. I want to teach you the regular way to say the numbers that come after 10. (Show 10 beads on the top row of the Rekenrek). Here is 10, 1 more than 10 is 11. (Slide over one more bead.) Say "eleven."

S: Eleven.

T: How many beads do you see?

S: 11.

T: 1 more than 11 is 12. (Slide over one more bead.) Say "twelve."

S: Twelve.

T: How many beads now?

S: 12.

Repeat this process to 13. Then continue with the following possible sequence: 11, 12, 11, 12, 13, 12, 13, 12, 11. Direct the students to gradually raise their hands as the numbers increase and lower their hands as the numbers decrease, mimicking the motion of a wave.

Note: This fluency anticipates the work of GK–Module 5. Developing automaticity with the counting sequence in conventional language will facilitate the work with teen numbers.

Lesson 25:	Model decompositions of 9 using a story situation, objects, and number bonds.
Date:	11/12/13

4.E.3

5-Group Flashes (5 minutes)

Materials: (T) Large 5-group cards (1–4) (S) 5-group cards

Note: This activity seeks to build on students' understanding of comparison in order to see the relationship between partner numbers.

> T: (Show 4 dots.) How many dots do you see?
> S: 4.
> T: How many more to make 5?
> S: 1.
> T: Say the number sentence.
> S: 4 plus 1 equals 5.
> T: Write the number sentence on your board. Get ready. Show me.
> S: (Display 4 + 1 = 5.)

Continue with the following possible sequence: 3, 2, 1, 4, 2, 3.

Take Apart the Array (5 minutes)

Materials: (S) Array of 9 fluency template, personal white board

> T: (Project or show a copy of the fluency template.) Let's count the dots. Ready?
> S: 1, 2, 3, 4, 5, 6, 7, 8, 9.
> T: So our job is to take apart?
> S: 9!
> T: We can take apart the 9 dots by drawing a straight line like this. (Demonstrate.) How many dots are in this part? (Point to indicate which part to count.)

> S: 3.
> T: The other part? (Provide wait time and a signal, such as a clap of the hands, for the answer of 6 to allow time for those students who need to count all 6 dots).
> S: 6.
> T: (Record the number bond.) We can read it like this: 9 is 3 and 6. Echo me, please.
> S: 9 is 3 and 6.
> T: (Erase the line, but do not erase the number bond.) We can also take apart the 9 dots with a line that looks like an L. (Demonstrate.) How many dots are in this part? (Point to indicate which part to count.)

> S: 2.
> T: The other part? (Provide wait time and a signal, such as a clap of the hands, for the answer of 7 to allow time for those students who need to count all 7 dots.)
> S: 7.
> T: (Record the number bond.) We can read it like this: 9 is 2 and 7. Echo me, please.

COMMON CORE™ | Lesson 25:   Model decompositions of 9 using a story situation, objects, and number bonds.
Date: 11/12/13

4.E.4

S: 9 is 2 and 7.

T: Now, it's your turn to take apart 9!

If necessary, complete another example with the class, or direct students to work independently on drawing lines and recording decompositions of 9 as number bonds. After some time, invite students to explain how they know they've found all of the ways to take apart 9.

Note: This activity prepares students to work with decomposing 9 at the pictorial level.

Application Problem (4 minutes)

There were 9 flowers in Casey's beautiful garden. She had 2 vases. Draw one way she could have put all of the flowers into the vases. Show your picture to your partner. Did he draw the flowers in the vases the same way? Are both ways right? Are there other ways you could have shown the flowers?

Note: Thinking about different ways to decompose 9 and discussing them with a partner sets the stage for today's lesson.

> **NOTES ON MULTIPLE MEANS OF ACTION AND EXPRESSION:**
>
> Give students who are below grade level and those with disabilities linking cubes or counting sticks (or another manipulative) to show the Application Problem before asking them to draw their results. Manipulatives make the conceptual transference from concrete to abstract easier.

Concept Development (25 minutes)

Materials: (S) 9 teddy bear counters or other manipulatives and 1 paper bowl per pair, personal white boards

T: There were 9 bears in the forest. Some bears went to sleep in their cave, and some left to find a honey tree. Use your counters to show the bears. How many bears were there in all?

S: 9.

T: I wonder how many bears were sleeping. Who would like to share an idea?

S: I think that 3 bears were sleeping and the other ones went to the honey tree.

T: Great! Let's use your set of counters show 3 sleeping bears and the rest of your counters to show the honey tree-hunting bears. Arrange your counters to show the different groups. (Allow time for the children to model the situation, circulating to ensure accuracy.)

T: Good work! Could we show this story in a number bond? How many bears are there in all? What number should go in the whole?

S: 9.

> **NOTES ON MULTIPLE MEANS OF ENGAGEMENT:**
>
> Make partner work easier for English language learners by providing sentence frames such as, "I see ___ bears outside, so there are ___ bears sleeping." Practice with them a few times so that they are more comfortable working with their partner.

COMMON CORE

Lesson 25: Model decompositions of 9 using a story situation, objects, and number bonds.
Date: 11/12/13

4.E.5

T: Good! Draw the number bond and the whole. What are our parts?

S: There are 3 sleeping and 6 hunting in the forest! → The parts are 3 and 6.

T: (Demonstrate.) Yes! We can make our 9 bears into parts of 3 and 6. Finish the number bond on your board.

T: Did anyone think about the story in another way?

S: Yes! → I imagined 7 sleeping and the rest hunting.

T: If more bears were sleeping in the story this time, do you think there will be more or fewer bears hunting for honey now? Let's show this new situation with your bears to find out!

S: More bears sleeping mean that there aren't as many hunting this time!

Allow time for other student ideas and discussion, modeling of the new situations, and creation of other number bonds representing the bears. Guide the discussion if necessary to find all of the partners making 9.

MP.4

T: You are going to play a game with your 9 teddy bears and your partner. While she closes her eyes, hide some of your bears under the bowl to show the sleepy bears in the cave. Then tell your partner to open her eyes. How many bears are outside? Can she figure out how many bears are hiding in the cave? If not, show her. Draw a number bond to show your story, and then switch! How many partners for 9 can you find? (Allow time for play and discussion.)

T: Let's show some of the number bonds you discovered on the board! What partners did you find?

S: We found 8 and 1! → We found 4 and 5. → 7 and 2 make 9, too! (Record student number bonds on the board.)

Problem Set (10 minutes)

Students should do their personal best to complete the Problem Set within the allotted 10 minutes.

Note: The teacher may first need to read each problem aloud, depending on the reading abilities of the students. After explaining the problem, allow time for the students to create the solution before moving on.

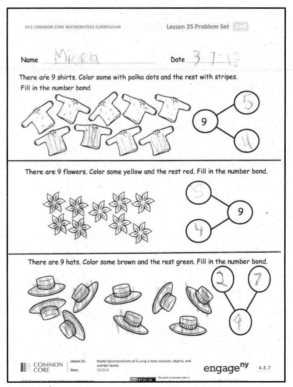

Student Debrief (8 minutes)

Lesson Objective: Model decompositions of 9 using a story situation, objects, and number bonds.

The Student Debrief is intended to invite reflection and active processing of the total lesson experience.

Invite students to review their solutions for the Problem Set. They should check work by comparing answers with a partner before going over answers as a class. Look for misconceptions or misunderstandings that can be addressed in the Debrief. Guide students in a conversation to debrief the Problem Set and process the lesson.

COMMON CORE™ | Lesson 25:   Model decompositions of 9 using a story situation, objects, and number bonds.
                    Date: 11/12/13

4.E.6

You may choose to use any combination of the questions below to lead the discussion.

- What strategies did you use to fill in the number bonds in the problem set? Did you count each of the parts, or did you think in a different way?

- How did you figure out how many bears were in the cave during your partner game?

- How did know you where you should write each part when you were drawing your number bonds on your personal board?

- Seven bears are sleeping and 2 are in the honey tree. Here is the number bond. What if there were 2 bears sleeping and 7 in the honey tree? Would the number bond change? Does the story change?

- Thumbs up if you think you are getting really good and putting together and taking apart numbers to 5. (Ask a few addition and subtraction questions such as $3 + 2$, $5 - 1$, $4 + 1$, and $3 - 2$.)

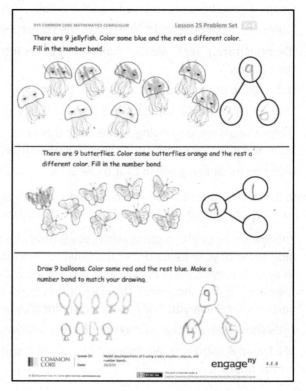

4.E.7

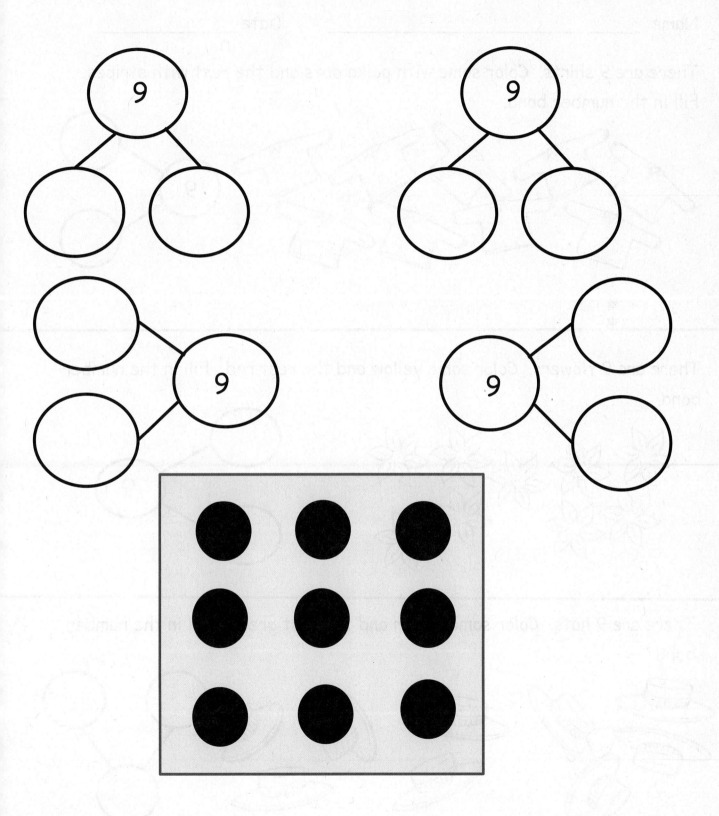

COMMON CORE™   Lesson 25:   Model decompositions of 9 using a story situation, objects, and
                                      number bonds.

                     Date: 11/12/13   4.E.8

Name _____ Date _____

There are 9 shirts. Color some with polka dots and the rest with stripes.
Fill in the number bond.

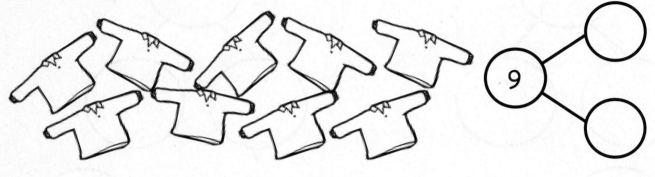

There are 9 flowers. Color some yellow and the rest red. Fill in the number
bond.

There are 9 hats. Color some brown and the rest green. Fill in the number
bond.

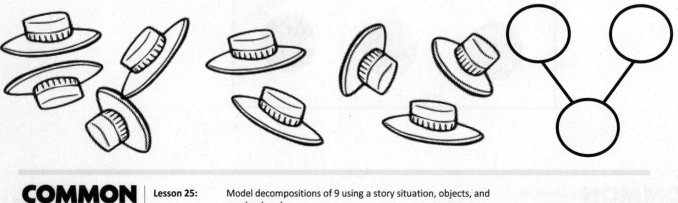

COMMON CORE™

Lesson 25: Model decompositions of 9 using a story situation, objects, and
number bonds.
Date: 11/12/13

4.E.9

There are 9 jellyfish. Color some blue and the rest a different color. Fill in the number bond.

There are 9 butterflies. Color some butterflies orange and the rest a different color. Fill in the number bond.

Draw 9 balloons. Color some red and the rest blue. Make a number bond to match your drawing.

Lesson 25:   Model decompositions of 9 using a story situation, objects, and number bonds.

Date: 11/12/13

Name _____   Date _____

There are 9 leaves. Color some of them red and the rest of them yellow. Fill in the number bond to match.

There are 9 acorns. Color some of them green and the rest yellow. Fill in the number bond to match.

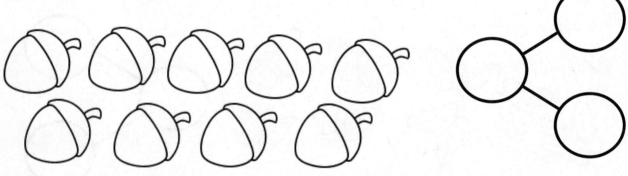

Draw 9 birds. Color some of them blue and the rest red. Fill in the number bond to match.

On the back of your paper, draw 9 triangles. Color some red and some brown. Draw and fill in a number bond to match.

Lesson 26

Objective: Model decompositions of 9 using fingers, linking cubes, and number bonds.

Suggested Lesson Structure

■ Fluency Practice   (12 minutes)
■ Application Problem   (5 minutes)
■ Concept Development   (25 minutes)
■ Student Debrief   (8 minutes)
   Total Time   **(50 minutes)**

Fluency Practice (12 minutes)

- Rekenrek Wave **K.NBT.1**   (3 minutes)
- Race to 5 Addition Game **K.OA.5**   (4 minutes)
- Make 9 Matching Game **K.OA.3**   (5 minutes)

Rekenrek Wave (3 minutes)

Materials: (T) 20-bead Rekenrek

Count with the Rekenrek the Say Ten way as described in GK–M4–Lesson 25, but this time, continue to 15. After introducing each new number name, use the following sequence while students use the wave hand motions to indicate increasing and decreasing quantities: 10, 11, 12, 11, 12, 13, 12, 13, 14, 13, 14, 15, 14, etc.

Note: This fluency anticipates the work of GK–Module 5. Developing automaticity with the counting sequence in conventional language facilitates work with teen numbers.

Race to 5 Addition Game (4 minutes)

Materials: (S) Die with the 6-dot side covered

1. Both partners roll their dice and state their numbers respectively.
2. Both partners roll again, and add the previous number to the new number on the die. Both partners state their new equations.
3. Continue the addition race, rolling the die and adding with speed and accuracy until one of the partners reaches 5 as the total.
4. They must reach 5 exactly, so if either partner reaches a total more than 5, they can roll again.

Lesson 26:	Model decompositions of 9 using fingers, linking cubes, and number bonds.
Date:	11/12/13

4.E.12

Here is an example of how the game might unfold:

Partner A: Rolls a 2, and says 2.

Partner B: Rolls a 3 and says 3.

Partner A: Rolls a 1, and says 2 + 1 = 3.

Partner B: Rolls a 2, and says 3 + 2 = 5, and wins the race to 5.

Begin a new round if time permits.

Extension: The next time this fluency activity is done students can record the addition sentences on their personal boards.

Note: This activity develops automaticity with addition within 5, part of the fluency goal for this grade.

Make 9 Matching Game (5 minutes)

Materials: (S) Cards with quantities of 0–9 (use only dots, dice, and fingers) per pair (cards from GK–M4–Lessons 1 and 7)

Note: Students will find the hidden partners of 9 in support of the day's work with composition and decomposition.

1. Shuffle and place the cards face down in two equal rows.

2. Partner A turns over two cards.

3. If the total of the numbers on both cards is 9, then partner A collects both cards. If not, then Partner A turns them back over in their original place face down.

4. Repeat for Partner B.

NOTES ON MULTIPLE MEANS OF ENGAGEMENT:

Have students who are performing below grade level and having difficulty finding partners to 9 practice with interactive technology tools such as the one found at http://www.ictgames.com/save_the_whale_v4.html.

Such practice will help students feel more confident and better able to participate in the lesson.

Scaffold: Provide each partner with a stick of 9 cubes to help them determine the missing part. For example, a student turns over 4, then breaks off 4 cubes, revealing 5 as the missing part, that way they know to look for the card with the number 5.

Application Problem (5 minutes)

Materials: (S) Paper, green and blue crayons

It is laundry day. We have 9 extra socks! Some are green and the rest are blue. Draw the set of green socks and the set of blue socks. Make a number bond to help tell about your picture.

Turn and talk to your partner about your drawings and number bonds. Do they look alike? Are your sets of socks different?

Turn your paper and show the story a different way.

Note: Use this time to see which students might need support finding partners for 9 prior to identifying decomposition patterns in today's lesson.

Lesson 26:	Model decompositions of 9 using fingers, linking cubes, and number bonds.
Date:	11/12/13

4.E.1

Concept Development (25 minutes)

Materials: (S) 9 linking cubes (groups of 5 blue and 4 red), personal white board

T: Lee had 9 blocks. Hold up 9 fingers to show how many blocks she had. Show me the Math way!

T: Five of her blocks were red and the rest were blue. Show me her red blocks with your fingers. How many?

S: (Show 5 fingers.)

T: Show me the blue blocks. How did you know how many blue blocks she had?

S: I needed the other 4 fingers to get to 9! → 5 red and 4 more make 9 blocks in all. → 9 is the same as 5 and 4 together.

T: Could we draw a number bond showing our story? Where would we put our whole and our parts in our number bond? (Demonstrate the number bond on the board and ask students to recreate the bond on their boards.)

S: 9 goes in the place for the whole number of blocks! → The parts are 5 and 4 for the different colors.

T: Take out your linking cubes and put them in a stick. Use all of the blue cubes first, and then use the rest of the cubes. How many cubes are in your stick?

S: 9.

T: Take off 1 red cube. Do you still have 9 cubes in all? What are the parts now?

S: We still have 9 cubes. → We made it into 8 and 1.

T: Draw the number bond on your board. (Demonstrate.)

T: Now take another cube off your long stick and put it together with the one cube. Do we still have 9 cubes? What are your new parts?

S: We still have 9 in all, but now we have a 7-stick and a 2-stick.

T: Great! Let's make a number bond with the new parts. (Continue the exercise with new situations and number bonds, removing one cube at a time until the students end with 1 and 8.)

T: Did anyone notice a pattern while we did this with your cubes or with the number bonds?

S: Every time we take off a cube, the other part gets bigger! → The other part gets smaller. → One gets one less and the other gets one more. → The 9 in the number bond doesn't change!

T: Put your 9-stick together again. Using your cubes, turn and work with your friend to find hidden partners inside 9. Could you think of a story to tell about the cubes? Be sure to write each set of partners in number bonds on your personal board! (Allow time for sharing and discussion.)

NOTES ON MULTIPLE MEANS OF REPRESENTATION:

Make sure English language learners are clear about the meaning of the term *pattern* so that they can participate in that part of the lesson. Show examples of patterns and non-patterns so that when asked if anyone noticed a pattern, they will be able to answer.

P.8

Problem Set (10 minutes)

Students should do their personal best to complete the Problem Set within the allotted 10 minutes.

Student Debrief (8 minutes)

Lesson Objective: Model decompositions of 9 using fingers, linking cubes, and number bonds.

The Student Debrief is intended to invite reflection and active processing of the total lesson experience.

Invite students to review their solutions for the Problem Set. They should check work by comparing answers with a partner before going over answers as a class. Look for misconceptions or misunderstandings that can be addressed in the Debrief. Guide students in a conversation to debrief the Problem Set and process the lesson.

You may choose to use any combination of the questions below to lead the discussion.

- How did you know which cube sticks matched the number bonds on the first page of the Problem Set?
- How did the cube sticks you colored help you to finish the number bonds on the second page of the Problem Set?
- How is using your fingers like using cubes to solve a problem?
- When you were working with the cube sticks in today's lesson, did you notice any patterns?
- What are some of the partners you found to make 9? Tell me using an **addition sentence** starting with 9. (As students list the partners, write them on the board to help them see the pattern.)

$$9 = 8 + 1 \qquad 9 = 4 + 5$$
$$9 = 7 + 2 \qquad 9 = 3 + 6$$
$$9 = 6 + 3 \qquad 9 = 2 + 7$$
$$9 = 5 + 4 \qquad 9 = 1 + 8$$

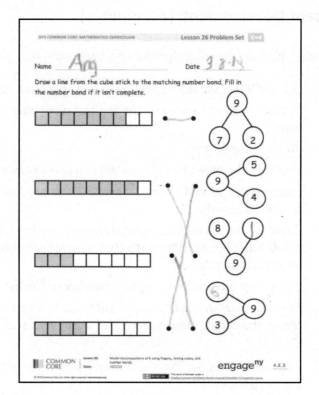

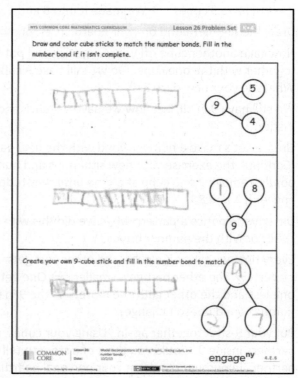

COMMON CORE™   Lesson 26:   Model decompositions of 9 using fingers, linking cubes, and number bonds.
              Date: 11/12/13

4.E.1

Name _____ Date _____

Draw a line from the cube stick to the matching number bond. Fill in the number bond if it isn't complete.

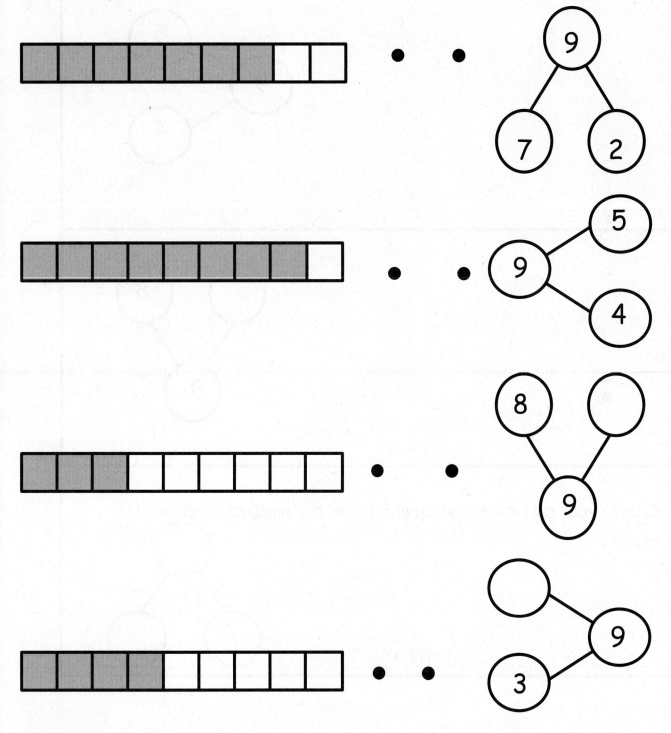

Lesson 26: Model decompositions of 9 using fingers, linking cubes, and number bonds.
Date: 11/12/13

4.E.16

Draw and color cube sticks to match the number bonds. Fill in the number bond if it isn't complete.

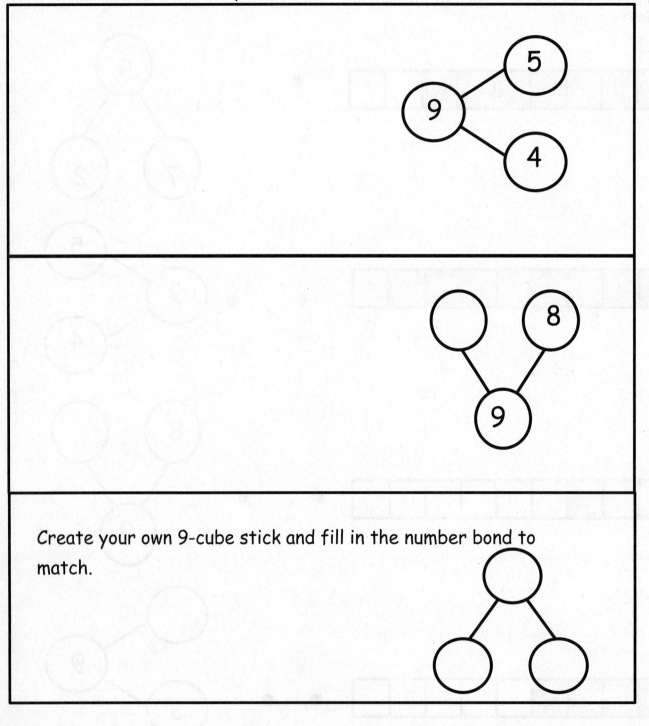

Create your own 9-cube stick and fill in the number bond to match.

Lesson 26: Model decompositions of 9 using fingers, linking cubes, and number bonds.

Date: 11/12/13

4.E.1

Name _____ Date _____

Do the linking cubes sticks match the number bond? Circle yes or no.

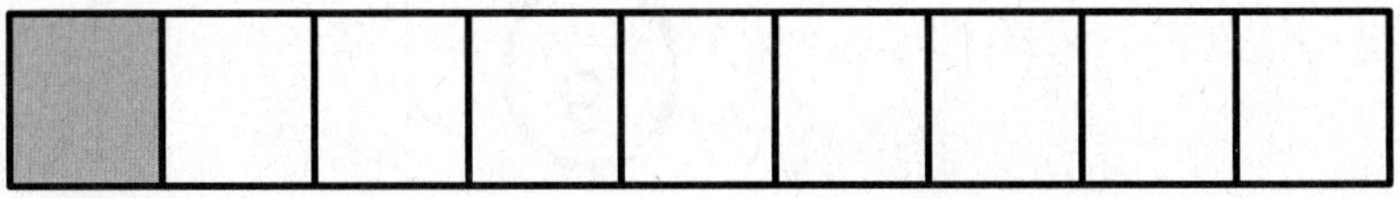

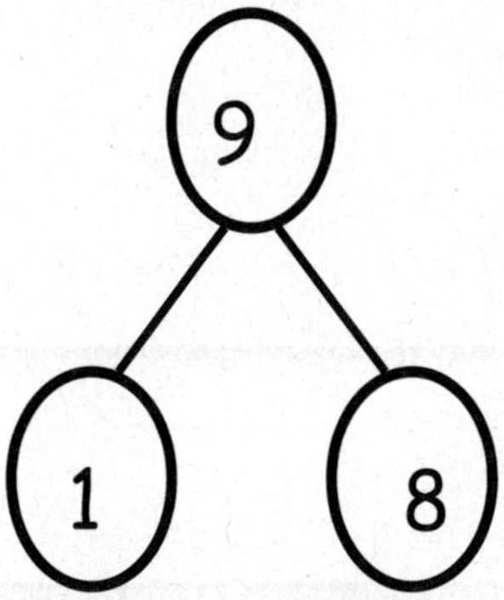

Yes   No

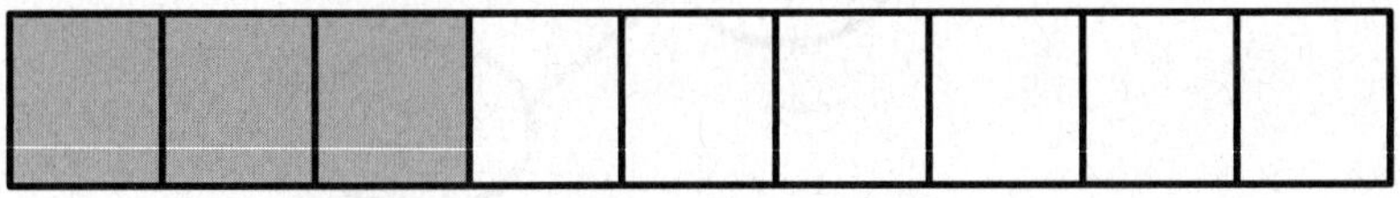

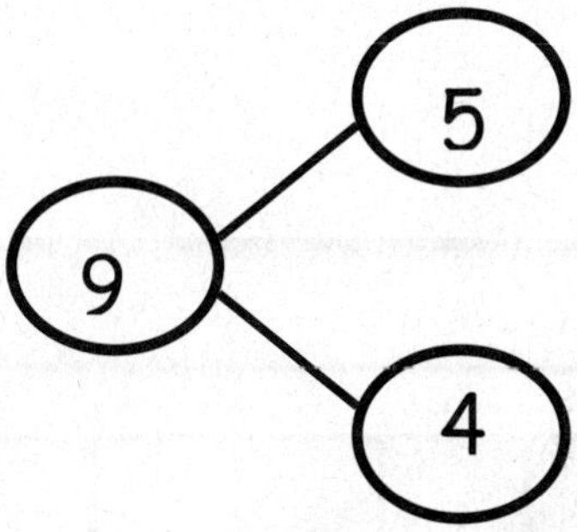

Yes   No

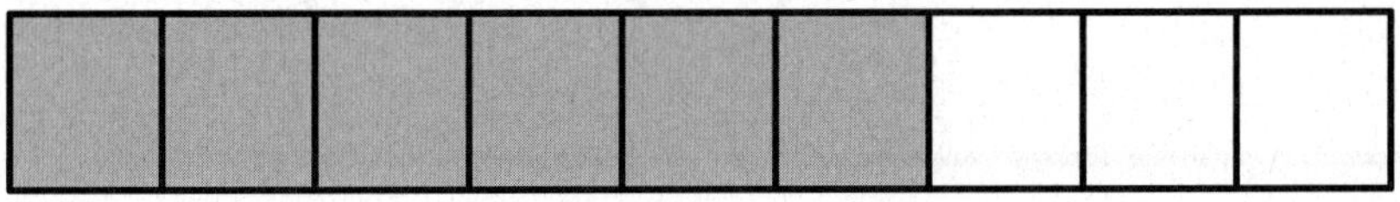

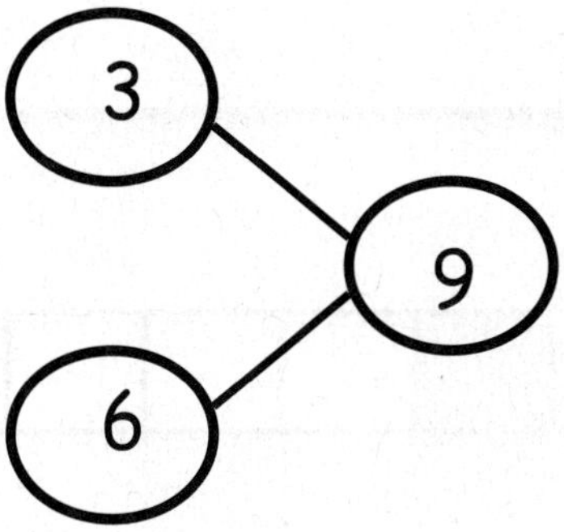

Yes   No

Make the number bond match the cube stick.

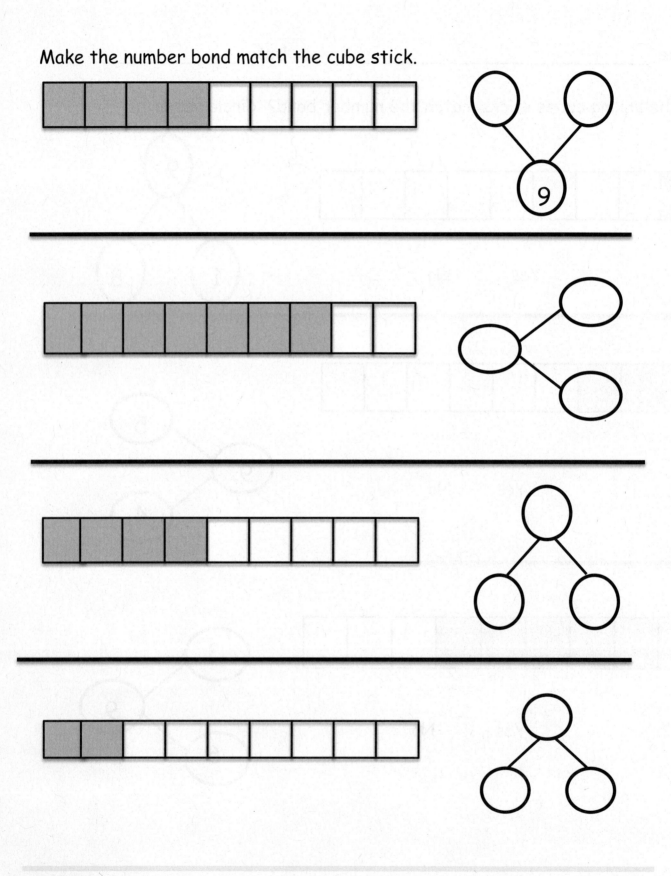

COMMON CORE™   **Lesson 26:**   Model decompositions of 9 using fingers, linking cubes, and number bonds.
Date: 11/12/13

4.E.1

Lesson 27

Objective: Model decompositions of 10 using a story situation, objects, and number bonds.

Suggested Lesson Structure

- ■ Fluency Practice   (12 minutes)
- ■ Application Problem   (5 minutes)
- ☐ Concept Development   (25 minutes)
- ■ Student Debrief   (8 minutes)
- **Total Time**   **(50 minutes)**

Fluency Practice (12 minutes)

- Rekenrek Wave **K.NBT.1**   (3 minutes)
- What Is Less? **K.OA.1**   (5 minutes)
- Take Apart the Array **K.OA.3**   (4 minutes)

Rekenrek Wave (3 minutes)

Materials: (T) 20-bead Rekenrek

Count with the Rekenrek the Say Ten way as described in GK–M4–Lessons 25, but now continue to 20 if students are ready. After introducing each new number name, use a similar sequence as before, while students use the wave hand motions to indicate increasing and decreasing quantities.

Consider showing the numbers in the 5-group orientation as well, so that students can gain flexibility in recognizing the quantities. For example, 13 would be 5 red on the top row, 5 red on the bottom row (mimicking a 5-group arrangement of 10), plus 3 white beads on the top row.

Note: This fluency anticipates the work of GK–Module 5. Developing automaticity with the counting sequence in conventional language facilitates work with teen numbers.

What Is Less? (5 minutes)

Materials: (S) Personal white boards

- T: (Write 2 on the board.) Think of a number that is less than 2. Write it on your board and show me.
- S: (Write 1 or 0.)
- T: Write this **subtraction sentence** on your board: 2 minus 1.

COMMON CORE™ | Lesson 27: Model decompositions of 10 using a story situation, objects, and number bonds.
Date: 11/12/13

4.E.20

S: (Write 2 – 1.)

T: Write the answer and show me.

S: (Write 2 – 1= 1.)

T: Say the subtraction sentence.

S: 2 minus 1 equals 1.

Repeat with 3, 4, and 5. Use each of the smaller numbers students identify to build a subtraction equation (e.g., 3 – 1, 3 – 2). Invite students who choose zero to write a subtraction equation using zero and show it to the class. Addition and subtraction of zero will be covered in GK–M4–Lesson 37.

Note: This activity builds on students' understanding of comparison and builds fluency with subtraction facts for numbers to 5.

Take Apart the Array (4 minutes)

Materials: (S) Array of 10 fluency template inserted into personal white boards

Conduct as described in GK–M4–Lesson 25, but now with decompositions of 10.

Note: This activity prepares students to work with decomposing 10 at the pictorial level.

Application Problem (5 minutes)

Materials: (S) Paper, crayons

You are having a birthday party! You need to have 10 party hats for your friends. Draw 10 simple hats. Color some hats red and some blue. Make a number bond about your picture.

Turn and talk with your partner. Do your pictures look the same? Explain to your partner how you decided which way to color your hats. Talk about how your number bonds are the same or different.

Note: Thinking about different ways to decompose 10 serves as the anticipatory set for the lesson.

Concept Development (25 minutes)

Materials: (T) White board and colored markers (S) 1 chenille wire stem, 10 pony beads of one color, personal white board

T: We were just talking about birthday parties! What if you had a birthday party and received 10 presents? Let me draw squares on the board to show your presents. (Demonstrate.) I have 10 presents on the board. I want to color some yellow and some red. Who has an idea to help me?

S: This is like the party hats! → Let's make 5 yellow and 5 red. → We can show them both on our fingers that way.

COMMON CORE™   Lesson 27:   Model decompositions of 10 using a story situation, objects, and
                                      number bonds.
                       Date: 11/12/13   4.E.21

© 2013 Common Core, Inc. All rights reserved. **commoncore.org**

T: OK, we will make 5 yellow and 5 red. (Demonstrate.) How could I make a number bond about my picture?

S: Put a 10 in the place for the whole because there are 10 presents. → We have 5 yellow and 5 red. → Each of the parts would be 5!

T: Yes, our parts are both 5 this time and we have 10 altogether. Would someone like to come up and make the number bond on the class board for us? The rest of you can show your work on your personal boards. (Allow a student to volunteer to demonstrate. At this point, students should be confident enough in their ability to create number bonds that they should be enthusiastic about demonstrating their work, though offer encouragement and assistance freely!)

T: Did anyone think about the picture in a different way? (Allow several opportunities to create other visual situations with the gifts; each time either demonstrating or allowing individual students to play the role of teacher and model the coloring of the squares and the number bonds on the class board.)

T: Ten is a very special number, isn't it? What seems different about this number from the other ones we have looked at so far?

S: It is bigger! → There are two numerals now! → It takes all of our fingers.

T: Yes! Now, we have 10 ones! You have some beads on your table. Count your beads.

S: 1, 2, 3, 4, 5, 6, 7, 8, 9, 10.

T: We are going to make bracelets to celebrate this very special number! Count your beads again while you lace them onto the chenille stem. I will come around to help you finish your bracelets. (Assist students in tying the bracelets, circulating to ensure accuracy in counting.)

T: Your bracelets are beautiful! Let's play with the beads. What happens if we slide 1 bead to this side and all of the other beads to the other side of the bracelet? Show me on your bracelets.

S: We still have 10 beads on our bracelet. → Now we have 9 on 1 side and just 1 on the other.

T: Interesting! Let's make the number bond for what you just did. Please write it on your personal board while I do it up here. (Demonstrate.) Can anyone help me fill in the parts?

T: I wonder if we could make a number sentence.

S: 10 is 9 and 1. → 10 = 9 + 1.

T: Great job! What if we slide another bead over?

MP.4

NOTES ON MULTIPLE MEANS OF REPRESENTATION:

Give students performing below grade level and students with disabilities who have processing issues a number bond graphic to fill out. This will keep the focus on the math content and with more practice, students will be able to accomplish the task with less scaffolding.

NOTES ON MULTIPLE MEANS OF REPRESENTATION:

Scaffold the lesson for English language learners by pointing to the number sentences "10 is 9 and 1" and "10 = 9 + 1" on the board or word wall as the class discusses them. Refer to the visuals of *parts* and *whole*.

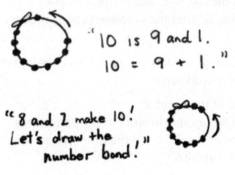

"10 is 9 and 1.
10 = 9 + 1."

"8 and 2 make 10!
Let's draw the
number bond!"

COMMON CORE | Lesson 27:   Model decompositions of 10 using a story situation, objects, and
                    number bonds.
              Date: 11/12/13

4.E.22

© 2013 Common Core, Inc. All rights reserved. commoncore.org

MP.4

S: Now we have 8 on one side and 2 on the other. → We made our 10 into parts of 8 and 2 this time.

T: Let's think about the number bond. What are our parts now? Did our whole change? Draw the new number bond on your personal board.

Repeat the activity, discussion, and drawing of the number bonds on the boards for the whole sequence of partners to 10.

T: With your friend, spend some time being number detectives with your bracelets. Practice this again. Talk about the groups of bead partners you find hidden in 10, and practice drawing the number bond each time. Do you notice any patterns? (Allow time for sharing and discussion.)

T: You may take your bracelets home to show your friends and family. Don't forget to tell them about the number partners! Be sure to bring them back so we can work with them again tomorrow.

Problem Set (10 minutes)

Students should do their personal best to complete the Problem Set within the allotted 10 minutes.

Note: Encourage students to use circles when drawing dragons. They can use the cloud and grass to show which dragons are flying and which are on the ground.

In this lesson, it may again be beneficial for the teacher to read each problem aloud and then to allow the students to work on that exercise. Students with higher-level reading ability could be encouraged to make additional decomposition pictures for 10 on the back of their papers if they finish early.

Student Debrief (8 minutes)

Lesson Objective: Model decompositions of 10 using a story situation, objects, and number bonds.

The Student Debrief is intended to invite reflection and active processing of the total lesson experience.

Invite students to review their solutions for the Problem Set. They should check work by comparing answers with a partner before going over answers as a class. Look for misconceptions or misunderstandings that can be addressed in the Debrief. Guide students in a conversation to debrief the Problem Set and process the lesson.

You may choose to use any combination of the questions below to lead the discussion.

- Look at the baseball problem. How did you know which numbers to write in the parts of the number bond? Are there other ways you could have done it?

COMMON CORE | Lesson 27: Model decompositions of 10 using a story situation, objects, and number bonds.
Date: 11/12/13

4.E.23

© 2013 Common Core, Inc. All rights reserved. commoncore.org

- What strategies did you use when you were making up your own story?

- How did the bracelets help in finding the partners to 10?

- Who can use this bracelet to teach someone how to make number bonds at home tonight? Tell me how you will do it.

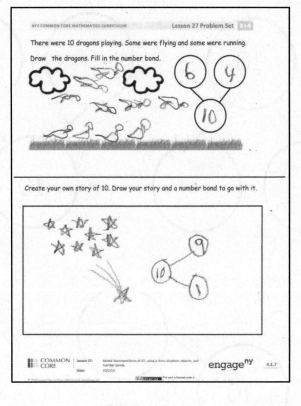

COMMON CORE™ | Lesson 27: | Model decompositions of 10 using a story situation, objects, and number bonds.
| Date: | 11/12/13

4.E.24

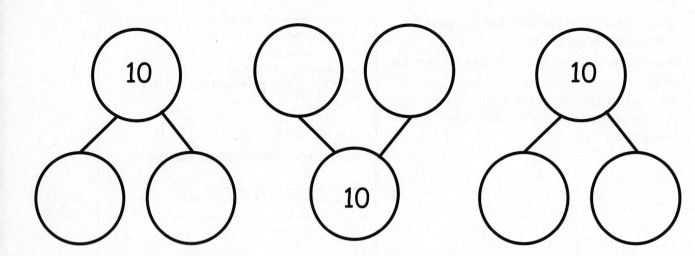

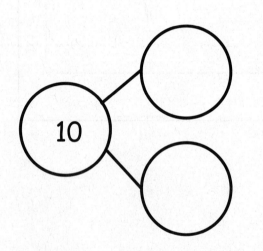

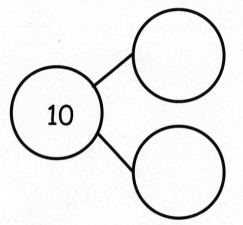

Lesson 27: Model decompositions of 10 using a story situation, objects, and number bonds.

Date: 11/12/13

4.E.25

Name _____   Date _____

Benjamin had 10 bananas. He dropped some of the bananas. Fill in the number bond to show Benjamin's bananas.

Savannah had 10 pairs of glasses. 5 are green and the rest are purple. Color and fill in the number bond.

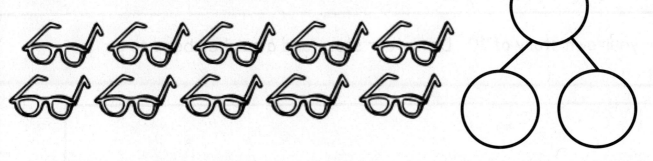

Xavier had 10 baseballs. Some were white and the rest were gray. Draw the balls and color to show how many may be white and gray. Fill in the number bond.

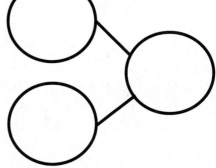

COMMON CORE™

Lesson 27:   Model decompositions of 10 using a story situation, objects, and number bonds.

Date: 11/12/13

4.E.26

There were 10 dragons playing. Some were flying and some were running.
Draw the dragons. Fill in the number bond.

Create your own story of 10. Draw your story and a number bond to go with it.

Lesson 27:   Model decompositions of 10 using a story situation, objects, and
number bonds.

Date: 11/12/13

4.E.27

Name _____   Date _____

Pretend this is your bracelet.

Color 5 beads blue and the rest green. Make a number bond to match.

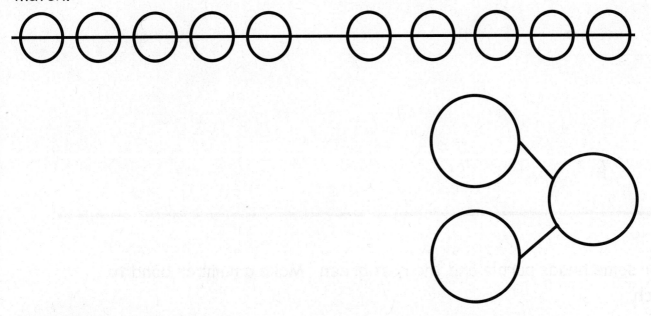

Color some beads yellow and the rest orange. Make a number bond to match.

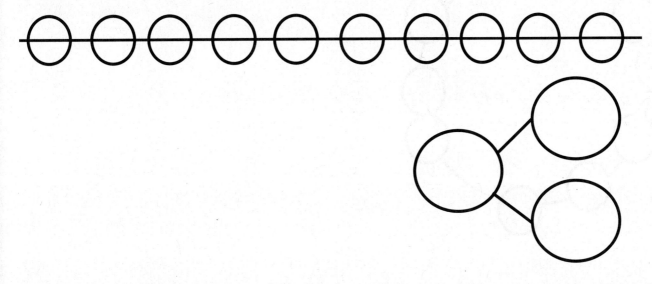

Lesson 27:   Model decompositions of 10 using a story situation, objects, and number bonds.

Date: 11/12/13

4.E.28

Color some beads yellow and the rest black. Make a number bond to match.

○━○━○━○━○━○━○━○━○━○

Color some beads purple and the rest green. Make a number bond to match.

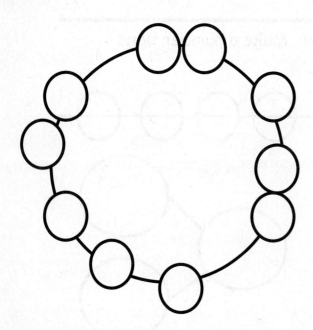

Lesson 27:	Model decompositions of 10 using a story situation, objects, and number bonds.
Date:	11/12/13

4.E.29

Lesson 28

Objective: Model decompositions of 10 using fingers, sets, linking cubes, and number bonds.

Suggested Lesson Structure

■ Fluency Practice   (12 minutes)
■ Application Problem   (5 minutes)
■ Concept Development   (25 minutes)
■ Student Debrief   (8 minutes)

   Total Time   **(50 minutes)**

Fluency Practice (12 minutes)

- Race to 0 Subtraction Game **K.OA.5**   (4 minutes)
- Number Bond Bracelet **K.OA.4**   (3 minutes)
- Make 10 Memory Game **K.OA.3**   (5 minutes)

Race to 0 Subtraction Game (4 minutes)

Materials: (S) Die with the 6-dot side covered

1. Both partners roll their dice and subtract the number on their die from 5. Both partners state their equations respectively.

2. To win the game, subtract a number from 5 that equals 0 (only by rolling a 5). If neither partner rolls a 5 they both state their subtraction sentence out loud.

3. Both partners roll again and subtract the new number on the die from 5. Both partners state their respective new equations.

4. Continue the subtraction race, rolling the die and subtracting with speed and accuracy until one of the partners rolls a 5 and says, "5 − 5 = 0."

5. They must reach 0 exactly, stating each subtraction equation before they roll again.

Here is an example of how the game might unfold:

Partner A: Rolls a 2, and says 5 − 2 = 3.

Partner B: Rolls a 3, and says 5 − 3 = 2.

Partner A: Rolls a 4, and says 5 − 4 = 1.

Partner B: Rolls a 5, and says 5 − 5 = 0, and wins the race to 0.

Begin a new round if time permits.

Lesson 28:	Model decompositions of 10 using fingers, sets, linking cubes, and number bonds.
Date:	11/12/13

4.E.30

Note: This activity develops automaticity with subtraction within 5, part of the fluency goal for this grade.

Number Bond Bracelet (3 minutes)

Materials: (S) Number bonds of 10 bracelet from GK–M4–Lesson 27, personal white board

> T: Do you remember how many beads are on your number bond bracelets?
>
> S: 10!
>
> T: Is 10 the whole (emphasize with hand gesture, two hands clasped together) or part of the beads? (Pull two hands apart to reinforce the meaning.)
>
> S: Whole.
>
> T: Yes. Take 1 of the beads, and slide it away from the rest. Is 1 the whole, or a part? (Emphasize with gestures as before.)
>
> S: Part.
>
> T: Good. Raise your hand when you know the other part. (Wait for all hands to go up, then signal.) Ready?
>
> S: 9.
>
> T: Yes, now write the number bond.

Continue to provide guidance as necessary, then direct students to work independently through the partners of 10 using their bracelets.

Note: This activity helps students develop automaticity with partners to 10, crucial to learning more efficient methods of addition in Grade 1.

Make 10 Memory Game (5 minutes)

Materials: (S) Cards with quantities of 0–10 (use only dots, dice, and fingers) per pair, 1 extra 5-card (so one of the partners can be 5 and 5), (cards can be found in GK–M4–Lessons 1 and 7)

Conduct activity as outlined in GK–M4–Lesson 26 but now have students find partners of 10.

Scaffold: Provide each partner with a stick of 10 cubes to help them determine the missing part. For example, a student turns over 4 then breaks off 4 cubes, revealing 6 as the missing part. Students then know to look for the card with the number 6.

Note: Students will find the hidden partners of 10 in support of the day's work with composition and decomposition.

Application Problem (5 minutes)

Materials: (S) Small ball of clay, personal white board

Use your clay to make 10 tiny grapes. With your marker, draw a pretty plate on your board. Now, put some of the grapes on the plate.

Lesson 28:   Model decompositions of 10 using fingers, sets, linking cubes, and
              number bonds.
Date: 11/12/13

4.E.31

How many grapes do you have in all? How many grapes are on the plate? How many are not on the plate?

Draw a number bond about your work and talk about it with your partner. Did she do it in the same way?

Take the grapes off and try it again!

Note: Continuing yesterday's practice with the decomposition of 10 leads into further work with this topic in the Concept Development.

Concept Development (25 minutes)

NOTES ON MULTIPLE MEANS OF ACTION AND EXPRESSION:

Challenge above grade level students by asking them how they would complete their number bond if all the grapes were placed on the plate, and as a follow-up, if all the grapes remained on the table.

Materials: (S) 2 linking cube 5-sticks, a half sheet of red construction paper to represent a picnic blanket, personal white board

T: You just did a lot of work with your grapes! Who can tell me one way they grouped them?

S: I had 8 on my plate and 2 not on the plate.

T: Everyone, show me a pretend set of 8 grapes using your fingers. Show me in the Math way. How many fingers are you still holding down?

S: I have 2 down!

T: How many fingers are up?

S: There are 8 fingers up. → 8 up and 2 down. → That is just like the parts in the number bond.

T: You are right! You have 10 fingers in all, but you showed the 8 and the 2 in different ways with your fingers. This time, the up-and-down fingers make the parts of 10. Who arranged their grapes in a different way? Could you show your idea to us with your fingers?

S: I made 1 and 9. → I had 5 and 5.

T: Let's practice showing these number partners with our fingers, too. (Allow time for practice and discussion.) How are your fingers like number bonds for 10? (Allow students to describe the relationship.)

T: You have some cubes in front of you. Count your cubes.

S: There are two 5-sticks. → I just counted mine all up: 1, 2, 3, 4, 5, 6, 7, 8, 9, 10. → Fives are partners to 10! I had a 5-stick and 5 more.

T: Put all of your linking cubes together. Now imagine with me for a minute. It is a beautiful summer day at the park, and you are having a picnic with your friends. Now imagine that 10 ants come to share your picnic!

T: Let's pretend your paper is a little picnic blanket. It is not wise to play with real ants, so we will act

NOTES ON MULTIPLE MEANS OF ACTION AND EXPRESSION:

As students are invited to imagine the picnic story, scaffold for English language learners by pointing to or showing a visual of an ant, and illustrate how the ants crawled away from the picnic blanket. Students will be able to tackle the math if they understand the story situation being created.

out the story using our linking cubes instead. How many ants do we have?

S: 10!

T: Put all of the ants on your blanket. Now, pretend 1 ant got full and crawled away. Break off a linking cube and make it crawl off the blanket. How could we talk about this with math words?

S: There are still 10 ants in the whole story, but now we have parts of 1 and 9. → This is just like what we did with our bracelets! → One is off the blanket and 9 are on the blanket.

T: Good thinking! Draw a number bond to tell about the ant that crawled away. Hold your boards up so I can see your work. (Quickly scan for accuracy.)

MP.8

T: Imagine that another ant got full, too, and left the blanket. Break off another cube and put it with its full friend. Who can tell me about what you see now?

S: We still have 10 cubes, but now our parts are different. → Now we have 2 and 8. → It is like a pattern, the same with as the bracelets. → This one is growing and this one is getting shorter!

T: Draw a new number bond to show the new parts. (Circulate to ensure accuracy.)

T: With your partner, continue to act out the story as the ants get full one by one! Each time, make a new number bond about the hidden partners you find for 10. (Allow time for sharing, modeling, and discussion.) Now, put your 10-sticks together again, and act out a picnic new story. You can choose how many are on the blanket each time. Don't forget to make your number bonds! (Allow time for extra partner practice.)

Problem Set (10 minutes)

Students should do their personal best to complete the Problem Set within the allotted 10 minutes

Student Debrief (8 minutes)

Lesson Objective: Model decompositions of 10 using fingers, sets, linking cubes, and number bonds.

The Student Debrief is intended to invite reflection and active processing of the total lesson experience.

Invite students to review their solutions for the Problem Set. They should check work by comparing answers with a partner before going over answers as a class. Look for misconceptions or misunderstandings that can be addressed in the Debrief. Guide students in a conversation to debrief the Problem Set and process the lesson.

You may choose to use any combination of the questions below to lead the discussion.

- How did you know which number bond to match with which linking cube stick in your Problem Set?
- What did you think about when you had to draw your own linking cube sticks?

COMMON CORE   Lesson 28:   Model decompositions of 10 using fingers, sets, linking cubes, and number bonds.
    Date: 11/12/13

4.E.33

© 2013 Common Core, Inc. All rights reserved. commoncore.org

- How is what we did today like what we did yesterday with our bracelets?
- How are your fingers like number bonds of 10?
- How can you show 6 and 4 as partners of 10 on your fingers? Is 6 a part or a whole? (Part.) What is the other part? What is the whole?

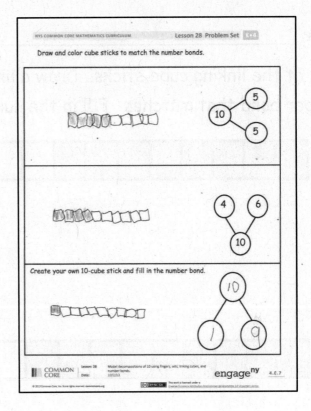

 **Lesson 28:**   Model decompositions of 10 using fingers, sets, linking cubes, and number bonds.

Date: 11/12/13

4.E.34

© 2013 Common Core, Inc. All rights reserved. **commoncore.org**

Name _____ Date _____

Look at the linking cube sticks. Draw a line from the cube sticks to the number bond that matches. Fill in the number bond if it is not complete.

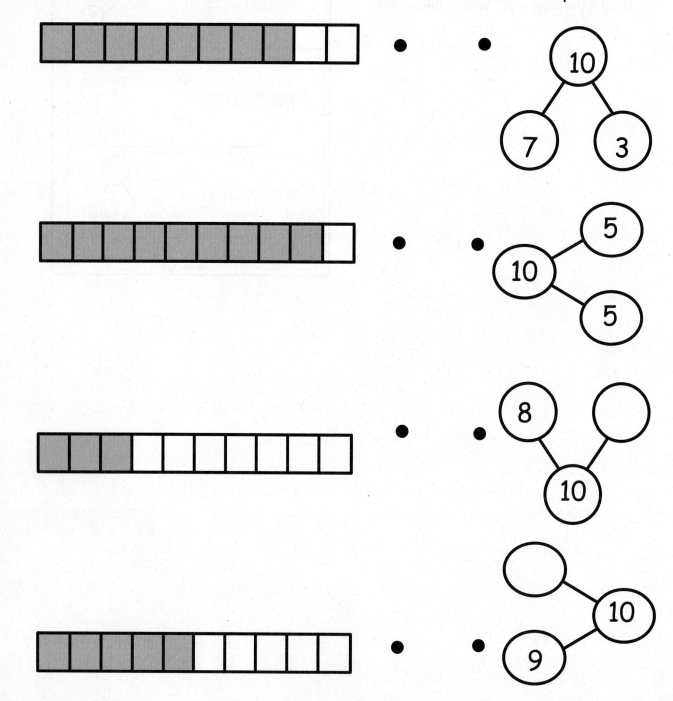

COMMON CORE™

Lesson 28: Model decompositions of 10 using fingers, sets, linking cubes, and number bonds.

Date: 11/12/13

4.E.35

Draw and color cube sticks to match the number bonds.

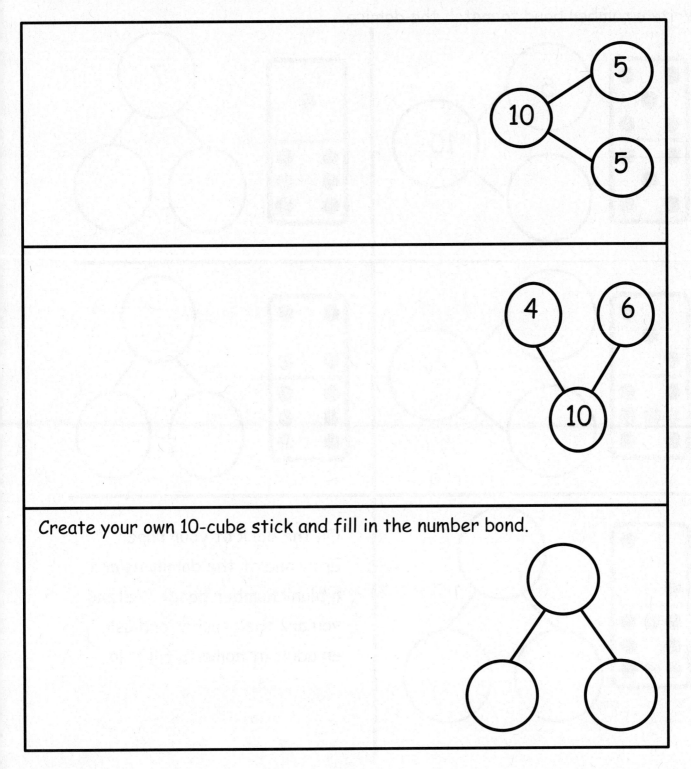

Create your own 10-cube stick and fill in the number bond.

Lesson 28:   Model decompositions of 10 using fingers, sets, linking cubes, and
number bonds.

Date: 11/12/13

4.E.36

Name _____   Date _____

Write a number bond to match the domino.

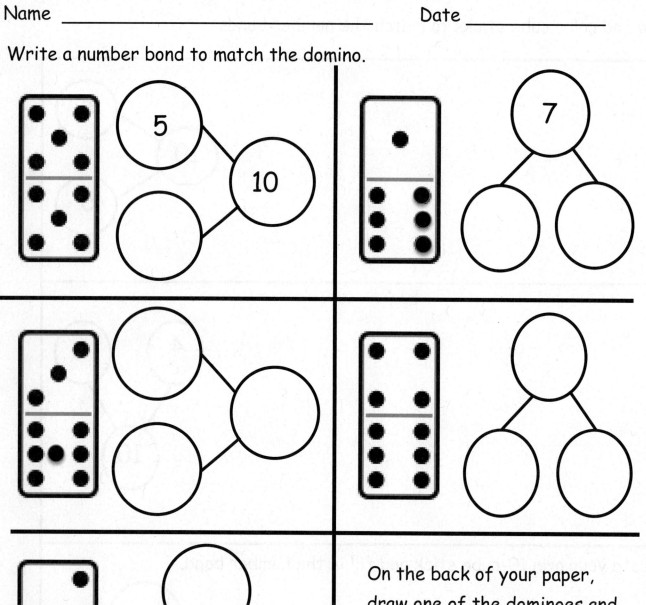

On the back of your paper, draw one of the dominoes and a blank number bond. Pretend you are the teacher and ask an adult at home to fill it in.

COMMON CORE™

Lesson 28:   Model decompositions of 10 using fingers, sets, linking cubes, and number bonds.

Date: 11/12/13

4.E.37

Topic F

Addition with Totals of 9 and 10

K.OA.2

Focus Standard:	K.OA.2	Solve addition and subtraction word problems, and add and subtract within 10, e.g., by using objects or drawings to represent the problem.
Instructional Days:	4	
Coherence -Links from:	GPK–M5	Numerals to 5, Addition and Subtraction Stories, Counting to 20
-Links to:	G1–M1	Sums and Differences to 10

Topic F asks students to connect their understanding of number pairs for 9 and 10 to addition expressions and equations. Core Fluency Practice Sets and Sprints are introduced in this topic to give students practice adding and subtracting numbers to 5 quickly and accurately (**K.OA.5**).

In Lessons 29 and 30, students pictorially represent composition and decomposition addition stories using 5-group drawings and equations with no unknown. Decomposition: "There were 9 flowers. Five were red and 4 were yellow." Composition: "Bob picked 6 red flowers. Then he picked 4 yellow flowers, now he has 10 flowers."

Lesson 31 has opportunities for students to solve *add to with result unknown* and *put together with total unknown* problems with totals of 9 and 10. Both of these problem types are represented by the same equation, A + B = C, with the difference being that *add to result unknown* problem types embed an action within the story. Conversely, *put together with total unknown* problem types join parts with no action. The latter situation is a more complex problem type for kindergartners to consider because there is no movement of one of the parts to support the mental act of joining inherent in addition (e.g., counting on one part to the other one at a time).

The final lesson in the topic deals with the last addition situation for kindergartners, solving *put together* with *both addends unknown* word problems (C = ___ + ___) with totals of 9 and 10 using 5-group drawings, pictures, and equations. All four lessons in this topic correspond to those of Topic C, but with totals of 9 and 10.

This topic builds student understanding of addition within 10 while providing practice with multiple addition situations appropriate for kindergarteners. Due to the length of this module, there is the option to take a day and a half to administer Topics E and F of the end-of-module assessment at the end of Lesson 32. This will identify students who may need more support and allow more time to reassess these students throughout the module.

A Teaching Sequence Towards Mastery of Addition with Totals of 9 and 10

Objective 1: Represent pictorial decomposition and composition addition stories to 9 with 5-group drawings and equations with no unknown.
(Lesson 29)

Objective 2: Represent pictorial decomposition and composition addition stories to 10 with 5-group drawings and equations with no unknown.
(Lesson 30)

Objective 3: Solve *add to with total unknown* and *put together with total unknown* problems with totals of 9 and 10.
(Lesson 31)

Objective 4: Solve *both addends unknown* word problems with totals of 9 and 10 using 5-group drawings.
(Lesson 32)

Topic F: Addition with Totals of 9 and 10
Date: 11/12/13

4.F.2

Lesson 29

Objective: Represent pictorial decomposition and composition addition stories to 9 with 5-group drawings and equations with no unknown.

Suggested Lesson Structure

- ■ Fluency Practice   (13 minutes)
- ■ Application Problem   (4 minutes)
- ■ Concept Development   (25 minutes)
- ■ Student Debrief   (8 minutes)

    Total Time   **(50 minutes)**

Fluency Practice (13 minutes)

- Grade K Core Fluency Differentiated Practice Sets **K.OA.5**   (5 minutes)
- 1, 2, 3, Sit on 10 and 20 **K.CC.2**   (4 minutes)
- 5-Group Flashes **K.CC.5**   (4 minutes)

Grade K Core Fluency Differentiated Practice Sets (5 minutes)

Materials: (S) Core Fluency Practice Sets

Note: During GK–M4–Topic F and for the remainder of this module, each day's fluency includes an opportunity for review and mastery of the sums and differences with totals through 5 by means of the Core Fluency Practice Sets or Sprints. Five options are provided in this lesson for the Core Fluency Practice Set, with Sheet A being the most simple addition fluency of the grade and Sheet E being the most complex (including addition and subtraction). Start all students on Sheet A. Keep a record of student progress so that you can move students to more complex sheets when they are ready.

Students complete as many problems as they can in 96 seconds (6 seconds per problem). We recommend 100% accuracy and completion before moving to the next level. Collect any Practice Sheets that have been completed within the 96 seconds and check the answers. If students did not finish, encourage them to take the sheets home and continue their work. The next time Core Fluency Practice Sets are used,

**NOTES ON
MULTIPLE MEANS OF
ENGAGEMENT:**

Timing students' work in kindergarten is a sensitive issue. Work through any social or emotional issues that surface.

- Encourage students to enjoy practice; show them that practice leads to improvement. For example, "Today you got 4 + 1 quickly whereas yesterday you got stuck on that one. How did you practice to get better?"

- Support them in focusing on their own improvement rather than competing with their peers.

- Have conversations about how we are all different and that our job is to do our personal best.

COMMON CORE | Lesson 29: | Represent pictorial decomposition and composition addition stories
            | | to 9 with 5-group drawings and equations with no unknown.
            | Date: | 11/12/13

4.F.3

students who have successfully completed their set today can be provided with the next level and the other students can work on a new Sheet A.

Consider assigning early finishers a counting pattern and start number (e.g., count forward starting at 5, count backward starting at 10). Celebrate improvement as well as advancement. Students should be encouraged to compete with themselves rather than their peers. Interview students on practice strategies. Notify caring adults of each child's progress.

1, 2, 3, Sit on 10 and 20 (4 minutes)

Note: In this activity, students improve on rote counting to 20, a necessary skill for success in Module 5.

> T: (Call students to stand in a circle on the rug. Refer to GK–M1–Lesson 22 for 1, 2, 3, Sit on 10.) We're going to play a fast counting game. You remember we used to play 1, 2, 3, Sit on 10. Well, now you can count to 20! Remember, each person says the next three numbers. So, if you come after 10 you say?
>
> S: 11, 12, 13.
>
> T: Then the next person says?
>
> S: 14, 15, 16.
>
> T: And the next person?
>
> S: 17, 18, 19.
>
> T: Here comes the change. The next person says 20, and they have to?
>
> S: Sit.
>
> T: That's right! Should you be sad if you have to sit?
>
> S: No.
>
> T: Wait until you see what happens at the end. Ok, let's get started.
>
> S: 1, 2, 3.
>
> S: 4, 5, 6.

Proceed around the circle to 20, and then start again at 1. Continue until all students are sitting.

5-Group Flashes (4 minutes)

Materials: (T) Large 5-group cards (1–4) (S) 5-group cards

Note: This activity gives students practice subitizing or counting quantities in 5-group configurations in preparation for the day's objective.

Conduct activity as described in GK–M4–Lesson 25. This time, work with numbers to 8.

NOTES ON MULTIPLE MEANS OF ACTION AND EXPRESSION:

Some students may not be ready for Practice Sets. Invite them to join you in a "get ready" group, beginning with effectively using their fingers to model the problems, as the others solve the problems. Consider allowing any students to join the group even if you feel they are ready. This may diffuse the stress so that they can bridge to the Practice Set.

COMMON CORE

Lesson 29: Represent pictorial decomposition and composition addition stories to 9 with 5-group drawings and equations with no unknown.

Date: 11/12/13

4.F.4

Application Problem (4 minutes)

Materials: (S) 9 pennies, pencil, paper

Emma had 9 pennies. Show her pennies in the middle of the desk.

She wanted to use 4 of her pennies to buy some gum and 5 pennies to buy a balloon. Count and slide apart the pennies she needs to buy the gum and for the balloon. On your paper, show the number bond that tells about her pennies now.

Now slide your groups of pennies together again. How many pennies in all? Would you need to create a new number bond about what you just did? Turn and talk to your partner about your work.

Note: The physical decomposition and composition of 9 with the pennies, and the subsequent thinking about the number bond, will serve as the anticipatory set for representations with equations in this lesson.

> **NOTES ON MULTIPLE MEANS OF REPRESENTATION:**
>
> Model the Application Problem for students with disabilities. As you ask students to count and slide apart the 4 pennies and 5 pennies, count 4 pennies as you move these to one side and count 5 pennies as you move these to the other side. Have students practice a few times in front of you until you are satisfied that they can carry on independently.

Concept Development (25 minutes)

Materials: (S) Personal white boards

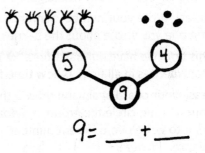

T: Listen to my story. Toby had 9 tasty berries. Five were strawberries and 4 were blueberries. How many berries did he have in all?

S: 9.

T: How many strawberries?

S: 5.

T: How many blueberries?

S: 4.

T: Excellent listening! Draw Toby's berries on the blank side of your white board and I will draw them here. (Demonstrate.)

T: Count the strawberries and write that number underneath them. Now count the blueberries and write that number. We want to use your numbers to make a number bond and a number sentence about Toby's berries. How many berries in all?

S: 9!

T: Great! Let's make a number bond with those numbers. (Demonstrate using the 5 and 4 previously written under the drawings.)

T: Let's make our number sentence now. We could begin our number sentence with 9, to show how many berries in all. (Write 9 = ___ + ___.) How do I know what numbers to write in the blanks?

S: Put in the strawberries and the blueberries! → Those are the parts!

Lesson 29: Represent pictorial decomposition and composition addition stories to 9 with 5-group drawings and equations with no unknown.

Date: 11/12/13

4.F.5

T: (Demonstrate.) Yes! Write the number sentence on your board, too. Turn to your partner and read the number sentence. Talk about how you knew which number should go where. (Circulate to ensure understanding.)

T: Erase your board. I have another story for you. Kate had 6 beads. Her friend gave her 3 more beads. Now Kate has 9 beads. How many beads did Kate have at first? (6.) How many did her friend give her? (3.) How many beads does Kate have all together? (9).

T: On your personal board, draw the number of beads Kate had at first in the 5-group way. Let's fill in these beads to help us keep track of them. (Demonstrate.) Now, draw the beads her friend gave her using empty circles. (Demonstrate using empty circles.) How could we make a number sentence about the story and your drawing?

S: Write the numbers for the parts first! Then, we can put the total at the end after our equal sign.

T: (Write ___ + ___ = 9 on the board.) What number should go in the first blank?

S: Six for how many beads she had at first.

T: And the second blank?

S: Three for the ones her friend gave her.

T: Great! Write your number sentence on your board. How is this number sentence different from the first one you wrote about the berries?

S: This time we have our parts first. → Last time we put how many berries in all first. (Allow time for discussion.)

MP.7

T: Erase your board again and draw 9 the 5-group way. With your marker, circle the group of 5 dots at the top. We want to write two different number sentences about your picture. (Write 9 = ___ + ___ and ___ + ___ = 9 on the board.) Who can help me fill in the blanks? (Allow time for discussion.) Write the number sentences on your board and show your partner.

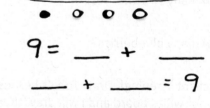

T: Erase your board. Work with your partner to draw 8 the 5-group way. See if you can find the 5 inside the 8, circle it, and create number sentences about your picture. (Allow time for partner work, allowing students to share their equations with the class. If time permits, ask them to work with 5-group pictures and decompositions for 7 and 6 as well.)

Problem Set (10 minutes)

Students should do their personal best to complete the Problem Set within the allotted 10 minutes.

COMMON CORE™

Lesson 29:   Represent pictorial decomposition and composition addition stories to 9 with 5-group drawings and equations with no unknown.

Date: 11/12/13

4.F.6

Student Debrief (8 minutes)

Lesson Objective: Represent pictorial decomposition and composition addition stories to 9 with 5-group drawings and equations with no unknown.

The Student Debrief is intended to invite reflection and active processing of the total lesson experience.

Invite students to review their solutions for the Problem Set. They should check work by comparing answers with a partner before going over answers as a class. Look for misconceptions or misunderstandings that can be addressed in the Debrief. Guide students in a conversation to debrief the Problem Set and process the lesson.

You may choose to use any combination of the questions below to lead the discussion.

- How did the number bonds help you to make your number sentences in the Problem Set?
- How do you know where the whole or total goes in your number sentence? The parts? (Check for understanding that the sum can be represented on either side of the equation.)
- When you drew your marbles, was it helpful to make them in the 5-group way?
- How did circling the group of 5 help you with your counting when using 5-groups? What were your strategies?

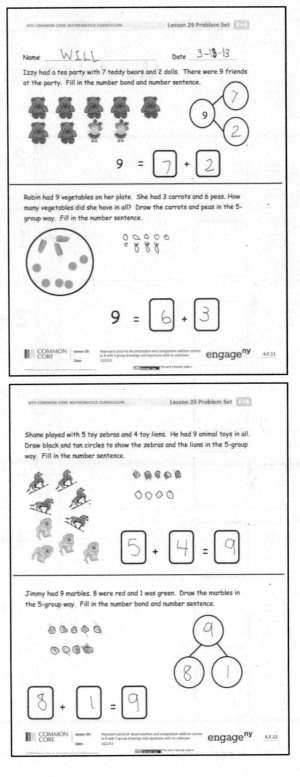

COMMON CORE™   Lesson 29:   Represent pictorial decomposition and composition addition stories to 9 with 5-group drawings and equations with no unknown.

Date: 11/12/13

4.F.7

Name _____   Date _____

My Addition Practice

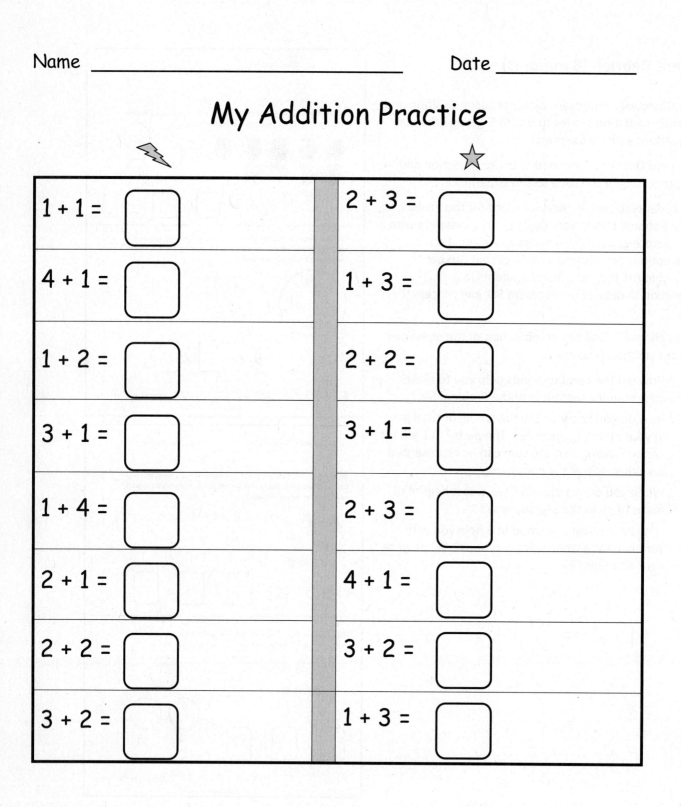

1 + 1 =	2 + 3 =
4 + 1 =	1 + 3 =
1 + 2 =	2 + 2 =
3 + 1 =	3 + 1 =
1 + 4 =	2 + 3 =
2 + 1 =	4 + 1 =
2 + 2 =	3 + 2 =
3 + 2 =	1 + 3 =

Lesson 29:   Represent pictorial decomposition and composition addition stories
to 9 with 5-group drawings and equations with no unknown.

Date: 11/12/13

4.F.8

Name _____   Date _____

My Decomposition Practice

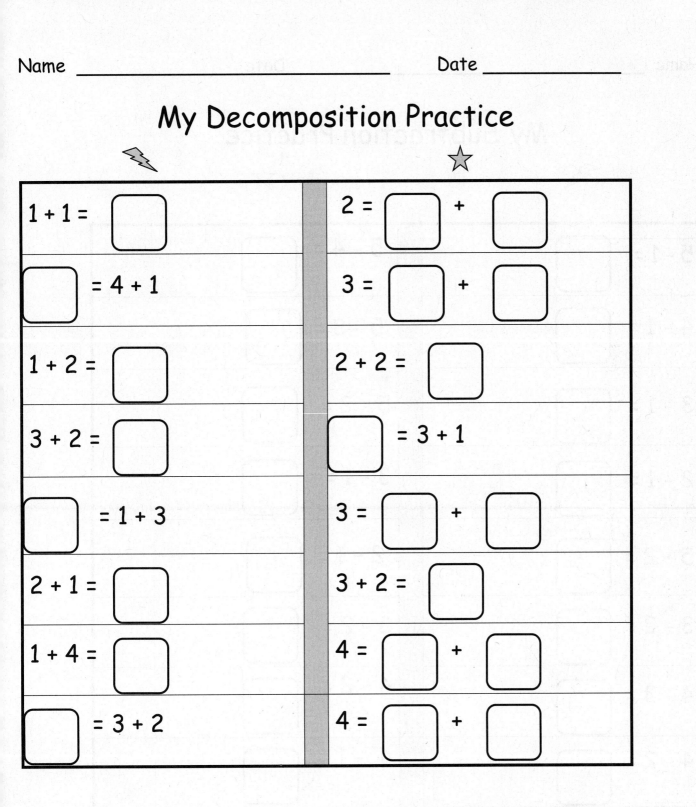

1 + 1 = ☐

☐ = 4 + 1

1 + 2 = ☐

3 + 2 = ☐

☐ = 1 + 3

2 + 1 = ☐

1 + 4 = ☐

☐ = 3 + 2

2 = ☐ + ☐

3 = ☐ + ☐

2 + 2 = ☐

☐ = 3 + 1

3 = ☐ + ☐

3 + 2 = ☐

4 = ☐ + ☐

4 = ☐ + ☐

COMMON CORE™

Lesson 29:

Date: 11/12/13

Represent pictorial decomposition and composition addition stories
to 9 with 5-group drawings and equations with no unknown.

4.F.9

Name _____   Date _____

My Subtraction Practice

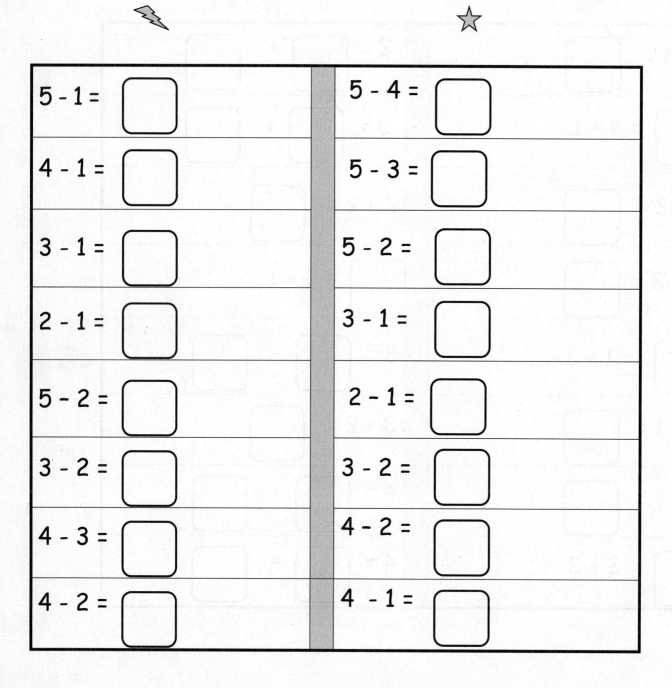

5 - 1 = ☐   5 - 4 = ☐

4 - 1 = ☐   5 - 3 = ☐

3 - 1 = ☐   5 - 2 = ☐

2 - 1 = ☐   3 - 1 = ☐

5 - 2 = ☐   2 - 1 = ☐

3 - 2 = ☐   3 - 2 = ☐

4 - 3 = ☐   4 - 2 = ☐

4 - 2 = ☐   4 - 1 = ☐

COMMON CORE ™   **Lesson 29:**   Represent pictorial decomposition and composition addition stories
                                          to 9 with 5-group drawings and equations with no unknown.

                  Date: 11/12/13   4.F.10

Name _____   Date _____

My Subtraction Practice

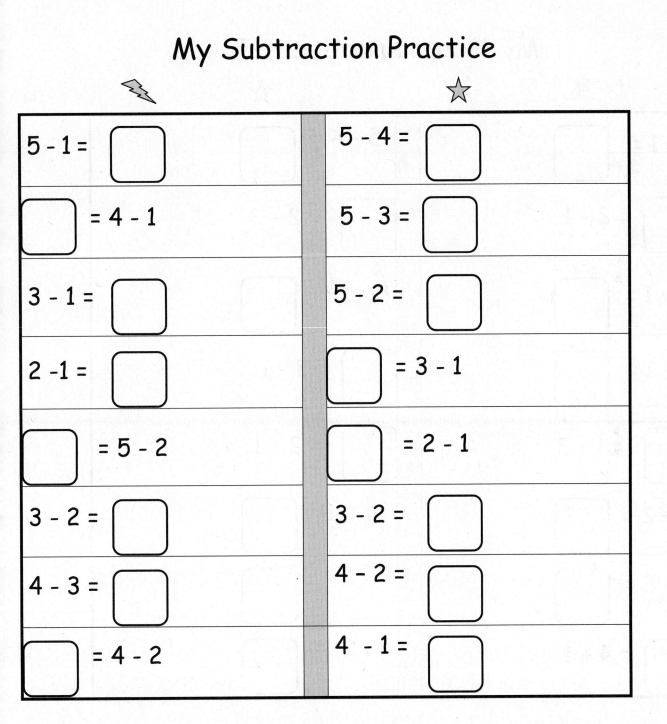

5 - 1 = ☐

☐ = 4 - 1

3 - 1 = ☐

2 - 1 = ☐

☐ = 5 - 2

3 - 2 = ☐

4 - 3 = ☐

☐ = 4 - 2

5 - 4 = ☐

5 - 3 = ☐

5 - 2 = ☐

☐ = 3 - 1

☐ = 2 - 1

3 - 2 = ☐

4 - 2 = ☐

4 - 1 = ☐

COMMON CORE™   **Lesson 29:**   Represent pictorial decomposition and composition addition stories
                                      to 9 with 5-group drawings and equations with no unknown.

                     Date: 11/12/13

4.F.11

Name _____   Date _____

My Mixed Practice to 5

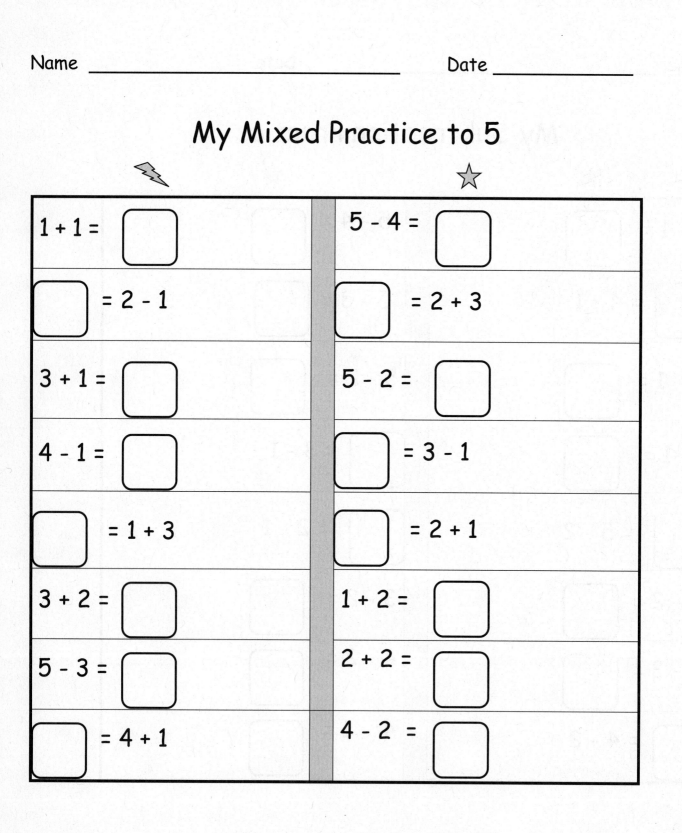

$1 + 1 =$ ☐	$5 - 4 =$ ☐
☐ $= 2 - 1$	☐ $= 2 + 3$
$3 + 1 =$ ☐	$5 - 2 =$ ☐
$4 - 1 =$ ☐	☐ $= 3 - 1$
☐ $= 1 + 3$	☐ $= 2 + 1$
$3 + 2 =$ ☐	$1 + 2 =$ ☐
$5 - 3 =$ ☐	$2 + 2 =$ ☐
☐ $= 4 + 1$	$4 - 2 =$ ☐

COMMON CORE™

Lesson 29:   Represent pictorial decomposition and composition addition stories to 9 with 5-group drawings and equations with no unknown.

Date: 11/12/13

4.F.12

Name _____   Date _____

Izzy had a tea party with 7 teddy bears and 2 dolls. There were 9 friends at the party. Fill in the number bond and number sentence.

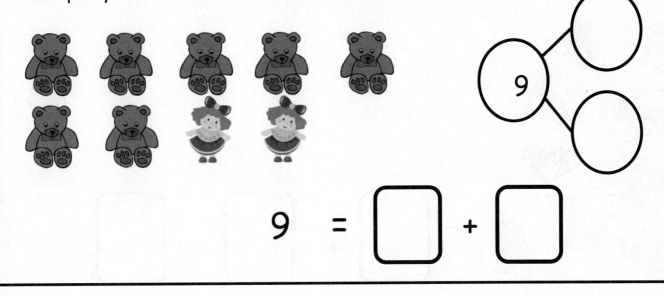

9 = ☐ + ☐

Robin had 9 vegetables on her plate. She had 3 carrots and 6 peas. How many vegetables did she have in all? Draw the carrots and peas in the 5-group way. Fill in the number sentence.

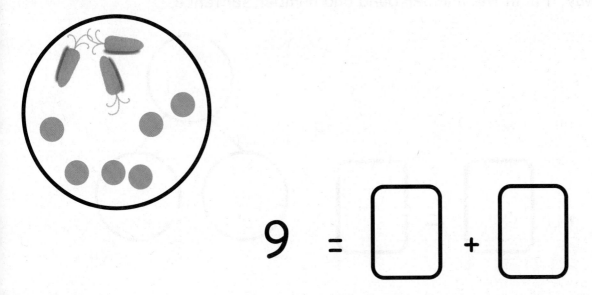

9 = ☐ + ☐

COMMON CORE™   Lesson 29:   Represent pictorial decomposition and composition addition stories
                                    to 9 with 5-group drawings and equations with no unknown.   **4.F.13**
                          Date: 11/12/13

Shane played with 5 toy zebras and 4 toy lions. He had 9 animal toys in all. Draw black and tan circles to show the zebras and the lions in the 5-group way. Fill in the number sentence.

Jimmy had 9 marbles. 8 were red and 1 was green. Draw the marbles in the 5-group way. Fill in the number bond and number sentence.

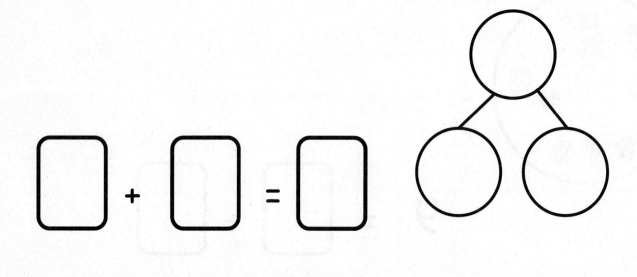

Lesson 29:   Represent pictorial decomposition and composition addition stories
                to 9 with 5-group drawings and equations with no unknown.

Date: 11/12/13

4.F.1

© 2013 Common Core, Inc. All rights reserved. commoncore.org

Name _____ Date _____

Jack found 7 balls while cleaning the toy bin. He found 6 basketballs and 1 baseball. Fill in the number sentence and the number bond.

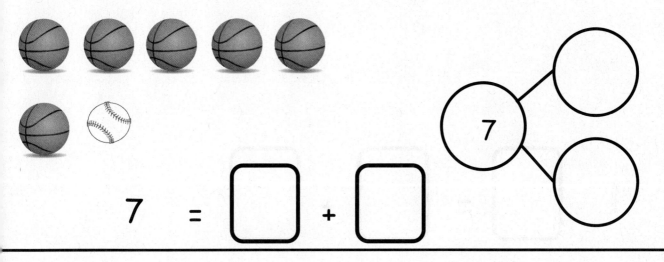

Jack found 7 mitts and 2 bats. He found 9 things. Fill in the number sentence and the number bond.

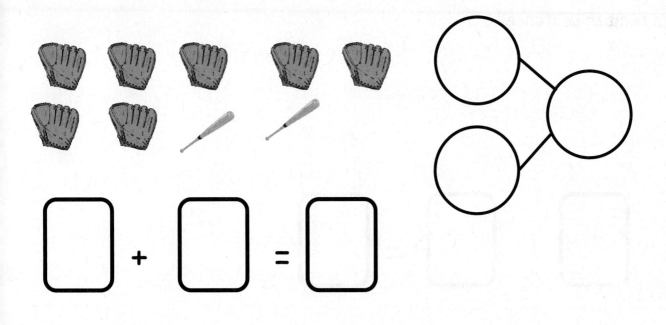

COMMON CORE™   **Lesson 29:**   Represent pictorial decomposition and composition addition stories
to 9 with 5-group drawings and equations with no unknown.

Date: 11/12/13

4.F.15

Jack found 8 hockey pucks and 1 hockey stick. He found 9 hockey things.
Draw the hockey pucks and stick in the 5-group way. Fill in the number
sentence.

Jack needs a snack. He found 9 pieces of fruit. 5 were strawberries and
4 were grapes. Draw the strawberries and grapes in the 5-group way. Fill
in the number sentence.

Lesson 29:   Represent pictorial decomposition and composition addition stories
               to 9 with 5-group drawings and equations with no unknown.
Date: 11/12/13

© 2013 Common Core, Inc. All rights reserved. commoncore.org

4.F.1

Lesson 30

Objective: Represent pictorial decomposition and composition addition stories to 10 with 5-group drawings and equations with no unknown.

Suggested Lesson Structure

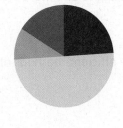

■ Fluency Practice   (12 minutes)
■ Application Problem   (5 minutes)
■ Concept Development   (25 minutes)
■ Student Debrief   (8 minutes)
Total Time   **(50 minutes)**

Fluency Practice (12 minutes)

- Grade K Core Fluency Differentiated Practice Sets **K.OA.5**   (5 minutes)
- Spill the Beans **K.OA.5**   (4 minutes)
- Flash Five **K.OA.2**   (3 minutes)

Grade K Core Fluency Differentiated Practice Sets (5 minutes)

Materials: (S) Core Fluency Practice Sets from GK–M4–Lesson 29

Note: This activity assesses students' progress toward mastery of the required addition fluency for kindergarten.

Give Practice Set B to students who correctly answered all questions on Practice Set A in the previous lesson. All other students should try to improve their scores on Practice Set A.

Students complete as many problems as they can in 96 seconds. Assign a counting pattern and start number for early finishers, or have them play an independent game such as the Make 10 Memory Game. Collect and correct any Practice Sets completed within the allotted time.

NOTES ON MULTIPLE MEANS OF REPRESENTATION:

If students need concrete materials to complete the Practice Sets, encourage them to use their fingers. Most will naturally stop the practice as they master the grade level fluency in order to move quickly. Some students may want to create drawings to solve. Encourage them to find faster, accurate ways to solve the equations.

Spill the Beans (4 minutes)

Materials: (S) 5 beans painted red on one side or 5 two-sided counters, cup, personal white board

Note: This activity leads students to mastery of adding and subtracting within 5, a fluency goal for kindergarten.

Lesson 30: Represent pictorial decomposition and composition addition stories to 10 with 5-group drawings and equations with no unknown.
Date: 11/12/13

4.F.17

1. Take 3 beans out of the bag, and place them in the cup.
2. Shake the cup gently, and then spill the beans onto the personal board.
3. Count the number of red and the number of white, and record as an addition sentence.
4. Erase, and repeat a few more times.
5. If students demonstrate mastery with addition to 3, then direct them to place 4 beans in the cup to practice addition to 4 and similarly with 5.

Challenge students to solve by counting on or subitizing to add more efficiently.

Flash Five (3 minutes)

Note: This activity allows students to practice more efficient methods of addition using fingers.

T: Quick, show me 5 as fast as you can!
S: (Open one full hand quickly to show 5.)
T: Now show me 5 on the other hand.
S: (Show 5 on the other hand.)
T: Great. Show me 1 the Math way.
S: (Show the left pinky finger.)
T: We want to add 5 to it. I could do it this way. (Reveal the 4 remaining fingers, plus 1 more from the other hand.) 1, 2, 3, 4, 5. Can you think of a faster way? (If students are unsure, elicit a response by flashing five, or opening and closing the full hand, to show 5.)
S: We can just open the other hand! We have 5 fingers on the other hand!
T: That's right! We can flash five! How many fingers are you showing now?
S: 6.
T: Say the addition sentence starting with 1 please.
S: $1 + 5 = 6$.

Repeat the procedure with $2 + 5$, $3 + 5$, $4 + 5$, and $5 + 5$.

Application Problem (5 minutes)

Materials: (S) Tree template, 10 linking cubes, paper and pencil or personal white board

Pretend your linking cubes are pears from the pear tree! How many pears do you have in all? Using your linking cubes, put 5 pears in the tree and 5 pears on the ground. Make a number bond about the pears in your picture. Use your math words to tell your partner about the pears. Can you think of a number sentence?

NOTES ON MULTIPLE MEANS OF ACTION AND EXPRESSION:

Help students with disabilities and students performing below grade level by asking them comprehension questions before they attempt the Application Problem. This will serve as a review and help students solve the problem.

- How many pears are there all together?
- How many pears are on the ground?
- How many pears are on the tree?
- Where do we put the total number of pears on the number bond?
- Where do we put the parts?

COMMON CORE

Lesson 30: Represent pictorial decomposition and composition addition stories to 10 with 5-group drawings and equations with no unknown.
Date: 11/12/13

4.F.18

Now, show another pear falling out of the tree. How many cubes are in the tree now? Would your number bond change? Is there a different number sentence you would use to tell about what you just did? Talk about your ideas with your partner. (If students focus on the pears in the tree, e.g., 5 – 1 = 4, confirm that work and ask them to show a number bond or number sentence that includes all of the pears on the page.)

Note: Again in this lesson, using concrete objects at first to decompose and then compose the number serves as the anticipatory set for the more formal equation work during the lesson.

Concept Development (25 minutes)

Materials: (S) Personal white boards

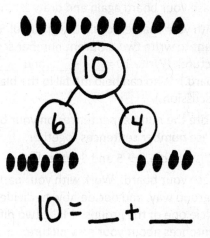

T: Listen carefully to my story. Nancy had 10 beans. She picked up 6 in one hand and 4 in the other.

T: How many beans did she have in all?

S: 10.

T: How many did she pick up in each hand?

S: She picked up 6 in one and 4 in the other!

T: You are good listeners. Draw Nancy's 10 beans on your board. I will draw them here. Write the number for Nancy's beans. (Demonstrate.)

T: Now, let's draw the beans she had in each of her hands. (Demonstrate.) We will write the number for each of the groups and use our numbers to make a number bond. (Demonstrate.)

T: We want to make a number sentence about the beans. How could we begin our number sentence?

S: Let's begin it with how many in all. Then we can put our parts! → This is like what we did yesterday!

T: Good idea. (Write 10 = ___ + ___.) How do we know which numbers should go in the blanks?

S: The 6 and the 4! → They are the parts.

T: Finish your number sentence. Turn to your partner and read the number sentence. Talk about how you knew which number should go where. (Circulate to ensure understanding.)

T: Listen to our next story.

T: Shelly had 8 presents. Her friend gave her 2 more presents! Shelly has 10 presents now.

T: How many presents did Shelly have at first? (8.) How many did her friend give her? (2.) How many presents did Shelly have all together? (10.)

NOTES ON MULTIPLE MEANS OF REPRESENTATION:

Scaffold the lesson for English language learners by pointing to visuals on the board or word wall when terms such as *number bond*, *number sentence*, and *parts* are mentioned

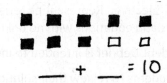

COMMON CORE

Lesson 30:   Represent pictorial decomposition and composition addition stories
             to 10 with 5-group drawings and equations with no unknown.
Date: 11/12/13

4.F.19

T: Draw 8 little squares to show the presents Shelly had first. Make sure you draw them in the 5-group way. Color in the little squares. Now, draw 2 empty squares to show the 2 presents her friend gave her. How could we make a number sentence about the story?

S: Write the numbers for the parts first! Then, we can put the total at the end after our equal sign.

T: Great! (Write ___ + ___ = 10.) Write this on your board. How should we fill in the blanks?

S: We will put in the parts! → Put an 8 in the first and a 2 in the second to show her new presents.

T: Finish your number sentence. Let's read the number sentence together.

S: 8 + 2 = 10.

T: How is this number sentence different from the first one you wrote today? How are they the same? (Allow time for discussion about the types of equations.)

T: Erase your board again and draw 10 the 5-group way.

T: With your marker, circle the group of 5 dots at the top. We want to write two different number sentences about your picture. (Write 10 = ___ + ___ and ___ + ___ = ___ on the board.) Who can help me fill in the blanks? (Allow time for discussion.)

T: Write the number sentences on your boards. Let's read these number sentences together.

MP.2

S: 10 is 5 and 5. → 5 and 5 make 10.

T: Erase your board. Work with your partner to draw 10 in the 5-group way, and decide how to divide it into two groups. Circle one of the groups. Make two different number sentences about your new picture.

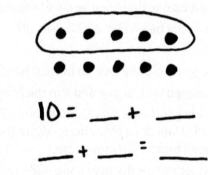

T: (Pause as students work.) Read your number sentences with your partner. How many different number sentences for 10 can we find? (If desired, allow pairs of students to model their work on the board for the group.)

T: Who would like to share their pair of number sentences with the class?

List all different number sentences for 10 on the board. Allow time for sharing and discussion. If time permits, allow students to repeat the exercise with groups of objects less than 10 for additional review.

Problem Set (10 minutes)

Students should do their personal best to complete the Problem Set within the allotted 10 minutes.

Student Debrief (8 minutes)

Lesson Objective: Represent pictorial decomposition and composition addition stories to 10 with 5-group drawings and equations with no unknown.

The Student Debrief is intended to invite reflection and active processing of the total lesson experience.

Invite students to review their solutions for the Problem Set. They should check work by comparing answers with a partner before going over answers as a class. Look for misconceptions or misunderstandings that can

	Lesson 30:	Represent pictorial decomposition and composition addition stories to 10 with 5-group drawings and equations with no unknown.
	Date:	11/12/13

4.F.2

be addressed in the Debrief. Guide students in a conversation to debrief the Problem Set and process the lesson.

You may choose to use any combination of the questions below to lead the discussion.

- How did you know which were the parts and which were the wholes in your Problem Set?
- In the Problem Set, were the parts easier for you to see in the 10-frame? Why or why not?
- How did the number bonds help you with your number sentences?
- What helps you most when you are writing number sentences? Do you prefer to use pictures, cubes, fingers, or number bonds?
- Do you have any other strategies?

Lesson 30:   Represent pictorial decomposition and composition addition stories to 10 with 5-group drawings and equations with no unknown.
Date: 11/12/13

4.F.22

Name _____   Date _____

Fill in the number bonds and complete the number sentences.

Ricky had 10 space toys. He had 7 rockets and 3 astronauts.

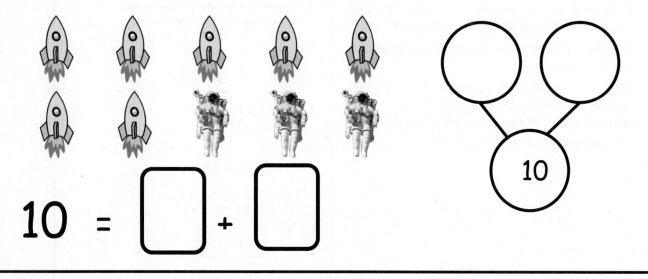

$$10 = \boxed{} + \boxed{}$$

Bianca had 4 pigs and 6 sheep on her farm. She had 10 animals all together.

$$\boxed{} + \boxed{} = \boxed{}$$

COMMON CORE™   **Lesson 30:**   Represent pictorial decomposition and composition addition stories
to 10 with 5-group drawings and equations with no unknown.   **4.F.2**

Date: 11/12/13

Danica had 5 green balloons. Her friend gave her 5 blue balloons. Draw all of her balloons in the 5-group way. Fill in both number sentences.

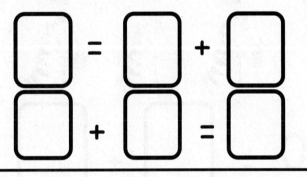

Jason is playing with 10 bouncy balls. He has 8 on the table and 2 on the floor. Draw the bouncy balls in the 5-group way. Fill in both number sentences.

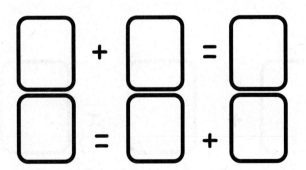

COMMON CORE™

Lesson 30:   Represent pictorial decomposition and composition addition stories
Date: 11/12/13   to 10 with 5-group drawings and equations with no unknown.

4.F.24

Name _____   Date _____

Fill in the number bonds and complete the number sentences.

Scott went to the zoo. He saw 6 giraffes and 4 zebras. He saw 10 animals all together.

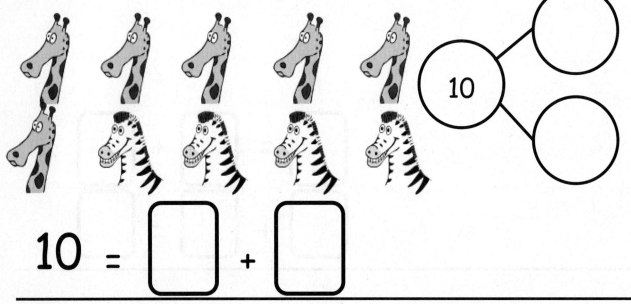

$10 =$ ☐ $+$ ☐

Susan saw 10 animals at the zoo. She saw 5 lions and 5 elephants. Draw the animals in the 5-group way.

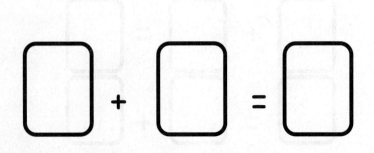

☐ $+$ ☐ $=$ ☐

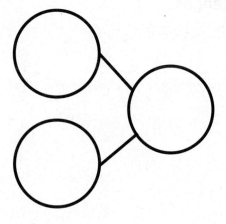

 | Lesson 30: | Represent pictorial decomposition and composition addition stories to 10 with 5-group drawings and equations with no unknown.
Date: | 11/12/13

4.F.2

© 2013 Common Core, Inc. All rights reserved. commoncore.org

Make 2 groups. Circle 1 of the groups. Write a number sentence to match.
Find as many partners of 10 as you can.

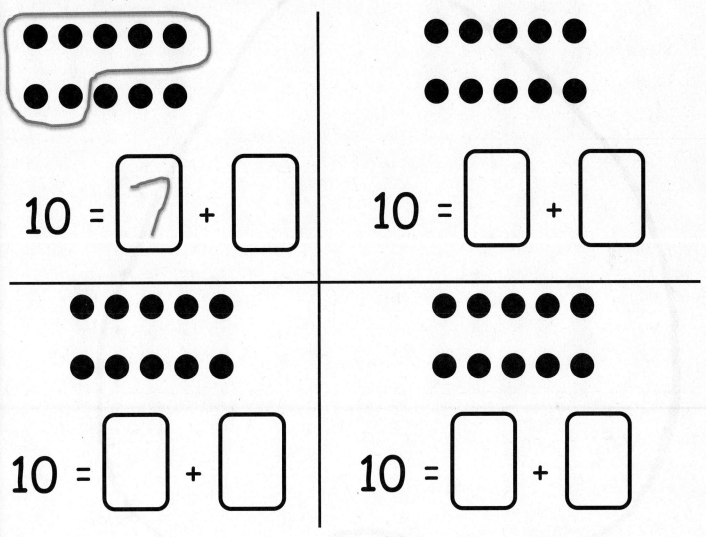

Draw 10 dots the 5-group way. Make 2 groups. Circle one of the groups.
Write a number sentence to match your drawing.

 | Lesson 30: | Represent pictorial decomposition and composition addition stories
to 10 with 5-group drawings and equations with no unknown. | 4.F.26

Date: | 11/12/13

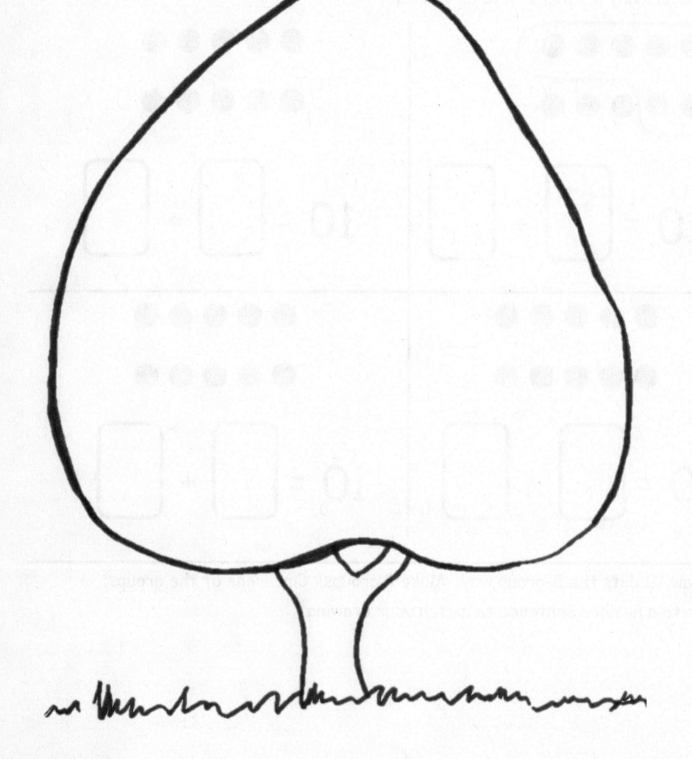

COMMON CORE™

Lesson 30: Represent pictorial decomposition and composition addition stories
to 10 with 5-group drawings and equations with no unknown.

Date: 11/12/13

4.F.2

Lesson 31

Objective: Solve *add to with total unknown* and *put together with total unknown* problems with totals of 9 and 10.

Suggested Lesson Structure

■ Fluency Practice	(12 minutes)
■ Application Problem	(5 minutes)
■ Concept Development	(25 minutes)
■ Student Debrief	(8 minutes)
Total Time	**(50 minutes)**

Fluency Practice (12 minutes)

- Sprint: Core Fluency **K.OA.5**   (9 minutes)
- Ready, Set, Add! **K.OA.5**   (3 minutes)

Sprint: Core Fluency (9 minutes)

Materials: (S) 1 copy of each Sprint per student

Note: During GK–M4–Topic F and for the remainder of the module, each topic includes an opportunity for review and mastery of the sums and difference with totals through 5 by means of the Core Fluency Sprints. Four sprints are provided in this lesson, with Sprint A being the most simple addition fluency of the grade and Sprint D being the most complex (including addition and subtraction). Select the Sprint that is most appropriate for your class. In order to correct the work as a class, all students should take the same Sprint.

> T: It's time for a Sprint! (Briefly recall previous Sprint preparation activities and distribute Sprints facedown.) Take out your pencil and one crayon, any color. For this Sprint, you are going to subtract to find how many are left. (Demonstrate the first problem as needed.)

Continue to follow the Sprint procedure as outlined in GK–M4–Lesson 3. Have students work on the Sprint a second time. Continue to emphasize that the goal is simply to do better than the first time and celebrate improvement.

Ready, Set, Add! (3 minutes)

Note: In this activity, students test their mastery of addition facts within 5, and when the total is greater than 5, they will be able to rely on the strategies of counting all or counting on with fingers.

1. Assign partners. Both students put one hand behind their back.
2. With the hand that is in view, they pump their fists two times as they say, "Ready, set," and then the

---

Lesson 31:	Solve *add to with total unknown* and *put together with total unknown* problems with totals of 9 and 10.
Date:	11/12/13

4.F.28

third time, they show a number of fingers as they say, "Add!" (The motion is similar to rock, paper, scissors.)

3. Partners race to say an addition sentence that matches the number of fingers shown. The first partner (fastest) repeats the addition sentence for both to hear.
4. The second partner flips the addition sentence.
5. Repeat.

At first, have students use only one, two, or three fingers. As they demonstrate mastery, invite them to include four and five fingers as well.

Application Problem (5 minutes)

Materials: (S) Paper, crayons, pencil

Five children were playing soccer in the park. Draw the children. Four more children came to play. Draw the new players. How many children were playing soccer? How did you know? Turn and talk to your partner about your answer. Do you agree?

Note: This practical example of an *add to result unknown* problem serves as the anticipatory set for today's lesson.

Concept Development (25 minutes)

Note: Today's problem-solving objective encourages students to work more independently. The lesson begins with whole-group work. With partners, students listen to and represent word problems through drawings, and finally, write and solve the related equations. Depending on the abilities of the students, the problems can be modeled by the teacher if necessary. Alternatively, students who demonstrate ability can be encouraged to complete their work on the board as an example and explain their thinking to their peers.

Materials: (S) 10 teddy bear or other counters, equation template, personal white board

Problem 1

T: (Write _____ + _____ = _____ on the board.) We are going to write more number sentences today. If you look at what I wrote on the board, what kind of number sentences do you think we will be talking about?

S: Add to number sentences. → Addition sentences!

T: Do you remember what we put in the box in our lessons before?

S: How many altogether! → The mystery number. → The number we didn't know.

NOTES ON MULTIPLE MEANS OF ACTION AND EXPRESSION:

To help your English language learners understand the lesson and participate, point to the appropriate part of the blank number sentence on the board as you ask students: "What number should I put in first blank? In the next blank? What about the blank after the equal sign?"

T: You are right! You have some counters on your desk. Listen to my story. Six bears were walking in the forest. Show the bears with your counters.

T: Three more bears came to walk with them. Show the new bears with your counters. How many bears were walking in the forest all together?

S: Now we have 9 bears!

T: How do you know?

S: I counted them all. → I started at 6 and counted 3 more!

T: You are right. We started with 6 bears and added 3 more bears to make 9 bears all together. How could we write a number sentence about the story? What number should I put in the first blank?

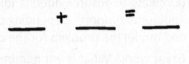

S: 6.

T: In the next blank?

S: 3.

T: What about the blank after the equal sign?

S: 9.

T: How did you know where each of the numbers belonged?

S: Six and 3 were the parts. → We put the 9 in the blank after the equal sign because that was how many bears there were in all.

Problem 2

T: Let's make up another story about the bears. This time, there were 3 bears sleeping and 7 bears playing. Show your groups of bears with your counters. How many bears in all?

S: I have 10 bears.

T: Can you tell me a number sentence about these bears?

S: Three bears and 7 bears make 10 bears. → Three plus 7 equals 10.

T: I will write that on the board, too. Help me fill in my blanks. (Again, allow students to explain which number would go in each of the blanks and how they knew.)

Problem 3

T: I'm going to let you try a problem with your partner now on your personal boards. Listen carefully to my story and draw a picture about what happens. When you have finished your picture, fill in the number sentence to solve the problem.

MP.1

T: Maggie had 4 pennies. Her mom gave her 5 more pennies. How many pennies does Maggie have now? Draw the pennies and make a number sentence. (Allow time for drawing and discussion, circulating to ensure understanding during this new, more independent phase of problem solving.)

> **NOTES ON MULTIPLE MEANS OF ACTION AND EXPRESSION:**
>
> Scaffold the lesson for below grade level students by giving them step-by-step directions. Be sure to ask students questions as they work to make sure they understand what they are doing.

COMMON CORE™ | **Lesson 31:**   Solve *add to with total unknown* and *put together with total unknown* problems with totals of 9 and 10.

   | **Date:**   11/12/13

4.F.30

MP.1

T: How many pennies does Maggie have now? What was the number sentence?

S: 4 + 5 = 9! → She has 9 pennies now.

Problem 4

T: Great! Erase your boards and listen to the next story. Work with your partner to draw a picture about what you hear and write the number sentence.

T: John had 2 circle magnets and 8 square magnets. How many magnets did he have all together? (Circulate to ensure understanding and to repeat the problem for students who might need additional support. Depending on students' abilities, choose pairs of students to work on the board and model the problem for the class.)

T: Great work! What is our number sentence?

S: 2 + 8 = 10!

T: How many magnets did he have in all?

S: 10.

T: I'm going to give you some time to think up an addition story with your partner. Draw the picture and write the number sentence. I will come around to hear your stories!

If time permits, allow students to create several *add to result unknown* and *put together total unknown* stories of their own. If the students work on paper at this point, the results can be collected for a bulletin board or as part of a class book.

Problem Set (10 minutes)

Note: Depending on the abilities of the class, it may be appropriate to continue using the protocol above with students working independently. Read one problem at a time and give students time to complete it, circulating to assist as necessary, prior to reading the next one. Early finishers can make up their own additional story problem drawings and number sentences on the back of their sheets.

Student Debrief (8 minutes)

Lesson Objective: Solve *add to with total unknown* and *put together with total unknown* problems with totals of 9 and 10.

The Student Debrief is intended to invite reflection and active processing of the total lesson experience.

Invite students to review their solutions for the Problem Set. They should check work by comparing answers with a partner before going over answers as a class. Look for misconceptions or misunderstandings that can be addressed in the Debrief. Guide students in a conversation

NYS COMMON CORE MATHEMATICS CURRICULUM   Lesson 31 Problem Set

Name _Darnell_   Date _3-15-13_

Draw the story. Fill in the number sentence.

Zayne had 6 round crackers and 3 square crackers. How many crackers did Zayne have in all?

6 + 3 = 9

Riley had 9 crayons. Her friend gave her 1 crayon. How many crayons did Riley have in all?

9 + 1 = 10

COMMON CORE | Lesson 31: Solve add to with result unknown and put together with result unknown problems with totals of 9 and 10.
Date: 10/2/13   engage^ny   4.F.10

to debrief the Problem Set and process the lesson.

You may choose to use any combination of the questions below to lead the discussion.

- How did the pictures you drew help you with your number sentences in the Problem Set?
- How did you decide where to put each number in the number sentences in your Problem Set? How did you know what numbers to put in the blanks?
- What do we call the types of number sentences that we were working on today? (Addition sentences.)
- Why is listening carefully very important when solving story problems?
- Were there lots of answers today or was there always one answer? Were there different ways to get to an answer?
- In the Problem Set, did someone create his own number story he would like to share? (Listen to the story and have students solve together.)

NYS COMMON CORE MATHEMATICS CURRICULUM   Lesson 31 Problem Set   K•4

Draw the story. Write a number sentence to match.

Jenny had 3 red and 7 purple pieces of construction paper. How many pieces of construction paper did Jenny have all together?

$3 + 7 = 10$

Rhett had 5 square blocks. His friend gave him 4 rectangle blocks. How many blocks does Rhett have all together?

$5 + 4 = 9$

COMMON CORE | Lesson 31: | Solve add to with result unknown and put together with result unknown problems with totals of 9 and 10.
Date: | 10/2/13

engage^ny   4.F.11

COMMON CORE™

Lesson 31: Solve *add to with total unknown* and *put together with total unknown* problems with totals of 9 and 10.

Date: 11/12/13

4.F.32

Name _____   Date _____

Write the missing number.   Number correct: ⭐

1	2 + 1 = ☐		11	☐ = 3 + 2
2	1 + 1 = ☐		12	1 + 3 = ☐
3	1 + 4 = ☐		13	☐ = 2 + 2
4	3 + 1 = ☐		14	☐ = 1 + 2
5	2 + 2 = ☐		15	1 + 4 = ☐
6	2 + 3 = ☐		16	☐ = 2 + 3
7	1 + 2 = ☐		17	☐ = 5 + 1
8	4 + 1 = ☐		18	5 + 2 = ☐
9	3 + 2 = ☐		19	1 + 0 = ☐
10	1 + 3 = ☐		20	5 + 0 = ☐

COMMON CORE™   Lesson 31:   Solve *add to with total unknown* and *put together with total unknown* problems with totals of 9 and 10.

Date: 11/12/13

4.F.33

Name _____   Date _____

Write the missing number.   Number correct:

1	$2 - 1 = \Box$		11	$\Box = 4 - 2$
2	$4 - 1 = \Box$		12	$5 - 3 = \Box$
3	$5 - 1 = \Box$		13	$\Box = 3 - 1$
4	$3 - 1 = \Box$		14	$\Box = 5 - 2$
5	$3 - 2 = \Box$		15	$4 - 1 = \Box$
6	$4 - 2 = \Box$		16	$\Box = 5 - 4$
7	$5 - 3 = \Box$		17	$\Box = 5 - 1$
8	$5 - 2 = \Box$		18	$6 - 1 = \Box$
9	$4 - 3 = \Box$		19	$1 - 0 = \Box$
10	$5 - 4 = \Box$		20	$5 - 5 = \Box$

Name _____   Date _____

Write the missing number.   Number correct: ⟨⟨⟨ ⟩⟩⟩

1	$2 + 1 =$ ☐	11	$3 + 2 =$ ☐
2	$2 - 1 =$ ☐	12	$3 - 2 =$ ☐
3	$3 + 1 =$ ☐	13	$4 + 0 =$ ☐
4	$3 - 1 =$ ☐	14	$4 - 0 =$ ☐
5	$4 + 1 =$ ☐	15	$5 + 0 =$ ☐
6	$4 - 1 =$ ☐	16	$5 - 0 =$ ☐
7	$1 + 1 =$ ☐	17	$5 - 5 =$ ☐
8	$1 - 1 =$ ☐	18	$4 + 1 =$ ☐
9	$2 + 2 =$ ☐	19	$5 - 4 =$ ☐
10	$2 - 2 =$ ☐	20	$5 - 1 =$ ☐

COMMON CORE™

Lesson 31:   Solve *add to with total unknown* and *put together with total unknown*
                problems with totals of 9 and 10.
Date: 11/12/13

4.F.35

Name _____   Date _____

Write the missing number.

Number correct: ⟨⟩

1	2 + 1 = ☐
2	4 + 1 = ☐
3	5 - 1 = ☐
4	3 + 1 = ☐
5	3 + 2 = ☐
6	4 - 2 = ☐
7	5 - 3 = ☐
8	5 - 2 = ☐
9	2 + 3 = ☐
10	5 - 4 = ☐

11	☐ = 1 + 2
12	5 + 0 = ☐
13	☐ = 3 - 1
14	☐ = 2 + 2
15	4 - 1 = ☐
16	☐ = 5 - 4
17	☐ = 5 - 1
18	3 + 0 = ☐
19	1 - 0 = ☐
20	5 - 5 = ☐

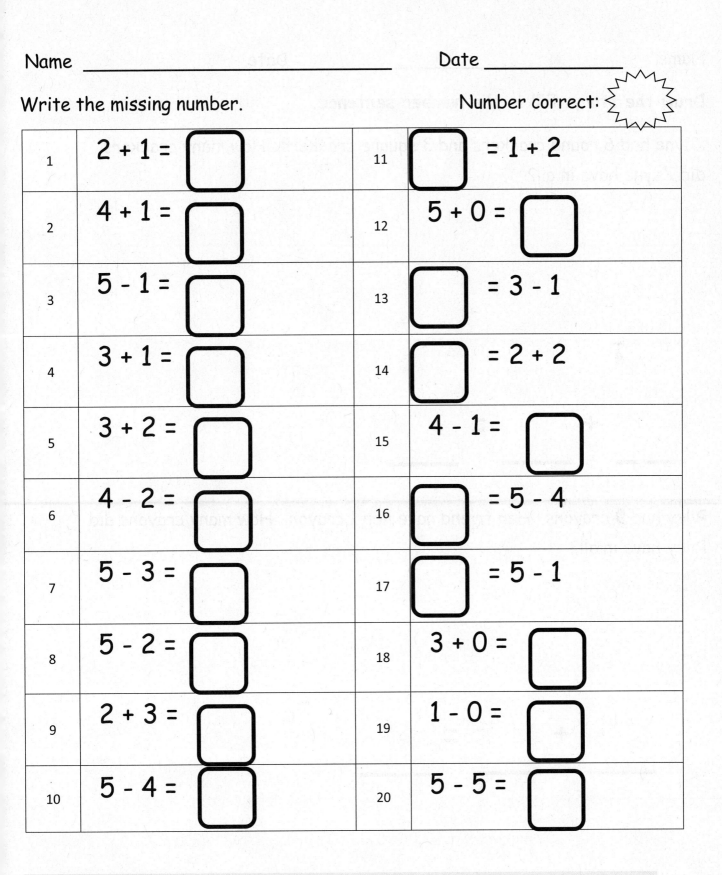

COMMON CORE™

Lesson 31:   Solve *add to with total unknown* and *put together with total unknown* problems with totals of 9 and 10.

Date: 11/12/13

4.F.36

Name _____   Date _____

Draw the story. Fill in the number sentence.

Zayne had 6 round crackers and 3 square crackers. How many crackers did Zayne have in all?

_____ + _____ = _____

Riley had 9 crayons. Her friend gave her 1 crayon. How many crayons did Riley have in all?

_____ + _____ = _____

Lesson 31:   Solve *add to with total unknown* and *put together with total unknown*
                 problems with totals of 9 and 10.

Date: 11/12/13

4.F.37

Draw the story. Write a number sentence to match.

Jenny had 3 red and 7 purple pieces of construction paper. How many pieces of construction paper did Jenny have altogether?

Rhett had 5 square blocks. His friend gave him 4 rectangle blocks. How many blocks did Rhett have altogether?

Lesson 31:   Solve *add to with total unknown* and *put together with total unknown* problems with totals of 9 and 10.

Date: 11/12/13

4.F.38

Name _____   Date _____

Draw the story. Fill in the number sentence.

Jake has 7 chocolate cookies and 2 sugar cookies. How many cookies does he have altogether?

+   =

_____   _____   _____

Jake's mother bought juice boxes. 4 were apple juice and 5 were orange juice. How many juice boxes did she have in all?

+   =

_____   _____   _____

Lesson 31:   Solve *add to with total unknown* and *put together with total unknown* problems with totals of 9 and 10.

Date: 11/12/13

4.F.39

Draw the story. Write a number sentence to match.

Ryan had 5 celery sticks and 5 carrot sticks. How many veggie sticks did Ryan have altogether?

Draw an addition story and write a number sentence to match it. Explain your work to an adult at home.

COMMON CORE™

Lesson 31: Solve *add to with total unknown* and *put together with total unknown* problems with totals of 9 and 10.

Date: 11/12/13

4.F.40

_____

=

_____

+

_____

Lesson 32

Objective: Solve *both addends unknown* word problems with totals of 9 and 10 using 5-group drawings.

Suggested Lesson Structure

■ Fluency Practice	(12 minutes)
■ Application Problem	(5 minutes)
■ Concept Development	(25 minutes)
■ Student Debrief	(8 minutes)
Total Time	**(50 minutes)**

Fluency Practice (12 minutes)

- Counting to 30 by Ones with the Rekenrek **K.CC.1**   (3 minutes)
- Break Apart Numbers **K.OA.3**   (4 minutes)
- 5-Group Puzzles **K.OA.3**   (5 minutes)

Counting to 30 by Ones with the Rekenrek (3 minutes)

Materials: (T) 100-bead Rekenrek

Note: Counting from 20 to 30 will prove easier than learning the linguistically challenging counting sequence of 11–20. Once students know the number word *twenty,* it becomes just a matter of extending a pattern.

    T: (Slide 10 beads over.) How many?
    S: 10.
    T: (Slide over 10 more for a total of 20.) How many?
    S: 20.
    T: (Slide over 10 more for a total of 30.) How many?
    S: 30.
    T: (Show 20 beads.) How many?
    S: 20.
    T: (Slide over 1 more.) 20. 1 more is 21. How many?
    S: 21.
    T: (Slide over 1 more.) 21. 1 more is 22. How many?
    S: 22.

COMMON CORE™	**Lesson 32:** Solve *both addends unknown* word problems with totals of 9 and 10 using 5-group drawings.
	Date: 11/12/13

4.F.42

Continue this process with as little or as much guidance as students require.

Break Apart Numbers (4 minutes)

Materials: (S) Break Apart Numbers template, personal white board

Note: Reviewing decomposing numbers to 5 supports kindergarten's required fluency of adding and subtracting within 5. The activity also prepares students to work with decomposition in today's lesson.

Students complete as many *different* number bonds as they can in one minute. Students can work in partners as needed. If students come up with number bonds including 0 as a part, invite them to draw more number bonds on their sheet so that they have enough to record all decompositions of a number. (They can even add a number bond with a total of 1.) Take a poll of how many students completed all decompositions for 2, 3, etc., and celebrate accomplishments.

5-Group Puzzles (5 minutes)

Materials: (S) 10 dot 5-group cards cut apart to show the decompositions of 10, personal white board

Note: Assembling the 5-Group cards gives students a way to visualize partners to 10, leading them to develop automaticity with this essential skill for Grade 1.

Students assemble the dot cards to make 10, and then write the number bond.

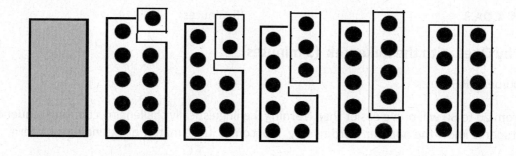

Application Problem (5 minutes)

Materials: (S) Paper, crayons

Chen had 9 pencils. Some of his pencils were red and some were blue. Draw Chen's pencils.

Make a number bond about your pencils. Now, turn and talk to your partner about your pictures and your number bond. Do your pictures look the same? Are your number bonds the same? Are they both correct?

Note: Decomposition of the number 9 and discussion about alternatives serve as the anticipatory set for today's *put together both addends unknown* objective.

NOTES ON MULTIPLE MEANS OF ENGAGEMENT:

Have blue and red pencils available for students who are performing below grade level and students with disabilities who might still be struggling with the part–whole relationship. Allow them to use the pencils to model the problem before asking them to draw the problem and represent it using number bonds.

COMMON CORE™

Lesson 32:   Solve *both addends unknown* word problems with totals of 9 and 10 using 5-group drawings.
Date: 11/12/13

4.F.43

Concept Development (25 minutes)

Materials: (S) 10-frame template, personal white board

Note: Today's problem-solving objective encourages students to work more independently. The lesson begins with whole-group work to exemplify the problem type. With partners, students listen to and represent variations of the word problem, then write and solve the related equations. Depending on the abilities of the students, the problems can be modeled by the teacher as necessary.

NOTES ON
MULTIPLE MEANS OF
ENGAGEMENT:

English language learners will benefit from speaking with their peers at key points in the lesson before their classmates are asked for responses. An opportunity to turn and talk to a partner to discuss how they knew that 7 and 2 are partners will give them a chance to practice their words and express their thinking, encouraging them to participate more fully in class discussions.

T: (Write 9 = ___ + ___ on the board.) Michael has 9 toy blocks. Some are large and some are small. Student A, how many of his blocks do you think were large?

S: 7!

T: I'm going to make a picture on the board of his large blocks. (Demonstrate.) I wonder how many of his blocks were small?

S: 2!

T: How did you know?

S: I used my fingers to count. → I counted on from 7. → I knew 7's partner was 2 to make a 9.

T: You are right! Let me put that into my picture. (Demonstrate.) I want to finish my number sentence. What does the 9 tell us, a part or how many he has in all?

S: How many blocks he has in all.

T: Which numbers should go in the blanks?

S: Those are for the parts! → Seven for the big ones and 2 for the small ones.

T: Yes! Now, let's read the number sentence together.

S: 9 = 7 + 2.

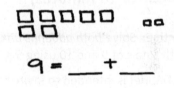

9 = __ + __

T: You and your partner are going to work together to do some more problems like this. Listen to my story: Susie had a plate of 9 cookies. Some were vanilla and some were chocolate. How many of each kind did she have?

MP.1

T: Do we know how many cookies she has of each kind?

S: No! → This is like the last one. There are lots of ways it could look.

T: With your partner, decide how many chocolate and how many vanilla cookies Susie had. Make a picture about your story in the 5-group way on your personal board and write the number sentence. Raise your hand when you are done and I will check your work. Then, try making a different story!

Lesson 32:   Solve *both addends unknown* word problems with totals of 9 and 10
using 5-group drawings.
Date: 11/12/13

4.F.44

Partners who demonstrate strong understanding could do their work on the board or on chart paper as class examples. Collect the number sentences as you assess the student work. List them on the board after the work time is over, ensuring that all sets of addends are represented.

T: You are good addition sentence detectives! Let's try another one!

T: Listen to my story: Jamal had a basket of 10 blocks. Some were white and some were grey. Work on this problem with your partner. Show Jamal's blocks and write the number sentence. Raise your hand when you are ready for me to see your work!

Follow the same procedure as for the previous problem. List the equations on the board to be reviewed before the Problem Set or during the Debrief.

Problem Set (10 minutes)

Students should do their personal best to complete the Problem Set within the allotted 10 minutes.

Note: Encourage students to use their math drawing for this activity. For example, instead of drawing nine elaborate trains, students can draw black and green rectangles to represent the trains.

There is an extra practice sheet for students who finish the first two pages of the Problem Set early. Make a few copies for early finishers.

Student Debrief (8 minutes)

Lesson Objective: Solve *both addends unknown* word problems with totals of 9 and 10 using 5-group drawings.

The Student Debrief is intended to invite reflection and active processing of the total lesson experience.

Invite students to review their solutions for the Problem Set. They should check work by comparing answers with a partner before going over answers as a class. Look for misconceptions or misunderstandings that can be addressed in the Debrief. Guide students in a conversation to debrief the Problem Set and process the lesson.

You may choose to use any combination of the questions below to lead the discussion.

▪ What did you think about when you were drawing the picture of trains in the Problem Set? How did you start?

COMMON CORE

Lesson 32:
Date:

Solve *both addends unknown* word problems with totals of 9 and 10 using 5-group drawings.
11/12/13

engage^ny   4.F.6

4.F.45

- Did you notice any patterns when you were working today? (Refer students to the list of equations showing decompositions of 9 and 10. They may also see patterns in the 5-groups.)

- How did you decide where to put the numbers in your number sentence blanks?

- You were able to choose your own groups when you were solving the problems about the cookies. When you chose your first part, did you have a lot of choices for the second part? How did you know what it had to be?

- How are 5-group drawings helpful when you are solving story problems?

NYS COMMON CORE MATHEMATICS CURRICULUM   Lesson 32 Problem Set K•4

Kate has 9 princess wands. Some are yellow and the rest are green. Show two different ways Kate's wands could look. Fill in the number sentences to match.

$$9 = 3 + 6$$ $$9 = 2 + 7$$

Danny has 10 robots. Some are red and the rest are gray. Show two different ways Danny's robots could look. Fill in the number sentences to match.

$$10 = 5 + 5$$ $$10 = 2 + 8$$

COMMON CORE   Lesson 32:   Solve both addends unknown word problems with totals of 9 and 10
              Date: using 5-group drawings.
                           10/2/13

engage^ny   4.F.7

Lesson 32:   Solve *both addends unknown* word problems with totals of 9 and 10
Date: using 5-group drawings.
             11/12/13

4.F.46

Name _____   Date _____

Listen to the word problem.   Fill in the number sentence.

Cecilia has 9 bows. Some have polka dots and some have stripes. How many polka dot and how many striped bows do you think Cecilia has?

Keegan has 10 train cars. Some are black and some are green. How many black and green train cars do you think Keegan has?

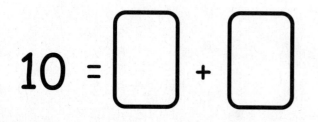

Lesson 32:   Solve *both addends unknown* word problems with totals of 9 and 10 using 5-group drawings.

Date: 11/12/13

4.F.47

Kate has 9 princess wands. Some are yellow and the rest are green. Show two different ways Kate's wands could look. Fill in the number sentences to match.

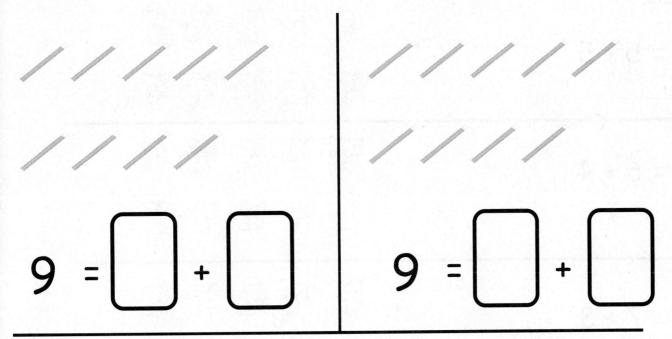

9 = ☐ + ☐   9 = ☐ + ☐

Danny has 10 robots. Some are red and the rest are gray. Show two different ways Danny's robots could look. Fill in the number sentences to match.

10 = ☐ + ☐   10 = ☐ + ☐

COMMON CORE™

Lesson 32: Solve *both addends unknown* word problems with totals of 9 and 10 using 5-group drawings.

Date: 11/12/13

4.F.48

Name _____ Date _____

Color the robots to match the number sentence. Tell a story about the robots.

$10 = 5 + 5$

$10 = 6 + 4$

$10 = 7 + 3$

$10 = 8 + 2$

$10 = 9 + 1$

COMMON CORE™

Lesson 32:   Solve *both addends unknown* word problems with totals of 9 and 10 using 5-group drawings.

Date: 11/12/13

4.F.49

© 2013 Common Core, Inc. All rights reserved. commoncore.org

Name _____ Date _____

Jerry has 9 baseball hats. Draw the hats the 5-group way. Color some red and some blue. Fill in the number sentence to match.

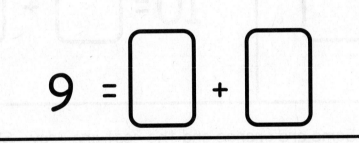

$$9 = \boxed{} + \boxed{}$$

Anne had 10 pencils. Draw the pencils the 5-group way. Color some pencils blue and some yellow. Fill in the number sentence to match.

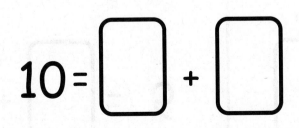

$$10 = \boxed{} + \boxed{}$$

Lesson 32:

Date:

Solve *both addends unknown* word problems with totals of 9 and 10 using 5-group drawings.

11/12/13

4.F.50

There are 10 apples. Color some red and the rest green. Then show a different way the apples could look. Fill in the number sentences to match.

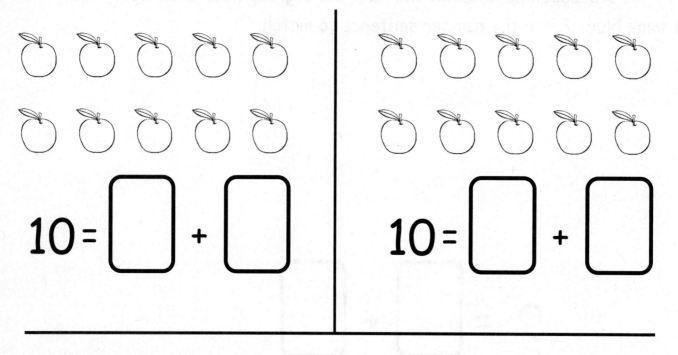

$$10 = \boxed{} + \boxed{}$$

$$10 = \boxed{} + \boxed{}$$

Anya has 9 stuffed cats. Some are orange and the rest are gray. Show two different ways Anya's cats could look. Fill in the number sentences to match.

$$9 = \boxed{} + \boxed{}$$

$$9 = \boxed{} + \boxed{}$$

COMMON CORE

Lesson 32: Solve *both addends unknown* word problems with totals of 9 and 10 using 5-group drawings.

Date: 11/12/13

4.F.51

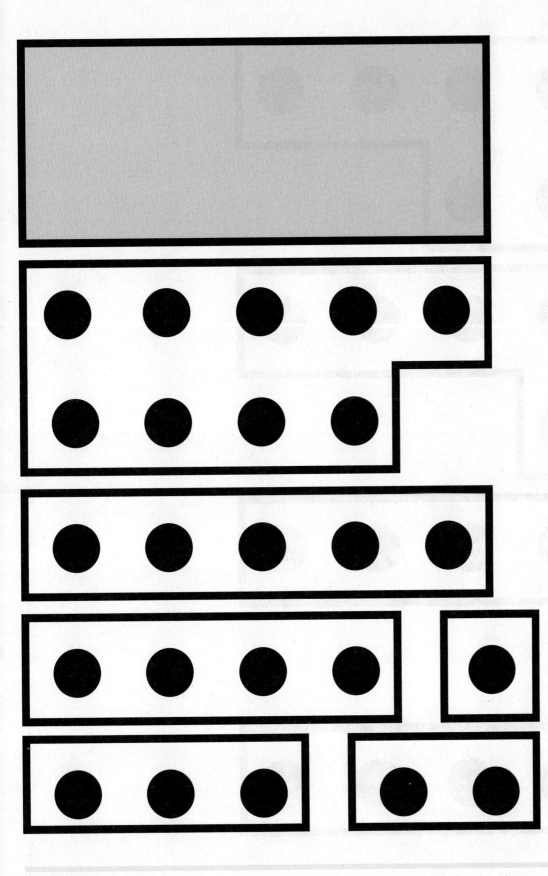

COMMON CORE™

Lesson 32:   Solve *both addends unknown* word problems with totals of 9 and 10
using 5-group drawings.

Date: 11/12/13

4.F.52

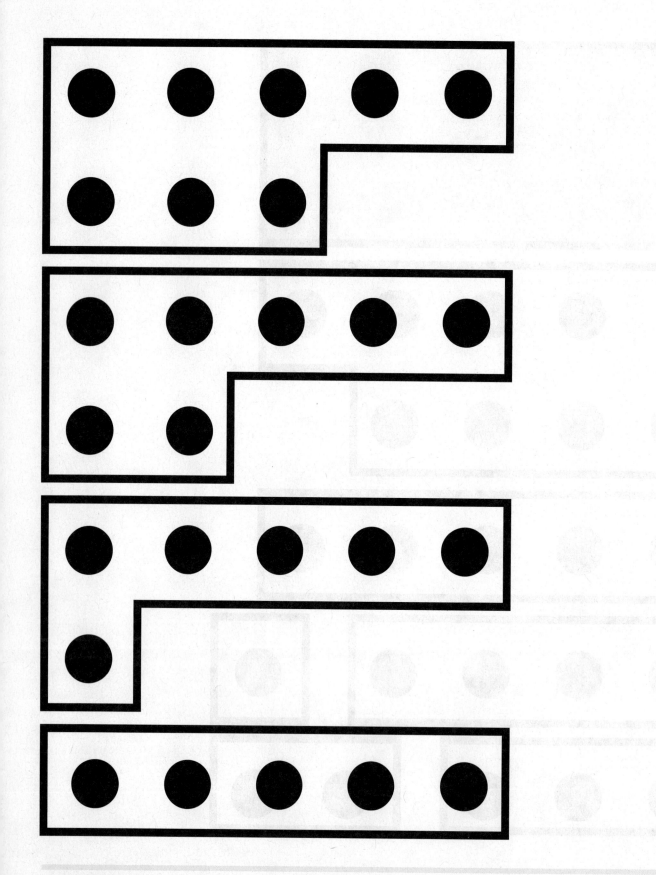

Lesson 32: Solve *both addends unknown* word problems with totals of 9 and 10 using 5-group drawings.

Date: 11/12/13

4.F.53

Break apart the numbers.

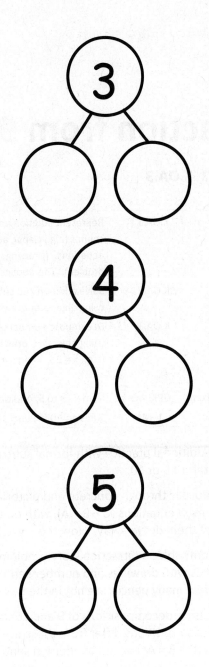

COMMON CORE™

Lesson 32: Solve *both addends unknown* word problems with totals of 9 and 10 using 5-group drawings.

Date: 11/12/13

4.F.54

Topic G
Subtraction from 9 and 10

K.OA.1, K.OA.2, K.OA.3

Focus Standard:	K.OA.1	Represent addition and subtraction with objects, fingers, mental images, drawings, sounds (e.g., claps), acting out situations, verbal explanations, expressions, or equations. (Drawings need not show details, but should show the mathematics in the problem. This applies wherever drawings are mentioned in the Standards.)
	K.OA.2	Solve addition and subtraction word problems, and add and subtract within 10, e.g., by using objects or drawings to represent the problem.
	K.OA.3	Decompose numbers less than or equal to 10 into pairs in more than one way, e.g., by using objects or drawings, and record each decomposition by a drawing or equation (e.g., $5 = 2 + 3$ and $5 = 4 + 1$).
Instructional Days:	4	
Coherence -Links from:	GPK–M5	Numerals to 5, Addition and Subtraction Stories, Counting to 20
-Links to:	G1–M1	Sums and Differences to 10

Topic G provides additional practice with formal subtraction concepts, including writing and solving number sentences with totals of 9 or 10.

Lesson 33 moves quickly through concrete and pictorial representations of subtraction with students representing *take from* equations ($C – B = A$), with no unknown for totals to 10. "There were 10 cars in the parking lot. Two of them drove away. Now there are 8 cars left in the parking lot."

In Lesson 34, students solve subtraction story problems by breaking off, crossing out, and hiding a part and show their strategies with drawings and number sentences (**MP.5**). "I have 9 pencils. I'm going to hide 3 pencils in a box. How many pencils are not in the box?"

Lessons 35–36 focus on decompositions of 9 and 10 using 5-groups, which are recorded as number sentences (**K.OA.3**). These decompositions differ from those in Topic F in that they are represented as subtraction number sentences ($C – B = A$) instead of addition sentences ($C = \_\_ + \_\_$).

Students continue to focus on the grade level fluency goal during Fluency Practice, improving the speed and accuracy with which they can add and subtract numbers to 5 (**K.OA.5**).

COMMON CORE™

Topic G:	Subtraction from 9 and 10
Date:	11/11/13

4.G.1

A Teaching Sequence Towards Mastery of Subtraction from 9 and 10

Objective 1: Solve *take from* equations with no unknown using numbers to 10.
(Lesson 33)

Objective 2: Represent subtraction story problems by breaking off, crossing out, and hiding a part.
(Lesson 34)

Objective 3: Decompose the number 9 using 5-group drawings, and record each decomposition with a subtraction equation.
(Lesson 35)

Objective 4: Decompose the number 10 using 5-group drawings, and record each decomposition with a subtraction equation.
(Lesson 36)

Topic G:	Subtraction from 9 and 10
Date:	11/11/13

4.G.2

Lesson 33

Objective: Solve *take from* equations with no unknown using numbers to 10.

Suggested Lesson Structure

- ■ Fluency Practice   (12 minutes)
- ■ Application Problem   (5 minutes)
- □ Concept Development   (25 minutes)
- ■ Student Debrief   (8 minutes)

Total Time   **(50 minutes)**

Fluency Practice (12 minutes)

- Core Fluency Differentiated Practice Sets **K.OA.5**   (5 minutes)
- 1, 2, 3, Sit on 10, 20, and 30 **K.CC.2**   (4 minutes)
- Hide 1 **K.CC.4d**   (3 minutes)

Core Fluency Differentiated Practice Sets (5 minutes)

Materials: (S) Core Fluency Practice Sets from GK–M4–Lesson 29

Note: This activity assesses students' progress toward mastery of the required addition fluency for Kindergarten.

Distribute Practice Sets A, B, or C based on student performance in GK–M4–Lesson 30. Students who correctly answered all questions on a Practice Set in the previous lesson should move to the next Practice Set. All other students should try to improve their scores on Practice Set A.

Students complete as many problems as they can in 96seconds. Assign a counting pattern and start number for early finishers, or have them play an independent game like the Make 10 Memory Game. Collect and correct any Practice Sets completed within the allotted time.

1, 2, 3 Sit on 10, 20, and 30 (4 minutes)

Note: In this activity, students improve on rote counting to 30, a necessary skill for success in GK–Module 5.

Conduct activity as described in GK–M4–Lesson 30, but now continue to 30 if students are ready.

Hide 1 (3 minutes)

Materials: (T) 5-group cards

Note: This activity prepares students to focus on subtraction in today's lesson.

T: (Show the 3 dot card.) Raise your hand when you know how many dots. (Wait for all hands to go up, then give the signal.) Ready?

S: 3.

T: Now, hide 1. You can use your hand to hide 1 of the dots from your eyes, or you can just see it in your mind. Now how many dots are left?

S: 2.

T: (Show the 4 dot card.) Raise your hand when you know how many dots. (Wait for all hands to go up, then give the signal.) Ready?

S: 4.

T: Hide 1. (Wait.) How many dots are left?

S: 3.

Continue with the following suggested sequence: 5, 1, 6, 7, 8, 9, 10.

Application Problem (5 minutes)

Materials: (S) 9 linking cubes and 1 construction paper "picnic blanket" per pair, paper and marker

You are going to play a game with your partner. Partner A, pretend your linking cubes are ants and your paper is a picnic blanket. Count your ants and put them all on the picnic blanket.

Now, pretend some of the ants crawled off the blanket. Slide some of your ants off the blanket to show the ones that crawled away.

Partner B, your job is to make a number bond showing the nine ants that were on the blanket, the ones that stayed, and the ones that crawled away. Partner A, check the number bond to see if you agree. Now, it is Partner B's turn to show some ants leaving the blanket!

NOTES ON MULTIPLE MEANS OF REPRESENTATION:

For below grade level students and students with disabilities who are still having difficulties with part–whole relationships, guide them step by step in making the number bond to represent the Application Problem. Pausing for student responses after each question, ask: "Where should you put the 9 ants? How many ants crawled off? Where should you put the 3 ants that crawled off?"

Note: This is a concrete representation of today's lesson and will serve as an anticipatory set.

Concept Development (25 minutes)

Materials: (S) 9 teddy bear or other counters, 10 linking cubes, subtraction equation template, personal white board

Lesson 33:   Solve *take from* equations with no unknown using numbers to 10.
Date: 11/12/13

4.G.4

Problem 1

T: (Write ___ – ____ = ____ on the board.) Let's pretend you have a family of 9 bears. Put 9 bears in front of you. One bear is hungry and wants to go to the honey tree! Take 1 bear and scoot him across your desk to show his adventure. Eight are left.

MP.4

T: Help me make a number bond about the story. (Allow students to guide in the creation of the number bond on the board.) Now, we want to make a number sentence about this story. Are we adding more bears in this story or taking some away?

S: Taking away.

T: Yes, we need to make a take away, or subtraction, number sentence. What number would we put in the first blank?

S: How many we started with! → 9.

T: What goes in the next blank?

S: The bear that went away. → 1.

T: What should we put in the blank after the equal sign?

S: How many bears are still at home. → 8.

T: Great! Let's write our number sentence. Fill in the blanks on your personal board and read with me. (Demonstrate.)

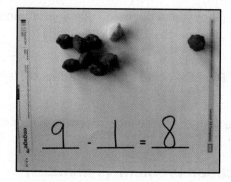

S: 9 minus 1 is 8. → 9 take away 1 leaves 8.

T: Send your bear back home. Let's pretend 2 bears are hungry this time. Send them to the forest. We need to write a new number sentence. What would we write this time? (Ask the students to help you fill in the blanks again, explaining why they chose each number.) Read the number sentence with me.

S: 9 – 2 = 7!

Continue with the activity several times, repeating the pattern through 9 – 8 and having the students write and read the equation each time.

Problem 2

T: Put your bears away and take out your linking cubes. How many do you have?

S: 10.

T: Let's pretend your linking cubes are little cars. You have 10 cars. Nine of them drove away. One is left. Slide 9 of your cars to the other side of the desk to show the ones that drove away. How would we write a number sentence about this story? Please help me fill in the blanks.

S: Put the 10 first to show how many we started with. → Next write the 9 to show the ones that drove

NOTES ON MULTIPLE MEANS OF REPRESENTATION:

Introduce unfamiliar words to English language learners by holding up a counting bear when you say *a family of bears* and showing pictures for *tree* and *forest*. This will allow them to focus on the math and also expand their vocabulary, which will in turn help them explain their thinking during partner shares.

COMMON CORE   Lesson 33:   Solve *take from* equations with no unknown using numbers to 10.
                   Date: 11/12/13

4.G.5

away. → Then you put 1 to show the car that was left!

T: Great! Write the number sentence on your personal board, too! Read it with me.

S: $10 - 9 = 1$.

T: Put your 10 cars back together. This time, use your cubes to show that 8 cars drove away. How many are left?

S: There are still 2.

T: Let's all fill in the blanks for our new number sentence. (Allow students to guide in creating the new equation and have them recreate it on their personal boards.) Read with me.

S: $10 - 8 = 2$.

Continue activity through $10 - 1$, each time asking students to act out the story and write and read the number sentence.

Problem 3

T: Now pretend your 10 linking cubes are trains in the station. Some of them drive off into the roundhouse. With your partner, act out this story several times. Each time, write the new number sentence on your personal board and whisper-read it together. (Allow time for exploration and discussion. Circulate to ensure accuracy in representing the equation.)

Problem Set (10 minutes)

Students should do their personal best to complete the Problem Set within the allotted 10 minutes.

Note: The Problem Set does not specify whether students should cross off or hide to solve. At this point, students can select the strategy that works best for them. Provide suggestions about strategies for students who are struggling to represent subtraction using concrete or pictorial methods.

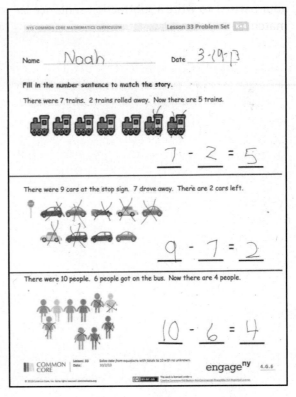

Student Debrief (8 minutes)

Lesson Objective: Solve *take from* equations with no unknown using numbers to 10.

The Student Debrief is intended to invite reflection and active processing of the total lesson experience.

Invite students to review their solutions for the Problem Set. They should check work by comparing answers with a partner before going over answers as a class. Look for misconceptions or misunderstandings that can be addressed in the Debrief. Guide students in a conversation to debrief the Problem Set and process the lesson.

You may choose to use any combination of the questions below to lead the discussion.

- Look at the first problem about the trains. What strategy did you use to find out how many trains were left? What does the 7 tell about? What does the 2 tell about? The 5?

- Look at the last problem about the planes. Compare your drawing with your partner's. How are they alike? How are they different? Did you use the same strategy to find out how many planes are still in the air?

- How did you know where to put each number in your number sentences?

- How are subtraction number sentences different from addition sentences? Are there any ways in which they are similar? (Note: Using a number bond at this point in the Debrief can help students gently begin to see the relationships between addition and subtraction.)

- Look at the number bond you created for the ants during the Application Problem. Work with your partner to write a subtraction sentence to match.

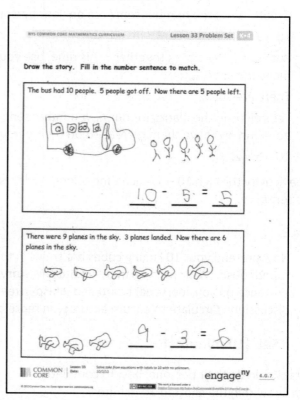

Name _____   Date _____

Fill in the number sentence to match the story.

There were 7 trains. 2 trains rolled away. Now there are 5 trains.

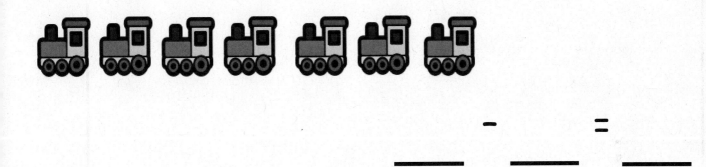

$$\underline{\hspace{3cm}} - \underline{\hspace{3cm}} = \underline{\hspace{3cm}}$$

There were 9 cars at the stop sign. 7 drove away. There are 2 cars left.

$$\underline{\hspace{3cm}} - \underline{\hspace{3cm}} = \underline{\hspace{3cm}}$$

There were 10 people. 6 people got on the bus. Now there are 4 people.

$$\underline{\hspace{3cm}} - \underline{\hspace{3cm}} = \underline{\hspace{3cm}}$$

Draw the story. Fill in the number sentence to match.

The bus had 10 people. 5 people got off. Now there are 5 people left.

_____ - _____ = _____

There were 9 planes in the sky. 3 planes landed. Now there are 6 planes in the sky.

_____ - _____ = _____

Lesson 33:   Solve *take from* equations with no unknown using numbers to 10.
Date: 11/12/13

4.G.9

Name _____   Date _____

Fill in the number sentence and the number bond.

There are 10 teddy bears. Cross out 2 bears. There are 8 bears left.

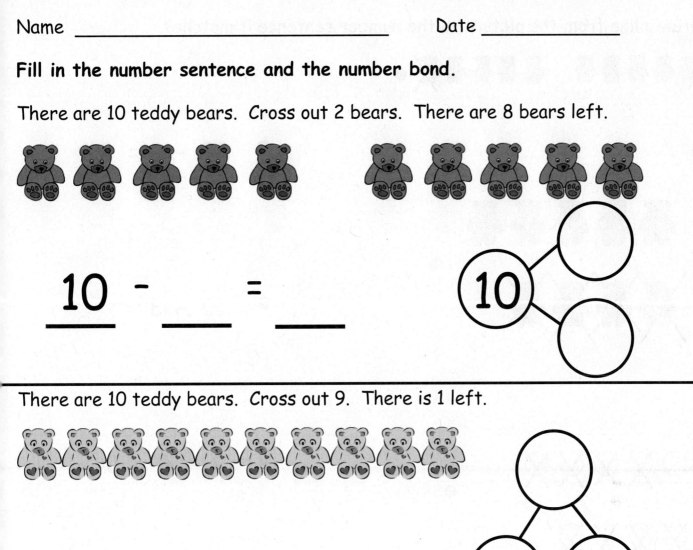

$$\underline{10} - \underline{} = \underline{}$$

There are 10 teddy bears. Cross out 9. There is 1 left.

$$\underline{} - \underline{} = \underline{}$$

There are 10 Teddy bears. Cross out 3. There are 7 bears left.

$$\underline{} - \underline{} = \underline{}$$

Draw a line from the picture to the number sentence it matches.

• 10 – 1 = 9

• 10 – 3 =

• 9 – 4 = 5

• 9 – 8 = 1

 | Lesson 33:   Solve *take from* equations with no unknown using numbers to 10.

Date: 11/12/13

4.G.1

Lesson 34

Objective: Represent subtraction story problems by breaking off, crossing out, and hiding a part.

Suggested Lesson Structure

■ Fluency Practice   (12 minutes)
▨ Application Problem   (5 minutes)
▢ Concept Development   (25 minutes)
▨ Student Debrief   (8 minutes)
   Total Time   **(50 minutes)**

Fluency Practice (12 minutes)

- Hide 2 **K.CC.4d**   (3 minutes)
- What is Less? **K.OA.3**   (4 minutes)
- Snap **K.OA.3**   (5 minutes)

Hide 2 (3 minutes)

Materials: (T) 5-group cards

Note: This activity prepares students to focus on subtraction in today's lesson.

  T: (Show the 4 dot card.) Raise your hand when you know how many dots. (Wait for all hands to go up, then give the signal.) Ready?

  S: 4.

  T: Now, hide 2. You can use your hand to hide 2 of the dots from your eyes, or you can just see it in your mind. Now how many dots are left?

  S: 2.

Continue with the following suggested sequence: 3, 5, 6, 7, 8, 9, 10.

What is Less? (4 minutes)

Materials: (S) Personal white boards

Note: This activity builds on students' understanding of comparison and builds fluency with subtraction facts for numbers to 5.

  T: (Write 2 on the board.) Think of a number that is less than 2. Write it on your board and show me.

Lesson 34:   Represent subtraction story problems by breaking off, crossing out, and hiding a part.
Date: 11/12/13

S: (Write 1 or 0.)

T: Write this **subtraction sentence** on your board: 2 minus 1.

S: (Write 2 – 1.)

T: Write the answer and show me.

S: (Write 2 – 1 = 1.)

T: Say the subtraction sentence.

S: 2 minus 1 equals 1.

Repeat with 3, 4, and 5. Use each of the smaller numbers students identify to build a subtraction equation (e.g., 3 – 1, 3 – 2). Invite students who choose zero to write a subtraction equation using zero and show it to the class. Addition and subtraction of zero will be covered in GK–M4–Lesson 37.

Snap (5 minutes)

Materials: (S) 5-stick of linking cubes per student

Note: This fast-paced game will serve as a concrete review of the composition and decomposition of numbers to 5. It also supports the part–whole thinking needed in the upcoming lesson.

1. Partner A shows Partner B her 5-stick, and then puts it behind her back.
2. When Partner B says, "Snap!" Partner A quickly breaks her stick into two parts.
3. Partner A shows Partner B one part.
4. Partner B tries to figure out the hidden part.
5. Partner A shows the hidden part and checks Partner B's guess.
6. Both partners say the subtraction sentence together (e.g., "5 take away 2 equals 3!").

Partners take turns, continuing with the 5-stick. If time permits, students can also play with a 4-stick, 3-stick, etc.

Application Problem (5 minutes)

Materials: Personal white boards

Tony had 8 checkers. His friend took 3 away. How many checkers did Tony have left?

Draw a picture of the story. (Draw.) Make a number bond and a number sentence about the story.

Show your work to your friend. Did you both do it the same way?

Note: Thinking about a *take from* problem and discussing the work with a partner provides an anticipatory set for today's lesson.

NOTES ON
MULTIPLE MEANS OF
ENGAGEMENT:

Have students who are performing below grade level and students with disabilities act out the Application Problem before asking them to make a picture of it and before explaining their thinking.

Lesson 34:   Represent subtraction story problems by breaking off, crossing out, and hiding a part.

Date: 11/12/13

4.G.14

Concept Development (25 minutes)

Materials: (S) Linking cube 10-stick with a color change at the five, 10 teddy bear or other counters, paper bowl per pair, personal white boards

Problem 1

T: Take out your linking cube stick. How many cubes do you have?

S: 10.

T: Break off 3 cubes from the end. Now how many do you have left?

S: 7.

T: Let's make a number bond about what we just did. What was our whole? (10.) What are our parts now? (7 and 3.) How would we talk about what we just did?

S: We had 10 and broke off 3. → We took away 3. Now we have 7 left. → We made 10 into parts of 3 and 7.

T: Yes! Draw the number bond on your personal board. (Demonstrate.) How could we make a number sentence about this?

S: 10 take away 3 is 7! → 10 − 3 = 7. (If students say 7 + 3 = 10, acknowledge the correct addition sentence and ask them to say the subtraction sentence.)

Write the number sentence on the board and ask students to represent it on their personal white boards. Repeat with several different iterations of breaking off, asking students to record number bonds and number sentences each time.

Problem 2

T: Put your linking cubes away. Listen to my story and draw the picture on your personal board.

T: Ellie had 9 grapes. Draw the grapes on your board. (Allow time for drawing; circulate to ensure accuracy.)

T: She shared 4 grapes with a friend. How could we show that in your drawing?

S: We could cross them out like we did before!

T: Cross out the number of grapes that she shared. How many grapes does Ellie have left?

S: 5! → We crossed out 4, now we have 5 left.

T: How would we make a subtraction sentence about what we did?

S: 9 − 4 = 5.

T: Write the number sentence on your personal board. Whisper-read it to your partner.

T: Let's tell the story in a different way. This time, Ellie had 10 grapes. She shared 8 grapes. How will your picture and your number sentence change? (Repeat several iterations of the story, each time

NOTES ON MULTIPLE MEANS OF ACTION AND EXPRESSION:

Scaffold your lesson for English language learners by showing them what you are asking them to do. Draw nine grapes (with a picture of grapes) and cross off the number of grapes as you instruct students to cross out the number of grapes shared. As you continue your lesson, use gestures to illustrate what you want students to do.

| Lesson 34: | Represent subtraction story problems by breaking off, crossing out, and hiding a part. |
| Date: | 11/12/13 |

4.G.15

changing the minuend and subtrahend and asking the students to record the drawing and the results in a number sentence.)

Problem 3

T: Get out your bears! Now it is time to work with your partner. How many bears do you have?

S: 10.

T: Let's pretend four bears went to sleep in a cave. Hide 4 bears under the bowl to show the sleepy bears. How many bears do you have left?

S: We have 6.

T: Draw a number bond on your personal board. Show the 10 bears you had and the 4 sleepy bears. How many bears were still awake? (6.) Finish the number bond and write the number sentence. Let's read it together.

S: $10 - 4 = 6$.

T: Great job! Let's do some more of this work together. Take turns with your partner hiding some sleepy bears. Each time, write the number bond and the number sentence. Let's see how many *take away* sentences we can make! (Circulate to ensure understanding and accuracy. As students create number sentences, list them on the board to be reviewed at the end of the lesson or during the Debrief.)

Problem Set (10 minutes)

Students should do their personal best to complete the Problem Set within the allotted 10 minutes.

Student Debrief (8 minutes)

Lesson Objective: Represent subtraction story problems by breaking off, crossing out, and hiding a part.

The Student Debrief is intended to invite reflection and active processing of the total lesson experience.

Invite students to review their solutions for the Problem Set. They should check work by comparing answers with a partner before going over answers as a class. Look for misconceptions or misunderstandings that can be addressed in the Debrief. Guide students in a conversation to debrief the Problem Set and process the lesson.

You may choose to use any combination of the questions below to lead the discussion.

- How did the pictures in your Problem Set help you to make your number bonds?

COMMON CORE   Lesson 34:   Represent subtraction story problems by breaking off, crossing out,
                             and hiding a part.
                  Date: 11/12/13

4.G.16

© 2013 Common Core, Inc. All rights reserved. **commoncore.org**

- How were the number bonds related to your subtraction sentences?
- How did you know where to put the different numbers in your *take away* sentences?
- How are the number sentences we wrote on the board similar? How are they different?
- Think back to Tony's checkers in the Application Problem. What would it look like if we hid the checkers his friend took? What would it look like if we crossed off the ones his friend took? Is there a way that we could break off a part? (Breaking off a part could entail lining up all of the checkers and pulling 3 away from the rest, or students could represent the checkers using an 8-stick and breaking off 3.)

COMMON CORE™

Lesson 34:   Represent subtraction story problems by breaking off, crossing out, and hiding a part.
Date: 11/12/13

4.G.1

Name _____   Date _____

Fill in the number sentences and number bonds.

There are 9 babies playing. 2 crawl away. How many babies are left?

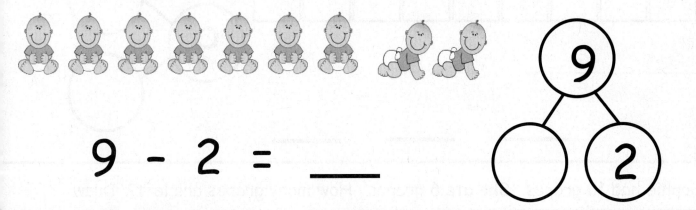

9 – 2 = ___

There are 10 babies playing. 1 crawls away. How many babies are left?

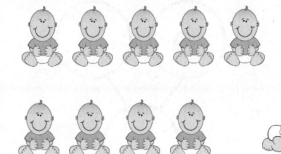

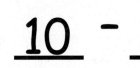

<u>10</u> – ___ = ___

There are 9 babies playing. 6 crawl away. How many babies are left?

___ – ___ = ___

Lesson 34: Represent subtraction story problems by breaking off, crossing out, and hiding a part.
Date: 11/12/13

4.G.18

Carlos had a 9-stick. He broke off 4 cubes to share with his friend. How many cubes are left? Draw a line to show where he broke his stick.

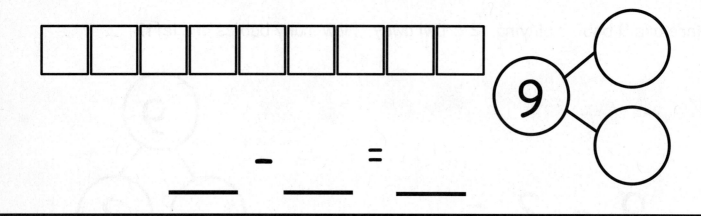

_____ - _____ = _____

Sophie had 10 grapes. She ate 6 grapes. How many grapes are left? Draw her grapes and cross off the ones she ate.

_____ - _____ = _____

Spot had 10 bones. He hid 8 bones in the ground. How many bones does he have now? Draw Spot's bones.

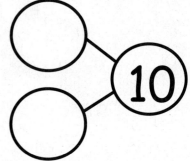

_____ - _____ = _____

 Lesson 34: Represent subtraction story problems by breaking off, crossing out, and hiding a part.

Date: 11/12/13

4.G.1

© 2013 Common Core, Inc. All rights reserved. commoncore.org

Name _____ Date _____

There were 8 penguins. 2 penguins went back to the ship. Cross out 2 penguins. Fill in the number sentence and the number bond.

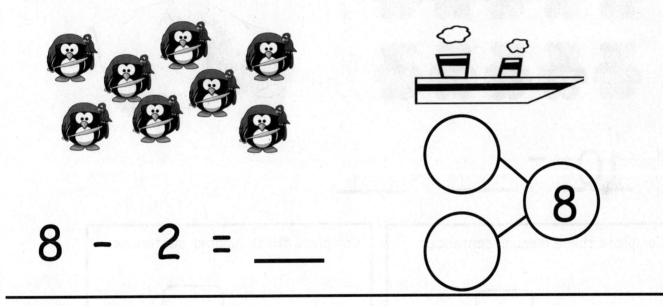

8 – 2 = ___

Count the cubes. Draw a line to break 4 cubes off the train. Fill in the number sentence and the number bond.

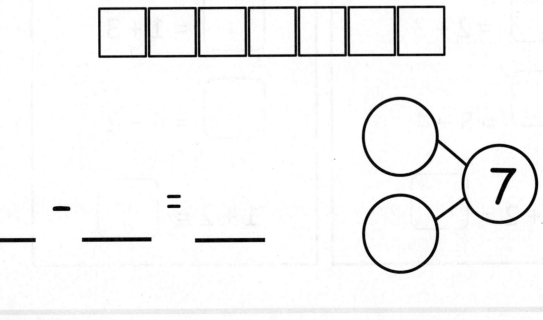

___ – ___ = ___

Lesson 34: Represent subtraction story problems by breaking off, crossing out, and hiding a part.

Date: 11/12/13

4.G.20

There are 10 bears. Some go inside the cave to hide. Cross them out.
Complete the number sentence.

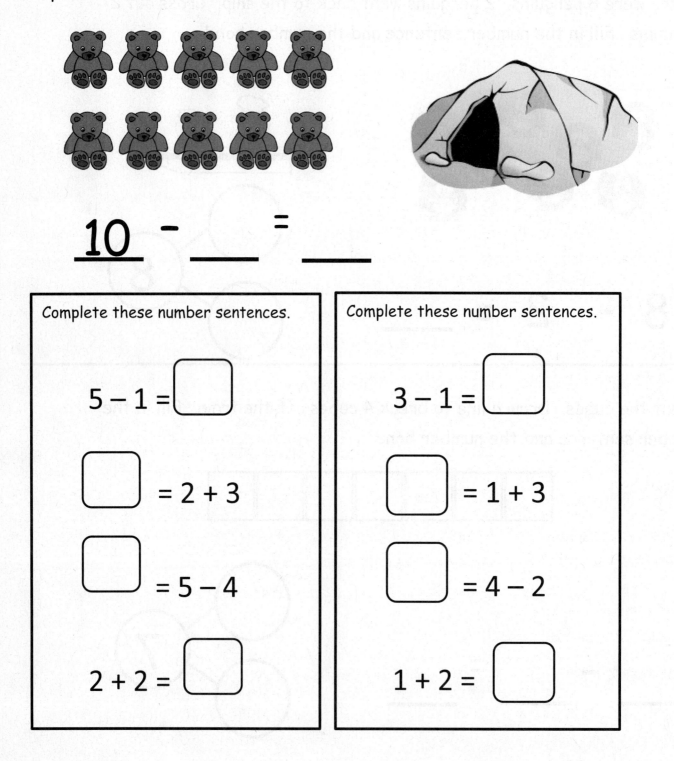

$$10 - \underline{\hphantom{0}} = \underline{\hphantom{0}}$$

Complete these number sentences.	Complete these number sentences.
5 − 1 = ☐	3 − 1 = ☐
☐ = 2 + 3	☐ = 1 + 3
☐ = 5 − 4	☐ = 4 − 2
2 + 2 = ☐	1 + 2 = ☐

Lesson 35

Objective: Decompose the number 9 using 5-group drawings, and record each decomposition with a subtraction equation.

Suggested Lesson Structure

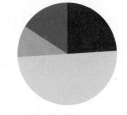

- ■ Fluency Practice   (12 minutes)
- ■ Application Problem   (5 minutes)
- ☐ Concept Development   (25 minutes)
- ■ Student Debrief   (8 minutes)
  - **Total Time**   **(50 minutes)**

Fluency Practice (12 minutes)

- Core Fluency Differentiated Practice Sets **K.OA.5**   (5 minutes)
- Spill the Beans **K.OA.5**   (4 minutes)
- Happy Counting **K.CC.2**   (3 minutes)

Core Fluency Differentiated Practice Sets (5 minutes)

Materials: (S) Core Fluency Practice Sets from GK–M4–Lesson 29

Note: This activity assesses students' progress toward mastery of the required addition fluency for Grade K.

Distribute Practice Sets A, B, C, or D based on student performance in GK–M4–Lesson 33. Students who correctly answered all questions on a Practice Set in the previous lesson should move to the next Practice Set. All other students should try to improve their scores on Practice Set A.

Students complete as many problems as they can in 90 seconds. Assign a counting pattern and start number for early finishers, or have them play an independent game like the Make 10 Memory Game. Collect and correct any Practice Sets completed within the allotted time.

Spill the Beans (4 minutes)

Materials: (S) 5 beans painted red on one side or 5 two-sided counters, cup, personal white board

Note: This activity leads students to mastery of the fluency goal for the grade, add and subtract within 5.

Have students complete the following steps:

Lesson 35:   Decompose the number 9 using 5-group drawings, and record each decomposition with a subtraction equation.

Date: 11/12/13

4.G.22

1. Take 3 beans out of the bag, and place them in the cup.
2. Shake the cup gently, and then spill the beans onto the board.
3. Take away the red beans, and record as a subtraction sentence (e.g., 3 – 2).
4. Erase, and repeat a few more times.

If students demonstrate mastery with subtraction to 3, repeat the process for 4 and 5.

Happy Counting (3 minutes)

Note: Fluidity with counting forward and backward builds students' number sense and sets the stage for counting on strategies used in Grade 1.

Conduct activity as described in GK–M4–Lesson 19, but continue to 15 or 20.

Application Problem (5 minutes)

Materials: 9 pennies, personal white board

Steve had 9 pennies. He wanted to put some pennies into each of his two pockets. Use your pennies to show one way he could have divided them. Make a number bond about your idea. Show your number bond to your partner. Did she do it the same way? How many different ways can you divide the pennies?

Note: A concrete review of the decomposition of 9 will prepare the students for a more formal decomposition of 9 with equations in today's lesson.

> **NOTES ON MULTIPLE MEANS OF ACTION AND EXPRESSION:**
>
> Challenge students performing above grade level by extending the Application Problem to showing all the ways Steve could divide his 9 pennies. Students can then share with the class how they went about finding the different ways to make 9.

Concept Development (25 minutes)

Materials: (S) Equation template, personal white board

MP.7

T: Connie had 9 bouncy balls. Let me draw her balls in the 5-group way on the board. (Demonstrate drawing the 5-group way.) Three of her balls were green. I will draw a circle around a group of 3 to show the balls that were green. (Draw the circle.) How many of her balls were not green?

S: 6!

T: How did you know?

S: I counted the ones that were not in the circle. → I took away the 3 to get 6. → I saw 5 and 1 more weren't green.

T: You are right! How do I make a number bond about this?

S: Our whole is 9. → We have parts of 3 and 6.

T: (Write the number bond on board.) We could also write this as a subtraction sentence, couldn't we? Let's find out how many balls are not green! Cross out the part of 3. Nine balls take away 3 green balls leaves…?

Lesson 35:	Decompose the number 9 using 5-group drawings, and record each decomposition with a subtraction equation.
Date:	11/12/13

4.G.2

S: 6 balls!

T: Please help me write the subtraction sentence. (Allow students to guide you in creating the sentence.) Let's read it together.

S: 9 – 3 = 6.

T: Let's try another. Doug had 9 special rocks. Draw the rocks.

T: He had 4 white rocks. This time, let's circle the 4 rocks to show the ones that were white. Let's cross off that part to see how many were left. How many rocks were another color?

S: 5! → I counted the 5 that were not crossed off. → I counted on from 4 to 9!

T: Who can give me a number sentence to tell me about the picture?

S: Nine rocks take away 4 white rocks leaves 5 rocks.

T: Let's write and read that together: 9 – 4 = 5.

T: Now it is time for partner work. Listen to my story and make the picture on your board. Then, you may work with your partner to make a number sentence about your story.

T: Calla had 9 apples. Draw her apples. (Allow students time to draw.) Seven of her apples were green. Circle and cross off the 7 green apples. Now, write a number sentence to tell me how many apples were not green. (Circulate to ensure accuracy and comprehension. If appropriate, choose pairs of students to model their work on the board or on chart paper and to explain their thinking to the class.)

T: Great! Let's do this another way! What if Calla had only 1 green apple? How would your picture and your number sentence change? Talk to your partner about the new story. (Allow time for sharing and discussion.)

T: Now, you and your partner can take turns deciding how many green apples Calla had. Each time, make a new picture and write the number sentence. Raise your hand when you and your partner have a new number sentence for me to look at, and I will collect them for the board! (Allow time for students to create several iterations of the story. Then, allow students to share their equations to be reviewed at the end of the lesson or during the Debrief.)

> **NOTES ON MULTIPLE MEANS OF ACTION AND EXPRESSION:**
>
> When it is time to share, allow English language learners to use their boards to point and show what they did in response to the story. Help them to produce language by providing them with sentence starters such as, "___ apples are green," and "I got my answer by…."

Problem Set (10 minutes)

Students should do their personal best to complete the Problem Set within the allotted 10 minutes.

Student Debrief (8 minutes)

Lesson Objective: Decompose the number 9 using 5-group drawings, and record each decomposition with a subtraction equation.

The Student Debrief is intended to invite reflection and active processing of the total lesson experience.

| Lesson 35: | Decompose the number 9 using 5-group drawings, and record each decomposition with a subtraction equation. |
| Date: | 11/12/13 |

4.G.24

Invite students to review their solutions for the Problem Set. They should check work by comparing answers with a partner before going over answers as a class. Look for misconceptions or misunderstandings that can be addressed in the Debrief. Guide students in a conversation to debrief the Problem Set and process the lesson.

You may choose to use any combination of the questions below to lead the discussion.

- Look at the first problem. Tell your neighbor what each dot represents. (You are looking for a response that each dot represents one of the balls.)

- How did you decide where to place each number in your number sentences?

- Do you always have to take time drawing a picture or can we represent pictures with something easier and faster to draw? Did we do this in the Problem Set?

- What strategy did you use to solve the subtraction sentences at the end of the Problem Set? (Answers will vary. Many students will know these facts after repeated experiences. Others may still be using fingers or drawings to solve.)

- What is similar about the number sentences we listed on the board? What is different?

- How does crossing out in a picture help you to find the numbers for a number sentence?

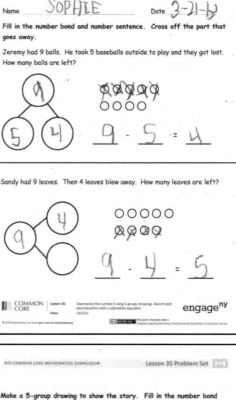

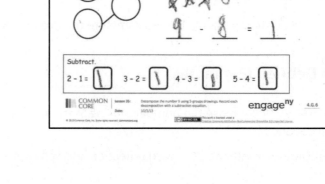

COMMON CORE™ | Lesson 35: Decompose the number 9 using 5-group drawings, and record each decomposition with a subtraction equation.
Date: 11/12/13

4.G.2

Name _____   Date _____

Fill in the number bond and number sentence.   Cross off the part that goes away.

Jeremy had 9 balls. He took 5 baseballs outside to play, and they got lost. How many balls are left?

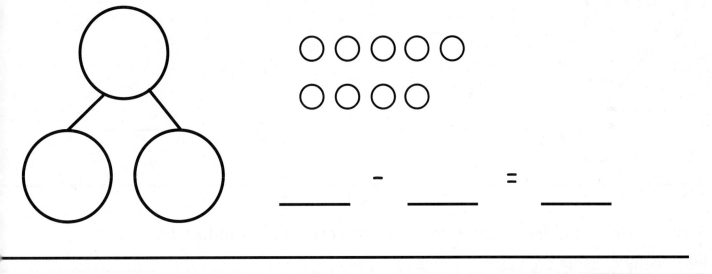

____ ‒ ____ = ____

Sandy had 9 leaves. Then 4 leaves blew away. How many leaves are left?

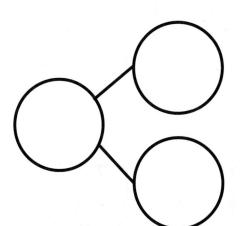

____ ‒ ____ = ____

Make a 5-group drawing to show the story. Fill in the number bond and number sentence. Cross off the part that goes away.

Ryder had 9 star stickers. He gave 3 to his friend. How many silver stickers does Ryder have now?

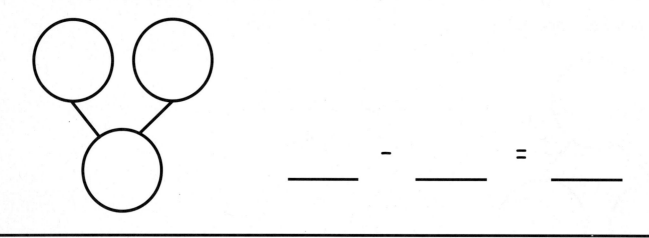

_____ - _____ = _____

Jen had 9 granola bars. She gave 8 of the granola bars to her teammates. How many granola bars does she have left?

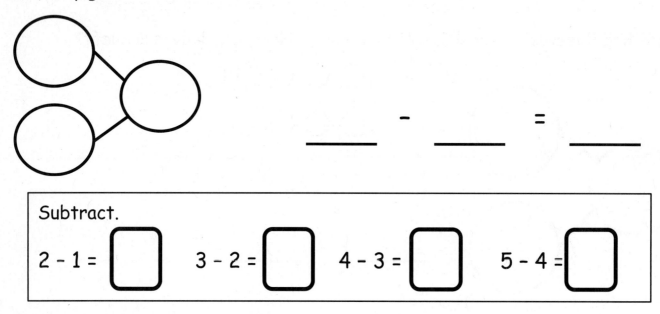

_____ - _____ = _____

Subtract.

2 – 1 = ☐   3 – 2 = ☐   4 – 3 = ☐   5 – 4 = ☐

 **Lesson 35:**   Decompose the number 9 using 5-group drawings, and record each
decomposition with a subtraction equation.   4.G.27
Date: 11/12/13

Name _____   Date _____

Fill in the number bond and number sentence. Cross off the part that goes away.

Mary had 9 library books. She returned 1 book to the library. How many books are left?

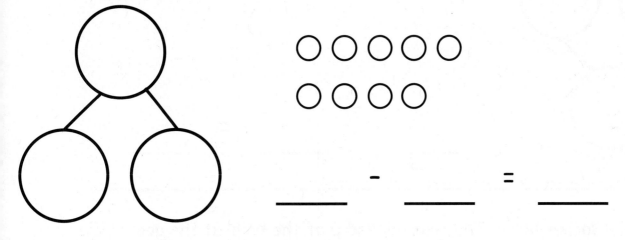

_____   -   _____   =   _____

There were 9 lunch bags. 3 bags were thrown away. How many bags are there now?

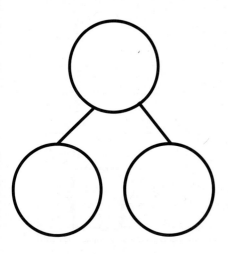

_____   -   _____   =   _____

Lesson 35:	Decompose the number 9 using 5-group drawings, and record each decomposition with a subtraction equation.
Date:	11/12/13

4.G.28

Make a 5-group drawing to show the story. Fill in the number bond and number sentence. Cross off the part that goes away.

Ms. Lopez has 9 pencils. 7 of them broke. How many pencils are left?

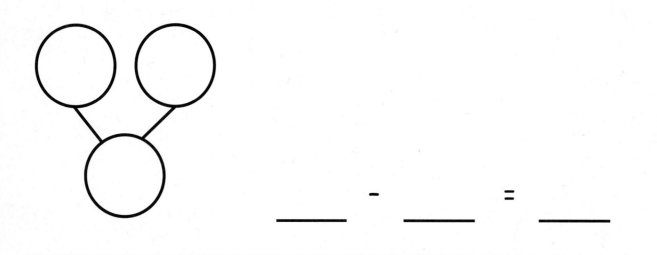

_____ - _____ = _____

There are 9 soccer balls. The team kicked 5 of the balls at the goal. How many soccer balls are left?

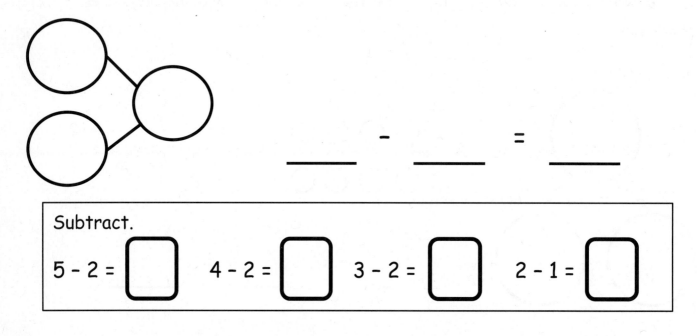

_____ - _____ = _____

Subtract.

5 - 2 = ☐   4 - 2 = ☐   3 - 2 = ☐   2 - 1 = ☐

 **COMMON CORE**™

Lesson 35:   Decompose the number 9 using 5-group drawings, and record each
decomposition with a subtraction equation.

Date: 11/12/13

4.G.29

Lesson 36

Objective: Decompose the number 10 using 5-group drawings, and record each decomposition with a subtraction equation.

Suggested Lesson Structure

■ Fluency Practice	(12 minutes)
■ Application Problem	(5 minutes)
■ Concept Development	(25 minutes)
■ Student Debrief	(8 minutes)
Total Time	**(50 minutes)**

Fluency Practice (12 minutes)

- Sprint: Core Fluency **K.OA.5**   (9 minutes)
- Counting to 30 by Ones with the Rekenrek **K.CC.1**   (3 minutes)

Sprint: Core Fluency (9 minutes)

Materials: (S) Core Fluency Sprints from GK–M4–Lesson 31

Note: This activity assesses students' progress toward mastery of the required addition fluency for kindergarten. Select the Sprint that is most appropriate for the class. In order to correct the work as a class, all students should take the same Sprint.

   T: It's time for a Sprint! (Briefly recall previous Sprint preparation activities, and distribute Sprints facedown.) Take out your pencil and one crayon, any color. For this Sprint, you are going to subtract to find how many are left. (Demonstrate the first problem as needed.)

Continue to follow the Sprint procedure as outlined in GK–M4–Lesson 3. Have students work on the Sprint a second time. Continue to emphasize that the goal is simply to do better than the first time and celebrate improvement.

Counting to 30 by Ones with the Rekenrek (3 minutes)

Materials: (T) 100-bead Rekenrek

Note: Counting from 20 to 30 will prove easier than learning the linguistically challenging counting sequence of 11–20. Once students know the number word *twenty,* it becomes just a matter of extending a pattern.

Conduct as described in GK–M4–Lesson 32.

	Lesson 36:	Decompose the number 10 using 5-group drawings, and record each decomposition with a subtraction equation.	
	Date:	11/12/13	**4.G.30**

© 2013 Common Core, Inc. All rights reserved. **commoncore.org**

Application Problem (5 minutes)

Materials: (S) 10 linking cubes, personal white board

Martin had 10 building blocks. Pretend your linking cubes are his blocks. Count to make sure there are 10!

He shared 4 blocks with his sister. Move 4 blocks to show the ones he shared. How many blocks did he still have? Make a number bond about the story. Now, make a number sentence. Show your work to your partner. Did she do it the same way?

Put your blocks back together. Act out the story again, sharing a different number of blocks this time. How does your number sentence change?

Note: Concrete work with decomposition of 10 prepares the students for today's lesson.

NOTES ON MULTIPLE MEANS OF ENGAGEMENT:

Scaffold the Application Problem for below grade level students and students with disabilities by asking them to act out the problem and asking questions as they go. For example, if Martin had 10 Lego blocks, ask, "How many Lego blocks does Martin have?" If he shares 4 blocks with his sister (have one student give her partner 4 blocks) ask, "How many blocks does his sister have? How many does Martin have left?"

Concept Development (25 minutes)

Materials: (S) Equation template, personal white board

T: Melanie had 10 peaches. Draw her peaches in the 5-group way on your board. (Demonstrate drawing the 5-group way.) Four of her peaches were not yet ripe. Circle and cross out the 4 unripe peaches. How many peaches were ready to eat?

S: 6! → She has 6 ripe peaches!

T: Let's make a number bond about this story. What is our whole? How many peaches does she have?

S: 10.

T: What would our parts be?

S: 4 and 6. → 4 are not ripe and 6 are!

T: (Demonstrate making a number bond.) What if we wanted to make a subtraction sentence from this number bond?

S: We would start with the 10 peaches. → We would take away the 4 that aren't ripe. → There are 6 left!

T: Write the number sentence on your board and read it with me: $10 - 4 = 6$.

NOTES ON MULTIPLE MEANS OF REPRESENTATION:

To support English language learners, teach the meaning of words they need to follow the lesson, such as *peach*, *ripe*, *car*, and *wheel*. Bring in examples of ripe fruit and fruit not yet ripe to help students get an orientation to the context of the problem. Allow non-native English speakers to make up stories in their native language to show on their personal boards.

Lesson 36:   Decompose the number 10 using 5-group drawings, and record each decomposition with a subtraction equation.
Date: 11/12/13

4.G.31

T: Erase your board. Listen to this next story: Chris had 10 toy cars. Draw squares in the 5-group way to show all of his cars. (Allow time for the students to draw, then demonstrate the process to ensure accuracy.) Two of the cars had no wheels. Circle and then cross off the cars with no wheels (demonstrate). Who can help me make a number bond about this story?

S: He had 10 cars, so the 10 would be the whole. → The parts would be 2 and 8 for the cars that didn't have wheels and the cars that did.

MP.4 T: Great! (Draw the number bond.) How will we make our number sentence? (Allow students to guide in the creation of the subtraction equation.) Write the equation and read with me.

S: $10 - 2 = 8$!

T: It's time for some partner work! With your partner, make up some *ten* stories of your own. Show your work on your board. When you have your number sentence, raise your hand so I can come add it to our collection! (Circulate to ensure accuracy and understanding. Pairs of students can be encouraged to show their work on the board or on chart paper. As you collect the equations, write them on the board to be reviewed at the end of the lesson or during the Debrief. If desired, allow students to work on paper for this part of the lesson and collect the lovely story problems for a class math book.)

Problem Set (10 minutes)

Students should do their personal best to complete the Problem Set within the allotted 10 minutes.

Student Debrief (8 minutes)

Lesson Objective: Decompose the number 10 using 5-group drawings, and record each decomposition with a subtraction equation.

The Student Debrief is intended to invite reflection and active processing of the total lesson experience.

Invite students to review their solutions for the Problem Set. They should check work by comparing answers with a partner before going over answers as a class. Look for misconceptions or misunderstandings that can be addressed in the Debrief. Guide students in a conversation to debrief the Problem Set and process the lesson.

You may choose to use any combination of the questions below to lead the discussion.

- Look at the first problem. Tell your neighbor what each dot represents. (Look for the response that each dot represents one of the blueberries.)

COMMON CORE™   Lesson 36:   Decompose the number 10 using 5-group drawings, and record each decomposition with a subtraction equation.

Date: 11/12/13

4.G.32

- How did you know which number belongs in the first blank in your number sentences?
- How did crossing out in your pictures help you to make your number sentences?
- Do you always have to take time drawing a picture or can we represent pictures with something easier and faster to draw? Did we do this in the Problem Set?
- How are the number sentences on the board alike? How are they different?

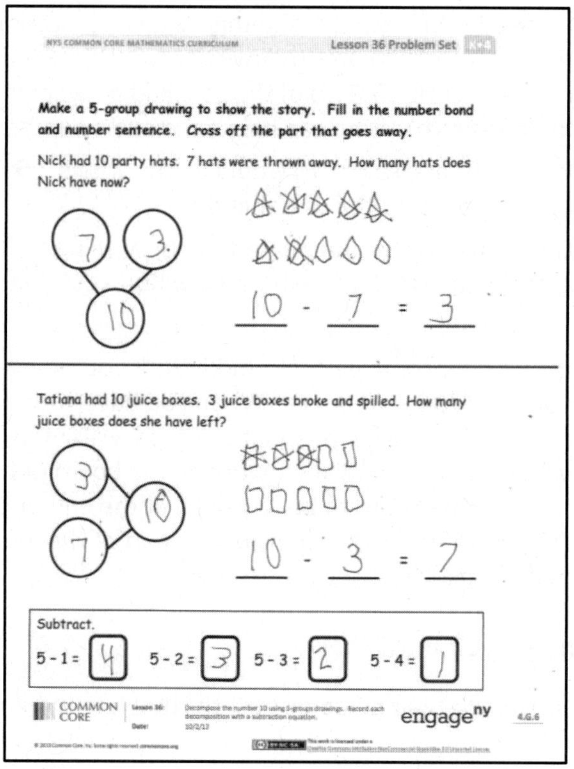
NYS COMMON CORE MATHEMATICS CURRICULUM Lesson 36 Problem Set K•4

Make a 5-group drawing to show the story. Fill in the number bond and number sentence. Cross off the part that goes away.

Nick had 10 party hats. 7 hats were thrown away. How many hats does Nick have now?

7, 3, 10

10 - 7 = 3

Tatiana had 10 juice boxes. 3 juice boxes broke and spilled. How many juice boxes does she have left?

3, 7, 10

10 - 3 = 7

Subtract.

5 - 1 = 4 5 - 2 = 3 5 - 3 = 2 5 - 4 = 1

COMMON CORE Lesson 36: Decompose the number 10 using 5-groups drawings. Record each decomposition with a subtraction equation. Date: 10/2/13 engage^ny 4.G.6

Name _____ Date _____

Fill in the number bond and number sentence. Cross off the part that goes away.

Stan had 10 blueberries. He ate 5 berries. How many blueberries are left?

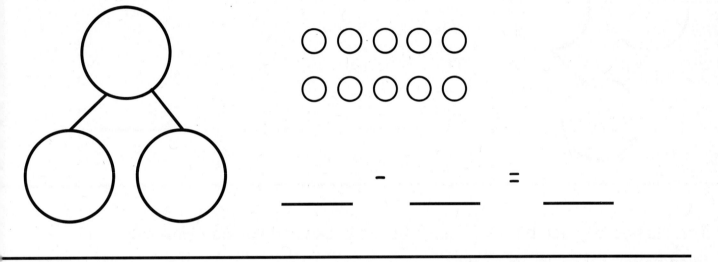

_____ - _____ = _____

Tracy had 10 heart stickers. She lost 1 sticker. How many stickers are left?

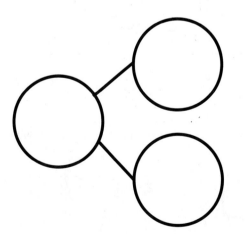

_____ - _____ = _____

Lesson 36:   Decompose the number 10 using 5-group drawings, and record each
                  decomposition with a subtraction equation.

Date: 11/12/13

4.G.34

Make a 5-group drawing to show the story.   Fill in the number bond and number sentence.   Cross off the part that goes away.

Nick had 10 party hats. 7 hats were thrown away. How many hats does Nick have now?

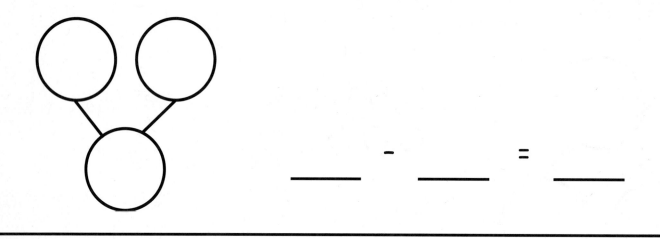

_____ - _____ = _____

Tatiana had 10 juice boxes. 3 juice boxes broke and spilled. How many full juice boxes does she have left?

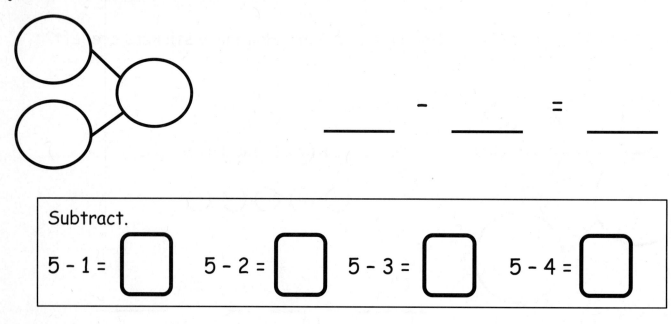

_____ - _____ = _____

Subtract.

$5 - 1 =$ ☐ $5 - 2 =$ ☐ $5 - 3 =$ ☐ $5 - 4 =$ ☐

Lesson 36:   Decompose the number 10 using 5-group drawings, and record each decomposition with a subtraction equation.

Date: 11/12/13

Name _____   Date _____

Fill in the number bond and number sentence. Cross off the part that goes away.

MacKenzie had 10 buttons on her jacket. 2 buttons broke off her jacket. How many buttons are left on her jacket?

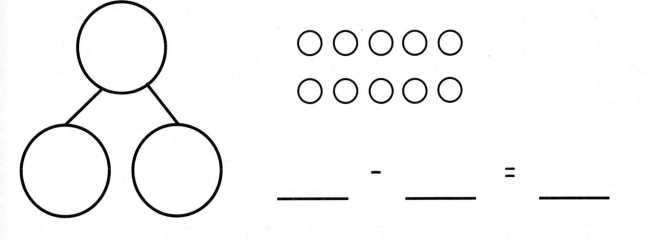

_____ - _____ = _____

Donna had 10 cups. 6 cups fell and broke. How many unbroken cups are there now?

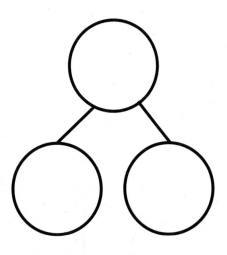

_____ - _____ = _____

Make a 5-group drawing to show the story. Fill in the number bond and number sentence. Cross off the part that goes away.

There were 10 butterflies. 9 butterflies flew away. How many are left?

_____ - _____ = _____

_____

Bob had 10 toy cars. 4 cars drove away. How many cars are left?

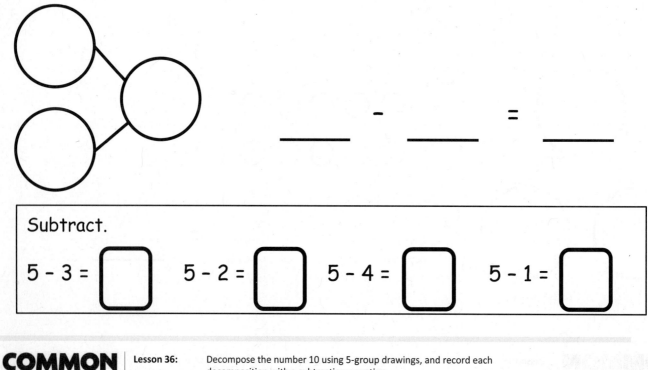

_____ - _____ = _____

Subtract.

5 – 3 = ☐   5 – 2 = ☐   5 – 4 = ☐   5 – 1 = ☐

Topic H

Patterns with Adding 0 and 1 and Making 10

K.OA.1, K.OA.2, K.OA.4

Focus Standard:	K.OA.1	Represent addition and subtraction with objects, fingers, mental images, drawings, sounds (e.g., claps), acting out situations, verbal explanations, expressions, or equations. (Drawings need not show details, but should show the mathematics in the problem. This applies wherever drawings are mentioned in the Standards.)
	K.OA.2	Solve addition and subtraction word problems, and add and subtract within 10, e.g., by using objects or drawings to represent the problem.
	K.OA.4	For any number from 1 to 9, find the number that makes 10 when added to the given number, e.g., by using objects or drawings, and record the answer with a drawing or equation.
Instructional Days:	5	
Coherence -Links from:	GPK–M5	Numerals to 5, Addition and Subtraction Stories, Counting to 20
-Links to:	G1–M1	Sums and Differences to 10

In Topic H students will begin to see patterns when adding 0 and 1, and find the number that makes 10 when added to a given number (**K.OA.4**). Lesson 37 explores the additive identity: zero. Students learn that adding or subtracting zero doesn't change the original quantity. In this lesson students will also begin to see the inverse relationship of addition and subtraction. "There were 8 children playing. Two more came to play. Then there were 10. But then 2 children had to go home. Then there were only 8 children playing." (8 + 2 = 10; 10 − 2 = 8.)

Lesson 38 uses 5-groups to see patterns when adding 1. Once again, focusing on the 5-group will help move students to Level 2 counting on strategies. Lessons 39 and 40 focus on making compositions to 10. "How many more does 6 need to make 10? Draw a picture of 6 in a 5-group. How many do you need to draw to make 10? Let's make a record of that with an addition equation." (6 + 4 = 10.)

This module is concluded with a culminating activity that calls on students to use what they have learned to teach others how to think about a part–part–whole situation. Students choose tools strategically to model and represent a stick of 10 cubes broken into two parts. This is an excellent opportunity to bring in another class, family members, administrators, or community volunteers to serve as enthusiastic "students" for individual student presentation.

	Topic H:	Patterns with Adding 0 and 1 and Making 10	
	Date:	11/12/13	**4.H.1**

A Teaching Sequence Towards Mastery of Patterns with Adding 0 and 1 and Making 10

Objective 1: Add or subtract 0 to get the same number and relate to word problems wherein the same quantity that joins a set, separates.
(Lesson 37)

Objective 2: Add 1 to numbers 1–9 to see the pattern of *the next number* using 5-group drawings and equations.
(Lesson 38)

Objective 3: Find the number that makes 10 for numbers 1–9, and record each with a 5-group drawing.
(Lesson 39)

Objective 4: Find the number that makes 10 for numbers 1–9, and record each with an addition equation.
(Lesson 40)

Objective 5: Culminating task—choose tools strategically to model and represent a stick of 10 cubes broken into two parts.
(Lesson 41)

Topic H: Patterns with Adding 0 and 1 and Making 10
Date: 11/12/13

Lesson 37

Objective: Add or subtract 0 to get the same number and relate to word problems wherein the same quantity that joins a set, separates.

Suggested Lesson Structure

■ Fluency Practice (12 minutes)
▨ Application Problem (5 minutes)
▨ Concept Development (25 minutes)
■ Student Debrief (8 minutes)

 Total Time   **(50 minutes)**

Fluency Practice (12 minutes)

- Imagine More to Add to 5 **K.OA.5** (5 minutes)
- Hide 1 **K.OA.1** (3 minutes)
- Cross Out 2 to Subtract Within 5 **K.OA.5** (4 minutes)

Imagine More to Add to 5 (5 minutes)

Materials: (S) Fluency Practice Set A

Note: This activity bridges the pictorial to the abstract as students make progress on the grade level fluency goal.

This activity is similar to GK–M4–Lesson 12 Draw More to Make 5, but now challenges students to add just by visualizing, and then write the addition sentence. Students who are struggling can show more on their fingers to solve, rather than drawing more.

After giving clear instructions and completing the first few problems together, allow students time to work at their own pace. Encourage them to do as many problems as they can within a given time frame. Go over the answers and direct students to energetically shout, "Yes!" for each correct answer.

Hide 1 (3 minutes)

Materials: (T) 5-group cards 0–5

Note: This activity helps students represent subtraction situations using number sentences.

 T: (Show the 2 dot card.) Raise your hand when you know how many dots are on the card. (Wait for all hands to go up, then give the signal.) Ready?

S: 2.

T: Now, hide 1. You can use your hand to hide 1 of the dots from your eyes, or you can just see it in your mind. Now how many dots are left?

S: 1.

T: Say the subtraction sentence starting with 2. (Pause.) Ready?

S: 2 − 1 = 1.

Continue with the following suggested sequence: 3, 4, 5, 1, then random numbers.

Variation: Students can write the subtraction sentence on their personal boards instead of verbally.

Cross Out 2 to Subtract Within 5 (4 minutes)

Materials: (S) Fluency Practice Set B

Note: Working with both addition and subtraction in fluency prepares students for today's lesson by gaining flexibility with both operations.

After giving clear instructions and completing the first few problems together, allow students time to work at their own pace. Encourage them to do as many problems as they can within a given time frame. Go over the answers, and direct students to energetically shout, "Yes!" for each correct answer.

Application Problem (5 minutes)

Materials: (S) Small ball of clay per student

Chico the puppy had 8 tennis balls. His owner threw two of them, but Chico brought them right back!

Make 8 balls with your clay. Show the story with the clay balls you created. (But don't throw them! Remember, he brought them right back!) Did Chico lose any of his tennis balls? Did he find any more balls? How many balls does Chico have at the end of the story?

Turn to your partner and talk about how you might be able to create number sentences about Chico's adventures. Then, act out the story with different numbers of balls.

Note: Thinking about inverse subtraction and addition situations in the story, and modeling them with concrete materials, provides the anticipatory set for today's lesson.

Concept Development (25 minutes)

Materials: (T) Construction paper number path (0–10) on the floor, additional number path for 0–10 drawn on the board (S) Number path template, personal white board

T: What do you notice on the floor and on the board? Do you remember what we call this?

S: There are squares with numbers on them, all in a row. → I see numbers from 0 to 10. → It is a number path!

| Lesson 37: | Add or subtract 0 to get the same number and relate to word problems wherein the same quantity that joins a set, separates. | 4.H.4 |
| Date: | 11/12/13 | |

T: Today we are going to show how we can use a number path to help us write a number sentence. Student A, please start at the beginning. (Point to the spot next to the number line by number 1.) Count and walk 5 spaces to get to the number 5. I want to make an addition sentence starting with the number 5. If I were thinking about an addition sentence, would I be adding more or taking some away?

S: Adding more.

T: I want to add 3. Student A, go forward 3 hops in the path to show 3 more. Where do you land?

S: Now I am on 8.

T: Yes. (Demonstrate on the class board number path as well.) We started at 5. Three more makes?

S: 8.

T: Let's make a number sentence about that together. I will write it here while you write it on your personal board.

S: 5 + 3 = 8.

T: Student B, please stand on the number 8. I want to make a subtraction sentence starting with my number 8. How do you think we might show that type of story on the number path?

S: You would go the other way! → This time the numbers would get smaller.

T: Good! Student B, could you subtract by going back 3 hops? Where do you land?

S: I'm back at 5! → We are right back where we started!

T: Write the number sentence with me: 8 – 3 = 5. Now, listen to the next story. I will ask someone to show it on our big number path while we show it on our personal board number paths.

T: There were 4 pigeons on the sidewalk. Five more pigeons came to join them. How many pigeons are there now? Student C, please show us how we could use our number path to help us solve this problem. Where would you begin?

S: I would start at the 4! → I would take 5 hops forward to show the 5 new pigeons. (Demonstrate.)

T: Show what Student C just did by hopping along your little number path with your finger. Where did you land?

S: I am on 9.

T: How many pigeons do we have now?

S: Now we have 9 pigeons!

T: Write and say the number sentence with me.

S: 4 + 5 = 9.

T: Pretend that the 5 pigeons flew away again. Show the new story on your number path with your finger while Student C shows us on the big number path. Where do you land this time?

COMMON CORE™

Lesson 37:   Add or subtract 0 to get the same number and relate to word problem: wherein the same quantity that joins a set, separates.

Date: 11/12/13

4.H.5

S: We had to go backwards. → We are back at 4! → We are right back where we started.

T: How many pigeons do we have now?

S: We have 4 pigeons left.

T: Write and say the new number sentence with me.

S: $9 - 5 = 4$.

T: Does anyone notice anything interesting?

S: We keep ending up back where we started. → The number sentences undo each other!

T: (Repeat several iterations of similar stories, showing inverse number sentences each time. Ask students to state and write a subtraction sentence that "undoes" the addition for each scenario or vice versa. If students demonstrate understanding, allow them to do some partner work in this manner.)

MP.8

T: Let's try a different kind of story this time. Student D, please come up to the number path to demonstrate while your friends work on their number paths.

T: David found 6 pine cones in the park. Show me 6 pine cones on the number path.

S: (Counts all the way to 6, or stands on the number 6.)

T: He looked and looked, but he couldn't find any more! Then, it was time to go, so he took his 6 pine cones home. How many pine cones does he have now? Hmmm. What should we do on our number paths?

S: We have to stay right here. → He didn't get any more, but he didn't lose any. → I don't have to go anywhere on the number path.

T: Who remembers the number that means *no more* or *none*?

S: Zero! → He has zero more pine cones!

T: I wonder how we could write an addition number sentence for this using zero.

S: Six pine cones and zero more pine cones is still 6 pine cones. → $6 + 0 = 6$.

T: How about a subtraction sentence?

S: Six pine cones minus zero pine cones is still 6 pine cones! → $6 - 0 = 6$!

T: (If needed, provide a few more examples of addition and subtraction number sentences with zero. If the students exhibit understanding, move to partner work.)

T: Turn to your partner. Use your number path to help you make up some more stories and number sentences using zero. When you have one, raise your hands so I may hear your story and collect your number sentences for our board. (Circulate to ensure understanding, listing equations on the board to be discussed during the Debrief.)

NOTES ON MULTIPLE MEANS OF ACTION AND EXPRESSION:

Build on English language learners' background knowledge by making the most of cultural and home experiences to help them bridge the language gap. For example, simply pair the terms *no more* with *no más* and pair *none* with *nada* and *ninguno* for native Spanish speakers. Point out that the Spanish word *cero* is a cognate of *zero*.

NOTES ON MULTIPLE MEANS OF ENGAGEMENT:

Extend learning for students performing above grade level by asking them to explain how the problems of adding and subtracting the same number are related to the addition and subtraction of zero problems.

COMMON CORE™   Lesson 37:   Add or subtract 0 to get the same number and relate to word problem: wherein the same quantity that joins a set, separates.   **4.H.6**

Date: 11/12/13

Problem Set (10 minutes)

Students should do their personal best to complete the Problem Set within the allotted 10 minutes.

Note: Depending on the abilities of the students, it may be necessary to read the problems individually and give students a time allotment to complete them. Early finishers can be encouraged to create additional story problems on the back if they have extra time.

Student Debrief (8 minutes)

Lesson Objective: Add or subtract 0 to get the same number and relate to word problems wherein the same quantity that joins a set, separates.

The Student Debrief is intended to invite reflection and active processing of the total lesson experience.

Invite students to review their solutions for the Problem Set. They should check work by comparing answers with a partner before going over answers as a class. Look for misconceptions or misunderstandings that can be addressed in the Debrief. Guide students in a conversation to debrief the Problem Set and process the lesson.

You may choose to use any combination of the questions below to lead the discussion.

- How did the number path help you in the first problem in your Problem Set?
- Did you notice any patterns in the Problem Set?
- How can addition and subtraction sentences undo each other?
- If we add or subtract zero in a number sentence, what happens?
- What new (or significant) math vocabulary did we use today to communicate precisely?
- Think about our Application Problem at the beginning of the lesson. Now could we write some number sentences about the adventures that Chico had with his tennis balls?

[Problem Set worksheet — top]

NYS COMMON CORE MATHEMATICS CURRICULUM   Lesson 37 Problem Set   K•4

Name NITANEL   Date 3-26-13

Listen to each story. Show the story with your fingers on the number path. Then fill in the number sentence.

1	2	3	4	5	6	7	8	9	10

Freddy has 3 strawberries for snack. His Dad gave him 2 more strawberries. How many strawberries does Freddy have now?

3 + 2 = 5

Freddy ate 2 of his strawberries. How many strawberries does Freddy have now?

5 - 2 = 3

Logan had 7 frogs. 2 frogs hopped away. How many frogs does Logan have now?

7 - 2 = 5

Pretend that Logan's 2 frogs hopped back. How many frogs does he have now?

5 + 2 = 7

COMMON CORE   Lesson 37:   Add or subtract zero to get the same number and relate to word problems wherein the same quantity that joins a set, separates.   engage^ny   4.H.8

[Problem Set worksheet — bottom]

NYS COMMON CORE MATHEMATICS CURRICULUM   Lesson 37 Problem Set   K•4

1	2	3	4	5	6	7	8	9	10

Stella had 4 pennies. She found 3 more pennies. How many pennies does Stella have now?

4 + 3 = 7

Stella gave the 3 pennies to her dad. How many pennies does she have now?

7 - 3 = 4

Marissa made 8 bracelets. She loved them so much she didn't give any away. How many bracelets does Marissa have now?

8 - 0 = 8

Jackson found 6 toys under his bed. He looked and didn't find any more toys. How many toys does Jackson have now?

6 + 0 = 6

Solve.

2 + 0 = 2   2 - 0 = 2   4 - 0 = 4   3 + 0 = 3

COMMON CORE   Lesson 37:   Add or subtract zero to get the same number and relate to word problems wherein the same quantity that joins a set, separates.   engage^ny   4.H.9

 Lesson 37:   Add or subtract 0 to get the same number and relate to word problems wherein the same quantity that joins a set, separates.

Date: 11/12/13

4.H.7

Imagine more to make 5, and write the addition sentence in the box.

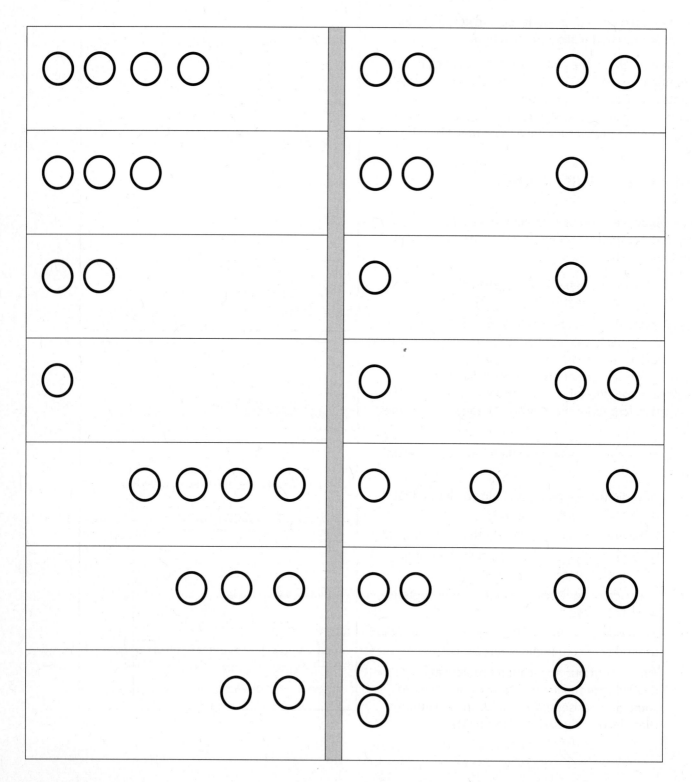

Lesson 37:   Add or subtract 0 to get the same number and relate to word problems
Date: 11/12/13   wherein the same quantity that joins a set, separates.

4.H.8

Cross out 2, and finish the subtraction sentence.

★ ★ ★	3 − 2 = ___
☾ ☾ ☾ ☾	4 − 2 = ___
★ ★ ★ ★ ★	5 − 2 = ___
☾ ☾	2 − 2 = ___
★ ★ ★ ★	4 − ___ = ___
☾ ☾ ☾ ☾ ☾	5 − ___ = ___

Name _____   Date _____

Listen to each story. Show the story with your fingers on the number path. Then fill in the number sentence.

1	2	3	4	5	6	7	8	9	10

Freddy has 3 strawberries for snack. His Dad gave him 2 more strawberries. How many strawberries does Freddy have now?

$$\underline{\quad3\quad} + \underline{\quad2\quad} = \underline{\qquad}$$

Freddy ate 2 of his strawberries. How many strawberries does Freddy have now?

$$\underline{\quad5\quad} - \underline{\quad2\quad} = \underline{\qquad}$$

Logan had 7 frogs. 2 frogs hopped away. How many frogs does Logan have now?

$$\underline{\qquad} - \underline{\qquad} = \underline{\qquad}$$

Pretend that Logan's 2 frogs hopped back. How many frogs does he have now?

$$\underline{\qquad} + \underline{\qquad} = \underline{\qquad}$$

| 1 | 2 | 3 | 4 | 5 | 6 | 7 | 8 | 9 | 10 |

Stella had 4 pennies. She found 3 more pennies. How many pennies does Stella have now?

Stella gave the 3 pennies to her dad. How many pennies does she have now?

_____ + _____ = _____

_____ - _____ = _____

Marissa made 8 bracelets. She loved them so much she did not give any away. How many bracelets does Marissa have now?

_____ - _____ = _____

_____ + _____ = _____

Solve.

2 + 0 = ☐   2 – 0 = ☐   4 – 0 = ☐   3 + 0 = ☐

Lesson 37:   Add or subtract 0 to get the same number and relate to word problems wherein the same quantity that joins a set, separates.

Date: 11/12/13

4.H.11

Name _____   Date _____

Listen to each story. Show the story with your fingers on the number path. Then fill in the number sentence and number bond.

1	2	3	4	5	6	7	8	9	10

Joey had 5 pennies. He found 3 pennies in the couch. How many pennies does Joey have now?

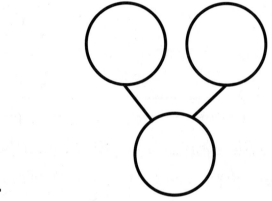

_____ + _____ = _____

Joey gave the 3 pennies to his dad. How many pennies does Joey have now?

_____ + _____ = _____

COMMON CORE™

Lesson 37:   Add or subtract 0 to get the same number and relate to word problems wherein the same quantity that joins a set, separates.
Date: 11/12/13

4.H.12

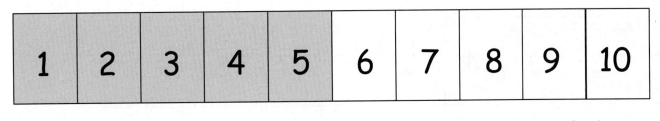

Siri had 9 pennies. She looked all around the house but could not find any more pennies. How many pennies does she have now?

_____ + _____ = _____

There were 8 children waiting for the school bus. No more children came to the bus stop. How many children are waiting now?

_____ + _____ = _____

Solve.

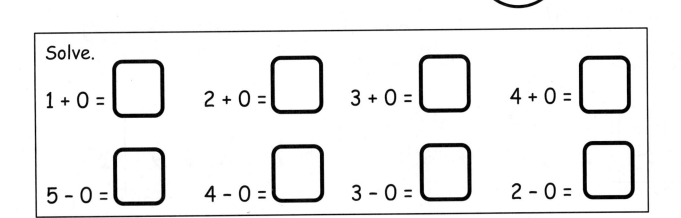

$1 + 0 =$ ⬜ $2 + 0 =$ ⬜ $3 + 0 =$ ⬜ $4 + 0 =$ ⬜

$5 - 0 =$ ⬜ $4 - 0 =$ ⬜ $3 - 0 =$ ⬜ $2 - 0 =$ ⬜

COMMON CORE™ | Lesson 37: Add or subtract 0 to get the same number and relate to word problems wherein the same quantity that joins a set, separates.

Date: 11/12/13

4.H.13

| 1 | 2 | 3 | 4 | 5 | 6 | 7 | 8 | 9 | 10 |

| 1 | 2 | 3 | 4 | 5 | 6 | 7 | 8 | 9 | 10 |

| 1 | 2 | 3 | 4 | 5 | 6 | 7 | 8 | 9 | 10 |

| 1 | 2 | 3 | 4 | 5 | 6 | 7 | 8 | 9 | 10 |

| 1 | 2 | 3 | 4 | 5 | 6 | 7 | 8 | 9 | 10 |

| 1 | 2 | 3 | 4 | 5 | 6 | 7 | 8 | 9 | 10 |

Lesson 37:   Add or subtract 0 to get the same number and relate to word problems
Date: wherein the same quantity that joins a set, separates.
             11/12/13

4.H.14

Lesson 38

Objective: Add 1 to numbers 1–9 to see the pattern of *the next number* using 5-group drawings and equations.

Suggested Lesson Structure

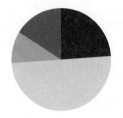

- ■ Fluency Practice   (12 minutes)
- ■ Application Problem   (5 minutes)
- ■ Concept Development   (25 minutes)
- ■ Student Debrief   (8 minutes)

  Total Time   **(50 minutes)**

Fluency Practice (12 minutes)

- Core Fluency Differentiated Practice Sets **K.OA.5**   (5 minutes)
- Imagine 1 More **K.OA.2**   (3 minutes)
- Building *1 More* and *1 Less* Towers **K.CC.4c**   (4 minutes)

Core Fluency Differentiated Practice Sets (5 minutes)

Materials: (S) Core Fluency Practice Sets from GK–M4–Lesson 29

Note: This activity assesses students' progress toward mastery of the required addition fluency for kindergarten.

Distribute the appropriate Practice Set based on student performance in GK–M4–Lesson 33. (All sets can be found in GK–M4–Lesson 29.) Students who correctly answered all questions on a Practice Set in the previous lesson should move to the next Practice Set. All other students should try to improve their scores on Practice Set A.

Students complete as many problems as they can in 96 seconds. Assign a counting pattern and start number for early finishers, or tell have them play an independent game like the Make 10 Memory Game. Collect and correct any Practice Sets completed within the allotted time.

Imagine 1 More (3 minutes)

Materials: (T) 5-group cards (0–5)

T: (Show the 2 dot card.) Raise your hand when you know how many dots. (Wait for all hands to go up, then give the signal.) Ready?

Lesson 38: Add 1 to numbers 1–9 to see the pattern of *the next number* using 5-group drawings and equations.
Date: 11/12/13

4.H.15

S: 2.

T: Now, imagine that there is 1 more. Now, how many dots with 1 more?

S: 3.

T: Say the addition sentence starting with 2. (Pause.) Ready?

S: 2 + 1 = 3.

T: Flip it!

S: 1 + 2 = 3.

To focus on the fluency goal of addition within 5, continue with the following suggested sequence: 3, 4, 5, 1, 0, then random numbers. If students are ready for a challenge, consider working up to 10.

Variation: Students can write the addition sentence on their personal boards instead of verbally.

Building *1 More* and *1 Less* Towers (4 minutes)

Materials: (S) 10 linking cubes per student

Note: Students practice counting up and down by 1 more or 1 less to support the addition of 1 using 5-groups and equations.

Guide students through the process of building a tower while stating the pattern as *1 more*. Maintain consistency in the language: (Place one block.) "1 more is 2." (Place another block.) "1 more is 3." (Place another block.) "1 more is 4." Continue to 10.

Disassemble the tower while stating the pattern as *1 less*. Challenge students to stop at a certain number and then change directions so that they state the pattern of 1 more or 1 less starting from numbers other than 1 or 10.

T: (Take apart your tower while saying 1 less.) Stop when you get to 5.

S: 10. 1 less is 9. 9. 1 less is 8. 8. 1 less is 7. 7. 1 less is 6. 6. 1 less is 5.

T: Stop! Now put it back together while saying, "1 more." Stop when you get to 7.

S: 5. 1 more is 6. 6. 1 more is 7.

T: Stop!

Continue changing directions several more times. It might be helpful to use a stick of cubes that show a color change at 5 to facilitate identifying the number of cubes in the tower.

Application Problem (5 minutes)

NOTES ON MULTIPLE MEANS OF REPRESENTATION:

To help English language learners follow the lesson, have pictures of dinosaurs and a watering hole on hand. This will help them to focus on the story of the Application Problem and the math.

Materials: 10 linking cubes per student, small square of blue paper to represent a watering hole (optional)

Pretend your cubes are dinosaurs. One dinosaur was thirsty and went to the watering hole. Move one of your cubes to the watering hole to show the thirsty dinosaur going to get his drink.

Lesson 38: Add 1 to numbers 1–9 to see the pattern of *the next number* using 5-group drawings and equations.

Date: 11/12/13

4.H.16

One more dinosaur got thirsty, too. Add another cube to the one by the watering hole. How many thirsty dinosaurs are there now? Turn to your partner and talk about an addition sentence that would tell what you just did.

Another dinosaur got thirsty! Take her to the watering hole too! Now how many dinosaurs are at the watering hole? Talk to your partner about the new addition sentence.

Keep acting out the story until all the dinosaurs are drinking water. Do you notice any patterns?

Note: Acting out the lesson objective with concrete materials gives students a conceptual understanding of the resulting number sentence which is fundamental to discussions about patterns during Concept Development.

Concept Development (25 minutes)

Materials: (T) Number path on the floor, large foam die (S) Number path template (GK–M4–Lesson 37), personal white board

   T: Student A, please come up and roll the die. What number did you get?

   S: 4.

   T: Show us the number 4 on the number path on the floor while the rest of the class finds it on their number path. We want to add 1 to our number. Find the answer on your number paths and raise your hand when you know. On my signal, you can tell me the answer together.

   S: 5!

   T: Yes! We need to make a number sentence. Let's write and read the number sentence together.

   S: 4 + 1 = 5.

   T: Good. Student B, please come up and roll the die.

   S: I got a 6.

   T: Show us the number 6 on the number path on the floor while the rest of the class finds it on their number path. We want to add 1 to our number. Find the answer on your number paths and raise your hand when you know. On my signal, you can tell me the answer together.

> **NOTES ON MULTIPLE MEANS OF ENGAGEMENT:**
>
> Scaffold the lesson for students with disabilities by providing them with linking cubes to use with their personal white board and number path template. Allow students to use the manipulatives until they are ready to work without them.

   S: 7!

   T: Read and write the number sentence.

   S: 6 + 1 = 7.

Repeat activity several times, having students act out and record the equation each time. Continue to list the equations on the number board as well.

   T: Does anyone notice any patterns?

MP.8   S: We just hopped to the next number each time on the path. → We added 1 on each time. → It's like finding the next bigger number.

Lesson 38:   Add 1 to numbers 1–9 to see the pattern of *the next number* using
                5-group drawings and equations.

Date: 11/12/13

4.H.17

T: I like your ideas! Turn your boards over to the blank side. We are going to talk about the pattern some more.

T: Draw 1 dot in the 5-group way. Now draw an empty circle next to it to show that we are adding 1. (Demonstrate.) How many circles do we have now?

S: 2.

T: What is our number sentence?

S: 1 + 1 = 2.

MP.8

T: Write your number sentence next to your picture. Now, draw 2 the 5-group way. Draw an empty circle next to it to show that we are adding 1 again. (Demonstrate.)

T: How many now?

S: 3!

T: What is the number sentence?

S: 2 + 1 = 3!

T: Yes! Write that number sentence under the picture. Now, work with your partner to see if you can keep going with the pattern until you have ten dots in all. Don't forget to draw the picture and write your number sentence each time. (Circulate during the exercise to ensure the students are understand. You may wish to ask pairs of students to present their work on chart paper or on the board.)

$$1 + 1 = 2$$
$$2 + 1 = 3$$
$$3 + 1 = 4$$
$$4 + 1 = 5$$
$$5 + 1 = 6$$
$$6 + 1 = 7$$
$$7 + 1 = 8$$
$$8 + 1 = 9$$
$$9 + 1 = 10$$

T: Who would like to tell something about patterns they noticed in their work?

S: It is like what we did on the number path. → When you are adding 1, the answer is always just the next number! → One more is the same as plus 1.

T: Let's read all of the number sentences that you made!

S: 1 + 1 = 2; 2 + 1 is 3; 3 + 1 = 4, etc.

Problem Set (10 minutes)

Students should do their personal best to complete the Problem Set within the allotted 10 minutes

Student Debrief (8 minutes)

Lesson Objective: Add 1 to numbers 1–9 to see the pattern of *the next number* using 5-group drawings and equations.

The Student Debrief is intended to invite reflection and active processing of the total lesson experience.

Invite students to review their solutions for the Problem Set. They should check work by comparing answers with a partner before going over answers as a class. Look for misconceptions or misunderstandings that can be addressed in the Debrief. Guide students in a conversation to debrief the Problem Set and process the lesson.

Lesson 38:	Add 1 to numbers 1–9 to see the pattern of *the next number* using 5-group drawings and equations.	**4.H.18**
Date:	11/12/13	

You may choose to use any combination of the questions below to lead the discussion.

- Look at the first page of your Problem Set. Do your 5-groups look exactly like your partner's? Why or why not?

- Look at the last two problems. Do your 5-groups and number sentences look exactly like your partner's? Why or why not?

- How is using the number path like using 5-group drawings? Which one do you like to use most? Why?

- Think back to building *1 more* and *1 less* towers. How are counting forward and adding 1 the same?

- Imagine that you are talking to an alien who does not know about adding 1. How would you tell the alien about what we did today? How would you describe the pattern we found?

- Think about the thirsty dinosaurs in our Application Problem. Was there a pattern in your addition sentences for that problem?

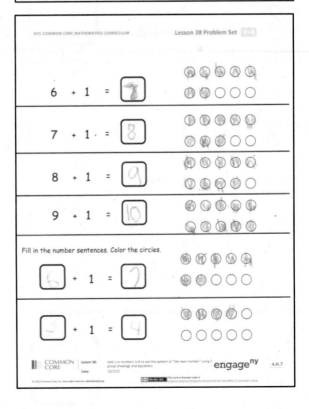

COMMON CORE™ | Lesson 38: | Add 1 to numbers 1–9 to see the pattern of *the next number* using 5-group drawings and equations.
Date: | 11/12/13

4.H.19

Name _____   Date _____

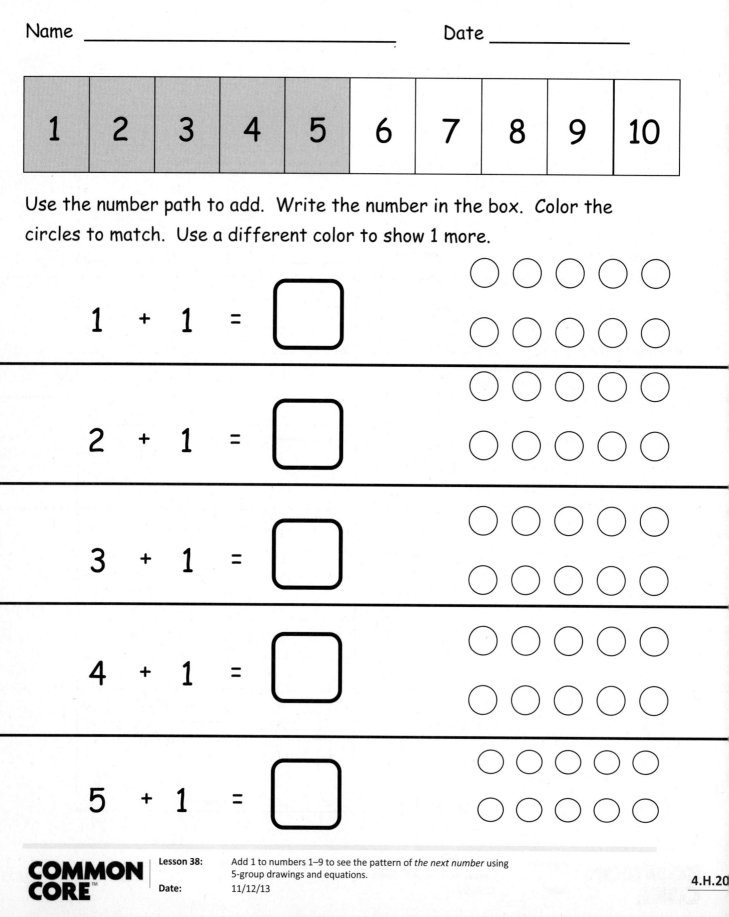

| 1 | 2 | 3 | 4 | 5 | 6 | 7 | 8 | 9 | 10 |

Use the number path to add. Write the number in the box. Color the circles to match. Use a different color to show 1 more.

1 + 1 = ☐

2 + 1 = ☐

3 + 1 = ☐

4 + 1 = ☐

5 + 1 = ☐

COMMON CORE   **Lesson 38:**   Add 1 to numbers 1–9 to see the pattern of *the next number* using 5-group drawings and equations.

Date: 11/12/13   4.H.20

6 + 1 = ☐   ○ ○ ○ ○ ○
                       ○ ○ ○ ○ ○

7 + 1 = ☐   ○ ○ ○ ○ ○
                       ○ ○ ○ ○ ○

8 + 1 = ☐   ○ ○ ○ ○ ○
                       ○ ○ ○ ○ ○

9 + 1 = ☐   ○ ○ ○ ○ ○
                       ○ ○ ○ ○ ○

Fill in the number sentences. Color the circles.

☐ + 1 = ☐   ○ ○ ○ ○ ○
                       ○ ○ ○ ○ ○

☐ + 1 = ☐   ○ ○ ○ ○ ○
                       ○ ○ ○ ○ ○

COMMON CORE™   Lesson 38:   Add 1 to numbers 1–9 to see the pattern of *the next number* using
                                5-group drawings and equations.   4.H.21
                   Date: 11/12/13

Name _____   Date _____

Follow the instructions to color the 5-group. Then fill in the number sentence or number bond to match.

Color 9 squares green and 1 square blue.

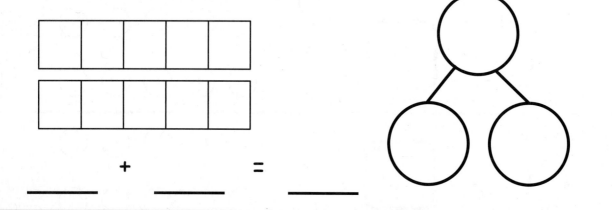

_____ + _____ = _____

Color 8 squares green and 1 square blue.

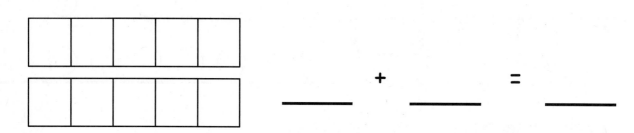

_____ + _____ = _____

Color 7 squares green and 1 square blue.

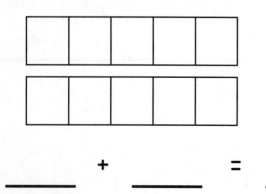 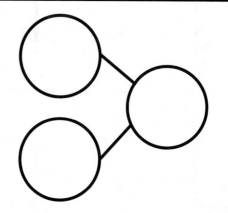

_____ + _____ = _____

COMMON CORE   **Lesson 38:**   Add 1 to numbers 1–9 to see the pattern of *the next number* using 5-group drawings and equations.

Date: 11/12/13

4.H.22

Color 2 squares green and 1 square blue.

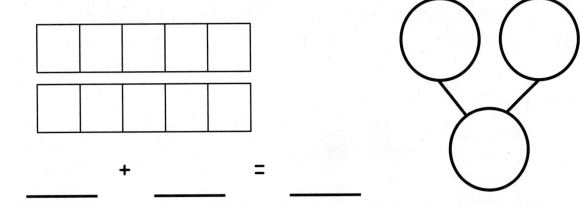

+ _____ = _____

_____

Color 1 square green and 1 square blue.

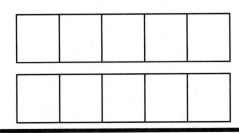

_____ + _____ = _____

Color 0 squares green and 1 square blue.

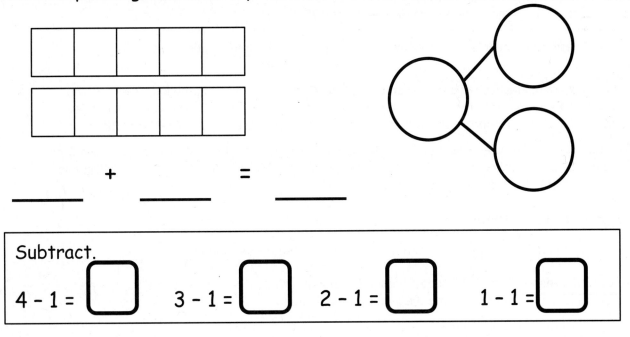

+ _____ = _____

_____

Subtract.

$4 - 1 =$ ☐ $3 - 1 =$ ☐ $2 - 1 =$ ☐ $1 - 1 =$ ☐

COMMON CORE™

Lesson 38:   Add 1 to numbers 1–9 to see the pattern of *the next number* using
5-group drawings and equations.

Date: 11/12/13

4.H.23

Lesson 39

Objective: Find the number that makes 10 for numbers 1–9, and record each with a 5-group drawing.

Suggested Lesson Structure

■ Fluency Practice   (12 minutes)
■ Application Problem (5 minutes)
□ Concept Development (25 minutes)
■ Student Debrief   (8 minutes)
 Total Time   **(50 minutes)**

Fluency Practice (12 minutes)

- Core Fluency Differentiated Practice Sets **K.OA.5** (5 minutes)
- Growing Apples to 10 **K.OA.4**   (4 minutes)
- 5-Group Peek-a-Boo **K.OA.4**   (3 minutes)

Core Fluency Differentiated Practice Sets (5 minutes)

Materials: (S) Core Fluency Practice Sets from GK–M4–Lesson 29

Note: This activity assesses students' progress toward mastery of the required addition fluency for kindergarten.

Distribute the appropriate Practice Set based on student performance in GK–M4–Lesson 38. Students who correctly answer all questions on a Practice Set in the previous lesson should move to the next Practice Set. All other students should try to improve their scores on the same set they used in GK–M4–Lesson 38.

Students complete as many problems as they can in 96 seconds. Assign a counting pattern and start number for early finishers, or tell have them play an independent game like the Make 10 Memory Game. Collect and correct any Practice Sets completed within the allotted time.

Growing Apples to 10 (4 minutes)

Materials: (S) Apple tree fluency template, 10 red beans, die with 6-dot side covered

Note: This activity prepares students for today's lesson by providing the opportunity to practice partners to 10 at the concrete level, before moving onto the pictorial and abstract.

Have students follow the directions below:

Lesson 39: Find the number that makes 10 for numbers 1–9, and record each with a 5-group drawing.
Date: 11/12/13

4.H.24

1. Roll the die.

2. Use the number on the die to determine how many red beans are placed on the apple tree. Arrange the beans in 5-groups.

3. Count how many more are needed to make 10.

4. Say, "I have _____. I need _____ more to make 10."

5. Do not remove the beans. Roll the die again. Count to see if there are enough spaces left over for that many beans. If the number goes over 10, and there are not enough spaces, roll again to get a smaller number. Then, place that many beans on the apple tree.

6. State the new amount and how many more it needs to make 10.

Continue until 10 is made. Remove the beans and start again from 0 if time permits. This game can be played with a partner, and a spinner can be substituted for the die.

5-Group Peek-a-Boo (3 minutes)

Materials: (T) 5-group cards

T: I'm going to show you my 5-group cards, but only for a second! Like this. (Hold up the card briefly, and then quickly take it out of view.) Quickly count the dots, and raise your hand when you know how many. Remember to wait for the snap. (Wait for all students to raise hands, and then give the signal.)

S: 9!

T: Raise your hand when you know how many more to make 10. (Wait for all hands to go up, then signal.) Ready?

S: 1.

Continue with the following possible sequence: 8, 5, 10, 7, 6, 1, 4, 3, 5, 2, 9, 0.

Variation: Have students play with a partner. Give each pair of students a set 5-group cards.

Application Problem (5 minutes)

Tim had 10 friends. Draw his friends.

Tim had 7 oranges. He wanted to give an orange to each of his friends. Does he have enough? Draw his 7 oranges. Now, draw more oranges so there are enough for all of his friends. Circle the new oranges. How many more oranges did he need?

Check your work by drawing a line to match each friend with an orange. Now, show your work to your friend. Did she do it the same way? Talk about what would have happened if Tim had started with 8 oranges.

Note: Thinking about *Are there enough?* and *How many more do I need?* serves as the anticipatory set for the lesson.

NOTES ON
MULTIPLE MEANS OF
REPRESENTATION:

Teach English language learners the meaning of *Are there enough?* and *How many more do I need?* by practicing their use. A possible conversation follows below:

- Are there enough pencils for 10 students?

- Let's count together.

- We only have 6 pencils. How many more do we need?

- Let's count: 1, 2, 3, and 4.

Concept Development (25 minutes)

Materials: (S) 1 set of 5-group cards, personal white board

T: Mittens the cat had 6 mice. She needed 10 mice in all to take home to her family for dinner. How many mice did she have?

S: 6.

T: How many did she need in all?

S: 10. → She doesn't have enough!

T: You are good listeners! Mittens will be happy for your help. What are some ways we could find out how many more mice she needs?

S: We could use a number path. → We could use our fingers and count up from 6. → We could make a picture.

T: Those are all good strategies. Today, let's make a picture. I will draw 6 in the 5-group way. (Demonstrate.) Now, count with me while I draw more empty circles until we have 10 in all. Tell me when to stop!

S: 1, 2, 3, 4 more. Stop! → Now we have 10!

T: Let me draw a ring around the extra circles that I drew. (Demonstrate.) How many extra circles?

S: 4.

T: How many did we begin with?

S: 6.

T: Could we make a number bond about our picture?

S: Yes! → 10 is the whole. → 6 and 4 are the parts.

T: Let's draw that number bond by the picture. (Demonstrate.) 6 needs 4 to make 10!

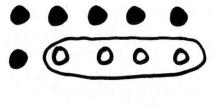

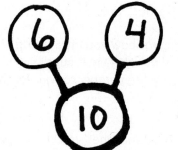

MP.7

T: I am going to tell this story again, but this time you do the 5-group drawing on your boards. Mittens has 7 mice, but she still needs 10 for dinner for her family. How many more mice will she need?

T: With your partner, draw Mitten's mice the 5-group way. Finish the picture to find out how many more mice she will need. Circle the extra mice that you drew, and make a number bond to match your picture. (Allow students time for partner work, circulating to ensure accuracy and understanding.) How many more mice did she need this time?

S: 3!

NOTES ON MULTIPLE MEANS OF ENGAGEMENT:

Scaffold the lesson for students with disabilities by providing linking cubes to model the lesson. A 10-frame template for their personal white boards may also allow them to follow along with the lesson more easily.

Lesson 39:   Find the number that makes 10 for numbers 1–9, and record each with a 5-group drawing.

Date: 11/12/13

4.H.26

T: Yes! 7 needs 3 to make 10. What if Mittens had started out with 8 mice? Draw the new picture and make the new number bond. (Allow students time to work with their partners.) How many more did she need this time?

S: 2!

Continue with this process, increasing Mitten's beginning number of mice by 1 each time until students have recorded all the ways to make 10 with 5-group drawings and number bonds. Allow pairs of students to present their work on the board or on chart paper, if desired.

T: Mittens is very grateful for your help! I'm going to let you play a game with your partner. Take out your 5-group cards. One partner will secretly choose a card to show his friend. The other partner will look at the card and will use his personal board to make a picture about how many more you need to make 10. Then, together you will make a number bond about your picture. When you are done, you can switch.

Allow students to play several iterations of the game. Circulate among them to ensure accuracy and understanding. Again, pairs of students may work on the board or chart paper.

Problem Set (10 minutes)

Students should do their personal best to complete the Problem Set within the allotted 10 minutes.

Student Debrief (8 minutes)

Lesson Objective: Find the number that makes 10 for numbers 1–9, and record each with a 5-group drawing.

The Student Debrief is intended to invite reflection and active processing of the total lesson experience.

Invite students to review their solutions for the Problem Set. They should check work by comparing answers with a partner before going over answers as a class. Look for misconceptions or misunderstandings that can be addressed in the Debrief. Guide students in a conversation to debrief the Problem Set and process the lesson.

You may choose to use any combination of the questions

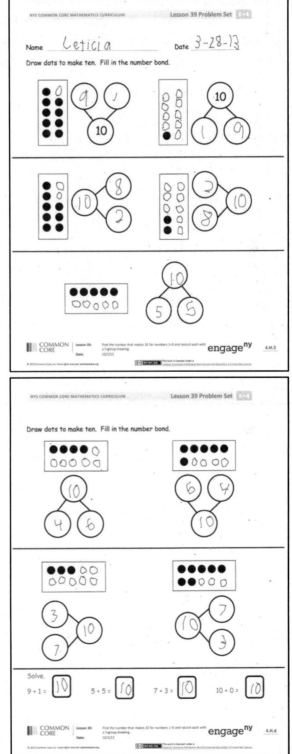

COMMON CORE™

Lesson 39:   Find the number that makes 10 for numbers 1–9, and record each
              with a 5-group drawing.
Date: 11/12/13

4.H.27

below to lead the discussion.

- Look at the first row of your Problem Set. What do the number bonds have in common?
- Do you see any patterns on your Problem Set?
- Pretend our alien friend is back again. Tell him how to make 10 with a number smaller than 10.
- How did you use 5-groups to find how to make 10?
- How did Tim's oranges from the Application Problem help you understand how to make 10?

Lesson 39:   Find the number that makes 10 for numbers 1–9, and record each with a 5-group drawing.

Date: 11/12/13

4.H.28

Name _____ Date _____

Draw dots to make 10. Fill in the number bond.

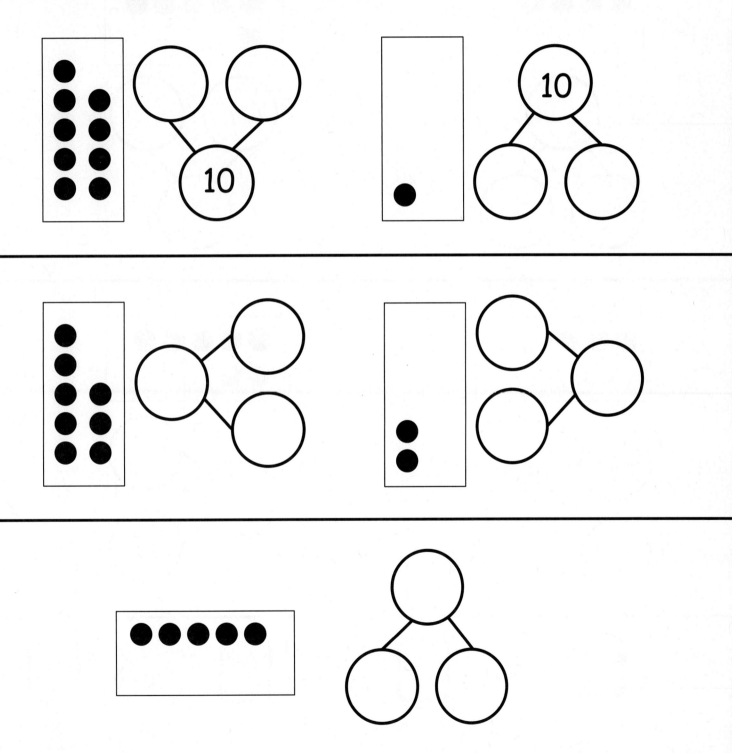

COMMON CORE™

Lesson 39: Find the number that makes 10 for numbers 1–9, and record each with a 5-group drawing.

Date: 11/12/13

4.H.29

Draw dots to make 10. Fill in the number bond.

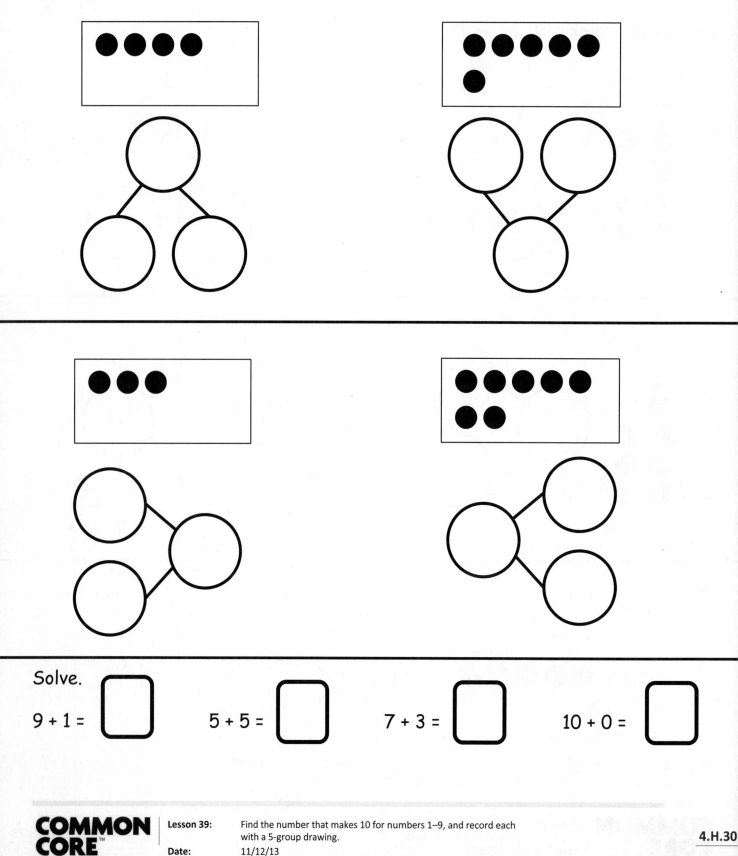

Solve.

$9 + 1 =$ ☐ $5 + 5 =$ ☐ $7 + 3 =$ ☐ $10 + 0 =$ ☐

COMMON CORE   Lesson 39:   Find the number that makes 10 for numbers 1–9, and record each
with a 5-group drawing.

Date: 11/12/13

4.H.30

Name _____   Date _____

Draw dots to make 10. Finish the number bonds. Draw a line from the 5-group to the matching number bond.

Lesson 39:   Find the number that makes 10 for numbers 1–9, and record each
              with a 5-group drawing.
Date: 11/12/13

4.H.31

© 2013 Common Core, Inc. All rights reserved. commoncore.org

Lesson 39:   Find the number that makes 10 for numbers 1–9, and record each
with a 5-group drawing.

Date: 11/12/13

4.H.32

Lesson 40

Objective: Find the number that makes 10 for numbers 1–9, and record each with an addition equation.

Suggested Lesson Structure

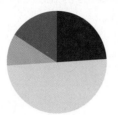

- Fluency Practice   (12 minutes)
- Application Problem   (5 minutes)
- Concept Development   (25 minutes)
- Student Debrief   (8 minutes)

Total Time   **(50 minutes)**

Fluency Practice (12 minutes)

- Ready, Set, Add! **K.OA.5**   (3 minutes)
- Beep Number **K.CC.4a**   (4 minutes)
- Draw More to Make 10 **K.OA.4**   (5 minutes)

Ready, Set, Add! (3 minutes)

Note: In this activity, students test their mastery of addition facts within 5, and when the total is greater than 5, they will be able to rely on the strategies of counting all or counting on with fingers.

Conduct activity as outlined in GK–M4–Lesson 31.

Beep Number (4 minutes)

Note: This activity extends students' proficiency in number order, anticipating the work of the next module.

- T: Let's play Beep Number! Listen carefully while I count. Instead of saying a number, I'll say *beep*. When you know what the beep number is, raise your hand.
- T: 16, 17, beep! (Wait until all hands are raised, then give the signal.)
- S: 18!
- T: 21, 22, beep, 24! (Wait until all hands are raised, then give the signal.)
- S: 23!

Continue in a thoughtful sequence, but return to a simpler sequence if students have difficulty. Numbers after will be easier to determine than numbers before, and crossing decades will prove difficult.

Lesson 40:	Find the number that makes 10 for numbers 1–9, and record each with an addition equation.	4.H.33
Date:	11/12/13	

Draw More to Make 10 (5 minutes)

Materials: (S) Fluency Practice Set

Note: This activity gives students practice with partners to 10 at the pictorial level in preparation for today's work in recording how many more to make 10 with an addition sentence.

After giving clear instructions and completing the first few problems together, allow students time to work at their own pace. Encourage them to do as many problems as they can within a given time frame.

Application Problem (5 minutes)

Materials: (S) Personal white boards

Ming has 3 baseball caps, but there are 10 girls on her team. Use your personal board and a 5-group drawing to find out how many more caps her team will need. Make a number bond about your picture.

Share your work with your partner. Do your pictures and number bonds look the same?

Note: Review of yesterday's work serves as preparation for today's lesson. Use this as a quick assessment to see if any students might need additional work with the 5-group drawings.

NOTES ON MULTIPLE MEANS OF ENGAGEMENT:

If students performing below grade level have difficulty with the Application Problem, scaffold it for them by having students act out the problem. Ask 10 students to line up the 5-group way, give 3 of them baseball caps before guiding students to make a number bond.

Concept Development (25 minutes)

Materials: (S) Linking cube 10-stick, personal white board, recording sheet, 1 set of 5-group cards per pair

T: Count the cubes in your stick. How many?

S: 10.

T: Break 1 cube off the end of your stick and put it on your desk. Do you still have 10 cubes in all?

S: Yes!

S: What are your parts now?

S: 1 and 9.

T: How much does one need to make 10?

S: 9.

T: If we started with 1, what would our number sentence be to record how much 1 needs to make 10?

S: 1 + 9 = 10.

T: Good! Complete that number sentence on the top of your recording sheet. Put your stick back together.

T: This time, break off 2 cubes from the end of your stick and put them on your desk. How many cubes

Lesson 40: Find the number that makes 10 for numbers 1–9, and record each with an addition equation.

Date: 11/12/13

4.H.34

does 2 need to make 10? How do you know?

S: 8. → I counted the ones that were left. → I used my fingers. → I remembered the partners from the number bonds before.

T: Let's write and read the new number sentence on our sheet.

S: 2 + 8 = 10!

Continue exercise to complete the recording sheet as a class review prior to the partner work.

T: Time to play a game with your partner! We will play one round all together, and then you will play with each other. Student A, would you please close your eyes and choose a card from this 5-group card deck?

S: I picked a 6.

T: Think about the 6. Figure out how many more 6 needs to make 10 and write the number sentence on your personal board. You can use your cubes, your fingers, or a drawing to help you. Raise your hand when you have your number sentence written down. Then, on my signal, hold up your boards. (Pause until the majority of hands are raised.) Read your addition sentence together.

S: 6 + 4 = 10.

MP.4

T: Good! You and your partner each have a set of 5-group cards. Take turns closing your eyes and choosing a card. Then, find how much the number needs to make 10 using any of the strategies we talked about. Write the number sentence and compare it to your partner's. Then, it is your partner's turn to choose a card.

Circulate during the activity to check for accuracy. Note which students are dependent on manipulatives or drawings. For those who choose to use them, note what the most popular strategies are. Note also overall confidence in writing the number sentences.

Problem Set (10 minutes)

Students should do their personal best to complete the Problem Set within the allotted 10 minutes.

Student Debrief (8 minutes)

Lesson Objective: Find the number that makes 10 for numbers 1–9 and record each with an addition equation.

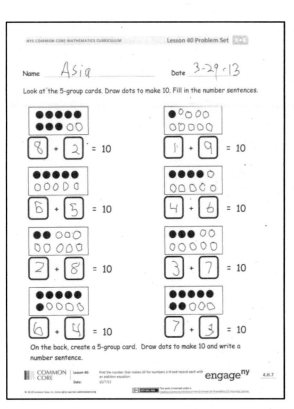

COMMON CORE | Lesson 40: | Find the number that makes 10 for numbers 1–9, and record each with an addition equation.
             | Date: | 11/12/13

4.H.35

The Student Debrief is intended to invite reflection and active processing of the total lesson experience.

Invite students to review their solutions for the Problem Set. They should check work by comparing answers with a partner before going over answers as a class. Look for misconceptions or misunderstandings that can be addressed in the Debrief. Guide students in a conversation to debrief the Problem Set and process the lesson.

You may choose to use any combination of the questions below to lead the discussion.

- How did you figure out how to make 10 from your number?
- How did thinking about parts help you to make a number sentence?
- Think back to Ming's baseball caps. Tell me an addition sentence about her caps.
- Do you remember our story with Mittens the cat yesterday? What is the same about the story of Mittens and our lesson today?
- Today we learned how to make 10 and record that with an addition sentence. Do you think we could make other numbers like 8 or 7?

Lesson 40:   Find the number that makes 10 for numbers 1–9, and record each
             with an addition equation.
Date: 11/12/13

4.H.3

Lesson 40: Find the number that makes 10 for numbers 1–9, and record each
with an addition equation.

Date: 11/12/13

4.H.37

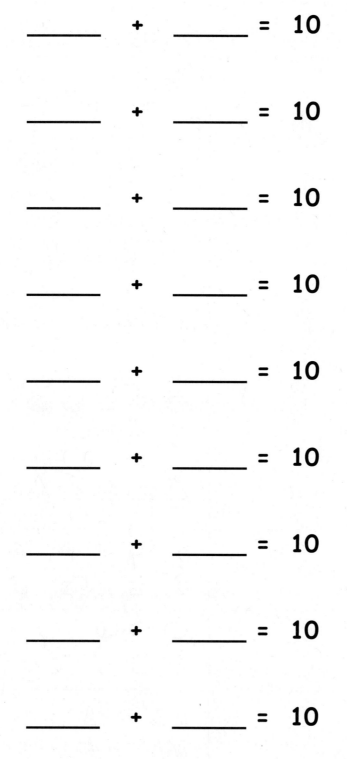

_____ + _____ = **10**

_____ + _____ = **10**

_____ + _____ = **10**

_____ + _____ = **10**

_____ + _____ = **10**

_____ + _____ = **10**

_____ + _____ = **10**

_____ + _____ = **10**

_____ + _____ = **10**

COMMON CORE™

Lesson 40: Find the number that makes 10 for numbers 1–9, and record each with an addition equation.

Date: 11/12/13

4.H.38

Name _____   Date _____

Look at the 5-group cards. Draw dots to make 10. Fill in the number sentences.

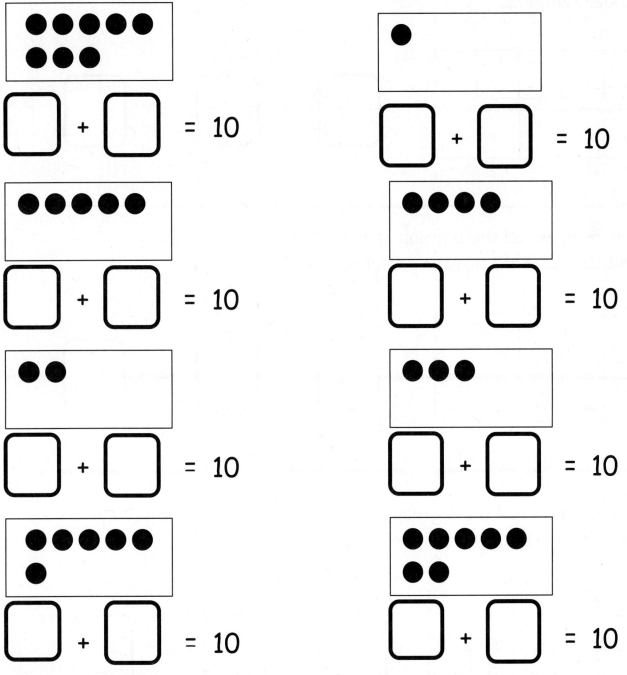

On the back, create a 5-group card. Draw dots to make 10 and write a number sentence.

Lesson 40:   Find the number that makes 10 for numbers 1–9, and record each
               with an addition equation.
Date: 11/12/13

4.H.39

Name _____   Date _____

Color 2 boxes red the 5-group way. Color the rest blue to make 10. Fill in the number sentence.

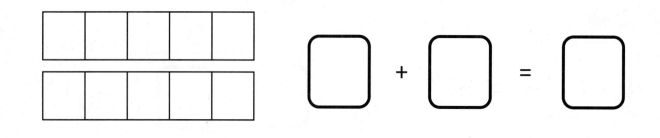

Color 5 cubes red the 5-group way. Color the rest blue to make 10. Fill in the number sentence.

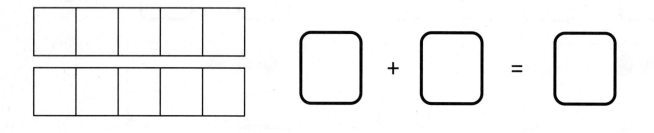

Color 7 cubes red the 5-group way. Color the rest blue to make 10. Fill in the number sentence.

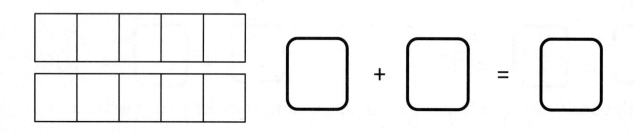

Lesson 40:   Find the number that makes 10 for numbers 1–9, and record each with an addition equation.

Date: 11/12/13

4.H.40

Match.

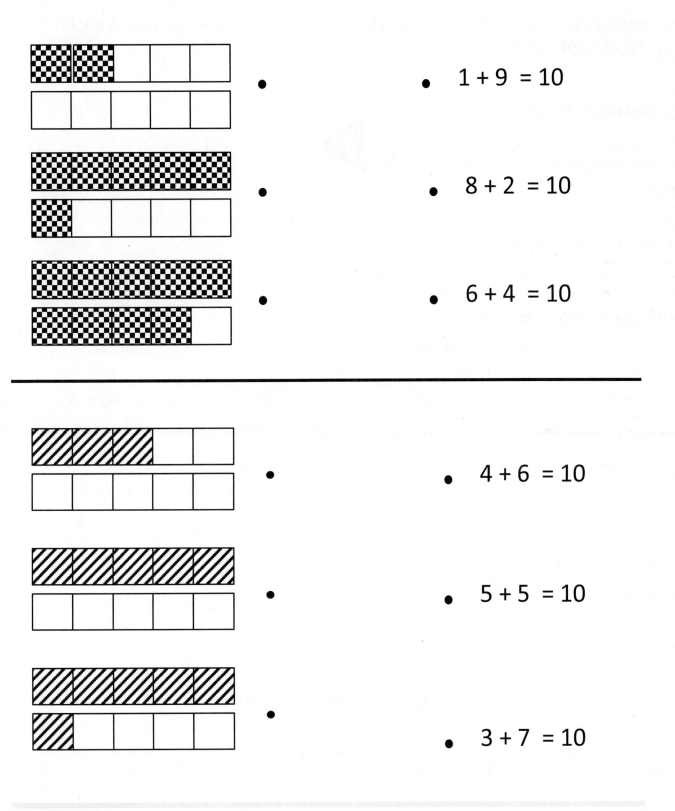

COMMON CORE™

Lesson 40: Find the number that makes 10 for numbers 1–9, and record each with an addition equation.

Date: 11/12/13

4.H.41

Lesson 41

Culminating task—choose tools strategically to model and represent a stick of 10 cubes broken into two parts.

Suggested Lesson Structure

■ Fluency Practice   (9 minutes)

  Concept Development   (41 minutes)

  Total Time   **(50 minutes)**

Fluency Practice (9 minutes)

▪ Sprint: Core Fluency **K.OA.5**   (9 minutes)

Sprint: Core Fluency (9 minutes)

Materials: (S) Core Fluency Sprints from GK–M4–Lesson 31

Note: This activity assesses students' progress toward mastery of the required addition fluency for kindergarten. Select the Sprint that is most appropriate for your class. In order to correct the work as a class, all students should take the same sprint.

    T: It's time for a Sprint!

Briefly recall previous Sprint preparation activities and distribute Sprints facedown.

    T: Take out your pencil and one crayon, any color. For this Sprint, you are going to subtract to find how many are left.

Demonstrate the first problem as needed.

Continue to follow the Sprint procedure as outlined in GK–M4–Lesson 3. Have students work on the Sprint a second time. Continue to emphasize that the goal is simply to do better than the first time and celebrate improvement.

Concept Development (41 minutes)

Materials: (T) A few sets of large plastic glasses, pointers, or other props for students to use as they become the "teachers" (S) Personal white board, linking cube 10-stick, colorful markers, 11" × 17" sheets of sturdy paper (construction or white)

Note: As this lesson represents the culmination of a great deal of learning in this module, it is suggested that a younger class or other members of the learning community be invited to act as the "students" for the

Lesson 41:   Culminating task—choose tools strategically to model and represent
                  a stick of 10 cubes broken into two parts.

Date: 11/12/13

kindergarteners to instruct. See details at the end of the lesson.

Preparation

T: Let's all count the cubes in this linking cube stick.

S: 1, 2, 3, 4, 5, 6, 7, 8, 9, 10.

T: (Break the stick into two parts, one of 3 and one of 7. Hold up the stick of 3.) How many are here?

S: 3!

T: How many are cubes are in the other part? Take your time. Raise your hand when you know. Wait for the signal. (Pause until all hands are raised.)

S: 7!

T: Who can tell me what these two parts make you think about?

S: I think about a number bond! → That makes me think of my 5-group drawings. → I think about an addition number sentence. → I think about a subtraction sentence. → I have a story about that!

T: (Hold up a piece of 11" × 17" paper.) Talk to your partner about all the ways you might show your ideas on paper! (Allow time for student discussion.)

MP.5 T: You have so many different ideas. Now it is your turn to share them! You have a big piece of paper and some markers. You have a linking cube stick, too. (Pass out a linking cube stick to each student.)

T: When I say to start, break your stick into two parts! Then, use as many ideas as you can to show your students and visitors different ways you think about your 10-stick and its two parts. Write or draw all of them on your poster. Then you will get a chance to share the work you did on your poster with someone else. You will be the teacher!

Note: Circulate during the activity to assess the students informally. Note areas of emerging understanding with individual students and support students who might need repetition of the directions. If students need support developing ideas for their posters, provide hints rather than ideas, e.g., "Look around the room. Do you see any drawings or number sentences that could help you think of ideas for your poster?"

Presentation

Student presentations take the place of the Debrief in this lesson. This is an opportunity to *celebrate* the intensive learning that has taken place during this module. The students can use their teacher prop as they present their work. If possible, invite parents, administrators, older students, or community volunteers to serve as enthusiastic "students" for individual presentations. Alternatively, your students can share with a partner or a small group, teaching about their selected number pair, explaining the various representations, and telling the related story. As the students make their presentations, ask the other students in the small groups to try to solve the problems on their personal white boards to ensure engagement.

Accelerated students could make additional posters with other addends.

The posters could be used as room decorations or bulletin board highlights. Alternatively, they could be made into a class *Book for Ten*.

Lesson 41:   Culminating task—choose tools strategically to model and represent
           a stick of 10 cubes broken into two parts.
Date: 11/12/13   **4.H.43**

Name _____   Date _____

Complete a number bond and number sentence for each problem.

Color 6 blocks blue. Color the rest red. All of the blue blocks fell off the table. How many blocks are still on the table?

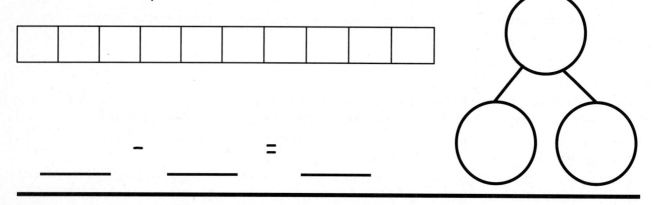

_____ - _____ = _____

Color some blocks orange and the rest yellow to make 10. All of the yellow blocks fell off the table. How many blocks are left?

_____ - _____ = _____

Draw 5 dogs and some cats the 5-group way.

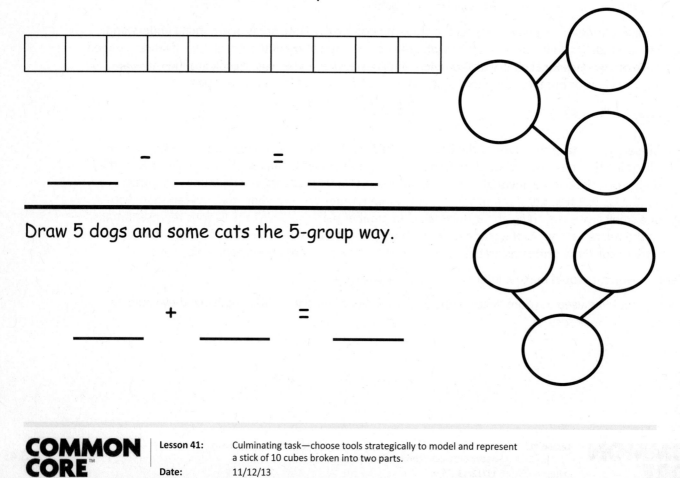

_____ + _____ = _____

COMMON CORE™   Lesson 41:   Culminating task—choose tools strategically to model and represent
                                a stick of 10 cubes broken into two parts.   4.H.44
                 Date: 11/12/13

There were 10 horses. Some were brown and some were white. Draw the horses the 5-group way. The brown ones went back into the barn. How many horses were still in the yard? Draw a number bond and write a subtraction sentence.

Solve.

1 + 1 = _____   1 + 2 = _____

2 + 1 = _____   _____ = 2 + 2

3 + 1 = _____   1 + 4 = _____

4 + 1 = _____   _____ = 3 + 2

5 + 1 = _____   2 + 3 = _____

Lesson 41:   Culminating task—choose tools strategically to model and represent a stick of 10 cubes broken into two parts.
Date: 11/12/13

4.H.45

Kindergarten Mid-Module 4 Assessment (Administer after Topic D)

Kindergarten End-of-Module 4 Assessment (Administer after Topic H)

Assessment time is a critically important component of the student–teacher relationship. It is especially important in the early grades to establish a positive and collaborative attitude when analyzing progress. Sit next to the student rather than opposite, and support the student in understanding the benefits of sharing and examining her level of mastery.

Please use the specific language of the assessment and, when possible, translate for non-English speakers (this is a math rather than a language assessment). If a student is unresponsive, wait about 15 seconds for a response. Record the student's results in two ways: (1) the narrative documentation after each topic set, and (2) the overall score per topic using A Progression Toward Mastery. Use a stopwatch to document the elapsed time for each response.

Within each assessment, there is a set of problems targeting each topic. Each set is comprised of three or four related questions. Document what the student did and said in the narrative, and use the rubric for the overall score for each set.

If the student is unable to perform any part of the set, her score cannot exceed Step 3. However, if the student is unable to use her words to tell what she did, do not count that against her quantitatively. Be aware of the difference between a non-native English speaker's and a native English speaker's ability to articulate something. If the student asks for or needs a hint or significant support, provide either, but the score is automatically lowered. This ensures that the assessment provides a true picture of what a student can do independently.

If a student scores at Step 1 or 2, repeat that topic set again at two-week intervals, noting the date of the reassessment in the space at the top of the student's record sheet. Document progress on this one form. If the student is very delayed in her response but completes it, reassess to see if there is a change in the time elapsed.

House the assessments in a three-ring binder or student portfolio. By the end of the year, there will be 10 assessments for each student. Modules 1, 3, 4, and 5 have two assessments each whereas Modules 2 and 6 only have one. Use the Class Record Sheet following the rubric for an easy reference look at students' strengths and weaknesses.

These assessments can be valuable for daily planning, parent conferences, and first grade teachers preparing to receive these students.

| Module 4: | Number Pairs, Addition and Subtraction to 10 |
| Date: | 11/12/13 |

4.S.1

Student Name _____

Topic A: Compositions and Decompositions of 2, 3, 4, and 5

Rubric Score: _____ Time Elapsed _____

	Date 1	Date 2	Date 3
Topic A			
Topic B			
Topic C			
Topic D			

Materials: (S) Number bond mat in a personal white board, tub of loose linking cubes, 4 plastic toy animals

T: (Put 4 toy animals in the whole's place on the number bond. Orient the whole toward the top.) Tell me a story about part of the animals going here (point to part of the number bond) and part of the animals going here (point to the other part of the number bond). Move the animals as you tell your story.

T: (Turn the number bond mat so that the parts are on top. Put 3 connected linking cubes and 2 connected linking cubes in the parts of the number bond.) Use these linking cubes (present the tub) to complete this number bond. (Students should put 5 linking cubes into the whole's place.)

T: Replace your cubes with numbers.

What did the student do?	What did the student say?
1.	
2.	
3.	

Topic B: Decompositions and Compositions of 6, 7, and 8 into Number Pairs

Rubric Score: _____Time Elapsed _____

Materials: (S) 2 5-sticks of same colored linking cubes, number bond mat in personal white board, tub of loose linking cubes

T: (Put 5-stick of same colored linking cubes and tub of loose same colored linking cubes in front of the student.) Show me 6 with the cubes. Show me 6 fingers the Math way.

T: (Place the tub of loose linking cubes, two 5-sticks, and the number bond mat in front of the student.) Use the cubes to show me a number bond for 7.

T: (Put the number bond in a different orientation. Write 8 in the whole of the number bond in front of the student. Be sure that linking cubes are accessible, so that the student may use linking cubes or drawings as support if needed.) Use your marker to complete this number bond. (Note how the student strategizes to solve the problem. What is she using to decompose 8, e.g., mental math, cubes, fingers, drawings? How does she know the quantities for each part: subitizing, counting all, counting on, etc.?)

What did the student do?	What did the student say?
1.	
2.	
3.	

Topic C: Addition with Totals of 6, 7, and 8

Rubric Score: _____ Time Elapsed _____

Materials: (S) Personal white board, story problem templates 1–3, 10 linking cubes (5 red and 5 blue)

T: (Place Template 1 in front of the student and give him the unconnected linking cubes.) Listen to my story, and watch as I record what I say. Use the cubes to help you to remember my story. I had 6 cubes. Two were red and 4 were blue. (Write $6 = 2 + 4$ on the white board as you talk.) Tell me what the 6 is telling about in my story. Tell me what the 2 is telling about in my story. Tell me what the 4 is telling about in my story.

T: (Place Template 2 in front of the student.) Listen to my story, and use the cubes to help you to remember the numbers. There were 5 white puppies and 3 brown puppies in the yard. How many puppies were in the yard? (Write ____ + ____ = ____ on the personal board.) Write the numbers in the addition sentence that matches this story.

T: (Place Template 3 in front of the student.) Listen to my story, and use the cubes to help you remember the numbers. Jacob had 7 toy cars. He puts some on the shelf and the rest in his toy box. How many could be in each place? Write an addition sentence that matches your story.

What did the student do?	What did the student say?
1.	
2.	
3.	

Topic D: Subtraction from Numbers to 8

Rubric Score: _____ Time Elapsed _____

Materials: (S) Personal white board, story problem templates 2–4, 10 red linking cubes

T: (Place Template 4 in front of the student in the personal board.) Listen to my story, and watch as I record what I say. Use the cubes to help you to remember my story. I had 7 cubes. A boy came and took 2 away. (Cross out 2 cubes and write 7 – 2 = 5 below the cubes.) Tell me what the 7 is telling about in my story. Tell me what the 2 is telling about in my story. Tell me what the 5 is telling about in my story.

T: (Place Template 2 in front of the student.) Listen to my story, and use the cubes to help you to remember the numbers. There were 8 puppies in the yard. Five went into the doghouse. How many puppies were still in the yard? (Write ___ – ___ = ___ on the white board.) Write the numbers in the subtraction sentence to match this story.

T: (Place Template 3 in front of the student.) Listen to my story, and use the cubes to help you remember the numbers. Jacob had 7 toy cars. He put 4 cars away in his toy box. How many cars was Jacob still playing with? Write a subtraction sentence that matches this story.

What did the student do?	What did the student say?
1.	
2.	
3.	

Mid-Module Assessment Task
Standards Addressed

Topics A–D

Understand addition as putting together and adding to, and understand subtraction as taking apart and taking from.

K.OA.1 Represent addition and subtraction with objects, fingers, mental images, drawings, sounds (e.g., claps), acting out situations, verbal explanations, expressions, or equations. (Drawings need not show details, but should show the mathematics in the problem. This applies wherever drawings are mentioned in the Standards.)

K.OA.2 Solve addition and subtraction word problems, and add and subtract within 10, e.g., by using objects or drawings to represent the problem.

K.OA.3 Decompose numbers less than or equal to 10 into pairs in more than one way, e.g., by using objects or drawings, and record each decomposition by a drawing or equation (e.g., $5 = 2 + 3$ and $5 = 4 + 1$).

K.OA.5 Fluently add and subtract within 5.

Evaluating Student Learning Outcomes

A Progression Toward Mastery is provided to describe and quantify steps that illuminate the gradually increasing understandings that students develop *on their way to proficiency*. In this chart, this progress is presented from left (Step 1) to right (Step 4). The learning goal for each student is to achieve Step 4 mastery. These steps are meant to help teachers and students identify and celebrate what the student can do now, and what they need to work on next.

A Progression Toward Mastery				
Assessment Task Item and Standards Assessed	STEP 1 Little evidence of reasoning without a correct answer. (1 Point)	STEP 2 Evidence of some reasoning without a correct answer. (2 Points)	STEP 3 Evidence of some reasoning with a correct answer or evidence of solid reasoning with an incorrect answer. (3 Points)	STEP 4 Evidence of solid reasoning with a correct answer. (4 Points)
Topic A K.OA.1 K.OA.3 K.OA.5	The student shows little evidence of understanding that the parts of the number bond comprise the whole, and is unable to complete most of the tasks.	The student: ▪ Tells a story about the animals that does not match their movements or numbers. ▪ Puts a quantity of linking cubes other than 5 in the number bond. ▪ Fills in the number bond with 5, 3, and 2 incorrectly or puts other numbers in the number bond.	The student correctly: ▪ Tells a decomposition story without using numbers. ▪ Selects 5 linking cubes but is confused about where to put them. ▪ Fills in the number bond with 5, 3, and 2, and is hesitant when writing the numerals in the number bond, looking to the teacher for support in writing the numbers in the correct place.	The student correctly: ▪ Tells a decomposition story saying numbers that match their movement of the toy animals. ▪ Selects 5 linking cubes and puts them in the whole of the number bond mat. ▪ Correctly fills in the number bond with numerals 5, 3, and 2.
Topic B K.OA.3	The student shows little evidence of understanding the relationship between the parts and the whole of the number bond, and is unable to complete most of the tasks.	The student: ▪ .Shows a number other than 6 with the linking cubes. ▪ Shows a number other than 6 with fingers. ▪ Puts a random number of cubes in the parts and whole of the number bond for 7. ▪ Writes random numbers in the parts of the number bond	The student: ▪ Counts out linking cubes to show 6, may or may not use the 5-stick, and holds up a different combination of 6 fingers to show 6. ▪ Uses linking cubes to make the correct parts for 7, but leaves the whole blank or confuses the parts and whole of the number bond.	The student correctly: ▪ Shows 6 cubes. (Make note if the student uses the 5-stick, which shows more advanced counting.) ▪ Holds up left hand and thumb of right hand to show 6 with fingers. ▪ Makes a number bond for 7 using any correct combination for the parts of 7.

A Progression Toward Mastery

		for 8.	• Needs teacher support and more time to identify partners of 8 and write correct parts in the number bond.	(Again, make note if the student uses the 5-stick.) • Fills all parts of the number bond. • Writes a correct combination of parts for the number 8.
Topic C **K.OA.1** **K.OA.2**	The student shows little evidence of understanding the addition expressions or addition equations, and is unable to complete most of the tasks.	The student: • Incorrectly states some or all of what each number represents. • Writes incorrect numbers in the blanks or puts the correct numbers in the wrong places. • Writes an incorrect addition sentence for the story.	The student requires teacher support to correctly answer the questions and/or misses one out of the three questions.	The student correctly and independently: • States what each number in the number sentence refers to. • Writes all the correct numbers in the blanks: $5 + 3 = 8$. • Writes an addition sentence to match own story, e.g., $7 = 3 + 4$.
Topic D **K.OA.1** **K.OA.2** **K.OA.3**	The student shows little evidence of understanding subtraction expressions or subtraction equations, and shows little understanding that the same number can be decomposed in different ways. He is unable to complete most of the tasks.	The student: • Incorrectly states some or all of what each number represents. • Writes incorrect numbers in the blanks or puts the correct numbers in the wrong places. • Writes an incorrect subtraction sentence for the story.	The student requires teacher support to correctly answer the questions and/or misses one out of the three questions.	The student correctly and independently: • States what each number in the number sentence refers to. • Writes all the correct numbers in the blanks: $8 - 5 = 3$. • Writes an addition sentence to match own story, e.g., $7 - 3 = 4$.

Class Record Sheet of Rubric Scores: Module 4					
Student Names:	**Topic A:** Compositions and Decompositions of 2, 3, 4, and 5	**Topic B:** Decompositions of 6, 7, and 8 into Number Pairs	**Topic C:** Addition with Totals of 6, 7, and 8	**Topic D:** Subtraction from Numbers to 8	**Next Steps:**

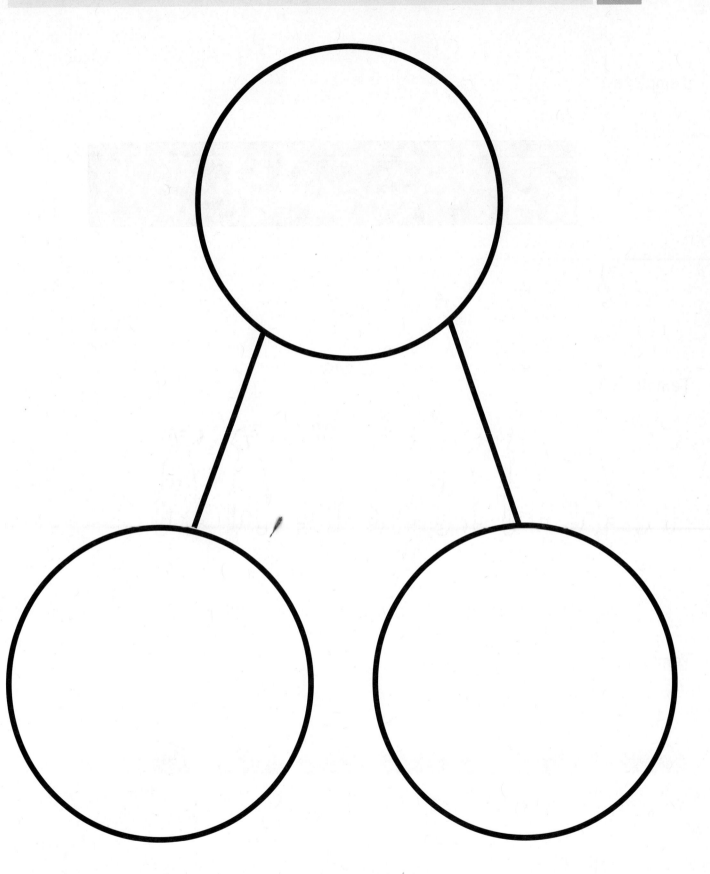

Template 1

Template 2

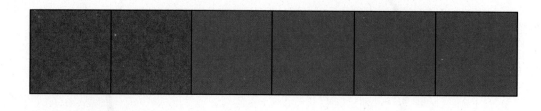

Template 3

Template 4

Student Name _____

Topic E: Decompositions of 9 and 10 into Number Pairs

Rubric Score _____ Time Elapsed _____

	Date 1	Date 2	Date 3
Topic E			
Topic F			
Topic G			
Topic H			

Materials: Personal white board, number bond mat, 10 loose cubes, 2 pieces of construction paper

T: (Put the number bond mat in the personal white board and write 10 in the whole's place.) Use your marker to complete this number bond.

T: Anya's friends brought her 9 presents. They put some of the presents on one table and the rest on the other table. (Place the two pieces of construction paper in front of the student to represent each table.) Use the cubes to show me how Anya's presents could look. Now draw a number bond about Anya's presents.

What did the student do?	What did the student say?
1. 2. 	

Topic F: Addition with Totals of 9 and 10

Rubric Score: _____   Time Elapsed _____

Materials: Personal white board, Template 1, 10 linking cubes, picture templates   5–6

- T: (Show Template 1 to the student and write 9 = _____ + _____ on the personal white board.) Look at the 5-group dots. How can the dots help you fill in the blanks of the equation? Fill in the blanks.

- T: (Place Picture Template 2 in front of the student.) Listen to my story, and use the cubes to help you remember the numbers. There were 6 orange cars in the parking lot. Four green cars drove in. How many cars are in the parking lot now? (Write ___ + ___ = ___ on the board.) Write the numbers in the addition sentence to match the story.

- T: (Place Picture Template 3 in front of the student.) Listen to my story, and use the cubes to help you remember the numbers. There were 10 flowers. Eight of them were red and 2 of them were blue. Write an addition sentence that matches this story.

What did the student do?	What did the student say?
1.	
2.	
3.	

Topic G: Subtraction from 9 and 10

Rubric Score: _____ Time Elapsed _____

Materials: 10 linking cube stick (5 cubes one color, 5 cubes a different color), 9 crayons, brown paper bag, personal white board, paper, and pencil

- T: (Give the student a piece of paper and a pencil.) Listen to my story, and watch what I do. When I'm finished you are going to record what you hear and see on your paper. You can use a drawing or a subtraction sentence. I have 9 crayons. I'm going to put 1 in this paper bag. How many crayons are left?

- T: (Give the student the 10-stick of linking cubes.) How many cubes? Break off some cubes and put them on the table. How many did you break off? How many are still in your hand? (As the student tells you how many cubes, write ___ – ___ = ___ on the personal white board.) Write the numbers in the blanks that tell what you did with the linking cubes.

- T: (Connect the cubes and erase the board. Place both items in front of the student.) Break off a different number this time and record your work by writing a subtraction sentence.

What did the student do?	What did the student say?
1.	
2.	
3.	

Topic H: Patterns with Adding 0 and 1 and Making 10

Rubric Score: _____   Time Elapsed _____

Materials: Template 1, Template 4, linking cubes, personal white board

   T: (Place 5 loose linking cubes of the same color in front of the student.) Count and put the cubes together. How many cubes are there? Take zero cubes away. How many cubes are left? Put zero cubes on your stick. How many cubes are there in all?

   T: (Student is still holding their 5-stick from the previous question. Put 5 loose linking cubes of different colors in front of the student.) Put 1 more cube on your stick. How many cubes are there? Put 1 more cube on your stick. How many cubes now?

   T: (Place Template 4 in front of the student.) Listen to my story. Hold up the equation that matches my story. Five fish were swimming in a pond. Then 3 frogs jumped in the pond. Now there are 8 animals in the pond. Which equation matches my story?

       Listen to some more. There were 8 animals in the pond. The 3 frogs jumped out and went home. Now there are 5 animals in the pond. Which equation matches my story?

   T: (Put Template 1 in front of the student.) How many more does 9 need to be 10? Write an equation that shows how many 9 needs to make 10.

   T: (Give the student the personal white board and marker.) Draw the number 7 using a 5-group. How many more does 7 need to make 10? Write an equation that shows how many 7 needs to make 10.

What did the student do?	What did the student say?
1.	
2.	
3.	
4.	
5.	

End-of-Module Assessment Task
Standards Addressed

Topics E–H

Understand addition as putting together and adding to, and understand subtraction as taking apart and taking from.

K.OA.1   Represent addition and subtraction with objects, fingers, mental images, drawings, sounds (e.g., claps), acting out situations, verbal explanations, expressions, or equations. (Drawings need not show details, but should show the mathematics in the problem. This applies wherever drawings are mentioned in the Standards.)

K.OA.2   Solve addition and subtraction word problems, and add and subtract within 10, e.g., by using objects or drawings to represent the problem.

K.OA.3   Decompose numbers less than or equal to 10 into pairs in more than one way, e.g., by using objects or drawings, and record each decomposition by a drawing or equation (e.g., 5 = 2 + 3 and 5 = 4 + 1).

K.OA.4   For any number from 1 to 9, find the number that makes 10 when added to the given number, e.g., by using objects or drawings, and record the answer with a drawing or equation.

Evaluating Student Learning Outcomes

A Progression Toward Mastery is provided to describe and quantify steps that illuminate the gradually increasing understandings that students develop *on their way to proficiency*. In this chart, this progress is presented from left (Step 1) to right (Step 4). The learning goal for each student is to achieve Step 4 mastery. These steps are meant to help teachers and students identify and celebrate what the student can do now, and what they need to work on next.

Module 4:	Number Pairs, Addition and Subtraction to 10
Date:	11/12/13

4.S.17

A Progression Toward Mastery

Assessment Task Item and Standards Assessed	STEP 1 Little evidence of reasoning without a correct answer. (1 Point)	STEP 2 Evidence of some reasoning without a correct answer. (2 Points)	STEP 3 Evidence of some reasoning with a correct answer or evidence of solid reasoning with an incorrect answer. (3 Points)	STEP 4 Evidence of solid reasoning with a correct answer. (4 Points)
Topic E **K.OA.3**	The student: • Writes random or no numbers in the number bond. • Is unable to represent story using cubes or number bond.	The student: • Writes two numbers that are close but an incorrect number pair for 10 in the number bond. • Represents the story incorrectly with cubes and number bond. **OR** The student performs one of the tasks correctly with some teacher support.	The student: • Writes a correct number pair for 10 in the number bond. • Represents the story correctly using cubes or a number bond.	The student correctly: • Writes a number pair for 10 in the number bond. • Represents the story using cubes and a number bond.
Topic F **K.OA.2**	The student shows little evidence of understanding addition sentences and is unable to complete most of the tasks.	The student: • Writes an incorrect number pair for 9. • Writes random numbers in the addition sentence and shows little understanding of the story. • Is unable to write an addition sentence or the addition sentence is not understandable. **OR** The student performs one or more of the	The student: • Identifies and writes 5 for the dark dots and 4 for the light dots in the equation or writes a different, correct number pair for 9. • Writes correct numbers in the addition sentence, with some confusion about parts and whole. • Writes an addition sentence that matches the story, with some confusion about	The student correctly: • Identifies and writes 5 for the dark dots and 4 for the light dots in the equation or writes a different, correct number pair for 9. • Writes all the correct numbers in the addition sentence: $6 + 4 = 10$ or $4 + 6 = 10$. • Writes a correct addition sentence that matches the story: $10 = 8 + 2$ or

4.S.18

A Progression Toward Mastery

		tasks correctly with some teacher support.	parts and whole.	8 + 2 = 10.
Topic G **K.OA.1** **K.OA.2** **K.OA.3**	The student shows little evidence of understanding subtraction sentences and is unable to complete most of the tasks.	The student: ▪ Represents the story using pictures, numbers, or symbols that are not related to the story. ▪ Orally answers the questions incorrectly and writes random numbers in the blanks of the subtraction sentence. ▪ Is unable to break off a different amount of cubes, and writes random numbers in the equation or is not able to write an equation. **OR** The student performs one or more of the tasks correctly with some teacher support.	The student: ▪ Represents the story using pictures, numbers, or symbols that are incorrectly related to the story (e.g., 9 + 1 = 8 or showing 9 pencils with one more added). ▪ Orally answers the questions being asked, counts all the cubes when asked the questions, and writes incorrect numbers in the blanks of the subtraction sentence (e.g., 8 – 1 = 9). ▪ Breaks off a different number of cubes and records work with an equation but may get numbers mixed up in the equation.	The student correctly: ▪ Represents and records 9 – 1 = 8 clearly using a drawing and/or equation. ▪ Orally answers the questions being asked and writes numbers in the blanks of the subtraction sentence that represent what happened with the cubes. ▪ Breaks off a different number of cubes and records work with an equation.
Topic H **K.OA.1** **K.OA.2** **K.OA.4**	The student shows little evidence of understanding zero, 1 more, and the relationship between numbers and addition and subtraction. He is unable to complete most of the tasks.	The student: ▪ Counts one-to-one incorrectly or is confused about zero. ▪ Adds more than 1 or takes cubes off the stick, and is confused about how many cubes after adding, stating an incorrect number of cubes.	The student: ▪ Counts 5 cubes correctly but has some confusion about zero. ▪ Answers 6 and 7 as they put one more cube on their 5-stick (must count all cubes every time). ▪ Selects the correct equation for only one part of the	The student correctly: ▪ Counts 5 cubes and answers 5 to each of the questions about zero. ▪ Answers 6 and 7 as she puts 1 more cube on the 5-stick. ▪ Selects the correct equation for both parts of the story: 5 + 3 = 8 and 8 – 3 =5.

A Progression Toward Mastery

		<ul><li>Selects incorrect equations and is clearly guessing.</li><li>May answer 1 orally but is unable to write a related equation.</li><li>Draws 7 dots but not in a 5-group, or draws a different number of dots, and provides the wrong answer, and/or has difficulty writing the equation.</li></ul>	<ul><li>story.</li><li>Answers 1 but may write the numbers or symbols incorrectly.</li><li>Correctly draws 7 dots in a 5-group pattern OR answers 3 orally and writes 7 + 3 = 10, but may have some difficulty with the drawing or writing the equation.</li></ul>	<ul><li>Answers 1 and writes 9 + 1 = 10.</li><li>Correctly draws 7 dots in a 5-group pattern, and answers 3 orally and writes 7 + 3 = 10.</li></ul>

Class Record Sheet of Rubric Scores: Module 4					
Student Names:	**Topic E:** Decompositions of 9 and 10 into Number Pairs	**Topic F:** Addition with Totals of 9 and 10	**Topic G:** Subtraction from 9 and 10	**Topic H:** Patterns with Adding 0 and 1 and Making 10	**Next Steps:**

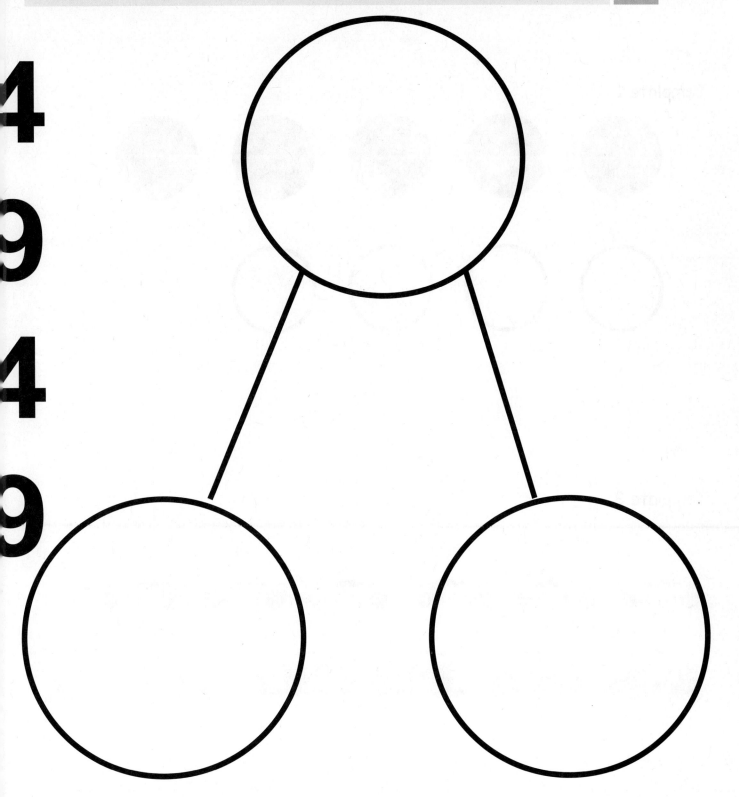

Template 1

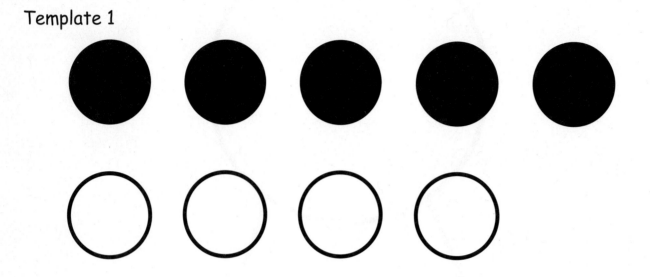

Template 2

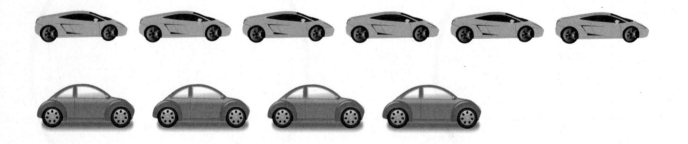

Template 3

Template 4

$$5 + 3 = 8$$

$$8 - 3 = 5$$

$$5 - 3 = 2$$